LEADERSHIP OF DISCUSSION GROUPS

LEADERSHIP OF DISCUSSION GROUPS
Case Material and Theory

Gertrude K. Pollak

S P Books Division of
SPECTRUM PUBLICATIONS, INC.
New York, N.Y.

Distributed by Halsted Press
A Division of John Wiley & Sons

New York   Toronto   London   Sydney

SPECTRUM PUBLICATIONS, INC.
86-19 Sancho Street, Holliswood, N.Y., 11423

Distributed solely by the Halsted Press division of John Wiley & Sons, Inc., New York

Library of Congress Cataloging in Publication Data

Pollak, Gertrude K
    Leadership of discussion groups.

    Bibliography: p.
    Includes index.
    1. Family life education. 2. Group counseling.
I. Title.
HQ10.P57   808.53   75-22050
ISBN 0-470-69175-1 (Halsted)

Printed in the United States
1 2 3 4 5 6 7 8 9

LEADERSHIP OF DISCUSSION GROUPS

LEADERSHIP OF DISCUSSION GROUPS
Case Material and Theory

Gertrude K. Pollak

S P Books Division of
SPECTRUM PUBLICATIONS, INC.
New York, N.Y.

Distributed by Halsted Press
A Division of John Wiley & Sons

New York   Toronto   London   Sydney

SPECTRUM PUBLICATIONS, INC.
86-19 Sancho Street, Holliswood, N.Y., 11423

Distributed solely by the Halsted Press division of John Wiley & Sons, Inc., New York

Library of Congress Cataloging in Publication Data

Pollak, Gertrude K
    Leadership of discussion groups.

    Bibliography: p.
    Includes index.
    1. Family life education. 2. Group counseling.
I. Title.
HQ10.P57   808.53   75-22050
ISBN 0-470-69175-1 (Halsted)

Printed in the United States
1 2 3 4 5 6 7 8 9

II
Purpose and Scope of the Family
Life Education Program

The Program was established with prevention of problems of family and social relationships as its primary goal. The underlying assumption was that learning in these areas can be achieved through group discussions with an educational emphasis. Following through on this assumption, members of community groups were given opportunities to discuss their questions and concerns regarding their family and social relationships under the leadership of the writer, who was in charge of the Program, of her associates, or of other staff members of the agency who worked for the Program part time and on a voluntary basis. The writer offered consultation and supervision to these leaders of the Family Life Education group discussions; this rounded out the training and expertise in counseling families and individuals which staff members brought to the task.

A second goal was to offer help to persons who had problems in these areas, but who were hesitant to use the resources of the community, by reaching out to them with this service. Such hesitancy may be based on distrust of what society has to offer, on apathy, or on being too threatened to turn to existing resources.

The third goal of the Program was to make available to persons who had such problems help of a different nature than any counseling or other treatment experience. This was based on the theory that help can be offered in a variety of ways, and that one can work on these problems on various levels. While it is often important to get at the root of the trouble, through psychiatric or analytical treatment, this is not always feasible. Such treatment may not be available at the time when it is needed; financial or other problems--of time, of location, of family responsibilities--may preclude seeking it; again, the potential patient or client may be too threatened to look for such help, or to follow through when it is suggested. Any or all of these factors may change at some later point but, in the meantime, the problems exist, and the person who has them usually--but not always--seeks some solution or alleviation in the here and now.

Examples of persons who are often looking for some ways of coping with their problems, without being ready to take steps involving them in treatment experiences, are widowed or divorced or separated persons who must reconstruct their lives, parents who find it diffi-

cult to raise their children, or older persons who cannot make the
adjustment to the later years with ease.

In some instances, the problems faced by the persons who were
in difficulties were less obvious to them than to the professional people who knew and dealt with them.   Three situations described in this
book fall into that category: the retarded teenagers in a school, the
parents of children with problems of acting out behavior, and a group
of retired persons from low socioeconomic background.   They also
belonged to the previously mentioned part of the population which
would not have used the community's resources, if left to their own
devices.   Although they had not actively sought help and were partly
also resistive to such help, they were offered opportunities to participate in the discussions of the problems which were facing them, and
of possible solutions.   All three groups used the group discussions
well; they were exposed to new points of view, some of which they
could accept; many group members learned better ways of coping
with their problems and found new and/or different solutions which
were applicable in their life situation.

THE DIFFERENCE BETWEEN FAMILY LIFE EDUCATION AND
TREATMENT EXPERIENCES

Group discussions with educational goals, such as Family Life
Education discussions, have different goals than therapy has; this
has been well defined by Dr. Peter Neubauer who said the following

> ...[therapy] aims to effect change in individual
> pathology. Making use of a specific technique
> consciously applied, it approaches conflicts in
> order to free the energies bound within them,
> thus making these energies available for healthy
> growth.
> Education is aimed at those faculties of the ego
> which are undisturbed by conflict. It is oriented
> toward the healthy factors of the personality and
> appeals to the ability to judge, to learn by experience,
> to gain understanding, to plan, to make choices, to
> adapt to changing circumstances.
> The term education, in connection with group
> experiences, is not used in the traditional sense of
> applying only to the intellectual capacities of the
> group members. Here the educational experience
> takes on a broader meaning. It recognizes the
> importance of feelings and attitudes and uses
> emotional mobilization as well as intellectual stimu-
> lation. It uses all the potent psychic factors of the
> educational process while maintaining an awareness
> of the difference between education and therapy.

And while in group education there is an awareness
of individual problems and their effect on the person's
functioning, the unconscious motivations of emotional
problems are not explored nor are attempts made to
resolve these problems. (Neubauer, 1952, p. 12).

The service described in this book was educational in nature
in the sense of the above definition. This does not mean that change
on a deeper level, for instance, by acquiring insight into oneself,
was precluded; such change did occur, mostly when group members
were motivated to change, had the capacity for strong relationships
to each other and to the group leader, and were exposed to repeated
experiences of such group discussions. When such change occurred,
however, it was a by-product and not the goal of the service.

It should be mentioned that some groups had members who had
been, or were, in individual treatment, be it with psychiatrists or
with counselors in family or other community agencies. These group
members used the discussions in a different way, namely to supplement the treatment experience and to apply any learning which occurred
in the meetings to the problems of daily life. If they acquired some
insight also in the group educational setting, this helped to strengthen
them and to speed them on the way to better functioning.

It was interesting that none of these group members ever played
the well known game of pitting one helping person against the other.
This was due mostly to the fact that the therapists who were treating
the group members approved of their patients' participating in these
discussions, while the leader did not feel called upon to compete with
the therapists. Clarity about one's professional sphere and respect
for another person's competence result in an atmosphere where the
patient, who is also a member of such educational groups, can benefit from help offered on different levels and by different persons.
Jealousy between such persons, their conscious or unconscious competitiveness, however, is sensed by the patient and group member
and leads to confusion and lack of progress on his part. Where such
situations develop, conferences between the professionals involved
are indicated.

THE SCOPE OF THIS PROGRAM

The preceding statements are based on twenty years of experience in leading discussions of problems of family and social relationships. Most of them evolved from a series of meetings where group
members got together, usually once a week, for a number of times,
so that their questions and concerns could be explored in detail and
from a variety of angles. Such repeated contacts with each other and
with the leader also fostered the development of closer and more
sustaining intergroup relationships as well as similar relationships
to the leader. (This will be discussed at a later point.) Many mem-

bers of such groups attended several discussion series which offered them additional experiences to learn and opportunity to develop such relationships. In addition, many of the groups with whom the writer had extended contacts also progressed in their choice of topics and questions, from the areas of their immediate concerns to areas which were likely to become important to them in the future. Some parent groups, for instance, took up the problems of school age children first, turned to the problems of adolescent children next, and then moved on to the discussions of marital adjustments in later adulthood, when children are grown up. When such development occurred, it contributed to the scope and depth of the group members' learning experience, as well as to the breadth and variety of the Program.

In average years, the writer offered leadership for ten to twelve discussion series, that is for a total of sixty to seventy meetings with community groups. She also supervised staff members who led similar group discussions, as well as a Family Life Educator who worked part-time for the Program in earlier years, and full-time later on to meet increasing demands for the service. Their combined activities added an average of twenty to twenty five discussion series; totalling one hundred twenty to one hundred fifty meetings added to the yearly volume of work. In addition to the meetings with groups, the Program included approximately fifty planning conferences a year with cooperating agencies and organizations. These cooperative projects are discussed later in Chapter III.

LEADERSHIP BY MEMBERS OF OTHER PROFESSIONS AND PARAPROFESSIONALS

Although the theoretical formulations, practice suggestions and record discussions in this Handbook are drawn from the experience of a professional social worker, the material is presented in such a way so that it can also be used by members of other professions and by paraprofessionals. It is expected that professions geared to the service of special population groups will feel increasingly called upon to offer family life education to their clients. Occupational therapists may find it of value for the handicapped and family members responsible for them. Since rehabilitation seeks to make it possible for patients to return home and, since this frequently implies new problems and challenges for their families, physicians and nurses who work in Rehabilitation Centers may be similarly challenged. These professionals may find the description of the writer's experience in work with mothers of handicapped children to be of special interest. Guidance counselors in the schools may find the chapters describing the work with teenagers, the retarded, and unmarried mothers either indirectly relevant to their work and conducive to arranging family life education groups for them with leadership drawn from other professions, or helpful in leading groups themselves. Social gerontologists, of course, will be interested in the chapters on work with

retired persons. Such professionals may find it helpful to use the
general part of the Handbook concerned with mobilizing groups,
defining group goals and leadership, and then to turn directly to the
records of work with client groups of their interest.

Social workers and other professionals such as marriage
counselors, clinical psychologists, and clergymen may use the
Handbook in its totality by familiarizing themselves with the general
part and consulting special chapters in the second part when they are
called upon to lead groups falling into one of the categories of membership discussed in the records presented there. Or, they may use
the first part in adapting the principles presented there to other
client groups, such as foster mothers, parents of dropouts, etc.
They may want to use this guide truly as a Handbook for reference
according to the demands of their practice as they occur.

The work of paraprofessionals in Community Health Centers,
in Reach-out programs and in Methadone Clinics may also lead them
into Family Life Education as group leaders. It is hoped that in the
training and supervision of paraprofessionals for such functions this
Handbook will be found helpful as well.

In the expectation that people from such varied backgrounds
will use the Handbook, the writer attempted to bring the actual flow
of group discussions and the theory of leadership which directed them,
to the reader by using a specific format. The material in the second
part is presented in two columns. At the left the reader will find a
running record of an actual group discussion and at the right, the
comments of the writer. The latter will interpret the sequence of
events in the discussion process with special reference to the interaction between group members and their interactions with the leader.
These comments will also draw the reader's attention to the hidden
meaning--sometimes conscious, sometimes unconscious--of the
interactions. Finally, they will share the benefit of hindsight with
the reader in pointing out the writer's mistakes when they occurred
and what she should have done instead.

III

Outreach and Mobilization of Groups

One of the major concerns of professionals and paraprofessionals who offer group discussion leadership is how to reach the people to whom they wish to offer their services. It is unfortunately not true that those who could use help in the judgment of helpers are always waiting for it and eager to use it. When readiness and motivation are present, a group develops very easily, of course, and leader and group start from a better base because they agree that problems and conflicts exist, to which solutions should be found. When this is not the case, the first step is to reach the persons who are potential group members and to motivate them to attend the group meetings.

MAKING CONTACT AND THE USE OF LIAISON PERSONS

Nothing can take the place of meeting face to face the person who is offering help. If this can be done by the future leader's visits to potential group members, so much the better. Where this is too time consuming, professionals or paraprofessionals who are already in touch with them can act as liaison people and can visit in the leader's place. These persons can also offer valuable advice as to how to bring out this particular group. Very often a first exploratory meeting can be scheduled, the main purpose of which is to bring together potential members and the potential discussion leader for this particular group. Every possible device should be used to insure that the people one wishes to reach attend this meeting. Visits are again one of the most successful approaches, since they are evidence of concern on the part of the visiting person, and of his expenditures of time and effort on the person being sought out. Letters inviting potential group members to such a meeting, and follow-up visits to repeat such an invitation and to answer questions about the purpose of the meeting, as well as telephone calls a day or two before the meeting to stress the invitation and to repeat the date, time, and place, have brought many an undecisive person to a meeting, and often led to his or her involvement with and attendance at the group discussions which followed.

If this seems like a lengthy, laborious, and time consuming

approach, the writer can only agree that this is indeed so. It brings
results, however, in tackling such difficult tasks as reaching out to
extend one's sphere of professional activity when the reaching out
attempts to mobilize people who do not ask for help.

If the leader and the liaison person have agreed that a first
meeting should be planned, more to get the group members to meet
the leader than to offer any experience of learning through group discussion, it is essential to focus this meeting on one of the concerns
of this particular group, and to describe the purpose of the meeting
in these terms. Furthermore, the concern should be one which most
group members share and which is not too threatening. For instance,
if one wishes to bring out parents of the working class whose children
attend an elementary school, a meeting which centers on discipline
or on gang problems is more likely to bring out a good attendance
than one on how to motivate children to learn. Older persons with
limited incomes and little education are more vitally concerned with
financial problems in the later years and more likely to come out in
large numbers if a meeting deals with these concerns than if it focuses
on self-enrichment and on ways of attaining it in their time of life.

In brief, meetings of this kind must be related to the major
concerns of the group which one is approaching. Here the liaison
persons who are already in touch with the potential group members--
perhaps because they are active in the community, or in a church,
or are part of a school's faculty--can be very helpful. A leader must
realize, however, that the group's own concerns are not always
identical with what the persons who are in contact with them consider
them to be. While many persons who know a community or a specific
subgroup of the population can often pinpoint both the people in it who
could use a group discussion experience as well as the areas in
which it could be profitable to them, their own goals for the group,
or their own feelings, or conscious or unconscious motivation, may
blind them to that which they know. This is more likely to happen
if the professionals or paraprofessionals are overidentified with the
population they are serving, as this feeling usually leads one to project one's own wishes and hopes on the people to whom one offers
service.

In developing plans for a meeting as above-described, which
serves most of all as exposure to a potential leader, the writer has
found it best to combine the suggestions of the liaison persons with
some of the concerns which members of the future group express,
when it is possible to get them to do this. Added to these two factors
should be one's own professional knowledge of the possible and probable concerns of specific groups. In these times when professional
expertise is often looked upon with suspicion and disbelief, it is
doubly important to remain aware of what one has learned, not only
through one's training, but also through the accumulated experience
of years of doing one's job. This does not mean that one should not
be receptive to suggestions and ideas which may sound strange, or
even way out, when one is first exposed to them. They should not

be rejected out of hand but should be examined and, when they offer a chance for a new approach, they should be combined with those parts of one's knowledge which are applicable to that particular situation, and should be tried out.

Visual aids, such as movies--again they should be related to the group members and to their concerns--usually succeed in bringing out many persons who might otherwise not come. So do plays or slides, although the latter seem to have less appeal in the writer's experience. As a last resort, "sneaking in through the back door" is sometimes successful. In this instance, an activity of a very different kind, for instance, a Christmas party in a school, is used to introduce a future leader to a potential group. This needs to be followed up later on, needless to say, but it can serve the purpose of having group members and leader meet.

Sometimes questions are raised about the advisability of extending oneself in such fashion to mobilize people who do not wish to be reached. These questions are justified if the agency or organization by which one is employed does not include in its services reaching out into the community in such fashion, or if staff shortages or financial problems prevent one from doing this. Undoubtedly, many services are less time consuming and less frustrating than those extended to the nonmotivated client, patient or group member. If, however, the mandate of the agency requires service to the underprivileged who do not come to one's door asking for it, it will be necessary to use new and imaginative approaches to the nonmotivated potential client, patient or group member, and those described here have been effective. Furthermore, if one has chosen a helping profession, one's most important goal should be to help, even if this means conquering apathy or meeting with rebuff.

It is also important to see the lack of motivation in an objective fashion and not as a personal rejection. It is well known that apathy, inertia, anomie and a distrust of social agencies and other community organizations are often found in underprivileged persons (Minuchin et al, 1967, p. 22). These traits isolate them from potential sources of help which could bring to them some solutions to their problems so that instead of finding alleviation and, with it, hope, they continue to be faced by these problems. This leads to feelings of failure, despair, and of hopelessness (Gladwin, 1967, pp. 77, 105; Lewis, 1966, XIV), which, in turn, sap their strength and coping capacity so that a vicious circle is set in motion.

Mobilizing a group does not end after the potential group members have had a first meeting of whatever kind with the leader. If at all indicated, the leader should express interest in meeting with the group further to discuss some of their concerns and should inquire who among those present would like to attend such a meeting. If no one expresses interest--which is rare--the contact should be considered as terminated, at least at this time and with this leader. (At another time and, perhaps with another leader, a similar attempt may be successful.) In the same fashion, if the group members who came did not respond at all to the leader's attempts to reach them, or left before the meeting ended, the leader's expressing interest in future meetings is not appropriate.

Should some group members show an inclination to come to additional meetings, this can be reinforced if the leader conveys to them that such meetings are theirs to use, in any way they wish, as long as the leader's professional competence can be of service to them. Such questions as the content and focus of these meetings, their dates, time, and place can and should be decided by the group members at the first meeting, as this involvement in the planning process tends to assure their later participation. If for any reason-- such as unavailability of the leader at the time desired--the plans as suggested do not seem feasible, the leader's objections must be made tactfully and they should always be accompanied by positive sugges- tions, for instance, making another staff member available at the time which the planning group has selected for future meetings.

The leader will do well to confirm the plans which were devel- oped, and to arrange for those details of which the future group mem- bers cannot take care. He will be well advised to follow up by letters of invitations and telephone calls. It is better to do too much here than to trust the memory or the promises of the persons who expressed interest in future meetings. Many reality factors can intervene with their plans for attendance; if the father loses his job or if "the welfare check" does not arrive on time, of if one child in a large family gets sick, it is easy to forget a meeting. Furthermore, since the original motivation to attend was low, if there was any, the spark of interest which has been aroused needs to be carefully nurtured if the leader wishes to mobilize a group.

A word of reminder may be helpful in regard to later meetings: Attempts to keep a group alive do not end after the first meeting. Very often, a number of the people who attended it do not show up for the second meeting. This is often distressing to the leader who tends to regard this as a lack of interest, or as dissatisfaction with the service offered, or as a rejection of himself. While this may be true, other reasons may account for the failure of group members to come. Again, apathy and anomie may be among them but other factors need to be kept in mind, such as the demands made on parents by their large families, older people's fears of bad weather with its dangers of catching cold, or of slipping on ice, and the lure of parties for teen-agers. Last but not least, it is well known that many persons of low socioeconomic background have different attitudes toward time and toward keeping appointments. They do not consider time as a valuable commodity which should be used planfully and constructively (Mayer and Schamese, 1969, p. 141). Where this is the case, it is the by-product of an orientation toward the present and toward imme- diate gratification. Such an approach to planning ahead is in contrast to the prevalent attitudes of middle-class persons who tend to be future-oriented and to think in terms of long range goals (Gursslin et al, 1959-60, p. 213).

In situations where the group has lost some members between the first and the second meeting, or between later meetings, attempts to reinvolve the persons who were absent should be made by the leader or by any liaison person who is in contact with them or anyone else who can establish contact easily. Again, visits, letters or telephone calls are usually effective, probably most of all, because they are indications of the leader's interest in and desire to be helpful to the absentees. While such follow-up efforts should be made, they should not be continued ad infinitum. Since it is not possible to offer one's professional service in such a fashion that it will meet the needs of every potential user, one must consider whether absenting oneself means that this particular person does not find the experience of being a member of this group helpful. Where this is the case, the leader should not make further attempts to draw the person into the group. Instead he should indicate that a decision to leave a group may be changed at any time so that the group member who is withdrawing can return whenever he wishes to do this. The leader should also suggest, wherever possible and indicated, other resources to which the group member can turn.

JOINT PLANNING OF GROUP DISCUSSION SERIES WITH COOPERATING COMMUNITY ORGANIZATIONS

Another way of extending one's professional service, which is often also another way of mobilizing new groups, is to plan group discussion programs with other organizations. Many existing groups, as well as potential group members, are part of, or are related to such organizations which very often have close ties with the area which they serve. In attempting to develop such joint programs, one must bear in mind that large cities tend to consist of many smaller communities, because neighborhoods often have a character of their own. What is more, they regard themselves as entities within the larger context of the city. It is essential to know as much as possible about the specific characteristics of a neighborhood if one plans to offer professional service there, and the cooperating organization which is already functioning in this area is usually the best source of information about it.

Such organized groups, or such potential group members, can be found in churches, in recreation centers and in other group work agencies, such as Young Men's Christian Associations and Young Women's Christian Associations, Neighborhood Centers, to name only a few. Libraries, as well as schools, are often hosts to groups which come into being in connection with the main functions of the host agencies. Requests for discussions of family relationships come quite frequently from representatives of such groups; for example, from the parents whose children attend a school. They may also come from the professionals or paraprofessionals who are staff members of the host organizations, such as teachers or counselors or home visitors in a public school, or librarians in a branch library. Several of the meetings described in later chapters--for instance, the group discussion with the parents of acting out children and the meeting with a group of retired persons in a branch library--are examples of the formation of groups in response to services offered at the request of a host organization. The reader will find more information about this process in these chapters.

At this point the writer would like to deal in more detail with the positives and negatives of cooperative projects of this kind. The first advantage is undoubtedly the extension of one's work into a part of the community which was not reached so far and no more needs to be said about this. Next is the sharing of the tasks which are part of this service, since cooperation presupposes that all the parties involved participate in the labor as well as in the results of these cooperative ventures. Third, the cooperation with professionals or paraprofessionals from other fields is usually an enriching experience, because they bring to the situation not only their expertise and their knowledge of a specific community or group, but also a different point of view.

In this writer's experience, the major problem of cooperative services is the danger of being drawn into activities which serve only the purpose of the host organization. This does not mean that one can--or should--ignore this purpose; on the contrary, one should attempt to further it. Needless to say, one would not cooperate with an organization if one disapproves of the goals which it pursues. There is a distinction, however, between furthering a goal and giving up one's own goal, and this distinction must be upheld. To give an example, in the discussion series with the parents of acting out children, the school's goal was the better adjustment of the children to the classroom situation and, while the leader and the agency employing her agreed that this was desirable, the leader's goal was to help the parents understand their children's needs and problems better and to help them find better solutions to the conflicts which existed in the parent-child relationships, as well as in their own marriage relationships. This was necessary because the acting out behavior was a symptom which reflected these more basic conflicts in family life (Pollak, 1964, pp. 489-494; Reiner and Kaufman, 1959, pp. 15-17; Rexford and van Amerongen, 1957, pp. 75-85). In the cooperative ventures with the Free Library of Philadelphia, the Library staff's professional goal was to develop new and more inventive uses of their facilities in the Branches by the communities which they served. The writer agreed that this was important, but when she offered leadership to the group of older persons in a library branch, her professional goal was to help them examine some of the necessary adjustments which aging brings and to use better the resources which were at their disposal--both within themselves and in the world around them--to make the later years a more fruitful and more enjoyable part of their lives. As a result, many older persons developed stronger ties to their libraries, greater interest in reading, and in attending the

other programs which these branches had, just as the acting out
behavior problems of the children in school grew less as family tensions decreased, and the interaction in their families became more
positive.

A second problem may arise if these ventures affect one's
professional functioning in ways which are contrary not only to the
requirements of one's profession, but are also contrary to the
justified expectations of the recipients of one's services. A good
example is confidentiality which is a principle in the helping professions in that clients, patients, and group members have a right
to expect that what they reveal to the therapist or group leader will
not be disclosed without their permission. If one plans cooperative
projects, it is often necessary to spell out very clearly, both to the
group members and to the host organizations, professionals and
paraprofessionals with whom one works, what kind of information is
to be shared and what kind of information will not be shared. The
line is sometimes finely drawn, but it has to be recognized, and
material brought out which is confidential must be treated as such.

A third problem is presented by requests for additional leadership assignments which one sometimes receives which are well meant
and are, perhaps, the result of a successful experience, but which
do not fall within one's field of professional competence. While one
may be tempted to acquiesce--it is hard not to feel flattered if one is
asked back!--it is not sound to do this. Any request for professional
work which would take one into another profession's area of functioning
should be referred to a member of that profession, irrespective of
who happens to make this request.

A fourth possible disadvantage of such projects is the feeling
of competitiveness between the cooperating persons which arises
sometimes and which may lead to strange results. Highly competent
teachers may feel that they should be competent also in understanding
and coping with the dynamic phenomena at work in a disastrous marriage which affects the children's behavior, and group discussion
leaders of recognized ability may desire to acquire teaching skills
or the special tools with which librarians work in their profession.
Such feelings are most likely to develop if the person from another
field impresses one favorably so that the wish to emulate and, if
possible, to outdo, arises. Again, it is important to recognize one's
own sphere of professional activity, to respect that of the other person, and to contain one's wishes to move into it. These wishes are,
in the last analysis, not so much complimentary as they seem to be,
but express a strong hostile desire to rob that person of their own
specialty, along with the satisfactions that it brings to them.

By giving these examples, the writer is attempting to outline
some of the pitfalls which may result, especially if cooperative ventures are successful. One's desire to continue to keep them that way
may lead one astray, and so may one's gratification at being appreciated. Furthermore, just as group members and the group leader
interact--much more will be said about this later--so do the cooper-

ating persons and many sometimes conscious and often unconscious feelings and attitudes result from this.

One last point should be made, if cooperative projects with other agencies or organizations are to be successful, and that is the importance of making cooperation a two-way street. There are many ways of doing this, such as sharing information on these ventures with those directly involved in planning them, reporting on them to other staff members of these agencies if this will be helpful from their point of view, or to the members of their Board of Directors, if desired. In many instances, Board members are somewhat removed from the day by day operations of the agencies or organizations with which they are connected, and it is often of considerable interest to them to have a representative of another agency describe such projects. This also exposes them to new points of view and makes them aware of other agencies which serve the community (Pollak, 1963, pp. 335-342).

IV
Group Goals and Group Composition

The goals toward which a group works should be clearly defined; they should be formulated in positive terms; they should not be threatening; they should make it clear that the meetings are a joint endeavor of the group members and of the leader. The writer wishes to stress that any formulation of goals in negative or punitive terms--"to help you to be better parents" is an example--will be self-defeating since most human beings react with anger or with feelings of failure and defeatism to punishment. This is contrary to what one wishes to accomplish in working with a group, which is to arouse in the group members a desire to change and to do better. An example of the statement of goals for a parent group formulated in line with the above-mentioned criteria would be: "We are getting together to find some solutions to the problems which many parents have, because it is difficult to raise children today." This statement is clear, nonpunitive and nonthreatening. It stresses the group's part by the use of "we;" it leaves the parent the option of assuming that he does not have a problem and is only coming to the meetings because of a mild interest in what other parents are doing, for instance. Last but not least, the parent is assured that if he has problems, he is not alone, a generalization which is reassuring but also true.

If we examine this statement of goals more closely, we will find that it avoids several pitfalls. The first one is that of the punitive approach, which was mentioned above. The second one is that of lying, by denying that problems exist. The third and most dangerous pitfall is that of not setting reachable goals. It is always sound to set one's sights realistically, and not to expect nor to lead the group members to expect that miracles will happen as a result of the group's working together and with the leader. If the expectations of the group members are raised too high, the results are bound to be disappointing. Furthermore, this prevents appreciation of whatever gains were achieved and, as a result, the group members-- and very often the professionals who are involved in the planning of such a program--become discouraged with what they consider small gains only. Since change in the area of family and social relationships is slow, if it comes about at all, and since the solutions of problems in these areas involve prolonged efforts on the part of all

concerned, it is more helpful to face this at the beginning than at the
end of an endeavor which has such goals. This approach will not only
prevent everyone involved in it--including the leader!--from becoming
discouraged, but will also enable the group and the leader to continue
to work together toward these goals until they are reached as far as
this can be done.

The limits within which help can be offered and change brought
about must be kept in mind by the leader when group goals are formulated. They should, of course, also be kept in mind by the group
members, but the latter may tend to be more inclined to set goals
too high than is the leader. This is due to their understandable
desire for an alleviation of the situation or to fantasies about their
or the leader's powers to bring about change. The leader has the
responsibility to assess and to evaluate the reality situation in which
the group members live, its assets as well as its liabilities, which
of the latter are amenable to change and which are not and what the
likely optimum potential for change is at this point. Factors which
are not amenable to change are for instance being old, or having
certain responsibilities like a large family, or having a child with a
physical handicap. How these factors are incorporated into the person's or the family's life will decide what their impact will be, but
that is a different matter, which is discussed in detail in the chapters
dealing with group members who are old, or mothers of large families, or who have children with physical handicaps.

An example of the setting of limited goals, that is of goals
which incorporate the reality with its assets and liabilities will be
mentioned here. It is taken from the discussions with the mothers
of acting out children, but is not the one which appears later in this
book. Most of these mothers had large families, they were middle
aged and, generally speaking, not too attractive physically, probably
because the task of raising children on small incomes had left little
time, little money, and little energy to pay attention to one's appearance. References to their husbands were usually negative and belittling but when the leader asked if these husbands had any positive
qualities, one was described as bringing home the paycheck, the
other as being good with the children, etc. The leader could use
these statements to help the mothers realize the positive sides in
their marriages and to formulate the concept that "one must work
around things which one cannot change." She did this because she
thought it unlikely that these women would be able to establish more
satisfactory marriage relationships with other men--or even to find
such partners--at this stage in their lives, so that the realistic goal
in these discussions was to improve the quality of the existing relationships as much as possible. This could be achieved by avoiding
unnecessary quarrels and by giving to husbands some recognition
for what they were doing instead of harping on their deficiencies.
Such a change was based on gaining some understanding of the needs
of human beings for approval and praise and if this seems like a
small increase in insight, it did, nevertheless, result in improved

parent-child relationships in those families where the change took place. In other words, and in line with the findings of Spiegel, "a small gain in one or two family members was registered as a large gain the total functioning of the family" (Spiegel, 1964, p. 319). Incidentally, "working around what one cannot change became a favorite expression of many group members who used this approach in other situations also. It became helpful to them in their attempts to cope better with the problems they were facing, as it channelled to better purposes the strength they had devoted--mostly in vain-- to attempts to change the unchangeable.

If, as sometimes happens, the members of the group set their goals too high, the writer has found it helpful to break down these goals into those that can be worked toward in the immediate present and near future, while leaving aside the kind of goals which sound unrealistic at this point. This approach has two advantages: It gives group members something to strive toward in the here and now, while it does not discourage working toward higher or more difficult goals later on. It is important to do this, partly because group members should have opportunities to achieve as this gives them strength, encourages their self-confidence, and improves their self-image, but partly also because even the most experienced leader cannot estimate their potential at some future time. It is surprising how much understanding of others and of themselves some members of groups can develop, whom one would have judged unable to do this in initial contacts with them, and where that occurs, it would do them grave injustice to exclude them, even if this were only in the leader's mind, from moving ahead as far as they possibly can.

In some instances, the goals on which group members and leader had agreed may turn out later on not to be those toward which some of the former would have like to work and when this happens the group members whose needs are not met are likely to leave the group. Their decision to do so should be respected and can be handled by the leader in appropriate ways, which were discussed previously.

The composition of a specific group affects several aspects of discussion leadership, such as, the techniques used, the form of verbal communication which the leader selects, the goals toward which group and leader work. A group of parents who have school age children and who belong to "the silent majority"--similar to the group discussed in a later chapter--are likely to respond well to some presentation of material by the leader on any question discussed, especially if it is done in simple, nontechnical terms. Their discussions will, in all probability, concentrate on the immediate problem, that is on how to help the school age child, although most of them have both younger and older children. The goal of this group will be to learn better ways of raising their children, provided these better ways are in line with their own standards and mores.

A group of parents of physically handicapped children needs

much less presentation of material, but far more opportunities to
bring out their feelings of anxiety, of grief, of concern for the child's
future. Goals for their discussions have to take into account the
unalterable fact of the child's handicap. While some effects of the
handicap, such as parental overprotection, may be lessened or eliminated as a result of the group members' discussions and the
leader's--or some other helping person's--intervention, others can
only be modified and some factors, such as, the inability of some
handicapped children to become self-supporting later in life, cannot
be changed. If the members of such groups were presented with
didactic material in a routine fashion and if they would not have as
many opportunities as needed to ventilate their feelings, the group
discussions would not be helpful to them. Furthermore, if unrealistic goals are set for such a group, this would only reinforce the
anxiety and frustration of its members and would, therefore, do harm
to them and to their children. Needless to say, many parents in these
groups need to learn better techniques of raising their handicapped
children as well as the other children in their families, but such
learning has to focus on those parts of family life within which change
could occur, and it has to be limited to these areas.

Additional reference to the adaptation of techniques to be used
with specific groups will be found in the discussion of the preparation
of registration sheets and of questionnaires in the Chapter on Setting
and Tools and in the chapters dealing with the above-mentioned groups.
The writer would like to elaborate here, however, on the relationship
of the language, the terminology, the form in which the presentation
of material is couched to the composition of the group. The first
consideration is that the language selected should be understood by
the members of the group. Nothing is as frustrating and as futile as
the leader's showing his, or her, erudition to an audience which not
only cannot follow but is annoyed by this fact. One way of making
sure that one expresses oneself in ways which get across to the members of one's group is to ask: "Do I make clear what I am trying to
say? That is sometimes difficult to do, but I can try it another way,
if you would like me to do that. " Such a question puts the onus on the
leader--where it belongs, of course--and does not imply that group
members "do not come up to scratch. "

At the other end of the scale are the group members who are
eager to impress the leader by their knowledge, who have read many
books, are familiar with theories of parent-child relationships and
sometimes use Freudian terminology too--and quite correctly as well!
The separated, divorced, and widowed persons whose discussion is
described later on were a case of this kind. The writer has found it
useful not to show surprise, not to "kid" and certainly not to try to
outdo the erudite group members. If one works with such a group,
it is not only possible, but also indicated, to discuss more intricate
phenomena of family and social relationships, but one must also be
sure that every member of the group can follow. Again, a simple
question such as: "Does everybody here know what Mr. M. means?

There are other ways of discussing this problem and I can bring them to you, if you would like me to do that." This enables the group members who are less well informed to ask the leader to add to their fund of knowledge, a task which he should assume himself, by the way, because asking the group member who has used such a term or such a concept to do this might look like an acknowledgment of his superiority over those who were not familiar with it.

In regard to the use of appropriate language with groups, considerable discussion has taken place about the necessity of "speaking the group members' language" especially in working with adolescents from low educational background. In the author's experience, this is neither essential to the establishment of rapport, nor is it helpful to the group members. It is quite enough if a leader indicates with a smile, or with a few words of acknowledgment, familiarity with what used to be called "four letter words," but goes on to use the medical terminology for the parts of the body, or for sex relations in whatever form. The writer has always done this, with the explanation that this is the language which is used in clinics and hospitals by nurses and by doctors and that to know what one is asked gives one a feeling of competence, in addition to one's receiving more time and attention, if one does not need to ask unnecessary questions. If one operates from the assumption that a goal of one's work is to help people to a better coping capacity, to better functioning in the reality situation, and to a better self-image, the use of correct terminology is one way of enabling group members to move in that direction.

In attempting to get some clarity about the composition of a particular group, the registration sheets, which are taken up in a later Chapter are of great help to the leader. In addition, or in situations where such tools cannot be used--for instance, because writing skills are poor--a leader can try to elicit certain factors by asking questions either from the group members or from the liaison persons and last, but not least, he can draw on his own expertise and knowledge of the community for certain general background information. If one works with a group of parents, for instance, some elements of group composition which the leader would like to know are the age group of the children who are the immediate focus of parental concern, whether mothers only, or both parents will attend the meetings, to what social and economic group the parents belong, how much education they have, whether any special factors are at work in the situation, such as physical handicaps or acting out behavior of the children. Race and religion of group members are additional factors which must be taken into account. While much of this information can be elicited by asking for it on the registration sheets--or by discussing it with the liaison persons; for instance, the age of the children or the educational background of the parents--other factors can usually be supplied by the leader's knowledge and experience. This applies often to the race and to the religion of the future group members, and to their economic background, because one can expect that the future members of a group who live in a specific part of the city are likely to be members of certain racial and economic subgroups, and will often belong to certain religious groups also.

It is equally important to remember, however, that not all the above-mentioned factors which add up to the composition of a given group have the same weight and the same meaning. This leads us to the concept of group homogeneity, which is by no means always important for the development of good intragroup relationships, a sine qua non for a helpful group discussion experience. To give an example, the members of the discussion series in a Library Branch which dealt with the adjustments to the later years came from very different economic, social, and educational backgrounds. While their financial circumstances were brought up in the meetings occasionally, this did not affect group interaction and was not detrimental to the relationships of group members, because those who were more fortunate were tactful and helpful when these matters were discussed. Aging, and how to cope with the experiences which the aging process brings to everybody, was the common and often burning concern of all group members. This concern forged a bond which overcame these differences. A similar phenomenon was at work in the meetings of the parents of physically handicapped children. Here, too, the common experience of having a handicapped child united group members who came from very different social, economic, racial, religious and educational backgrounds.

In other words, the group's leader must be aware of the group's concerns and of the role they play in relation to group composition and group homogeneity. The experience of aging, or that of having a physically handicapped child, tend to arouse anxiety, which in turn leads to motivation to seek help. This sets the stage for mutual acceptance and mutual support of group members irrespective of group homogeneity in such areas as their social or economic or educational background.

It is also important that the leader be able to work with groups which are not homogeneous and accept the difference of group members in such areas as education or race or social background without being threatened by them. If the leader sets the tone in this fashion, most group members will follow this cue, while those to whom an inhomogeneous group is not acceptable will leave it, as they should do. This will be discussed in more detail in the Chapter on Leadership.

V
Setting and Tools

The setting for a meeting or a discussion series is important in many ways and must meet a variety of requirements. If a group already has a specific meeting place--such as, the school which the children of a parent group attend, or the recreation center which the older persons described later used--it is usually best to keep it for any new group activity which is being planned. Group members tend to become accustomed to their meeting place and are more likely to attend meetings in a place with which they are familiar.

SELECTING A SUITABLE SETTING

If a group is to be mobilized and has not had a meeting place so far, the leader and the persons with whom the meeting is being planned, must consider the location of the meeting place first of all in terms of its accessibility for the majority of group members. While this requirement depends somewhat on such factors as their economic situation--do they own cars? are they used to taking taxis? --it always looms large in the minds of the planners and group members alike.

Location is important not only in terms of accessibility but also in terms of safety. The latter factor will also affect the decision about the time of the meeting because certain locations, particularly in large cities, which are safe during the day, are not safe at night. The decision about a meeting place is, therefore, closely related to the decision about the time of the meeting. The place and time of a meeting seem to be more important in planning for teen-age groups and for groups of older people than for groups of other adults. In the case of old people especially, the fears of being attacked, or of having accidents, or of catching cold in bad weather if they must walk from public transportation to the meeting place, must be kept in mind. Teen-agers have similar fears if a chosen place requires them to move into "the turf" of another gang or group, a step which would be likely to bring upon them swift retribution for such trespass. If the leader is not aware of these conditions in a specific locality, the liaison people in that community can always provide information.

If the meeting place is not within walking distance for group members, or for some of them, the expenses for carfare can pose problems for low income groups. In a later chapter, the writer describes a meeting with young girls who came to a Library Branch after school hours. They went to a variety of schools and most of the girls came from families which were on public assistance. The agency made carfare available to the girls who needed it, and they responded to the trust placed in them with scrupulous honesty. It was touching to see them counting their pennies and dimes before they asked for additional money to enable them to get home after the meetings.

Beyond the factors of accessibility and safety, the comfort of the group members must be taken into account when one selects a meeting place. It is difficult to have interesting discussions in a place that is not well heated in the winter or well lit if the group meets in the evening. Large cavernous rooms have a discouraging effect, especially if a group is small. Sitting around a table encourages intimacy and the development of intergroup relationships and, even if the size of the group makes it necessary to have people sit in two circles around a table, this is preferable to having them sit in the more formal fashion of being lined up, row after row, as in an old fashioned schoolroom. Sitting around a table also makes it possible to put down one's handbag, or one's briefcase, or one's books, as well as making smoking more easily manageable, when permitted. Anything that makes the group members comfortable, conveys a feeling of being welcome to them, and contributes in this way to a positive group atmosphere. For this reason, armchairs or sofas, where available, should be used in preference to chairs which do not provide armrests.

This does not mean that a setting which does not offer any or all of these amenities should be discarded if it is the only one which is available, or if its advantages outweigh those of other possible meeting places. Very often, the group disregards the meeting place and its appearance or lack of comfort. An example of this is a group of parents to whom the writer offered leadership for several years. They met in the basement of an old elementary school where the boiler and pipes were located and which can only be described as dismal, even if one makes minimum demands on attractiveness and comfort. This was the only place available; the discussions were excellent and the group learned from them. It may be that being able to smoke--which could only be done in the school basement-- made up for some of the discomforts, since most group members were avid smokers.

The place where a group meets has other and less tangible effects on the discussions also. Meeting in a library or in a school stresses the educational part of the discussions because both institutions are associated with learning. Many persons in the writer's groups who would not readily admit, or not admit at all, that they might have problems in family or social relationships, felt safe in coming to meetings held in these locations. Educational activities and the pursuit of knowledge are not only safe, that is, nonthreatening, but are an indication of one's intellectual bent and are to one's credit. Very often, participants who came to the group with this aim moved beyond that in the discussions, while those who did not wish to investigate any problems which they had, either limited their participation or withdrew from the group. Undoubtedly, the selection of meeting places associated with learning attracted many persons who might not have come otherwise. The way in which they used the opportunity offered in this fashion depended on the individual as well as on the members of the group and the leader.

If the group met in the counseling agency which employed the writer, this affected the expectations of the participants also. This setting was associated not with learning but with having problems for which the agency offered its services. From the start all discussions held in this setting were geared more to the airing of problems, to the quest for the solution of interpersonal, and often intrapersonal, conflicts. Self-examination, along with examination of the other persons who were part of these conflicts, were the rule and not the exception. This was particularly true for the widowed, divorced, and separated group members who met there, whose meeting is described later in this book. It should be pointed out, however, that the setting may not have been the only reason for their approach to and the goals set in the discussions. The fact that many group members had had, or were having simultaneously with the meetings with the writer, experiences of counseling or of psychiatric treatment, may have accounted for some of this tendency. It is also possible that the writer, functioning in her own professional habitat, unconsciously led the discussions in a manner which reflected more closely her background as therapist.

REFRESHMENTS OR NOT

A brief word should be added here about the often controversial question of refreshments, which is closely related to the setting for a discussion series. If the group meets in the accustomed location so that the leader and the project move in, so to speak, it is usually best to let group members follow their custom in this matter. The leader should attempt to get the participants to time the serving of refreshments in such a fashion, however, that it will not interfere with the discussions, that is either at the end of the meeting or before it starts. If refreshments are available during the meeting, it is very easy for a group member to withdraw from the discussion by serving himself or other group members. Such activity interrupts the flow of the discussion which is, of course, what this particular participant wants at this particular point.

When a new group is forming and the desire for refreshments is expressed by its members, the above-mentioned principle should apply. Very often, however, the leader is the person who has to decide whether refreshments have a place in planning a discussion series, and such a decision must be based on the particular group which will come to the meetings. Food, its preparation, its serving, its consumption are usually equated with the giving of nurture, of support, of comfort, and of love. If one works with emotionally deprived persons, making food available often helps the group members to feel accepted, and to develop good relationships to their leader. Entrusting them with as much resonsibility as possible for shopping for, preparing, and serving it, and the subsequent cleaning up procedures also encourages the development of good intergroup relationships.

In deciding whether or not to include the serving of refreshments in the plans for a specific group, its mores also must be taken into account. Coffee and cake, for instance, were symbols of hospitality for the mothers of acting out children. Sitting down to this meant relaxing from a morning which was mostly confusion and upheaval, trying to get the children off to school and a husband off to work, if he was in the home and was working. Having coffee and cake with the group also meant to its members that their leader, who was a professional person and came from a different background, understood them and shared not only their problems but also one of their pleasures.

THE PLACE AND USE OF PUBLICITY MATERIAL

Publicity material, which consists in the main of flyers, letters, and posters, is an important tool if one wishes to mobilize a group. Its purpose is to notify potential group members of the service to be offered to them and to arouse their interest sufficiently so that they will wish to use it. Whether the material developed is simple or elaborate depends on funds available as well as on the ability of the person who develops it. It also depends on the kind of group one wishes to reach because very elaborate material sometimes scares people off who are not used to it. Another factor to take into consideration is whether the purpose of the material is to help form a new group, or whether it is addressed to an existing group; for instance, if it announces a second or third discussion series which is to be offered to the same group members. In the latter situation, and irrespective of group composition, the material can be both briefer and simpler than before, because one builds on the previous exposure of the participants to the service.

Whether these materials are simple or elaborate, printed, typed, handwritten, decorated with pictures, or plain, certain points are important to keep in mind. The first one is that the publicity must be geared to the specific group one wishes to reach in terms of statements about the purpose of the meetings, of language used, etc. The second is the timing of the distribution of such materials which should allow the potential participants to plan for attendance, but should not reach them so far ahead that they are likely to forget the meeting dates. Since planning one's time and keeping appointments is usually more part of the daily routines of group members from the middle or upper middle class, they may not need a second reminder a few days before the meeting date. An additional mailing of publicity materials is very helpful, however, for members of low socioeconomic background, and it may also be helpful to people from all backgrounds, if the initial response to the distribution of the publicity materials was not satisfactory.

Flyers or posters or letters announcing a meeting, or a series of meetings, should provide information about purpose, day of the week, date, time, and place. ("Wednesday, May 16" is easier to remember than "May 16" only.) If a movie or slides, or a play are to be shown, this should be mentioned, and the publicity should also give the name and professional affiliation of the discussion leader. Any additional statements which are likely to appeal to the persons one wishes to reach should be added, but one must beware of pre- paring material which is too long, or too wordy. Posters will, of course, have a briefer text than flyers or letters.

As to the distribution of publicity materials, sending out flyers or letters by mail is far more likely to mobilize a group than such techniques as giving them to children in a school with the request that they be handed to their parents. Children are likely to forget to do this, to lose the materials, and they may also be suspicious of the invitation contained in them. They are not far wrong if they assume that the meetings may have something to do with them, although their purpose is not to punish them. In some situations, liaison persons have called on prospective group members and handed out flyers at that time. This gives the person one wishes to reach opportunities to ask for additional information about the meet- ings. It goes without saying that the liaison persons should be well briefed on how to answer such questions.

Posters should be displayed in places to which the potential group members are likely to go. If one wishes to reach a parent group, for instance, posters in nursery schools, in schools, in library branches in the area in which the service is to be offered, will come to their attention. Pediatricians' offices, children's clinics, maternal health clinics, drugstores, shops selling children's clothes, and supermarkets are also excellent outlets for such publi- city. A knowledge of the community and of the life style of the future participants will suggest additional places for the display of publicity.

If this is the first attempt to mobilize a group, large numbers of flyers and letters are required, as well as considerable follow-up, both before the group meetings start, and between meetings. The latter is especially true if attendance has dropped. If a group has met for a number of times so that some group cohesiveness has developed, along with some intragroup relationships and some rela- tionship to the leader, much less publicity is needed to start a second or third series of meetings. Both the number of materials and the intensity of follow-up procedures can be sharply reduced.

TOOLS TO DETERMINE GROUP GOALS AND TO DEVELOP REGISTRATION SHEETS

Reference was made earlier to the importance of planning first meetings with a group so that they will be related to the members' major concerns, and how this can be achieved. If such a first meeting is to be held, the leader can, if he thinks it appropriate, use another way of bringing out the group members' concerns. This is the use of a very brief questionnaire at the end of the first meeting, asking whether the respondent enjoyed the meeting, whether he--or she--would like to attend additional meetings and, if so, which topics or questions should be discussed at that time. Such a questionnaire should not ask other questions, it should not require a signature, and it should be collected on the spot. It is also helpful to provide pencils if one thinks that the group members may not usually carry pens or pencils with them, as is often the case with some teen-agers, or with old people such as the ones described in a later chapter. The writer feels a little hesitant in mentioning some simple matters, such as bringing pencils to a meeting, or sending letters by mail to group members, and she hopes that the more experienced group discussion leaders will forgive her for doing this, but it is amazing how many apparently unimportant things are overlooked and, if they are not given adequate attention, how important they can suddenly become.

Suggestions received in this fashion will probably not be usable in their entirety, but they will give some clues as to what course this group wishes to take in later meetings. Needless to say, these questionnaires will also be the best indicators of a group's lack of interest in the service offered, thus saving valuable time and effort on the part of the leader and any persons with whom the meeting was planned.

Once a group has been mobilized, registration sheets are one of the most effective ways of finding out the concerns of the persons who are attending the meetings, and it is from them that the content and course the discussions should take, should be determined.

Registration sheets serve another important purpose also, namely, to give to the leader some information about the members of this particular group. In addition to the concerns and problems of group members, other factors affect group discussion leadership. If one works with a group of parents, it is helpful to know size and composition of the family, marital status, age, education, occupation of the group member or of the spouse. If one offers leadership to a teen-age group, questions about grade attended, name of school, age, number of brothers and sisters, would replace those about marital status or occupation. Should one be reasonably sure that such a question will not be embarrassing, one can inquire about the occupation of the father and the mother, as this gives valuable clues about the young person's background. In getting information of this nature from a group of retired persons, questions about siblings are not relevant, but information about past and any present occupation, as well as about the old person's living arrangements--does he, or she, live by himself? or with others? in a house? in an apartment? in a rented room?--is very meaningful. Needless to say, the leader should always try to obtain the addresses and telephone numbers of group members, so that they can be easily notified, for instance, if a meeting must be canceled.

Since one of the first requirements of good leadership is that one should not embarrass, and certainly not hurt people knowingly, the questions with which one seeks the above-mentioned information must be phrased very carefully, drawing on one's experience with similar groups, or on one's general knowledge about such groups. It is obvious that a group of parents from the working class are unlikely to have gone to college, and most of them will not have finished high school; questions about education might read: School attended, grade completed. Similarly, a group of black unmarried mothers from deprived backgrounds would probably resent being asked questions about their fathers, since many of them tend to come from fatherless homes.

Experience, or at least a theoretical knowledge of the characteristics of a given group, is again the most reliable guide, if one wishes to elicit their concerns and problems. It goes without saying that certain groups are likely to have overall interests--parents in their children, teen-agers in love, sex, and marriage problems-- and that this should be taken into account when one develops a registration sheet for a specific group. However, other factors must also be considered. In the writer's experience, group members with little education welcome more specific, "spelled out" questions, which should also be simply formulated. "Would you like to discuss the children's fighting at home?" needs little translating into the parents' own way of discussing their children, and gets a better response than "sibling rivalry." This term is, of course, very familiar to middle class or upper middle class parents and has its place on a registration sheet for such a group. Bringing the question close to their life experience, and making it specific, results in excellent clues as to where the group is and what it wishes to take up in the meetings.

Registration sheets on which group members have only to check off topics or questions are especially helpful to group members who find writing difficult, for instance, because they do not have a good command of the language, or because they do not see well, or because they are retarded. In such situations, the writer has never hesitated to offer a little help, in a tactful manner, and without putting pressure on the group members to fill the registration sheets out, or to check any questions listed, as this might be confusing or might alienate them. Other group members have often followed the writer's example, turning to their neighbors with such offers of help and, when this did not happen spontaneously, the writer often suggested such an approach. It is well known that most of us like the people to whom we can be helpful; furthermore, such interaction is a good way to "break the ice, " if group members do not know each other well.

Although the practice of leaders varies greatly, as it should in many areas of their work, this writer has found it best to ask group members to fill out registration sheets after some interaction among themselves and with the leader. The act of filling out registration sheets implies trust, a giving of the self, and requires also that any, or at least most, misconceptions which may have existed about the purpose and goals of the meetings have been clarified. For these reasons, the timing of that activity is important and deserves the leader's attention.

Once the registration sheets are filled out, the leader can and should put them to use in a variety of ways. If this is not done, and no reference is made to them again, group members feel cheated in that their efforts are not acknowledged. The writer's use of registration sheets will be discussed in more detail in the Chapter on Leadership.

THE PLACE AND USE OF MOVIES

Movies can be used to good advantage with groups, if they are carefully selected, are used with a definite purpose in mind, and if the showing of the movie is timed accordingly. The selection of a movie presupposes that one knows something about the questions and concerns of the group, or at least has some idea of what might appeal to this kind of group. It also presupposes that one tries to make it as easy as possible for the group members to identify with the movie's content and with the persons who appear in it. Any gap between what one sees on the screen and what one is oneself is more easily bridged by persons who have imagination, or who are used to dealing with ideas and concepts. This capacity is usually, although not always, closely related to the educational level of the members of a particular group. Since the leader who counts on the probable more than on the exception is likely to be more helpful to his group, it is wise to apply here the old convoy principle that the slowest ship must determine the speed with which the group proceeds. In other words, one will rarely go wrong if the movie is as close as possible to group mores and to the group's life style. If this is not the case, a careful introduction by the leader may help the group members to make the transition from themselves, their concerns and problems, to those presented in the movie. In this writer's opinion, however, this is second best only, although one may have to settle for it if the right kind of movie for a particular group is not available. Incidentally, it helps very much if the leader has seen the movie which he plans to use, instead of relying on the descriptions in catalogues, or on other persons. Unfortunately, this is not always possible due to such problems as the leader's schedule or previous bookings which make the movie available only for the time of the showing to the group.

The purposes a leader has in mind for the showing of a movie are usually twofold: The movie should be a stimulant for the group and help to get the discussion started, and it should attract an audience. Sometimes the first purpose is the dominant reason for showing a movie, sometimes it is the second and, in many instances, these two purposes are combined as was done with the group of older people who met in a Recreation Center. In that situation, the movie was shown at a first meeting of a group of retired persons who had little motivation to attend other meetings than social ones, such as parties. A third purpose for showing a movie may be to channel the discussions of an ongoing group into other directions. This was done with the group of retired persons who met in a library, who were highly motivated, but where the leader and the cooperating professional people wished to prevent too deep an involvement of group members in certain types of discussions. This is presented in more detail in the Chapter on Leadership and Leadership Training.

This writer found it helpful to make some notes on all the movies previewed or shown to a group, notes which covered the main topic, the helpful, or nonhelpful, way in which this topic or problem was presented, the quality of the movie, the interest it might arouse, and its suitability, or lack of it, for specific groups. Such notes make it possible to have on hand information about movies for the planning of meetings with other groups later on.

The timing of the movie showing is closely related to its purpose, which has been described above. A brief introduction of the movie by the leader is usually helpful. It should alert the group members to the main topic of the movie and often also to some special situations shown, or points made, which will be of interest to them and are likely to start off a good discussion. Again, the content of the introduction depends on the characteristics of the group in that the more alert and better educated group members usually need little preparation of this kind. Some introductory remarks, brief as they may be, however, set the stage and also draw the attention of the group members to the fact that the meeting is about to start.

THE PLACE AND USE OF BOOKS AND PAMPHLETS

Leaders differ widely in their use of materials of this kind, and the following statements reflect the opinion of the writer only. While it goes without saying that books and pamphlets, if used at all, must be related to the topics and questions with which the members of a particular group are concerned, more than this needs to be considered in deciding what kind and how much printed material one wishes to bring to them. Since learning in the area of family and social relationships is the principal reason why the group is meeting, one might think that such learning would always be enhanced by reading, but this is not true for all groups. The writer has found that the members of well educated groups tend to use books differently, not specifically to gain knowledge, but that they tend to consider reading a substitute for the changing of attitudes and the examination of oneself which is often a necessary, but painful, first step before the desired goals can be achieved. Also, many members of these groups are already familiar with professional publications in these areas; they may tend to quote from them in the meetings. While this can originate in an honest desire to be helpful to the other participants, it sometimes reveals competitiveness with the leader, an attitude which is not conducive to a positive group atmosphere. Leaders, being human, do not usually enjoy it if a group member competes with them, although some examination of one's own feelings mostly lead one to a resolution of such incipient conflicts. What is more important, however, is that any suggestions of additional reading materials might reinforce the tendency to avoid the difficult task of facing and of working on one's problems by escaping into intellectual pursuits.

Well chosen books and pamphlets have a place, however, with certain groups. In the area of sex education, a term which is commonly used to cover giving children information about conception, pregnancy, birth, and related matters, many parents who grew up in homes where such information was not forthcoming, find this a task for which they are unprepared. While discussing these questions brings out any feelings of reluctance and hesitancy which may be attached to these areas of parent-child relationships, and while such discussions also provide some information about these matters, reading and, if possible, owning a sound book or an appropriate pamphlet, can be most helpful to the parent as well as to the children in the family.

Some parents in groups led by the writer read these books with their children; others, who were more embarrassed, gave them to their children with the admonition to ask the parent if they had any more questions. Other parents again used such material as reference books; this was the case with the parents of acting out children, who are described later in this book. Because this group was very frank in admitting their embarrassment at the prospect of discussing these matters with their children, the writer "rehearsed" with them in several meetings the questions which children are most likely to ask, what the best answers would be, and explained why children should receive these answers. In addition to this preparation, she gave to the group members a copy of a paperback, "What to Tell Your Children about Sex," (Child Study Assoc. of Amer., 1965) as a little gift when this discussion series had ended. She did this because it was clear that most of the group members were poorly informed themselves about some of these phenomena although she did not, of course, make reference to this lack of knowledge. The paperbacks were put to good use, as group members reported later on; they read them and so did their children and, in some cases, their husbands.

Some readers of this chapter may--understandably--doubt that women who have given birth to children are uninformed about the physical aspects of pregnancy. Still, the writer was told many stories of such ignorance--always concerning other people, of course--by members of her groups. A member of the above mentioned group met a woman in the hospital who did not know that a baby is carried in the womb, although she had just given birth to her fourth child.

In summary, books and pamphlets can be very useful if they reinforce learning in the area of family and social relationships. This means that they should be used in addition to, but not in place of, the group discussions, as the latter would deprive group members of the opportunity to voice the feelings, and the fears and anxieties which had blocked them previously. Another benefit of making available materials on the topics under discussion is that group members who do not have necessary information will receive it in this fashion, incidentally, so to speak, and without having to admit their ignorance.

In certain specific situations, it was natural to encourage the use of books and pamphlets. This was the case when the group met in a library branch, as happened with several groups described in later chapters. For instance, the group of retired persons described later met in a library and, since reading is a recognized pleasure of many older people, they welcomed special exhibits of books which were of interest to them. Such exhibits contained books on adjustments to the later years, on health care, on diets, but also lighter fare, such as books on travel, crafts, and gardening, mystery stories, and recently published novels and biographies. The exhibits not only brought these publications to the attention of the group members, they also gave them a feeling of being important because special time, attention, and space were devoted to them.

In another situation, where a group of teen-age girls from economically, socially, and culturally deprived backgrounds met in a library, the exhibits presented books on grooming, on black history and biographies of famous black persons. They were selected partly to increase the girls' pride in their race as this, in turn, contributed to a better self-image and partly to encourage their interest in reading as an enjoyable activity which could also open new vistas to them. In addition to the exhibits, paperbacks dealing with the same subjects were also offered to the girls as door prizes with the same goals in mind. (Another purpose of giving out these door prizes was to encourage the girls to come to the meetings on time, but this was not achieved, due to the reasons discussed in a later chapter.)

QUESTIONNAIRES: HOW TO DEVELOP THEM AND HOW TO USE THEM

The counterpart of registration sheets, so to speak, are the questionnaires which group members fill out when a discussion series has ended. Such a questionnaire serves several purposes, the most important one being to get the reactions and suggestions of the participants about the meetings. This should be stated in the questionnaire, preferably in an introductory paragraph, so that the group members know how their responses will be used. A statement of this kind can be quite simple and the writer--whose lot it has been to fill out many questionnaires and who is aware that this can be quite a chore!--usually adds a brief thanks to the person who is taking the time to reply.

Developing a questionnaire should again take into account some group characteristics, especially the educational background and the ability of group members to express themselves. The questions should be phrased, keeping these factors in mind. Group members to whom writing does not come easily, will again prefer and will respond more readily to questions where they need only to check "yes" or "no." On the other hand, participants who have a good ability to express themselves will do very well with questions of a more general nature which leave them free to write comments of their own choosing and in their own wording.

Questionnaires may also be used for another purpose, namely, to reinforce any learning in the area which was under discussion, if the members of this particular group may benefit by some repetition of the concepts developed in the meetings. This depends on the leader's evaluation of the group, but here is an example of how such material can be brought again to the attention of the participants:

> We discussed a number of points in our meetings. I am listing a few below, just to bring them back to you. Please check if you agree or disagree and, if you would like to add some comments, please don't hesitate to do this.
> Children should be expected to come home from school at a certain time   Agree ( ) Disagree ( )
> A parent should know who his children's friends are.
>   Agree ( ) Disagree ( )

In addition to using the questionnaires to get the group members' reactions to the questions and problems discussed, and sometimes for the reinforcement of any learning, an important function of this tool is to determine the course and content of any future discussion series to be offered to this group. This presupposes that the leader, along with any persons with whom he may be collaborating in working with this group, has decided that such a continuation will be helpful to the group and is feasible in terms of leadership time and other considerations. This matter will be discussed in the Chapter on Leadership. A question:

> Would you like to attend another discussion series of this kind, if we could plan it? Yes_____ No_____.
> If so, what would you like to have discussed?

serves this purpose. If most participants would not wish to come, one would not proceed with further plans. If the response is positive, however, the suggestions for topics and questions to be taken up are almost always reliable indications of where the group is at this time as a result of the previous discussion series, and in which direction it wishes to move.

The questionnaires serve some additional purposes, such as to find out whether the meetings were helpful to group members, as well as to get their evaluation of the leadership. Questions which would elicit this information could be:

> Did you find the meetings helpful? Yes_____ No_____
> If so, in what ways? Was the leader helpful? Yes_____
> No_____ Did she present enough material _____
> too much material _____ not enough material _____
> Would you like to add any other comments about her
> leadership? (Where simpler language is helpful,
> the latter question can be phrased: Did she talk too
> much? _____ Not enough _____ Enough _____)

The answers to both sets of questions provide valuable clues, both as to whether the meetings met the group members' need and, if so, in what ways and, also, about their reactions to the leader and the leader's techniques. In the former area, much can be learned that will apply to any following discussion series, as well as to the work with other groups of comparable composition. In the second area, self-examination on the part of the leader, or other resources available to him for professional growth, will help him to use these replies to both his own and the group's best advantage. This will again be discussed in more detail in the Chapter on Leadership.

Another area which is often of interest to the leader, and which can be taken up in the questionnaires, is that of freedom to participate in the discussions.

> Were you free to participate in the discussions?
> Yes_____ No_____ Can you give your reasons?
> (Or: Were you free to speak up in the meetings?
> If that is more appropriate for a specific group.)

The answers to this question are helpful especially if a leader feels that the group members did not become sufficiently involved in the discussions.

Opinions differ as to whether questionnaires should be signed or not, but the writer has always asked group members to return questionnaires without signing them. Since the readers of this book will be quite familiar with filling out questionnaires, they will agree that this gives one greater freedom to express one's opinions, especially if they are negative. And while it is gratifying to hear positive comments about one's leadership, or about other aspects of one's professional work, they do not spur one on to do better as negative comments usually do. Anonymity is a great protector of truth.

This leads to "the grain of salt" with which all questionnaires should be read and the decision made to act upon them, or not to do so. It is very tempting to take positive, flattering comments about one's leadership at their face value, and to rest on one's laurels and, by the same token, to disregard negative comments about this or other aspects of the professional piece of work one has just terminated. The helpful truth lies, as so often, in between the two extremes. Careful sifting of the comments and suggestions, combined with what one knows about the group as a whole and its members, will enable one to make the best use of the replies on the questionnaires. For example, if two or three comments suggest that "we should cover more ground," that may be a valid suggestion if the leader comes to the conclusion that the group has bogged down in its discussions and that, for whatever reason, leadership has not been aware of this, or has permitted this to happen. If, on the contrary, this group had to move slowly because the majority of its members needed considerable time to examine a question and needed to do this from all angles, and repeatedly, the above mentioned comments represent "a minority opinion" only.

Timing, which was an important factor for the filling out of registration sheets, is just as important for the filling out of questionnaires. If this can be done by the group members at the end of the last meeting of a discussion series, the leader will have a larger number of questionnaires with which to work than if they are mailed to the group members. This has to do with the reluctance which many persons--not only the members of one's groups!--have to filling out such forms, the tendency to postpone this task until it seems too late to do it, the hesitancy to commit oneself, a hesitancy which is often reinforced by the feeling that the series which one is to evaluate is a thing of the past.

While results tend to be better if questionnaires are filled out at the last meeting of a discussion series, it goes without saying that the leader cannot, and should not, insist that everyone who is present fill out the questionnaire there and then. The group member who has to leave early, or who says that he wishes to think about the questions before answering them, has every right to take the questionnaire home, even if he conveniently forgets to send it back. By the same token, it is not advisable to return any questionnaire which is not fully completed, since every group member should feel free to write as much, or as little, as he is ready to.

Mailing questionnaires to group members is recommended, however, if they attended a number of meetings--half or more--but were not present at the last one. A letter explaining that these questionnaires are going out to a number of persons who did not attend the last meeting, explaining their use and stressing the fact that no signature is needed, is helpful, as is the enclosure of an addressed and stamped envelope for the return of the questionnaire.

If, for some reason, many group members took the question-naires along or, if a number of participants did not attend the last meeting so that questionnaires had to be sent to them, a second mail-ing of questionnaires is often productive, in the not unlikely situation that only very few such forms were returned. Such a second mailing should go out within a reasonable time, such as two weeks. Again, an explanatory letter and an envelope facilitate matters and so does the enclosure of another questionnaire form.

The leader will avoid disappointment if his expectations of such returns are not too high. If fifty percent of the questionnaires which group members took along, or which were mailed to them are returned, this can be considered an excellent response.

In summary, the writer would like to stress that first of all, no tool--be it a registration sheet, or a movie, or a publication--will ever solely by its use assure success in working with a group. Such use must be decided upon after careful examination of the pur-pose which a given tool is to serve in each specific instance. Further-more, every tool, whatever its nature, must be developed or must be selected so that it will fill the needs of the group as far as possible. Last, but not least, a tool must be as closely related to the group members' background and life experience as the leader can make it or, if a tool is used which the leader does not develop, such as a movie or a publication, as he can provide it.

PART TWO

GROUP DISCUSSION RECORDS WITH COMMENTS

VI
The Physical Side of Sex Relations

The meeting which will be discussed in this chapter is part of a discussion series on dating problems, problems of love and of pre-marital sex relationships, of planning for marriage, and of planning for one's future independently of marriage. An earlier discussion series with this focus had been offered to this group of young girls although it did not remain entirely constant, due to such unavoidable changes as parents moving to other areas of town, or to the group members going to live with other relatives. A process which can perhaps be called "outgrowing a group," that is, a group member's feeling that she has received optimum benefits from participation in the discussions over a period of time may also have accounted for some changes. This is different from a group member's dropping out of the group because it does not meet her needs, or because the discussions are too threatening, which usually takes place in the early meetings of a discussion series.

CHARACTERISTICS OF GROUP MEMBERS

The members of this teen-age group were fourteen and fifteen years old and can best be described as emotionally, socially, economically, and culturally deprived; this description applies also to their families. As the characteristics of these teen-age girls emerge from the numerous discussion series, totaling over 150 meetings, for which the author offered discussion leadership, they present a low self-image; distrust of other people; negative feelings about members of the opposite sex coupled with unrealistic expectations of what love and marriage can offer; fears of being rejected and hurt; considerable exposure to "life in the raw;" a desire to "shock adults;" a low attention span; equating disagreement with violence, which is usually seen as the only way to settle differences; a voluntary confinement to the part of town in which one lives; great interest in "the street" where "the action is;" a short range point of view which can also be defined as living by "the pleasure principle;" preoccupation with food, that is with oral needs, as well as with money and what it can buy; the great importance which is attached to trifles, if they are in any way conceived as being gifts; little awareness of the resources which the community offers. Some examples for the above characteristics are contained in the verbatim quotations of teenage girls from these discussion series:

"No one cares about me" which led to the statement: "Why should I care about what I do?"
"Why do you come to us? Why are we the ones with whom you meet?"
"Doctors make passes at you."
"If he does not work, he will hustle." "You should marry him if he goes into the service, so he won't cheat on you." "When you are married, he will beat you," or "he will run around with other women." "My cousin killed his wife." "If you do it, he will tell the other boys." "All old people drink." (This was probably also said to "bait" the discussion leader.) "If you have a baby, you take him to Court to get support." "His blood will tell if he is the father." "If I have a baby, my mother will say, 'It's just a mistake.'" "He will call you a whore if you have a fight."
"When I get married, I want a house with four bathrooms." "When we get married, he will give me all his money. He don't need any." "Married men make marvelous lovers." "Did you have sex before you were married?" (A question which was addressed to the discussion leader, probably as much to shock her as to test her. The former would be hard to achieve, of course, after many years of working with teen-age girls.) "If he would cheat on me, I would kill him."

In a discussion of the possibility of a young man's getting additional training or education after one's marriage:

"He will be tired when he gets home." "He won't have time for me."

(No mention was made of the possibility of his getting a better job, of the family's improving their standard of living as a result of getting additional skills, and when the discussion leader introduced this thought, group members had no desire to discuss it.)

"My mother is baking three potato pies for Thanksgiving." "Will we have candy when we come to your office?"

Any food which was provided for group discussion members disappeared within a few minutes, and the discussion leader's suggestion that some be saved for group members who would be coming a little later, met with surprise and sometimes with indignation suggesting the strength of their craving for the only form of love which many of them ever encountered.

The prizes for which the members of such a group drew, which were usually books, or records, or small bottles of perfume, were provided to stimulate new interests in the group members, or to encourage them to pay more attention to their own appearance. Whenever this happened, it led to a better self-image. These prizes were also an expression of the interest which the leader and the librarian had in the girls and fostered their positive relationships to these adults. This interest also furthered the development of a better self-image. The prizes were prettily wrapped, incidentally, and this was appreciated by the group members, since most of them rewrapped them spontaneously and carefully, after having shown them to the other participants and to the leader.

Babies aroused warm feelings in most group members, although a member of a large family would occasionally express her preference for a childless marriage of her own. On the other hand, having a baby--especially before marriage--was often regarded as one way of getting the attention which so many group members missed in their own childhood. This phenomenon has been described very vividly and very credibly by Kristin Hunter (1968, pp. 48-55 and pp. 98-105), a Philadelphia novelist, in "Pray for Barbara's Baby."

GENERAL GOALS OF THE DISCUSSION SERIES

The goals of offering discussions of their problems to teen-age girls were related to most of the characteristics cited above. If the discussions could help them to develop a better self-image, to develop sounder and, at the same time, more realistic goals for their dating, love and marriage relationships, to see a connection between what one does now and the kind of life one will in all probability lead later on, much would have been achieved. Conceivably, for some of the girls the vicious circle of poor family relationships, of poverty accompanied by hopelessness and despair, of large families in which no child receives sufficient nurture, love and attention might be broken. If it would be possible to help these teen-age girls to develop more ability to postpone immediate gratification for the sake of the greater rewards which a more solid future can bring, to get an education or skills which will lead to better paying jobs, or to select a mate whom one knows well and with whom one is likely to have a stable marriage relationship, we would have helped those group members who wanted to use this help to move out into lives of their own which would have greater chances for personal happiness, and for more stable relationships in their own families.

To put it more specifically, "structuring" a dating situation would, in all likelihood, help a girl to avoid embarrassing situations, or situations which are difficult to handle; interpreting one sex to another, for instance, by helping the girls to understand what anxieties, insecurities, or peer group pressures motivate some of their dates' approaches would probably make it possible to have more satisfactory dating experiences for both partners. Discussing the interaction of marriage partners, some of the realities of marriage relationships--that people get tired of each other, of their marriage, of their children--and the importance of evaluating the assets of the marriage partner as well as his unavoidable foibles and weaknesses, would probably reduce fantasies about husbands and marriage. Any of these discussions would contribute to the goals we outlined before and increase the teen-age girls' ability to handle their present life situation in a more realistic fashion, and also in ways more likely to lead to their greater happiness in the future. Greater competence in handling the problems of everyday life is also one way of helping one to feel more adequate and to develop a better self-image.

In similar fashion, developing greater social skills and learning to relate to other people would not only make the present lives of the teenage girls easier, richer, and more satisfactory, but it would help them to develop a better self-image. Most of us appreciate a "thank you" for anything we have done, a courtesy such as having someone pick up what we have dropped; beyond that, such things as passing food to other people at the table, or helping one's friend to wrap up a gift, are some of the small skills that facilitate interaction among people. If teen-agers, or young people, have some skills to offer in social situations, their place among their peers is usually more secure and they are more sought after in their own group.

Impulse control can be furthered, often starting in small ways, such as by asking "What do you think will happen if you do this?" "Is this what you want?" This approach was useful in a more important situation also when one teen-age girl advocated "killing the man who cheats on you," with reference to her aunt having done this.

"You will go to jail." "Who will take care of your kids?" "If you go to jail, he will go on cheating on you,"

were most helpful arguments which other group members brought out in reference to this problem. Again, the ability to control one's impulses is not only usually a way of better handling one's reality situation and current problems, but it also increases one's feeling of confidence in being able to handle future problems--another component of a good self-image.

Becoming familiar with such community resources as libraries and museums and encouraging their use, helps teen-agers from culturally deprived backgrounds to enrich their lives. When discussion series for teen-age girls were offered in branches of the Free Library of Philadelphia, teen-agers were greeted and welcomed by the Branch Librarians, were given exposure to exhibits of books dealing with dating and marriage problems, with black culture and history. This increased their willingness to use the facilities of a library and to read. Since we assumed that many of the teen-age girls with whom we met might in all likelihood have problems in later life for which they would need counseling help or would want to use other community resources, such as adoption agencies, free legal services, the services of visiting nurses, we arranged for certain groups of

teen-age girls from similar backgrounds to visit the agency's central
office at their last meeting. They were welcomed by the administrative staff of the agency, who met with the group for a few minutes
each and explained what they did. We also arranged to have the girls
visit the leader's office so that they could see what a family counselor's
office is like. As our central office was located in the Social Service
Building in which the Children's Aid Society, the Legal Aid Society,
and the Visiting Nurses Society had their offices, it was easy to discuss the services of these agencies also at the time of the girls'
visit. The visit was planned as the last meeting in a discussion series
of six weekly meetings because we thought that, by that time, the
members of the group would have developed a positive relationship
to the writer which would enable them to accept these new experiences
more readily and, perhaps, to transfer some of their positive relationship to her, to other services. It is well known that many members
of economically deprived groups of the population have negative attitudes to society and to its institutions as represented by schools and
social agencies (Pollak, 1964, pp. 489-494). If we could build a
bridge between some of our teen-agers and these institutions, we
thought that this would be helpful to them later on.

Getting an education was not only discussed as one way of getting a better job--for a young woman as well as for a young man--
so that one could move out of a difficult home situation, but it was
also explored as one way of meeting a new set of people of both sexes.
Many members of deprived groups have few if any social relationships
and do not belong to many organizations either. Since a variety of
relationships are another way of enriching one's life and of extending
one's horizons, it was important to bring out this by-product of
enhancing one's vocational skills.

In outlining these overall goals for a specific discussion series,
it is necessary to keep in mind that the individual group members have
goals of their own which are related to such factors as age, intelligence, personality, needs, appearance, family background, to name
only a few. Some teen-age girls who came from economically and
socially deprived families did not show the results of their deprivation and had sound expectations of love relationships and of marriage,
along with the ability to plan for their future within the realm of the
possible and likely. It is interesting to speculate why some young
people bring to their own lives strength and the potential to build a
better life for themselves, although their experiences in their own families have not provided them with any models for healthy family relationships (Pollak, 1957, pp. 369-378), while other young people, coming
from a comparable background and, sometimes from the same family,
do not have this potential. If one explores the reasons for these differences, one finds very often that the stronger young person had
received that little extra in his early years in the form of an accepting and supporting relationship--perhaps with a grandmother or with
another adult, a teacher, etc.--which has strengthened the ego, and
has affected the self-image of the young person positively.

THE RELATIONSHIPS OF THE LEADER TO THE GROUP MEMBERS

One of the basic tools of the helping professions is to offer to people who cope with problems of family relationships a relationship with an accepting, supporting professional or paraprofessional person, and we saw using a discussion leader as one approach to attempt to bridge the difference between the problem filled present of the group members and a better future as outlined by the goals of our work.

What one wants to achieve in any relationship with such a goal is a clarification of the problem with which the group members are coping, the identification of better solutions for these problems, and a strengthening of the individual group member's capacity to deal with them in a more positive fashion by applying these better solutions to the coping process. This requires strengthening of the ego, particularly in the areas of substituting a realistic assessment of one's life situation, with its liabilities as well as its assets, for fantasies, and of developing the ability to postpone immediate gratification for the rewards of the future--substituting the reality principle for the pleasure principle. It also requires the ability to tolerate some anxiety and some frustration and to withstand pressures of other people if they run counter to one's new plans for oneself. The latter is particularly important in working with teen-agers, because of the great importance which the approval of the peer group has for this age group. In addition, a poor self-image, feelings of worthlessness, of being unwanted and unloved, need to be replaced by a more realistic evaluation of the self, by the recognition that every human being is important and valuable to himself and to those other people with whom one can develop meaningful relationships, and that not having received the nurture and love which would have enabled one to grow up with more belief in oneself, does not mean that one is forever excluded from the more fortunate group of people who are able to develop their potential with less difficulty.

If we consider the professional relationship with the discussion leader as one tool which the group member will use to work toward these goals, we must outline the components of this relationship, state its boundaries, and describe its pitfalls. It is self-evident that acceptance of the teen-age girls, with the sometimes irritating quirks which most of them have in addition to their very real problem, is a sine qua non. The quirks, or perhaps we should call them general characteristics of this age group, are their restlessness, which is sometimes, but not always, caused by anxiety, the fluidity of their relationships with other members of their age and sex groups, their tendency to see things in black and white, their need to test the adults in their world, both as to their interest in them, but also as to the limits of what the adult is willing "to take" from the teen-ager. As a consequence, the discussion leader must have, beyond acceptance of the young people, firmness coupled with patience, a real conviction of his, or her, own worth, and the ability to introduce his, or her, own standards and values to the group members, slowly and in some relation to their own standards, as well as the ability to present to them new methods of coping with their problems. If these mandates sound too difficult, let us keep in mind not only the goals of working with deprived teen-agers--which surely are well worth one's efforts-- but also that many of these teen-agers are eager, and often starved, for relationships with warm and accepting adults. Once young people feel sure that the discussion leader wants to help, most of them let down their guards, talk freely, and are willing to listen to what the leader has to offer. Many young people go beyond that and identify with the helping person, accepting some of his ways of looking at, and of doing things, and some of his standards also. Again, some verbatim quotes will demonstrate this process:

"We had a nice group of young ladies - I enjoyed the meetings."

(This comment was made on one of the questionnaires which members of the discussion groups fill out at their last meeting, and return, without signing them. "Young ladies" was a term used by the leader with many groups to convey the image of being grown up, of having nice manners, and of knowing what to do. It had not been a term this group had used before.)

"Mrs. Pollak wants us to be grown up." This was the reason given by a teenage girl why she did not steal when her girl friend had just been apprehended in a store. "Thank you for coming to us to try and do what you could to give us a different and better look at life. Merry Christmas and may God bless you!" "I enjoy (sic) the meeting with you being as nice as you could. Please come back." "I want to become a counselor when I am grown up."

An example of identification with the leader occurred in another group, whose leader--not the writer--had, at one point, been a psychiatric nurse. One of its members decided to finish high school and went into a school of nursing. This was considerable achievement for a girl who came from a fatherless, poverty stricken family.

An indication of this need for a close relationship was the desire of some group members to sit in a tight circle and as close to the leader as possible, even though the group met in a large room. Also, those group members who came late but who usually sat next to, or close to the leader, would squeeze themselves into the places which they considered rightfully theirs.

SOME SPECIAL PROBLEMS OF THE LEADER FOR TEEN-AGE GROUPS

One of the pitfalls of working with these young girls, many of whom were appealing in their need for warm relationships, was the importance of containing the professional relationship which the leader offered within the appropriate limits. It is all too facile to be trapped by the desire to help into showing that one can do better than the parent, or the school, or what other people from the helping professions are doing, if the latter are also involved in working with the teen-agers. This overinvolvement is detrimental to all concerned because the rivalry affects not only the relationships of the leader to the other people who are part of the lives of the young people, but also the relationships of the teen-agers to the leader, to their parents, their teachers, school counselors, psychiatrists, or psychologists, since they are unconsciously aware of this rivalry, and get torn in their loyalties. This, in turn, damages their ability to relate positively to a variety of people in their life situation and to use the relationships which are offered to them to the best of their abilities.

Another pitfall is the need of young people to test adults, a need which results partly from the phenomenon called "adolescent rebellion," partly from a lack of security about being accepted. Since interracial tension had been increasing during the years when the author was working with teen-agers, some of that tension was also reflected in the testing of the leader. In coping with this testing, the author felt it important to clarify for herself, in every instance, what the purpose of the testing was. For instance, if the teenage group met in a school setting where there were definite rules for behavior--such as not leaving the room without saying where one was going and without a slip from the adult in charge discharging the girl--attempts to leave the room on one's own were blocked by the leader with such statements as: "You may leave to go to your counselor but if you leave without going there, please don't come back to our meetings." (These sessions took place in a special school for teen-age girls with such problems of behavior that the regular schools had not been able to keep them in the classroom.) Other rules which schools or libraries had--such as not making any noise in a library which would interfere with its use by its readers--were also observed by the discussion leader. This was done for a variety of reasons which go beyond the desire not to upset the normal functioning of one's host, that is, of the organization which has made its facilities available for the group meetings. An important element was the author's conviction that it was helpful to the group members to learn to accept certain limits, something which all of us have to do as adults, unless we choose to live outside of society and of its mores. While many people decide to do this, it seems sounder to make such decisions, which will affect the whole course of one's life, at a time when one has a little more clarity about one's goals and oneself than most adolescents have. Another consideration in deciding to adhere to most of the rules of the host organizations was related to the concept of maturity, since one of the components of the mature adult is his, or her, ability to live in harmony or at least with acceptance of some rules, and to be able to handle some of the unavoidable frustrations of adult life, of which having to face limits--one's own, one's life partner's, one's children's, to name only a few--is one.

Much testing of the leader was done in connection with such

rules of the organizations which were host to the discussion series.
It was quite possible that some of the group members found these
rules irksome and that they were trying to find relief from them,
but probably they also wanted to use the leader's greater leniency as
an argument for their point of view in any conflict with the authorities
of these organizations. This is the well-known phenomenon of "playing one parent against the other" and it stands to reason that no
responsible adult should lend himself to becoming involved with the
teen-agers' conflicts with authority in this insidious manner.

Testing the leader is often the result also of wanting to make
sure that she likes teen-agers, and likes the particular teen-ager
who is doing the testing. This is very understandable and is, of
course, the outcome of earlier experiences of rejection, of having
been hurt if one trusted people, and of having a low self-image. A
statement such as "I like you but I cannot let you do so and so for
such and such reasons" is often helpful in such situations, and it
also aids the teenager to recognize that liking somebody need not
mean giving in to all demands made upon one. This is an important
concept for teen-agers who have often heard "liking" or "loving"
used as a bribe by parents, or by boyfriends who wish to have sex
relations.

Sometimes questions which sound like testing are really attempts
to "translate" the leader's behavior into the forms of living, the mores
with which the group members are most familiar. The question of
a group member whether the leader has any children, very often leads
to the next question: "Why didn't you adopt any?", since the writer
is childless. While part of what is hidden behind these questions is
the fear that the leader might not like children and, more important,
might not like young people and the group members, part of it was
an attempt to find out why the leader did not act in ways with which
group members are familiar. It is well-known that adopting children,
or taking in foster children, or raising the children of other members
of one's family, if one is childless, is common practice in many
families in which group members had grown up and not conforming
to this way of life can be puzzling or even threatening to them.
Questions of this kind need to be answered in a truthful way, of course,
to reassure group members. It is interesting that no group member--
teen-ager or parent--has ever used this information for such statements as: "You don't understand me, you have no children."

The area of being asked personal questions is, in general, one
which needs careful attention, especially in working with teen-agers
and it is, by its nature, one area in which a great deal of testing of
the leader tends to take place. In answering such a question, it is
important not only to clarify why it is being asked but also in what
ways the answer may help the group members. For instance, the
question: "Are you married?" which the writer could answer by
saying that this was so, adding that she had been married for thirty
years, "and to the same man," led very often to very meaningful
discussions of marriage in general, what it takes to make marriage
work, some of the problems of marriage, the importance of recog-

nizing a marriage partner's assets, and of accepting his less desirable qualities also, the importance of evaluating what one must bring to marriage, oneself, to make it work. Such discussions were another way of helping group members to develop more realistic attitudes toward marriage, and their acceptance of and identification with the leader served to strengthen this learning process. The discussion of why some couples do not have children did not usually lead any further in meetings with teen-age girls, but groups of young adults very often went on from that factor to explore the variety of ways in which people can have full lives without having children, and also without getting married. These discussions were important since some young people do not consider motherhood, or fatherhood, as part of their life's plan, and because some young people do not intend to get married at all. Learning about other people's different point of view is often startling, especially to those young people who are rigid, or highly defended, and who need help to see that people differ in their goals, and in their concepts of "the good life."

Another question which the writer was sometimes asked, was whether she had had premarital sex relations. This question was always asked in an aggressive fashion and, since it was not desirable to encourage aggressive behavior in the group members, the writer ignored it. The question was never repeated, by the way, which was an indication that even aggressive group members "get signals" from the leader and act upon them. Had it been repeated, a statement to the effect that what we are discussing are their problems, their experiences, and their plans for their future, would have been the answer.

Questions about one's personal life tend to present problems to many persons in the helping professions, especially if they are young, are not very experienced, and if they have personal problems in these areas. Because of the limits of exploration which a Family Life Education discussion group has, such questions are usually more difficult to handle in these situations. Coping with these questions is one area in which the discussion leader needs to have clarified not only his standards, values, and goals for his own life, but also the goals of the work he is trying to do with the specific group so that his answers will be in line with these goals. One's own problems and uncertainties have no place in this professional situation, and should be explored in a therapeutic relationship where the discussion leader is the client or patient. The members of one's group have a right to receive answers to these questions which will help them move on toward the goals of the group meetings.

THE DISCUSSION SERIES: ITS PLANNING AND SETTING, GROUP SIZE AND GROUP COMPOSITION

The discussion series of which the following meeting was a

part, was planned in cooperation with the Free Library of Philadelphia (Pollak, 1963); the group met in a Branch of the Free Library. Representatives from a District Office of the Philadelphia County Board of Assistance helped also to plan these group meetings, and encouraged some of the teen-age girls whose families were receiving public assistance to come to the discussions. The group met in the afternoon after school hours. Since the library branch in which the meetings were held served primarily the black community in Philadelphia, the group consisted of black girls, with the addition of three Puerto Rican girls. While twenty girls belonged to the group, attendance at the meetings usually totaled fourteen girls; after school activities such as choir practice, or illness, or demands for help in the home, were the most frequent reasons for the absence of group members from the meetings. Also, the schools they attended had staggered closing hours. Eight girls had attended a discussion series which had been offered in the same library branch in the spring of that year; the other girls were new to this group. Half of the new group members had been referred to the group by the staff member of the Philadelphia County Board of Assistance; the other new group members were brought to the meetings by their friends who were already members of the group. The series had six weekly meetings; it started the last week in September to give group members a chance to settle down at school, and it ended before the Holiday Season with its extra activities and accompanying excitement, which tends to affect attendance at group meetings negatively.

Five of the twenty group members gave some information about the occupations of their fathers: "Elevator Operator, " "Army, " "Welder, " "Post Office, " "Construction Worker." The other group members did not fill out this space on their registration sheets, and it is likely that in most of these families the father did not live at home. The mothers of group members were working as factory workers, cooks or in similar occupations. Group members came from large families and had a total of 86 siblings. Five group members attended parochial schools; the other girls went to public schools.

In order to get some idea of the concerns and problems of group members, they had been asked to fill out registration sheets which listed a number of topics which are usually of interest to teen-age girls, such as: Having Fun, Earning Money, Dating Boys, Becoming a Woman, Planning Your Future, Getting an Education, Getting a Job, Getting Married, Love, Sex and Marriage. As could be expected, Dating Boys received the largest number of checkmarks--fourteen-- and Becoming a Woman the next largest--ten. Earning Money and Getting an Education received nine and eight checkmarks, respectively; Getting a Job was checked off eight times also, while Getting married received six checkmarks. Love, Sex and Marriage and Planning Your Future were checked off five and four times, respectively. It is perhaps indicative of the group members' awareness of life's problems that Having Fun did not receive any checkmarks. No other questions were listed for discussion the space provided for this, but group members may have thought that the topics they had checked off already would provide enough material for the discussions.

Since group members decided in every meeting what they wished to take up at that time, the questions which were discussed by this group varied considerably from those they had checked off on their registration sheets. Some practical aspects of dating-- where one should see a boy, if he came to visit, whether one's parents should meet him--were discussed in the first meeting of the group, probably because a movie was shown at the start of the session which showed the dating relationship of a young couple; three meetings took up menstruation, conception, and pregnancy, while marrying the father of one's child or giving the baby up for adoption, abortion, "low men" who do not support their children, whether a man can love his wife and still "run around" with other women, and whether a man of eighteen can support a wife and child, were the questions which group members brought up in the last two meetings of the series.

The opportunity to redefine content to be discussed makes it possible for group members to bring out their current concerns, and it contributes to the spontaneity of the discussions. It also encourages the relationship of the group members to the leader because it is proof of the leader's interest in the group members and of his or her readiness to follow their leads and of her desire to help them.

The following is the recording of the fourth meeting of this group, where the discussion of sex relations and related matter was continued. The recording is presented on the left and the writer's comments on the right.

GROUP PROCESS SESSION IV

Recording

Comments

October 16, 1969: Eighteen girls attended this session; three of them were new to the group: D.L. whom B.W. introduced: "I brought a friend," S.H. and J.T. S.H. had been a member of this group. The other group members present today were M.T., S.S., C.G., L.B., S.M., D.W., M.O., D.B., D.T., D.G., S.T., J.J.T., V.G., and N.W. Three group members, J.T., J.J.T. and S.T. are sisters. The girls sat around the table, as usual, and in that order.

Eighteen is a fairly large number for a teen-age girls discussion group, but all the girls were not present at every meeting.

Bringing friends to a group is evidence that the group member who does this finds the group helpful and enjoyable.

Neither the introduction of new group members at later meetings, nor the staggered arrivals were a problem for the group members, in part

because they were not a problem for the leader.

The attendance of sisters
could present problems, but
did not in this situation because
the sisters got along well together and the one who had come
first to the meetings brought
her other two sisters to the
group. Furthermore, in a
group which organized itself
to a large degree, as this one
did, it is best to go along with
the group composition. The
leader will always have opportunities to cope with any problems which may arise in
later meetings.

Teen-age girls often form
subgroups. Various factors
determine this; in this group
for instance, girls who attended
the same schools came together. Some relationships were
closer, for instance, that of
N.W. and V.G., who came and
left together, and where V.G.
was obviously the leader.
Three group members (J.T.,
J.J.T. and S.T.) were sisters
as mentioned before, and came
together. Other group members, however, always came
and left alone: M.O., L.B.,
D.B., were among them. If
the formation of subgroups
does not interfere with the discussions, that is, if there is
no heckling and no scapegoating,
as was the case here, the
leader does not need to deal
with this phenomenon.

The length of the actual
meeting usually varies from
the scheduled length, especially in the work with teen-
age groups, who are more
likely to be late, are more
easily distracted, and where

As usual most group members
came in small groups. B.W. came
with D.L., D.W. and C.G.: J.T.
and S.T. came with D.G., a little
before four o'clock when the meeting was under way. N.W. and V.G.
came together, as usual, a little
later. M.O. came by herself and
was early. The meeting lasted a
little over an hour. S.S. was the
first to come; see later recording.

D.W. won the book: "A Glorious
Age in Africa" and D.L. won the
record by Jack Jones. Most group
members needed and received carfare. The refreshments--potato
chips, pretzels, a fruit punch--
were enjoyed by group members as
usual.

a shorter meeting time may also be helpful in avoiding the the generation of too much anxiety.

Book prizes and records were made available to group members, the former to stimulate their interest in reading, the latter to give them pleasure. Both were related to teen-age interests, and also to the growing interest in black history, black culture, and soul music.

Carfare was provided by the agency. Most group members were very conscientious and would, for instance, count their money before announcing that they needed a dime or the full carfare of 35 cents.

I had, as usual, met with Mrs. D., the librarian, before the meeting and started the meeting by reporting to the group members that we would be seeing a movie, as they had requested, next time, and that we would have a Halloween party at our last meeting. This led to inquiries about how many meetings we will have, and if we will meet again in the spring as we did before. D.B. wanted to know if she could come back in the spring although she will have graduated from Junior High School. I told her that she was welcome to come as long as she would like to be with us, and I promised that I would notify her of the beginning of the next discussion series, as before.

Short, informal conferences of this kind were very helpful to settle details, to share impressions of group members, and to foster the cooperative relationships between the writer and the librarian. Group members, in turn, appreciated being informed of the plans for the following meetings, especially as some of them had asked to see again the movie which had been shown at their first meeting. This could not be arranged because the movie was not available for the date of the meeting, but a movie on a similar topic was reserved instead. It would not have been sound to change the date of the meeting in the writer's opinion, partly because that tends to affect attendance and continuity of meetings, but also because it is important for teen-agers to learn to accept some limits which reality imposes and the frustration which accompanies these limits.

Inquiries about the number of meetings can be used to offer an additional meeting if the leader's schedule permits it and if the meeting place is available, but that should only be done because the leader thinks that an additional meeting will further the goals of the group, or will make it possible to cover an important topic more thoroughly, or for similar realistic reasons. While it is flattering to feel that one is needed by group members, this is no basis on which to extend a professional service.

Letters notifying the girls of the start of a series and inviting them to attend were valued by most group members who did not receive much personal mail. These letters did much to encourage attendance. As a matter of fact, one grievance of two group members was based on the fact that each received two letters, due to an error of the leader: one of them had been meant for new group members -- and they were old ones!

Two group members (S.H. and J.T.) were better informed than the others and they were appreciative when the leader gave them opportunities to answer some of the questions other girls raised. They did this in a very pleasant way, and it was accepted by the other group members in the same fashion.

Recognition of knowledge or of achievement, when it is honest, is an Ego supportive experience for group members. If such knowledge would have been displayed in a patronizing manner by these two group members, it would not have been well received, and intergroup friction would have been one of its results. Members of this group had, for the most part, good intragroup rela-

Although the group was large and there were frequent interruptions because some members joined it after the meeting had started, the discussion went very smoothly. There was no "joshing" or "kidding" of group members, as if often the case when these topics are discussed. The pictures were passed around, looked at without giggling, and returned to me.

Many questions were asked by some of the more vocal group members who usually participated freely, such as S.S., B.W., D.T., but also by some who tended to be more quiet--D.B., L.B., C.G. The three group members who were here

tions, however, and there were only a few incidents of friction among them.

It is difficult to isolate the factors which will make for good intergroup relationships. Voluntary attendance is one; the setting--a library as opposed to a classroom, for instance--often is another. Voluntary attendance is not always identical with positive motivation, incidentally, because some teen-agers join a group with the intent to disturb. In the writer's experience the relationship which the group members form with their leader, their identification with a concerned, accepting and helpful professional person, is the most important factor in the development of good intragroup relationships.

Interruptions of meetings will be accepted by most group members following the cues of the leader. Some explanation by the leader may help, but the members of this group knew about the staggered school closings.

Joshing, kidding and giggling were usually the expression of anxiety which the discussion of the topics of sex relations often creates. These reactions of group members may also be expressions of hostility, which in turn can be directed at other group members or at the leader.

It is always easier for some group members to participate verbally than it is for others because the ability to verbalize and to interact in discussions varies greatly. This ability is not necessarily

for the first time participated readily.

Some of the questions were not very well phrased and often I could rephrase them. If I could not and looked startled, another group member helped by rephrasing the question. This was done seriously, again without giggling and also without "shaming" the girl who had asked such a question.

related to a higher, or lower, degree of intelligence, but it is related to the speed of a person's reactions to stimuli. It is also related to shyness, and sometimes to a low self-image. In no way is the ability to participate verbally related to gains from the experience of participating in a group discussion series, as the replies on questionnaires or individual contacts with such group members, often show.

The slurred speech of many teen-agers from deprived groups of the population may make it difficult to understand them, but most of these teen-agers are willing to explain what they mean, or a friend may interpret for them. In asking for such an explanation, it is important that the leader--and rightly so!-- assume the blame for not understanding, with a remark like: "I am sorry I did not catch what you said." Most group members resent being asked to repeat a comment or question more than once, and it is better to ignore the comment or question if one is still unable to understand it.

The inability to understand slurred speech is different from being unfamiliar with the current teen-age jargon, which a leader should know but need not use, especially as far as four letter words, or other popular terms for sex organs or sex relations are concerned. The writer has found it helpful to use such words as womb, vagina, penis, in answering questions of group members and to do this

One such question had to do with "the butt," and if one could get pregnant if one had sex relations "by the rectum" as S.H. rephrased it. Another was whether "greasing" was necessary for intercourse. I turned these questions over to group members: S.H. and J.T. answered the first one clearly and accurately, but had a little trouble with the second one so that I "spelled out" a little what they were trying to say, asking them if this was what they had had in mind.

casually with reference to the fact that these are the terms which doctors and nurses use, and that group members will find these helpful later on when they are grown up.

As previously mentioned, it is helpful to draw on the knowledge of group members where such knowledge is available. This is not only recognition of the individual group member who can share such knowledge with the others, but it is also assurance to those other group members that they will, in turn, be recognized when the occasion presents itself.

This approach also increases the awareness of group members that the leader sees them as able and contributive, and that the leader has no need "to be the sole authority" or "to know it all." If the leader needs to be the sole authority, this tends to provoke negative reactions in group members, often leading to the attrition or to the death of the group. Such a need is the expression of personal problems with authority, and professional help is indicated to cope with such problems.

While it is sound to draw on the knowledge of individual group members in the specific area which is being discussed, the leader will often find that some elaboration of the group member's contribution is necessary. Such elaboration-- or a correction of the answer, if that should be necessary-- must be offered in such a way as not to hurt the group member's feelings. A statement "that's very true, but perhaps our group members would also like to know..." permits the leader to add to the statement: "Many people believe this, because--giving reasons-- but what really happens is this" conveys the correct answer, without embarrassment of the group member who shared knowledge, or misinformation, as the case may be.

No leader would, of course, ridicule a group member--or permit other group members to do this--but if a group member is embarrassed, other group members may become apprehensive about exposing themselves and such reactions will inhibit their participation in the discussion.

Another question which group members discussed had to do with twins. How do twins happen--was this because one has intercourse several times the same night? How did they come out--together? One after the other? D.T. was very pleased when she could explain this: one of her aunts had just had twins.

Only one question made the other group members laugh. N.W. asked "if two cows can do it." (As I am recording this, I am wondering whether she was concerned about perversions, concerning animals, or whether a question about homosexual relations was on her mind. It may be helpful to discuss these matters with the group at a suitable opportunity.)

This is another instance of misinformation on a fairly common matter.

As previously recorded, many teen-age girls from deprived backgrounds have been exposed to experiences of which one would have preferred them to be ignorant. It is quite usual for them to be accosted and offered money for intercourse, or for fellatio; as one member of another group in a disciplinary school said shrugging her shoulders: "Five bucks is the going rate." Stories of homosexual approaches which have been made to them, or to their boy friends, in restrooms, on the subway,

etc. were often told by teen-
agers in other discussion
series, and this was done in
a very matter of fact way.

While members of the dis-
cussion series of which this
meeting was a part had not
made any reference to these
matters, they might well have
been a concern to them. This
is an instance where the
leader's experience is needed
in evaluating at what stage in
the growing up process the
members of a particular group
are, with what kind of reality
situations they have had to
cope, and also in picking up
any underlying, unspoken concerns. If the leader thinks it
appropriate, he can formulate
these concerns, generalizing
that "many young people have
had experiences of being
approached by men who expose
themselves"--or whatever
formulation may be appro-
priate, so that the group members will feel free to discuss
these questions also.

Other questions which group members asked were when the baby
started to kick in the womb, how
one would know it if the baby had
died (before birth), how many times
a man could have sex relations in
one night. As usual, I handled the
questions by turning them over to
the members of the group for discussion. Any addition or correction to the statements made by them
I made in my summarization of
these comments.

These questions are fairly
representative ones. Other
questions which one can expect
are likely to deal with additional anatomical details of
menstruation, conception,
pregnancy, ways of preventing
pregnancy and delivery. In
view of the fact that members
of any group may be Catholic,
it is important that the leader
mention the stand of the Catholic Church on birth control;
the writer usually adds that if
one would marry a practicing
Catholic, even if one were not
a Catholic, these teachings
would apply to the marriage
relationship. Additional ques-

tions which are often asked during these discussions take up abnormalities, babies who are born with deformities, and one also hears some weird stories about babies who are born "half baby, half dog," or about a woman's giving birth to ten children in one delivery. Some of these stories are the result of the group members' reading them in newspapers which cater to a sensation loving readership, but many are based on the exchange of misinformation among the group members or their hearing "scary stories" from older adults who may, or may not, be members of their families.

Recognition of a helpful contribution of a group member is Ego strengthening for the group member, and encourages the participation of other group members also, who may be shy or hesitant to ask questions, to expose their ignorance. Such recognition also strengthens the relationship of group members to the leader, who is seen as individualizing group members, and positively motivated to them.

In my summarization, I often mentioned the name of the group member who had made this comment, if it was a helpful one. This was usually very well received, with such comments as: "She remembers" or "She knows us." (The group members who had less education used "she" when talking about the leader.)

One of the answers in the discussion of the number of times a man can have sex relations brought a--rather optimistic!--reaction from a group member "twenty times" while another group member made reference to "black men" in that connection. Later in the meeting I made reference to the fact that we were talking about men and women in our discussions, and that love and sex are alike for all people, white or black.

A matter of fact reply here is that most men are not able to have intercourse that often, and that how many times a man can have intercourse depends on many factors: his age, whether he is tired, or worried, or not feeling well, and, most of all, on whether he loves his wife or not. Mentioning "wife" is another way of relating sex to love and marriage. (With a group of young teen-agers, it would be inappropriate to discuss that sex relations can be one way of expressing negative feelings, such as hate, contempt, control, etc.)

Whenever being black was mentioned by members of teenage discussion series, the writer agreed with realistic recognition of black achievement which was, of course, not the case in the statement about the number of times a man can have sex relations. It is important to stress the common base of life, of love and sex, of living together as a family, of being parents, which white, black, and the other members of our society share.

Other questions which group members asked dealt with "Spanish flies" and I used this to raise the question of using drugs in general. This led to a brief discussion of the reasons why people use drugs, and the dangers of using drugs. The girls were, of course, aware of the various drugs which are part of today's social scene. The reasons why one uses drugs were given as "because other kids do it," "for kicks," "not to be chicken;" the dangers were also described quite realistically, and also in a matter of fact way.

If the discussion seemed to be jumping around from topic to topic, this was due to the needs of the group members to find answers. It is sometimes helpful to put the questions of group members into some order, for instance by suggesting that we can discuss this question next week, "when we will talk about..." (mentioning related matter). Lack of time is one reason why one might do this, or the leader's need to think a little more about the question asked.

"Spanish flies" was a good way to introduce the topic of drugs. The leader might have raised the question of drugs, otherwise, but not in the context of a discussion of sex relations. If an opportunity for the discussion of an important topic presents itself as was the case here, a digression from the main topic is well worthwhile.

The members of this group

who discussed drugs were
well informed, probably also
because of the variety of programs on drugs offered in the
schools. Since the writer
does not get upset when drugs,
rape or crime are discussed,
her attitude often transmits
itself to the group members.
If most members of teen-age
discussion series--and quite
a few members of young adult
and of parent discussion series--
tend to be more anxious in the
discussion of sex relations, it
is due to the nature of this
topic. Here, too, the matter
of fact attitude of the leader--
granted that this needs considerable self-awareness and
self-control--is helpful to
group members.

Additional questions which group
members raised spontaneously were
whether one can feel the impact of
the sperm on the egg (my terminology of course); how long intercourse
lasts--D. B. commented "two hours;"
whether a girl could tell which of
her boy friends was the baby's
father. This, in turn, led to blood
tests and what they prove in regard
to paternity. A reference to interracial relationships was made in
this connection with regard to the
color of the eyes as proof of paternity. S. S.--a black group member--
said: "If he is white and has green
eyes, and the baby is white and has
green eyes, he is the father."

These questions are further
evidence of the lack of information which can, and often
does, accompany sexual
experience, although some of
the members of this group had
not had such experience yet in
the writer's opinion.

The leader missed a good
opportunity to tie in again love
and sex--if not love, sex and
marriage--when the third
question was asked.

Blood tests, proof of paternity, as well as the procedures
for getting support for one's
illegitimate child, are well
known to most members of
teen-age girls groups from
deprived families because
they have heard these topics
discussed by older sisters,
mothers, or other members
of their families or by friends.
The teen-age boys, in similar
fashion, are informed about
these matters, but they dis-

cuss them mostly from the point of view of how one can avoid the responsibility of having fathered a child.

Superstitions about ways in which a man would know that he has fathered a child abound. The writer has sometimes wondered if an unconscious wish to have a father for one's child is the basis for these superstitions. If S.H. had not corrected the erroneous statement, the leader would have had to do this, because group members tend to interpret the silence of the leader as agreement with a statement made, or a point of view expressed. This is different from treatment situations where silence of the therapist may be interpreted in different ways by the client or patient.

D.T. said: "The man gets sleepy and then he knows the girl is pregnant." It was helpful that S.H. said "The man cannot tell if the girl is pregnant, the doctor can tell her that," and I agreed with this statement. This remark of D.T.'s led to some negative statements about men in general. S.S. said: "They don't know and they don't care," while D.S. nodded and added: "It's all on the woman!"

These are two examples of the low opinion of men which teen-agers from deprived families tend to have, of what they think the attitudes toward and feelings for women are held by the men and of the lack of responsibility for their families which they expect from them.

The group members were reluctant to terminate the session, which we had to do because of the Library's closing time. I promised that we would continue to talk about these matters, and that I would also bring the pictures showing the male and

It is not always possible to have a discussion continue beyond the time when it is supposed to end. Had this been possible, the man's role in family life, one's expectations from a husband and father, and

female sex organs, the growth of the foetus and the birth of a child again, next week.

how to build up a good marriage relationship could have been explored further at this point.

****

****

OBSERVATIONS REGARDING INDIVIDUALS

Recording

Comments

When we were waiting for the group to assemble, S.S. talked with considerable feeling about her mother "who gets on my nerves." Her mother called the Library a few minutes later asking if S.S. was there, as she had not told her she would be home late. I did not have an opportunity to discuss this incident with S.S. because the other group members joined us and the discussion got under way.

The leader might have explored S.S.'s problem with her mother a little more, if time had permitted this, and could have asked S.S. if she would like to see a staff member of the agency for counseling help. On the other hand, few teen-age girls have ever followed through with such referrals, which have usually also led to their withdrawal from the group discussions. The situation would probably be different if the leader of the discussion group was also the person whom the group members can see for counseling with their more personal problems.

S.S. mentioned that she had "talked things out" with the girl who wanted her boy friend, but she added that she is "tired of him." I noticed that she was less vivacious than she had been last week, but she cheered up considerably when the Librarian brought the refreshments. She asked me if I would like some punch, helped herself also, and started to eat the pretzels and potato chips.

S.S. had discussed her conflict with the girl who wanted her boy friend at an earlier meeting. Reporting on what happened is helpful as an indication of a group member's positive relationship to the leader and it also showed that S.S. had learned something, since she had in her earlier discussion considered "fighting it out" as the solution to her conflict with her rival.

Food has, as previously recorded, considerable meaning for the members of this group, and its arrival was often greeted with expressions of pleasure, besides being consumed avidly. It was also easier for most group members to offer some refreshments to me, than to share them with other group members. Saving food for late-comers was out of the question, not so much because the girls needed the food but probably more because this would have indicated a willingness to include others into the welcoming setting of the meetings. Some members of this group were quite possessive, considered the meetings--and the leader?--as their own, and suggested not inviting the other group members when the attendance at one meeting had been quite small. The leader sent out these invitations in spite of this suggestion, explaining this as necessary, in case those group members who were present, would be unable to come the next time.

J.T. looks and acts in a more serious fashion than her sisters. She also expresses herself more clearly and more grammatically than they do. (S.T. listens mostly.) J.T. was nicely dressed and groomed; she has a much lighter skin than her sisters.

The descriptions of individual group members serve a variety of purposes: they are helpful in identifying the group members which, in turn, strengthens their relationship to the leader, because they feel important and valued. This also improves the low self-image of the group members, and the more positive their relationship to the leader is, the better is the leader able to win their confidence, and to help them with the problems with which they are coping.

These descriptions also enable a leader who is interested in professional writing, to bring back the group members long after the discussion series has ended. If one does not do this, it is much more difficult to outline the course which the discussion took, the contributions of individual group members, their interaction and similar phenomena. Physical characteristics are as important in these descriptions as descriptions of personality traits.

D. L. is tall and quite heavy; she wears her hair very short, and she seems to be shy, although she smiled pleasantly when I turned to her with a question which, incidentally, she did not answer.

In a larger group, it is not possible to remember and to describe all the group members, but this material can be added, as one is able to identify additional group members.

It is important, in the writer's experience, to respect the silence of a group member and not to insist that a question be answered. Needless to say, if members of the group attempt to force one of them into providing answers or information about themselves--"who has no boy friend?" is a good example of such a question--the leader should intervene by suggesting that "No one has to say anything in our meetings. If some of us prefer to listen, they are just as welcome to all of us as our friends who have more to say."

D. L. was hesitant to say if she needed carfare when I asked her about this. Before I could explain this matter further, B. W. said to her: "We all get it, she--she was pointing to me--doesn't want us walking the streets." B. W. said this very seriously and I thanked her for helping us. D. L. counted her money, and accepted the carfare.

B. W.'s explanation made it easier for D. L. to accept the carfare, and it also relieved any feeling that she was being singled out. The members of the group did not know, of course, whose family was receiving public assistance, as no reference was made to this by any group member, or by the leader.

This enabled the group members whose families were receiving such help to mingle with the other girls readily. If public assistance would have been brought up by a group member, we would have discussed it, like any other problem, in terms of advantages and disadvantages, possible choices, and solutions to the problem.

B. W. 's remark to D. L. was an indication of her positive relationship to the leader. On writing this, it seems that it would have been better to say "being out in the streets after dark, " since "walking the streets" could have been interpreted to mean "street-walking, " but this had not been in the leader's mind, and group members had accepted the somewhat awkward term in the sense in which she had used it in earlier meetings.

S. H. looks older than she is and could pass for eighteen. Part of this is due to the fact that she is very well developed, while some group members (D. W. , N. W. , L. B. are among them) are so small that they could pass for ten or eleven year olds. S. H. is also mature in her contributions, and expresses herself very well, as I remember from her participation in the Spring Discussion Series.

It is characteristic of many teen-agers from deprived families that they are physically not as well developed as teen-agers from more affluent groups of the population. Poor nutrition may be responsible for this or the fact that the mother's body is exhausted from pregnancies in quick succession. It is equally true that some of the teenagers from deprived families are obese which may be due to physical factors, such as poor health, glandular conditions, but which usually has an emotional basis as obesity tends to have.

The ability to express oneself well is helpful in a group discussion, and one sometimes

sees that group members
develop a better ability of
this kind as a result of being
exposed to the group discussions, in an accepting and
encouraging setting.

VII
Problems of Dating and Impulse
Control of Retarded Teen-Age Girls

The meeting which will be discussed in this chapter was part of a discussion series called "Senior Girls Forum on Dating and Family Living," which was offered to the girls who attended classes in a public school for retarded students. It is included in this presentation, partly because there seems to be a tendency to look upon anyone with even a slight degree of retardation, as unable to use help with personal problems and partly because the members of this group did not come to the meetings entirely of their own volition. Much has been written in the professional literature about the importance of motivation--or of the lack of it--in attempting to offer help to people in trouble (Ripple, 1964, pp. 25-28). This chapter describes a successful effort to overcome the difficulties of working with a group of low motivation.

The writer would not claim that discussions on family life could be led effectively with young people whose degree of retardation prevents them from living at home, and from attending special schools, if only for the reasons that she has not done this, and that this book is based entirely on her own experience in the field. Young girls who were members of this group had I. Q.'s of 65-70 and although they were fourteen to sixteen years old, their reading ability tended to be mostly at the third or fourth grade level. Some, but not all of them, had difficulty in writing down their names and addresses, and others were able to do this well. The lack of intellectual capacity did not interfere, however, with the ability of most group members to involve themselves in the discussions and to establish positive relationships with the leader. The quality of their intragroup relationships was different from that of the group members who were discussed in the preceding chapter, as we will see later.

The group members for participation in the meetings were selected by the school counselor. Although the girls were free to decide that they did not want to attend the meetings--which decision they could make before the meetings started, or after that time-- this served only to eliminate group members, but not to form the group itself. The preselection of group members was necessary, partly because meaningful discussions on the topics which were of concern to these teen-agers could only be offered to a small group, and partly because the more permissive setting of the meetings precluded the inclusion of girls who would have found it impossible to function in such a setting. In other words, a certain element of self control had to be part of a girl's personality to permit her to participate in such a project.

CHARACTERISTICS OF GROUP MEMBERS

The retarded teen-age girls who met for these discussions came from the same socioeconomic, culturally and emotionally deprived group as the teen-age girls described in the preceding chapter, and they showed the same general characteristics. Additional personality traits were a low attention span, as could be expected from retarded young people, as well as a low frustration tolerance, which was often coupled with considerable anxiety. The latter manifested itself most frequently in acting out behavior, in pushing and jostling other group members, or in shrieking, for instance, when they looked at the pictures showing the sexual organs. In line with their intellectual retardation, the concerns of group members were not on the level of the concerns of other girls in their own age group, but corresponded to the concerns of girls who were younger. It is well known that three or even two years of age difference affect the social and emotional maturity of teen-agers to a considerable degree and determine the problems of growing up with which they are coping. This difference in age, which is negligible once young people are in their twenties or older, determines to a great degree the content of the teen-agers' discussions, the extent to which they are able to explore problems, and to gain insight. The writer found that the retarded teen-agers were discussing questions which nonretarded girls in their own age group would have brushed aside, such as how to dress on a date or where to meet a boy. On the other hand, planning for marriage, which is of interest to most girls of fourteen to sixteen, was not a topic which was brought up spontaneously by the retarded group, nor were its discussions very productive when the writer started them. They did not go much beyond the desirability of the young man's having a job and "treating one nice." Marriage problems, on the other hand, were mentioned spontaneously, because troubled marriages were part of the life experience of most group members. It was important to keep in mind, while preparing oneself for the meetings and during the meetings as well, that the focus of the discussions would probably be comparable to that of a group of somewhat younger girls from the general teen-age population.

The physical appearance of the group members varied widely: some who were fifteen or older, were so small and undeveloped that they could pass for ten year olds, while others were very obese. The number of the girls who represented these extremes, however, was larger than in groups of normal teen-agers of the same age group.

Furthermore, many girls had additional physical handicaps, such as poor vision, poor hearing, cleft palates, or bone conditions, which no member of the other teen-age groups to whom the writer offered leadership happened to have. Mental retardation is often accompanied by other physical handicaps, and the unusually small size of so many group members may have been another example of this. The obesity of many group members may have been due to glandular deficiencies, but it was probably based on psychological factors also, showing again this compensatory mechanism of emotionally deprived persons.

A pervasive trait of the members of this group was the knowledge of being different, which led in turn to a very low self-image. Being different was an experience with which the group members had had to cope from the moment when they had been recognized as being retarded. However, the parents of these girls did not exhibit the inability to accept the child's handicap, the frantic "shopping" from doctor to doctor to find one who would give another medical opinion, which many parents of physically handicapped children from other social groups show, as described in a later chapter. The writer has often wondered whether the large families from which most of the group members came, families which are used to coping with many problems in their day by day living, may be more tolerant if one of the children is retarded, more able to accept this as another problem to cope with rather than to experience it as an intense, often devastating personal problem which requires one's utmost inner strength, and all one's inner--and outer--resources, so that it can be incorporated into the web of family life. This is hypothetical because the parents of the retarded teen-agers could not be mobilized to come to group meetings. As a result, the writer cannot evaluate their point of view and their reactions. This reluctance to identify themselves as parents of retarded children is a well known phenomenon, perhaps due to denial of the problem, and is again different from the anxiety with which the parents of physically handicapped children sought the comfort of each other's companionship and friendship, and the professional help which the writer was offering to them.

Even with this parental attitude, however, the retarded teen-agers were fully aware of being different. Their experiences in normal classes, which many girls had attended before their problem was recognized, the physical and psychological tests which they had to undergo, before their condition could be diagnosed and before they could find a place in the educational system, the fact that they attended a different school from that to which their friends were going all contributed to the group members' realization of their special situation. Added to this was the taunting of other young people about "going to a dummy school," or about "being dumb," experiences which were quite common, since cruelty is often part of the relationships of children to other children, and of teen-agers to other teen-agers.

The school which the girls attended provided every available service, such as counseling, training in a variety of occupations, being a nurses' aide or a waitress, or doing simple clerical work which would make the students self-supporting and give them the dignity of doing useful work and of joining the ranks of wage earners. Very occasionally one of the girls could be transferred to a junior high or a high school, but almost all the girls knew that they would not be able to move into such a situation and to live competitively and successfully in it.

A member of one of these groups expressed this feeling very touchingly when she said during her group's visit to the central office of the Agency: "I want to be important and to have an office, too." The leader's answer to such a statement was that there are many ways of being important, of which getting married and having children is one. Since this group member was very attractive and had been going out with a young man for some time, it seemed probable that she would get married and raise a family.

GOALS OF THE DISCUSSION SERIES

The goals for the discussion series with the retarded teen-age girls were not very different from the goals of discussion series with girls who are normal, but are slightly younger. Since we were dealing with emotionally, culturally, and socially deprived group members, helping them to develop a better self-image was one of these goals, and much of what has been presented in the preceding chapter about aiming at somewhat better impulse control, about gaining or improving social skills and becoming aware of community resources, were goals for the discussion series with the retarded teen-agers also. Equally important was the clarification of their misconceptions in the areas of sexual relations, of conceptions, pregnancy, and birth. As mentioned before, what one would look for in a future husband was discussed very sketchily only. Marriage itself, what to expect of it, how to adjust to a husband, and how to develop good family relationships, were too far removed from their present interests to be of concern to the group members.

THE RELATIONSHIP OF GROUP MEMBERS TO THE LEADER AND SOME SPECIAL PROBLEMS OF THE LEADER FOR GROUPS OF RETARDED TEEN-AGERS

As usual, the relationship which group members were able to develop with the leader was the vehicle through which such learning was accomplished, when it was accomplished. The retarded teen-agers were, if anything, more eager to relate to the leader than other teen-age girls had been, perhaps because they had fewer opportunities for relationships with adults who accepted them and liked them than normal teen-agers have. This was expressed in many ways, such as the solicitude for the leader's belongings--her papers, or

her umbrella, which were carried by group members when she came
or left the meeting room; positive comments about her clothes and
appearance; inquiries about her family life, her husband, the number of children she had, about her health, or her activities: where
was she going after the meeting? what would she be doing over the
weekend? could group members visit her?--and also by some physical contacts, such as taking her arm, or patting her on the back.
Some group members who had the ability to do this, wrote her letters
thanking her for what they had learned in the meetings and many
former members of these groups ran to meet the leader when she
returned to the school for a later discussion series, told her their
news, and expressed pride at having been "in your class." In a
school setting the members of a discussion series often have a tendency of viewing any activity offered to them as a class but if this
does not trouble the leader, it will not affect the group members'
ability to use the activity according to its real purpose which, in
this instance, was the discussion of their problems.

It may be well to discuss at this point one of the pitfalls of
working with a group of retarded teen-agers, because it belongs in
the area of the relationship of leader and group members. This is
a pitfall which exists also if one works with the parents of the physically handicapped children who will be described later on. The
pitfall is the overidentification, the desire to console, to gloss over
the difficulties of the situation, and to fall in line with the (understandable) desire of the members of such groups to deny their problems, or to seek solutions which do not exist. Such an attitude
on the part of the group discussion leader would be very destructive
for a variety of reasons. It would, first of all, encourage the flight
from reality, and it is never helpful if one does not face the actual
situation and the problems which it brings with which one must cope.
Second, such a withdrawal from reality prevents one from using
whatever it has to offer to alleviate the problem, even if it is not
possible to solve it. Third, and perhaps even more important, certain mechanisms of defense, such as denial, are damaging to the
Ego structure, while what the helping profession has to offer to
people who cope with problems which are by their nature unsolvable,
needs to be Ego supportive and Ego strengthening.

The low attention span and the frustration tolerance had also
to be taken into account in offering leadership to a group of retarded
teen-age girls. The first meant that it was often not possible to
explore any question raised for discussion from a variety of angles,
let alone in some depth; most members of these groups got restless
when the writer attempted to do this. Part of this restlessness may
also have been due to an unconscious fear that one would not get one's
share of the leader's attention, and of one's relationship to her. The
low frustration tolerance also necessitated some adjustment in the
quality of the leadership in that direct answers to questions were
often more helpful than attempts to involve the group members into
the kind of discussions where questions are "batted around," until

the answers emerge slowly and gradually but more meaningfully.

Many members of these groups had strong tendencies to acting out behavior; they would josh and push each other, if permitted, or would put their heads on the table, pretending to be sleepy or bored. Such behavior on the part of one group member would invariably be copied by several other girls in the group, who might try to outdo the girl who had first started to do this. The joshing and pushing was also an expression of their usually poor intragroup relationships. One could have expected that retarded girls might offer each other some support in coping with their problems of being different, might wish to be helpful to each other, or might develop some friendships among themselves, especially since it was often difficult for them to find friends among teen-agers who were not retarded. This was not the case in the writer's experience. Many members of these groups were likely to attempt to "tell on each other," for instance, by accusing each other of going with married men, or of having an illegitimate child; the pushing or hitting was often more than playful behavior and would in all probability have led to fights if the leader had not interfered. Some girls also enjoyed making negative comments about one of the group members, comments which made reference to her looks or to members of her family and here, too, the leader had to intervene for the protection of the attacked group member. However, no comment ever made reference to "being dumb," or "being stupid," a topic too painful to mention.

Any such activity quickly attracted a following. While most teen-agers are quite likely to follow the incentive which one of them has given, this tendency was far more pronounced in the members of retarded teen-age groups. Needless to say, in most instances, the initiative was for negative behavior.

These special problems which tended to emerge during the meetings with retarded teen-age girls made it necessary to adapt the leadership offered to these groups. It was important to cut short acting out behavior of any kind, preferably before it could spread, and in similar fashion, to interfere when some group members started to attack a girl in their midst. This required some very direct statements on the part of the leader about what group members can, and what they cannot do in the meetings because outer controls-- the leader's statements--had to take the place of the inner controls of the group members which were lacking in some instances. As previously mentioned, direct answers to the questions of group members were helpful because of the low frustration tolerance of many group members; in similar fashion, ground rules were helpful in establishing a less frantic and more orderly climate for the meetings.

Some additional safeguards were necessary in the discussion series with the retarded teen-agers. The concept of confidentiality of the meetings was foreign to them. The school counselor as well as the leader had to explain that no group member should mention what the content of the discussions had been, or quote what a group member had said, or had asked. Since many group members would be noisy, shout, or attempt to disrupt classes if an opportunity for this presented itself, they were asked to come to, and to leave the meeting room quietly. Both the school counselor and the leader were aware of the temptation which many group members might feel to disregard these suggestions, and a variety of approaches helped to encourage compliance with them. One was the use of the terms "Young Ladies," and "Senior Girls" in talking to, and referring to the group members, which they liked, as it appealed to their desire for being considered grown up, and "not kids," as one group member said. The other was the leader's appeal for their help: "If you are noisy, you are in trouble, and when you are in trouble, I am in trouble, too." The implication that group members could protect the leader, could do something for her, was attractive to many of them and helped to achieve the desired behavior in many instances.

Participation in the discussion series had come to be recognized as an honor, as something special which was not automatically available to all the students, as it could not be, because of the impossibility of finding staff members to lead additional groups. Some members of earlier discussion series would greet the leader--usually by kissing her, more about this later--as she came to the school; the school counselor included one or two members of the preceding discussion series in the following one, to help the new group members to relate to the leader. One of these "old" group members had the task of introducing the leader to the group, which served as a bridge between the leader and the new group members.

Obviously, being kissed is not one of the usual components of group discussion leadership, but in certain situations, such as the work with retarded teen-age girls, it is important that the discussion leader accept this expression of the girls' positive feelings. Furthermore, this should be done with some acknowledgment of these feelings, which may be a smile, or the statement: "I like you too," if the liking of the group member for the leader has also been expressed verbally. As always, the leader has to be very clear of the professional reasons for her reactions and, most of all, these reactions must be genuine. It is impossible to fake an acceptance of a feeling, if one rejects this feeling, or rejects its expression, because the unconscious of the group member will, every time, "pick up" the underlying rejection. The pitfall mentioned above of overidentification with the retarded teen-age girls on the other hand, might well lead to too many expressions of this kind of liking for the leader, and one does well to examine these phenomena carefully in regard to their frequency, their intensity, and also in the context of one's own conscious and unconscious attitudes, toward the group members.

The different reactions, concerns, intragroup relationships, and different characteristics of the retarded teen-age group members become particularly clear if one compares them with the group of girls who have been discussed in a preceding chapter. These differences should not lead one to the conclusion, however, that retarded teen-age girls are not able to use constructively the opportunity to meet in small groups and to discuss the questions and problems which are of concern to all teen-age girls. If these differences are given due consideration in the areas of group composition and of leadership offered to the group, their involvement and response will be comparable to that of other teen-age groups.

THE DISCUSSION SERIES: ITS PLANNING AND SETTING, GROUP SIZE AND GROUP COMPOSITION

In her selection of the group members, the school counselor took into account the recommendations of the teachers who usually knew the girls well because of the small size of the classes, and balanced these recommendations with her own evaluation of the individual group member's need for an opportunity to discuss her questions and concerns in the areas on which these discussions were focused, as well as her ability to function in the more permissive setting of a group discussion. Her summaries gave the leader some information about family background and family composition, about any unusual events in the group member's life, such as being raised in a foster home, as well as about the group member's reading level, her adjustment in the classroom and with her peer group, any additional physical problems of the group member, and any other community resources which were being mobilized on behalf of and used by the group member. These summaries, which were brief and to the point, were of great help to the leader in her work with the girls, although no reference was made to any of the information obtained in such fashion, unless a group member brought up her particular problem in a group discussion. Many of the concerns and questions raised by group members were more easily understood in the light of the background which these summaries provided.

The size of the groups varied, from 18 girls as a maximum to 12 as a minimum. These were the number of girls who were referred to the projects, but the number of group members present at each meeting was, of course, not identical with the numbers of girls who had been selected for attendance. Attendance of teen-agers at meetings tends to be more irregular than the attendance of adults, and the attendance of the retarded teen-agers in the school setting was affected to a somewhat higher degree, because of the greater problems of school attendance which many retarded teen-agers had. Such problems were, for instance, their lack of adjustment in classroom situations, the necessity of going to clinics or to doctors, along with the more usual problems of having to assume responsibilities for smaller children in the home, for doing household chores which affect the school attendance of many teen-agers from deprived families.

In the few instances when all 18 girls were present, it was necessary to be more alert than with smaller groups to the start of disturbances of group functioning, such as the above-mentioned "shoving" or pushing, as well as to the formation of subgroups, when three or four girls turned to each other and started to whisper or to giggle. In general, the admonition to tell everybody what they were talking about did not break up the subgroups; this is a technique which is more effective with adults than with teenagers. Breaking up the subgroups by inviting the most disruptive group member to sit next to the leader was a much better way of preventing further disturbance, but in a few instances, the only way to cope with the group member who was causing the greatest disturbance, was to ask her to leave the group. This was done only after repeated admonitions and after warning her that this might happen. But if one is faced with the spread of group unrest, it is best to exclude the group member, or group members, who are at the core of such unrest. This is particularly important in working with retarded teen-agers where unrest spreads more rapidly, because of the desire to achieve recognition, if only by causing trouble and because of the higher level of anxiety and of the lower impulse controls of most members of these groups.

The exclusion of a group member or of several group members usually causes more distress to the leader than to the group members who are being asked to leave the group. It is essential, however, to keep in mind one's responsibility to the majority of the group members, and not to permit them to be shortchanged because of the inability of a minority to function in the group discussion setting. This holds true whether this inability is due to their unrest, or to their dissatisfaction with the other group members, or to their negative feelings toward the leader. The existence of such feelings is always a possibility, painful as this realization may be, especially for the leader who is well motivated and eager to be of help to all the members in the group.

The following is the recording of the second meeting of a discussion series with retarded girls which was devoted to their relationships with boy friends and parents, and which also gives a very informative picture of the environmental and emotional problems with which they were coping.

SESSION II

Recording	Comments
March 10, 1965: Fourteen girls attended this session, three of them had not been here last week. I started the meeting by welcoming the new group members.	It is important to help girls who are new to the group to move into the discussions, and the leader's welcome makes it clear to the new and to the old group members that all of them are equally part of the group now. This prevents the group members who were

here at earlier meetings from feeling superior to the new-comers or from attempting to exclude them, which can be a danger, especially if new group members come when the discussion series had several meetings prior to their coming.

Next, I wrote down the names of the girls who were present in the order in which they were sitting; this was the only item I wrote down during the session.

Writing down the names of the group members in the order in which they are sitting is helpful in identifying them. Many retarded teen-agers are very suspicious, however, of notes taken by the leader, perhaps because of their greater familiarity with tests, doctors, and medical procedures which have a frightening effect at times. Occasionally, members of other teen-age groups also express interest in the notes which the leader takes-- which no group of adults has ever done--so that she has found it helpful to take only very brief notes, and sometimes only a list of the names when working with teen-agers.

The three girls who had not been present last week received and filled out registration sheets, and some of the girls who had done this at the first meeting, helped them to do this.

Part of helping the new group members to move into the group is to treat them in the same way as the girls had been treated who came to the first meeting, for instance, by asking them to fill out registration sheets.

If no one had volunteered to help the girls, the writer would have asked if one "of our young ladies who did this last week" would be willing to help "our new friends." If no one would have volunteered, the writer would have done this herself without further comment. Too much exhortation "to be nice" or to do this or that, does not work as well

Next, I asked group members if they would like me to explore those topics they had checked off for discussion last week and when they said yes, I reported that they had checked off "what kind of boy do you like for a date," "how to get a date," "how to keep a boy interested," seven times, and I asked how it would be if we talked more about "Boys" today? This met with expressions of pleasure.

The first question--about the kind of boy the group members like-- brought the following comments: "One who treats you nice," "one who has a nice personality," "one who does not have a foul mouth," "one who shows you respect." In answer to my questions as to how a boy should treat you, group members elaborated "he should not hit you" and "he should not curse you." The "nice personality" was explained by group members, again in answer to my question, as "talking to you, not watching TV," "being nice to your friends."

as the example of the adult's being helpful.

It is important to report back to group members what questions they checked off, or listed for discussion so that they get recognition for their efforts in filling out registration sheets. The leader can and should, however, exercise judgment in doing this, for instance by tying in this report with the topic which had been discussed at the previous session, if it had not been explored fully. Also, it is usually helpful if topics which are more threatening can be taken up in later sessions when group members have confidence in the leader's desire to be of help, and that too can be encouraged in the way in which this summary is presented to the group.

If group members had not wanted to discuss "Boys," we would, of course, have taken up other questions which were of more concern to them.

It is helpful if the leader takes the initiative in starting the discussion in working with a group of retarded teen-agers and beyond that, with any group of persons who do not have good facility in expressing themselves and are not used to discussing their problems. Although the explanations of what one means for instance by "treating one nice," were not very elaborate, any attempt made to explain what one means is a step forward, in that it leads one to clarify one's thinking. If group members can be helped to replace the use of cliches--such as

One comment, "one who is not a bum, " led to some discussion, prompted by me, as to what "being a bum" is; "hanging around with a gang" and "having been in jail" were mentioned. The latter point was contended by another group member, however, who described her boy friend as having been "picked up" when some other boys he knew had gotten in trouble with the police.

I commented that it can very well happen that someone who has not done anything himself, is in trouble because his friends are in trouble. I added that this would be quite different from "the boy who has been in jail many times," wouldn't it? One group member said: "you wouldn't go with him, " and I agreed that this would be sound.

"having a nice personality"-- by more concrete statements about specific behavior, this is one way of leading to better reality testing.

The discussion of "being a bum" showed how familiar group members were with gangs, with the boys' being picked up by the police and going to jail. These experiences would not be as likely to be mentioned by a group of middle class teen-agers, who would probably also have higher expectations of behavior from their dates than not being cursed, or not being hit.

It is important not to be defensive when one is told stories of police errors, or of police brutality. Neither should the leader fall into the opposite error of agreeing with criticism of the police because how the police--or other social institutions-- function is not the focus of these discussions. What is important, is to help group members cope with the problems of family relationships-- here of dating a boy who has been in jail, which is the result of brushes with the police.

In the discussion of similar situations with a group of teen-agers who would be better able to explore these matters from a variety of angles, the writer has often brought to group members the concept of "the second chance," which a person should have, particularly if it seemed likely that the young men might have had a brush with the police, or might have had a child before

At this point the discussion became more spontaneous because the group members started to ask questions. "How do you know if you love a boy?" led to the answers of "being jealous," "not wanting to see other boys" while one group member mentioned "feelings" which would tell you if you love him.

"How would you break off with a boy?" was another question which a group member raised, and it got quite aggressive reactions: "shut the door when he comes," "hang up when he calls you," "tell him, I don't want to see your stupid face again," "take off his ring, stamp on it, and throw it in his face." I remember also a rather awkward suggestion of one group member: "write on a piece of paper 'I am through with you' and give it to his sister." When I asked: "what will the sister do if she has such a message?" several group members spoke up: "she will make fun of him," "she will tell on him," "he will get mad."

marriage.

Discussions tend to become more spontaneous if the group has had a chance to settle down, to "warm up," and if the group members have become comfortable with each other and with the leader. This process usually takes less time as the number of group meetings increases. It is also sometimes affected by the introduction of new group members into the group; the latter tends to slow it down.

The process was hastened in this group by the low ability of most group members to concentrate, by their anxiety, and by the need of each group member who was able to participate verbally, to make sure that she got her turn.

Many boy-girl relationships, but also many friendships among girls in this group tended to be short lived, and swiftly changing, partly because of the low tolerance for frustration of group members--and frustration is an unavoidable part of all relationships--but partly also because of the craving for excitement which is characteristic of many persons (teen-agers and adults) from deprived homes (Miller, 1958, pp. 15-19; Pollak, 1964, pp. 489-494).

Terminating relationships with boys was one way of getting excitement into one's life. The techniques used showed little skill in social relationships, and no concern for the reactions of the rejected partner in the relationship. They also demonstrated the low ability of the girls to anticipate any effects of their

I agreed that all this might happen, but when I added: "what else could happen?" no replies came. I went on to say that boys have friends and that one would not want an "old" boy friend to tell his friends that he was badly treated, would one? This made sense to at least two group members who said "boys talk more than girls" and "he could scare his friends off you," respectively. I said that that was what I had been thinking of.

When I asked, could one perhaps say: "my mother says I am too young to go out with a boy," one group member answered that the boy might go to the mother and she would say, "I never said that," while another added: "My mother

actions, the reactions of the former boy friends, or of their boy friends' friends, for instance.

The leader could use the last suggestion to discuss with the group members some of the possible effects of their action, which some group members pointed out very helpfully.

This attempt to "take the discussion further" did not work out because group members did not understand what the leader was getting at; this may have happened because the question: "what else could happen?" was not concrete enough. The question: "do you think he would complain to his friends about his former girl friend?" might have been more helpful.

The silence of group members in answer to a question from the leader may have different meanings, but in working with retarded teen-agers--or with group members who have little education--it often helps to rephrase such a question, making it more concrete, or using different words.

"Boys talk more than girls" might have been picked up by the leader and could have led to a discussion of the ways in which boys and girls (and men and women) are different, but the leader did not recognize this opportunity.

The leader thought it worthwhile to explore the possibility of using parental veto as one way of breaking off a relationship more easily, but the group members who commented to the leader's remark did

would say to me--'you do your own dirty work!'"

not think that their mothers would be of help to them. This may have been true, perhaps because the mothers of large families may be too burdened to devote much time to the problems of one child, perhaps because of their hostility to the retarded teen-ager, perhaps because of envy of the growing-up young woman, or for any other number of reasons.

One group member then told a story which was a little involved about her former boy friend: "I feel I still belongs (sic) to him. " It seemed that he had turned to another girl, but now wanted to come back to the group member. When I asked the other members of the group what they thought, the girls who discussed this question agreed, and I agreed with them, that if one liked the boy very much, one might give him another chance but should explain to the boy friend that "this is the last time" (one takes him back) as one group member phrased it.

The stories of many teen-agers--not only of retarded teen-agers--are often a little difficult to follow, but the writer has found it best to try to get the main gist of the story, rather than to ask too many questions.

Asking the other members in a group what they think X should do, or, if that should not bring a reply, what they would do if this happened to them, often results in increased interaction in a group. The first question presupposes more of a positive intergroup relationship than the second, which involves group members on the level of their own potential problems. The leader, of course, uses whichever approach is most likely to bring about a good discussion, and the participation of as many group members as possible.

This conclusion was a sound one, and was therefore supported by the discussion leader.

It was interesting that one member of this group brought up a personal problem in the discussion. When this happens, it is usually an indica-

"Cheating" was brought up next by a group member and another girl who had not spoken up so far, said with great feeling: "I would kill him!" Several group members agreed that they would do this too, but one girl said: "you will go to jail" while another suggested: "you could show him the gun, and tell him you will kill him!" These comments enabled me to point out that going to jail would spoil a girl's life, and that other boys might not want to have anything to do with a girl who had killed someone, because they might be afraid the same thing might happen to them. Most group members looked startled when I made this point.

Does the boy ask a girl to be his girl friend, or does she tell him she likes him? was another question raised. Again, I turned this question over to the group members and the girls who commented on it, suggested that the boy should approach the girl. One way in which he could do this, would be by saying: "I am interested in you;" several group members also mentioned "asking you to go out" as a sign of the boy's interest.

What to say when a boy asks you: "Are you a virgin?" came up for discussion next and the question was raised spontaneously also by a group member. Several girls nodded when I asked if a boy would ask this; one said: "they wants (sic) to know;"

tion of the depth of the problem. The leader has to evaluate what is at work in any given situation.

Because of the rapidly changing relationships of many of the young people, who seem to lack a feeling of commitment to each other, cheating is almost always a topic which teen-agers, and especially teen-agers from deprived background, will bring up for discussion. The reactions to cheating tend to be violent, and to involve either the boy friend, or the other girl, or both.

It was interesting that those group members whose faces show their feelings--a few have a dull look, and their faces are devoid of expression--looked startled when the leader made this comment. This was another instance of the lack of ability to evaluate the possible effects of one's actions.

Some of the approaches to a member of the other sex, which are being discussed, sound a little awkward but they reflect the lack of social skills of these teen-agers. They may also be an expression of the anxiety which many adolescents have about their acceptability to the members of the opposite sex and about their sexual attractiveness.

It was quite obvious that this question is one which members of the group had been asked, and they had no doubt that it should be answered, if asked.

The leader's question,

another added: "you go out with him, he asks;" implied was, that this happens--or can happen--on a first date. I said, certainly we should discuss this: what would one say to the boy? No answer came, however, probably because this was a touchy topic, and whan I said "You know, there are some personal things which one does not have to discuss" several girls nodded again. One group member said: "you could say -- 'that's for me to know!'" and when I commented that that was a very good answer, there were again many nods, expressing agreement.

whether a boy would ask one this question reflects her surprise, which is due to the generation gap, no doubt, and she would have done better not to ask it. It was a sign of her acceptance by the group that this did not lead to her being ridiculed, or being accused of "not knowing what it's all about."

The attempt to involve the group members into a discussion of how to answer such a question failed for a number of reasons. One was that some group members had probably had sex relations and were not going to divulge this in the group--as they certainly should not!--and the other was that it was often quite difficult for many group members to discuss an abstract situation, to imagine what one would do in a given situation. The leader's reference to personal matters which one does not have to discuss "struck a chord" because many group members have probably been told by parents or other members of their families, that such matters as, e.g., where one's father is--if he has left the family-- or where the family gets its money--if they are on public assistance--are personal and should not be discussed with anyone.

The formulation which one group member suggested translated the leader's concept of personal matters of privacy into a form which was closer to the world of most group members, was helpful to the group, and to the leader also.

Any attempt by a group member to start a discussion of who was a virgin would have been inappropriate in view of the purpose of the discussions, and especially inappropriate in the setting of a school, and with a group of retarded teen-agers who might have used such information in a destructive way. If a group member had asked this question--this has happened--the leader would have cut the discussion off, again with reference to personal matters which one should not discuss. There is a difference between bringing personal problems to a group because members feel at home with the group and the leader and wish to use the group for help and asking group members for information about very personal matters of this kind. This is one of the instances where the leader determines what is "out of bounds" for a specific group.

What is "out of bounds" must be determined for each group. For instance, discussions of how to explain to a new boy friend that one has a child, on the other hand, were part and parcel of the discussion series with unmarried mothers, which are described in this book also.

The "hot dog" episode shows the deprivation of most members of this group, in the importance attached--by the receiver and apparently also by the giver--to the provision of such refreshment.

The exchange of small gifts--of food, of clothing or

What you can do "if he bought you a hot dog, and now he wants to do it, and you don't have any money" was another question which a group member raised, and I suggested that we discuss this problem. "Running away" was one suggested made by a group member but several other girls did not think this was a good idea, one with the comment: "He would beat me up." Another suggestion made was "tell him you'll give the money to him when you get your lunch money." There was apparently no question in the minds of the group members that a refund was due.

When no further suggestions came, I said, going out with a boy is an honor for him, and it does not give him any right to ask you for anything. Several group members stared at me, obviously quite surprised by this idea. Since no one disagreed, I waited a few moments to see if this would happen, and since no one laughed at me, I went on--encouraged by the lack of negative reactions--and said, if one knew something about the boy before going out with him on a date, had talked with him a few times, for instance, one would not get into such a difficult spot. Would the group members like to know what other girls had decided would be a good answer to such a question? As I expected, the girls who participated were eager to hear this, and I went on to say: "I am not that kind of a girl - I don't go out with a boy who treats me like that!" After having said that, one would get up and leave.

of money--for sexual intercourse is, of course, a phenomenon with which most teenagers from deprived backgrounds are very familiar. They have seen this happen among members of their families and among their friends, and it may well be that some members of the group have also participated in such exchanges.

The answer "he would beat me up" shows how violence is part and parcel of the lives of most group members.

The suggestion of later refund out of lunch money reflected again the economic deprivation of most group members who would not always have the price of a hot dog available.

Group members did not make any further suggestions, because they could not think of other ways of coping with the situation. Their silence did not have a rebellious quality, rather it reflected how baffled they were. The leader needs to use his judgment in interpreting the lack of further comments, but experience in working with groups helps to develop one's ability to evaluate what it means if there is no further discussion of a certain problem.

The leader had an opportunity here to present a new point of view to the group, one which reflected a different approach to dating, and a different evaluation of the self of the girls. If group members had shown disbelief that such an approach could be

The members of the group listened, again without disagreement, and that gave me an opportunity to say, casually: "you know if a girl can stay away from sex before she is married, that is really best for her!"

used, or had ridiculed the leader, she would have started a discussion of their reactions. Because the group members' silence meant acceptance--at least by some group members, and to some degree--it seemed better not to elaborate on this point too much, but to let it "sink in." Again, a quick "on the spot" decision had to be made here, but it was easier to make because the leader knew that there would be more meetings with this group and that the topic of premarital sex relations was certain to come up again in one of the later meetings. The new point of view was the leader's teaching of new concepts and of new attitudes.

It is very helpful if one can bring to group members the solutions which members of other groups have found for similar problems. Equally helpful is approaching group members in the form of a question, such as: "would you like to hear..." rather than saying: "I can tell you..." because the former formulation gives the group members a choice, and increases their conception of the leader as an accepting and nondictatorial person. If the group members had said that they did not want to hear this, the leader would, of course, not have presented the other group members' answers.

I did not "take this further" but I was pleased that one girl said approvingly: "if he bothers you more, you could slap him down!" I thought it was premature to go

If a leader is not willing to follow the leads--or most of the leads--of group members and is not comfortable doing this, such an approach would

into a discussion of the best ways to cope with such situations of which "slapping down" is not necessarily one.

"Boys who are in the service" were discussed next in response to a group member who brought this topic up. Her boy friend is in the service. I turned this question over to the group members who commented in detail, and thoughtfully, to this situation. The general agreement was that both the girl and the boy should go out with other people unless "they are serious." One group member volunteered the information that she had "two boy friends," one in the service and one "in jail;" she added that the latter was only a friend and that the charge of homicide--my formulation, not hers--was not true. Since our time was up, I did not "pick up" this comment, but it will probably be helpful to discuss with the group at a later session the problem of boys who get in trouble, how to evaluate this in terms of what the trouble was, whether the boy got in trouble once or repeatedly, etc.

not be helpful because the leader's unconscious rejection of it would be communicated to the group members. This invariably leads to the development of negative interaction between the leader and the group members.

It is always a sign of acceptance of and identification with the leader, if a group member "translates" the leader's statement into the group members' language, as happened here. "Slapping down" is a form of communication with which most members of deprived groups are very familiar, as actions tend to replace verbal communication for many members of these groups. This is equally true for adults, of course.

Since many teen-age girls have boy friends or know young men who are in the service, this topic is very likely to come up in the meetings with them. Depending on the age of the group members, and on their maturity, it usually gets explored from more angles than happened with this group. The time factor prevented the leader also from opening up this topic further.

It is helpful to record "Reminders" to oneself to explore a topic further or to bring a new topic up with a group at a later meeting, especially if a leader meets with several similar groups simultaneously.

If the leader can quote the remarks of group members, this adds authenticity to a record and it gives other staff members for instance, a feeling for a specific group which is often hard to convey in another fashion. One of the disadvantages of not being able to take notes--and of being under time pressure, which prevents immediate or extensive recording--is that some of this special quality of a group (and each group has its special quality!) gets lost. It is, however, more important, in the opinion of the writer, to free the group from any inhibitions which may be the consequence of taking notes, as was the case with the groups of retarded teen-agers who tended to be suspicious anyway, than to develop fuller material on the group sessions.

I was escorted downstairs by the two group members who were assigned this task. They offered spontaneously to carry my coat and my briefcase and they made "polite conversation" on the way to the school counselor's office. The two girls were very pleased when I mentioned to the counselor how helpful they had been, and what a nice talk we had had on the way down.

Escorting the leader was one of the ways of helping group members to develop a few social skills, such as carrying an older person's belongings, making "small talk." Beyond that, it was another way of teaching group members to accept responsibility and to fulfill assignments. Because of their low attention span, many group members tended to forget assignments, especially if there was a time lag between the time when the assignment had been made and the time when it was to be carried out.

Recognition for achievement is important, partly because it is disappointing not to get such recognition, partly because it usually encourages those who receive it to move on to greater achievement, but mostly because one of its consequences is often an improved

self-image.
****

Descripton of, and Information on, Some Group Members:

V.A. was one of a family of four siblings. She was 16 years old, had been born in the South and had had practically no education in her early years. Her retardation was recognized soon after attempts had been made to enroll her in school. She had had heart surgery, had defective vision, and her reading level was third grade.

V. had a pleasant smile, her skin was lighter than that of most of the other group members, she was nicely dressed and wore her hair in an upswept hairdo.

C.G. was sixteen years old, and one of a family of eight siblings. Her parents were separated; the father was unemployed. She often disturbed the class because she talked too much. She read at the fourth grade level. C.G. looked different from last year because her hair is now brown which seemed to be its natural color. Last year it was dyed red. C.G. was obese and not too attractive because she had a pasty skin with some blemishes as if she had had a bad case of acne. She was the girl who would "stamp on his ring" (when breaking off the relationship).

M.W., fifteen years old, had ten siblings. She had been an attendance and a behavior problem at school. She had poor eyesight, her reading level was primer to Book I. M.W. was so small that she could pass for ten years old. She had a listless expression and did not participate in the discussion.

This material is a combination of the referral summaries sent by the school counselor, the information--about siblings, for instance--which group members give on the registration sheets, and the leader's observations. Such material is helpful in a variety of ways, most of all as an aid in identifying the group members which, in turn, strengthens their relationship to the leader. The leader's observations may record details of physical appearance, facial expression, as well as comments made, or questions raised.

It is often not possible to identify more than a few group members at first, but additional ones can be identified in the later meetings. The ability to identify group members develops with increasing experience in group discussion leadership.

VIII
Talking about Love and Marriage
with Unmarried Mothers

Unmarried mothers and their problems have for a long time been a great concern to the helping professions. Teen-age mothers in particular have drawn their attention and efforts (Bernstein, 1971; Black, 1972, pp. 514-518; Kaufman and Deutsch, 1967, pp. 309-320; Kolodny and Reilly, 1972, pp. 613-622; Pochin, 1969, Young L., 1954). Many approaches have been tried to help these young women, and the group discussion approach was one of them. The meeting which will be presented and discussed in this chapter was held with unmarried mothers who participated in a special educational vocational program, part of which were Family Living classes. Health care for mothers and for young children, the use of community resources, and other similar topics were discussed in these classes, and nursery care was provided for the babies during class time. Counseling as well as group therapy was available to the young mothers. A first exploratory meeting showed that they were interested in discussing their problems in a group on a level different from group therapy, and a discussion series of four weekly meetings was therefore planned, following this first meeting. Because the response of group members was positive, a second discussion series of five weekly meetings followed.

CHARACTERISTICS OF GROUP MEMBERS

The girls ranged in age from fifteen to seventeen; some of them had one child, and some had two children. Two group members got married during the time the leader met with the group; neither of them married the father of her child. The group members were black, with the exception of one white girl who attended the second discussion series. They came from economically, socially, and culturally deprived families, many of whom received public assistance. One parent families were a common occurrence. The background of the group members was similar to that of the girls described in the preceding chapters.

The director and the counseling staff made ample information about the girls available to the leader; she, in turn, shared her impressions of individual group members and her evaluation of them with the staff. With few exceptions, the members of these groups had little Ego strength and little Superego; they acted out their instinctual drives which were primarily oral drives and lived by the pleasure principle. Their lack of thinking "in a time dimension," that is, of thinking beyond today and beyond the concern of the moment, was very noticeable. Many members of these groups were equally unable to think of others, to anticipate the feelings or possible reactions, of whatever kind, of those around them. This was equally true when they were involved with a young man--who might, or might not be the father of their child. Needless to say, attitudes of this kind did little to foster the development of love relationships. One reason for their lack of interest in the feelings, expectations, and reactions of others was their intense preoccupation with themselves and with their own needs.

Most group members had poor concepts of love and marriage relationships which were seen primarily in terms of what the other person should do for one, or can offer to one. The give and take, the mutual support which are part of such relationships were unknown quantities to them. When the leader introduced these concepts, the reaction was usually one of surprise, and often also one of disbelief.

Although the girls had given birth to children, many of them had little knowledge about the physical aspects of pregnancy, birth or correct information about the human body. It must be pointed out in all fairness that such ignorance is often found in women much older than the members of this group were.

Although all group members had children, they were, first of all, teen-age girls, whose problems centered around dating, love, and marriage relationships. These teen-age girls happened to have children also, and gave care--often excellent care--to these children, but they were not mothers in the sense in which this word is usually used. Care was seen as physical care and, while most group members loved their children, they did not feel responsible for them beyond this care, and they did not plan for their children's, or their own, future in realistic terms. These elements of mature motherhood were not part of the relationships of most group members to their children. In line with this, the latter were mentioned only in connection with the man whom group members were planning, or hoping, to marry, but were not seen as individuals in their own right.

GOALS OF THE DISCUSSION SERIES

The goals of the meeting with the unmarried mothers were not different from those described in the preceding chapters, with the exception of wanting to help the group members to see the implications of having a child for one's dating and love relationships, and for one's plans for a future marriage. It had not occurred to some group members, for instance, that having one's new boy friend meet one's child may bring a new element into the relationship, that a man's attitudes toward a girl may be in any way affected by the fact of her having a child, or that one's future husband may have a variety of reactions to one's child, if he is not the father. Also, since the involvement of group members which had led to their having an illegitimate child did not seem to have been based on a sound evaluation of their relationships to the young men who were the children's fathers, the opportunity to discuss their experiences might hopefully lead to more realistic planning for their future lives. The sharing of experiences with each other and with a leader who was not part of the staff was to provide a way of coping with their problems which the unmarried mothers would use in a fashion different from their use of counseling and group therapy services which were available to them.

It seems of value to point out that a variety of services can be offered in a complementary fashion, and can be used in different ways by the recipients of these services (Kolodny and Reilly, 1972, p. 616). If the professional people involved are clear about their respective areas of functioning, about the nature of the help they can, and wish to offer, and about the boundaries of their professional activities, such cooperation will not only work out well, but will also enrich the helping experiences of the clients, or patients, who use these services. While the basic problems of the clients or patients or group members are the same, they are brought out in different ways, with different intensity, and in different contexts in the different situations of being a client for counseling, a patient in psychiatric treatment, a group member in therapy, or a group member in a Family Life Education Discussion Series. It is only when the professional people involved are not clear about these matters, or worse, are consciously, or unconsciously, competitive with each other, that these cooperative projects fail. They fail because the users of these services tune in on the problems of the helping professionals and become confused, or use the competitive interrelationships of the helpers for their own destructive purposes.

THE RELATIONSHIPS OF GROUP MEMBERS TO THE LEADER

As before, the development of a relationship of group members--or at least of most of the group members--to the leader was seen as a sine qua non for enabling them to get help for their problems from the meetings. However, because the intragroup relationships and intragroup conflicts of the unmarried mothers were much more intensive than those of the teen-age girls who have been described in the preceding chapters, the relationship to the leader reflected these conflicts at points. Furthermore, many of these unmarried mothers were in conflict with some of the regulations of the setting in which they were meeting and of the nursery; some of these conflicts were also acted out in the relationship to the group discussion leader. In one instance, the leader was very neatly "conned" into permitting eating in the meeting room when she was told that the

mothers had not had time to get breakfast before bringing their children to the nursery. Later she found out that eating was restricted
to the dining room, where proper disposal of any food which was not
eaten could be made, because rats had been seen quite frequently in
the building.

THE DISCUSSION SERIES: ITS PLANNING AND SETTING, GROUP
SIZE AND GROUP COMPOSITION

The director and counseling staff were involved in the planning
of the discussion series, and selected the girls who were in their
opinion most likely to use this service well. As only about twenty
five unmarried mothers participated in the program, the pool from
which the group members were chosen was not large; the size of the
group did not exceed fourteen at maximum attendance.

The following four condensed descriptions are representative
of the backgrounds and problems of group members.

W.B. was fifteen years old, her two children were a year and
a half and six months old, respectively. The children's father was
three years older than the mother; he had dropped out of school.
W.B. was the sixth of seven children. Her father who had died a
few years ago had been her mother's common-law husband. One of
W.B.'s brothers was in prison, two others were in institutions for
delinquent boys. One of her unmarried sisters had a child and was
expecting a second. W.B. was short and heavy; while she was
described as lively and verbal by the staff, she was rather quiet in
the meetings.

H.M. was seventeen and had a three year old child. She was
one of three children; her sister had had a baby out of wedlock
recently. Records in social agencies told stories of neglect of H.M.
and her siblings. H.M. had refused to name the father of her child,
who was believed to be her mother's former paramour. Relationships between H.M. and her mother had been and continued to be
troubled, and the counseling relationship had started only a short
time before the meetings got under way. H.M. was quite attractive
although somewhat overweight; she was another group member who
was rather quiet in the meetings.

B.E. was seventeen, her two children were two years and
eight months old, respectively. The children had different fathers
both of whom had gotten married recently. B.E. had hoped to marry
the father of her second child. She lived with her mother and her
maternal grandmother; the latter was the dominant person in the
family. The mother's common-law husband was also part of the
family, as were three of B.E.'s younger siblings, the youngest of
whom was of the same age as B.E.'s older child. B.E. had a court
record of violence, having attacked some other girls. She had a
poor self-image and considered herself ignorant and stupid. In contrast to this opinion of herself--which she had shared with her

counselor--were her contributions in the sessions, which were
thoughtful and helpful to the other group members.

H.B. was sixteen, her two children were two and one years
old, respectively. The children had two different fathers, neither of
whom took an interest in his child or in the child's mother anymore.
H.B. was one of eleven children; her parents were separated but the
father contributed to the family's support through a court order.
H.B. had been in trouble at school, had been suspended for being
truant and for other infractions of school rules. She was quite hostile to many of her peers, but this did not manifest itself in the
meetings where she contributed only occasionally but helpfully.

SESSION V

December 8, 1966: Twelve group
members attended this meeting:
H.L., P.L., B.E., H.M., S.C.,
H.B., A.T., J.J., W.T., S.C.,
B.P., and J.G. All of them had
been present at our earlier meetings.

I started the meeting by mentioning that since this was our last
meeting, perhaps the group members would like to know what we had
discussed together so far so that
they could decide what we should
talk about today. When group members nodded, expressing agreement,
I covered very briefly the main
topics of the earlier meetings and I
ended with a reference to the discussion of reasons why married
people fought, which we had had last
week.

Next, I asked if the group members would perhaps like to talk today
about marriage, perhaps about how
one could tell ahead of time what
kind of a husband a man would be so
that one could find a man with whom
one would not have so many fights.
This was not what the group members wanted, however; a few said:
"No," and some made faces. W.T.
asked: "Could we talk more about
sex?" I said, certainly, if the other
group members wanted it also.
J.J., S.C., B.E., A.T. said

Since group composition is
affected when a new group
member joins a group, a
statement about whether this
is the case or not is a routine
part of the writer's recording
of a session.

It is good to review the
material covered so far and
to relate this to the fact that
this is the group's last meeting so that group members
have an opportunity to bring
out their most urgent questions
and problems. If group members would not have been
agreeable to the suggestion,
the writer would have asked
what they wished to discuss
that day.

This tie-in between the
topic of fights to married
couples and of looking at a
future marriage partner to
avoid marital conflict seemed
a natural one to the writer,
but the group members' concerns were of a different
nature.

"Yes," and when I asked what we should discuss about sex relations, W. T. took the initiative.

W. T.'s first question was "how" one could have sex relations, which she spelled out, in answer to my question: "In what positions?" (Since W. T. had two children, I was wondering at first if she was asking this and the following questions in earnest, but she was.)

The writer has sometimes been baffled by the meaning of a question and a simple question like: "What do you mean, Mary?" is usually the best way to handle this.

In working with teen-age groups, one sometimes thinks that one is being "kidded" especially when sexual relations or the physical factors connected with conception or pregnancy are being discussed, but actual experience does not necessarily assure accurate information.

I asked group members if they would like to ask questions about this matter, or if they would prefer me to explain this. J. J. replied: "No, you tell us," and S. C. and B. A. made similar remarks.

The leader asked a "loaded question," since she was sure that group members would prefer her to explain this question. It seemed better to use this slightly more didactic approach, partly because this would avoid the giggling which tends to accompany discussions of this sort, and partly because she was reasonably sure that the other group members would not have much correct information about these matters either.

I went on to outline briefly the different positions in which a man and a woman can have intercourse, and I asked at various points, if this was the information group members wanted to have. Most of them nodded or said "Yes." They were unusually quiet during this part of the discussion, except for W. T. and J. G. The latter whispered something to W. T. which made her laugh. When I asked what she had said, both girls shook their heads. W. T. said a little later: "Hanging around his neck;"

Listening in silence can indicate interest or boredom; in this case, it was interest. A leader learns to interpret silence as he gains in experience. If the silence had been an expression of boredom, it would have been an expression of hostility also in this situation since the group members had selected the topic. The leader would have challenged the group members if this had happened.

Silence may also indicate

She said this in a very low voice, but J.G. and A.T. laughed. H.M. was unusually quiet today; she put her head on her arms and closed her eyes. Although she said to me, in an apologetic tone, that she had been up all night, I wondered whether the discussion of sex relations was very difficult for her in view of her problems.

In discussing the different positions in which a man and a woman can have intercourse, I mentioned that sometimes if one was married and wished to have a child but could not get pregnant, the doctor might recommend certain changes in the way in which the couple had intercourse, and a change of position might be one of them. He would, of course, also want the couple to have medical examinations and, very often, he might find some physical problem which could be corrected quite easily and which had prevented the couple from having a child. Again, group members listened quietly.

My next comment, however--a comment which I had made casually only and not with the purpose of starting a discussion--got quite a reaction. I had said that a woman might be able to conceive a child by one man but not by another. B.E., S.C., and J.J. expressed their surprise, while P.L. said, in a sarcastic tone: "Who would want to have a child?" S.C. disagreed with her: "If you get married, you want

regret, for instance, because this was the last meeting of a group. Such a silence would presuppose a strong relationship of group members to the leader.

"Hanging around his neck" was a reference to cunnilingus which the leader would have discussed if group members would have reacted to this comment. It is often difficult to know whether one should pick up or ignore such comments, but the leader thought that group members might have other questions they wished to discuss in their last meeting.

Casual reference to "if one is married and wishes to have a child" might help to connect in the minds of group members marriage with having a family. Mentioning doctors in this statement was done in order to reinforce in group members the feeling that doctors were here to help them. In an earlier meeting the medical profession had come in for its share of negative comments by some group members, which is fairly usual when teen-agers from deprived backgrounds discuss doctors.

It would have been good if the leader would have added an explanation about some of the factors which may prevent conception, but the discussion went on and she was not quick enough to take hold of her opportunity. This was another case of hindsight--one knows after the meeting what one should have done and if that happens, one can only say to

to have children."

P.L. shook her head and said
that she did not want any more children. B.E. said: "But you have a
child; when you get married, he will
want to have a child too." P.L.
shrugged her shoulders and said:
"He would not know" (that she has
a child). This started an agitated
discussion, the main topic of which
was--as I formulated it, when I suggested that group members might
like to discuss this--"Do you tell a
man that you have a child and, if so,
when do you tell him about the
child?"

P.L. said: "The child can live
with your mother;" she added, "he
would not need to know." S.C.
replied that "Someone might tell
him," and B.E. said: "He would
not trust you." B.P. shrugged her
shoulders and said: "Who goes out
with me, knows I have children."
She explained that the children were
always around and that she introduced them to everyone who came to
the house. Since I knew that T.A.
was going to marry a man who was
not the father of her child, I asked
her what she had done about this.
T.A. explained that she had waited
"quite a while until I knew that he
was getting serious." At that time
she had told him about her little boy
"and about his father;" she became
very serious and quite sad also as
she mentioned the latter. As a
next step, she had arranged to have
her future husband meet her little
boy whom she had told that "He was
going to have a good father," and
the two had gotten along well when
they met.

H.L. asked T.A.: "Wasn't he
mad because you did not tell him
before?" and T.A. said, no, he had
not been mad "perhaps he was a

oneself: "Better luck next
time!"

How and when to tell a new
man in one's life that one has
had a child had not been discussed by the members of
this group in earlier meetings
and was a topic which needed
exploring with them.

Having the children around
and introducing them to everyone can be interpreted either
as a result of the lack of privacy in the homes of most
group members, but also as
acting out behavior, and perhaps also as an unconscious
desire for additional children.
(See the very interesting
article by Kristin Hunter (1968)
mentioned in Chapter VI about
getting pregnant as one way of
getting attention, of being
important, of "joining the
club.")

It was very helpful that a
member of the group reported
on a different, more planned,
and, incidentally, very successful way of handling this
particular situation.

One wonders if jealousy of
T.A. prompted the comments
by W.T. and J.G.

little hurt. " W.T. said: "I would tell him right away - he would feel like I kicked him right in the pants if I told him later, " and J.G. added: "He won't trust you if you don't tell him right away. "

I said, perhaps we should decide first whether things were different if one went out on a first or second date with a young man "who is really somewhat of an unknown quantity, isn't he? " A few group members nodded and I went on "and why does a young man go out with you? " Comments came "because he likes you, " "because he is curious, " while W.T. said, rather defiantly: "because he wants a piece of .... " Several group members giggled and I said, certainly, very often the purpose of a date was seen as having sex relations. On the other hand, if we agreed that requests for sex relations were likely to be made on a date, what was going to happen if a man knew from the start that one had a child? H.B. said: "He will say, why not me? " and B.E. added: "That's true. " Two other group members hooted and I remember one girl as saying: "Oh, come on!" J.W. said, sarcastically and shrugging her shoulder: "They ask anyhow, what difference does it make? "

I might add that several group members--J.G. was among them-- were more disruptive than usual but that may have been due to my having been delayed in getting to the meeting. An accident had held up the bus in which I was traveling. Although I apologized for being late and explained what had happened, several girls told me in a rather accusing fashion: "We thought you would not want to come today" and "We thought you had forgotten us. "

The technique of reformulating what group members are discussing and of sorting out different factors involved in different situations, can be used with good results in discussions with group members who do not think very clearly, and who have a tendency of seeing things in black or white, as is the case with many teenagers.

This discussion was, in the writer's opinion, a good example of the tendency of many members of this group of not thinking beyond the immediate moment and of their inability to anticipate the feelings and reactions of other people to them.

Because many fantasies develop about a leader, much and often too much, is expected of him. Being late or being ill are often interpreted as rejection, and the comments of the members reflected some of these unrealistic expectations of the leader, as well as their poor self-image.

The leader should have "picked up" these comments, more in terms of the underlying feelings than with an explana-

I was fortunate because B.E. said: "But it's your business if you have a child" and I commented that having a child was a personal matter which one need not discuss with a young man with whom one was starting to go out. I added that there were many other matters one would not discuss when one just started to get acquainted--the financial problems one might have or family problems. While it was true that requests for sex relations might be made, even if the new young man did not know that one had a child "why make it easier for him to ask?" Again, I received help from one group member (T.A.) who said: "Once he knows you better, he will respect you more." (Implied was that this will be helpful when the question of sex relations comes up.)

Although the other group members did not comment on my remarks, or on B.E.'s or T.A.'s statement, I had the impression that most of them had doubts about the desirability of not telling the new young man in one's life at once that one had a child. I have been wondering whether this need to share this experience was due to the desire to expose themselves to damaging experiences, which some unmarried mothers have, but it may also be that sex relations are used by some group members as one way of reassuring oneself about one's desirability. Since many unmarried mothers have a low self-image, this may have been one reason for their behavior in this particular situation. Also, if one craves excitement, as many members of deprived groups do, having sex

tion of the reality factors involved--another missed opportunity!

"It's nobody's business" is a statement with which many teen-age girls from deprived backgrounds are familiar, because they are often admonished not to discuss certain matters--that the family is receiving public assistance, for example-- outside of the immediate family.

B.E.'s and T.A.'s statements, which supported the leader's point of view, may have made some impact on group members, particularly since they knew that T.A. was going to get married, "had it made" as one girl had said, once, in reference to this matter.

The writer has found it helpful to add some impressions of group members' reactions, or of the underlying reasons for their actions, or her evaluation of common characteristics of members of certain groups whenever she had these impressions, or had thoughts about these reasons or was ready to formulate these characteristics. This material needs to be "caught" on the spot and it serves a variety of purposes, such as teaching, supervision, and professional writing.

relations--just as having fights--is one way of having thrills and of breaking the monotony of one's days.

I was ready to move the discussion along by asking what group members would like to talk about next when B.E. commented: "Not everybody likes children," and this started a very active discussion. Two other group members (H.M. and H.L.) disagreed; H.L. was quite shocked by this statement and H.M. said: "If he loves me, he loves my child. H.L. said: "Everybody likes children!" J.G. shook her head and mentioned her uncle "who doesn't like children"; he and his wife don't have any children. I said I was glad that J.G. had told us about her uncle, because it showed again that one would want to know a great deal about the man one was going to marry, such as, if he liked and wanted to have children. Group members did not pick up this comment, however.

S.C. said: "Some men don't like their own children," and T.A. added: "A man may like his own child--but that does not mean he must like your child." She added that she had worried about this before her future husband had met her child. I took my cue from her remark and said, perhaps we should ask, "What can it mean to a man if one has had a child by another man?" Several group members looked startled and H.L. said, somewhat defiantly, I thought: "That's none of his business!" B.E. replied: "Oh, come on--it is. The child lives with you." T.A. said, again a little sadly: "He knows now that you loved somebody else before you met him." S.C. added: "He knows he isn't the first one;" H.L. shrugged her shoulders and said: "He was probably running around, too!" T.A. shook her head and said:

The comment "everybody likes children" is another example of the unrealistic expectations of other people which some members of this had, of their tendency to see things and people in black and white only, and preferably in the way in which they wished to see them.

The leader's attempt to turn this part of the discussion toward the evaluation of a future marriage partner, toward planning for marriage, was a failure because most group members were fond of their children and the possibility of someone's not liking the child aroused their protectiveness.

As these comments of group members showed, the girls varied considerably in their maturity and in their ability to assess any reality situation.

The technique of using a question or a comment of a group member to explore a broader aspect of it which the leader used here, is helpful if one wishes to widen the group members' horizon and to encourage them to think more. This technique may not be helpful if one works with so-called "sophisticated" groups, which tend to use intellectualization to avoid facing their feelings and attitudes.

"but that is different, it's not the same for a man!" and B.E. added: "That's right. The child lives with you; if he has a child, it doesn't live with him."

I asked if I might say something; several group members told me to "go ahead," "you tell us what you think." I said, it seemed to me that the fact that one has a child was one which was important not only in one's own present life, but also important if one was getting serious also. Certainly "It is his business also. If you two are married and if your child is hungry or needs clothes, what is he going to do?" S.C. replied: "He will buy it food or clothes if he lives with you." Several group members nodded. I agreed and went on to discuss some of the other responsibilities of a good father. Again, several group members nodded, indicating agreement with the points I was making.

I went on to say that one's having a child also meant, as we had heard, that one had loved somebody else and, very often, one retained a special feeling for the man with whom one has had sex relations for the first time. Several group members nodded, but H.M. said: "No, what you're saying isn't true. I hate him--I hate him-- you're wrong!" No one picked up her remark.

I said, we had always agreed that we got together to talk about what were the concerns or problems or questions of the members of our group and, of course, these were different for different people. No one claimed that everything we said would sound right to everyone and, of course, "I can be wrong, too." (As usual, I made my comments in greater detail than I am recording them, and that applies also to many

This question is useful in gaining the attention of group members who also appreciate the courtesy extended to them by being asked this question.

The leader used the term: "good father" here, its purpose being to stress the positive components of fatherhood.

Some additional discussion of what it means to have a child, and of the meaning of having intercourse for the first time, would have been helpful but the reaction of H.M.--who spoke with agitation--made it undesirable to pursue this topic further.

Statement of this kind often need to be repeated, as was the case here.

It is impossible to record all the comments made during a meeting which lasts an hour or longer, partly because they are hard to remember, partly because verbatim recordings run into many pages. (So do transcriptions of tape recordings.) Partial recording, if

comments of group members.)

J.J. then turned to me and asked "Can we talk some more about sex?" I said, of course, and she went on to say: "How can one tell a man that he does not satisfy one?" This started a discussion which took up the balance of our time. J.J. added, in answer to a question from A.T. that she meant "sexually;" several group members (B.E., S.C. and S.C. were among them) said that you could not do this. W.T. disagreed, and explained how she had told her husband that he had "to go slow." H.B. laughed and said: "He was too quick for you, you could not keep up with him!" W.T. replied in a rather annoyed tone: "No, you don't understand!" B.E. nodded and said: "Men and women are different," and P.L. added: "Some people are slower." W.T. said: "That's right" and, turning to me, asked if I could explain this? She added: "And will you also repeat the word you told us the last time you were here? You know, the man has an erection, but I mean what the woman has." Group members nodded when I asked if I should do this; I outlined briefly what an erection was and the physical factors of sex relations as far as woman and a man are concerned-- climax, ejaculation, etc. W.T. said: "Climax is what you told us-- I couldn't remember it!"

Group members listened quietly while I explained these matters. I then turned to P.L. and said, she was right some people's reactions in sexual relations were slower, and I used this to outline the different speed with which a man or a woman might react to sexual stimulation. I tied this in with the fact that one's

carefully done, is usually sufficient to reflect the mood and flavor of any group.

This particular question had not been raised before, neither by the members of this or of any other group of unmarried mothers with whom the leader had met.

W.T. was one of the members of this group who were now married; quite often when she mentioned her husband-- which she did rather casually and not in a boastful way-- she got hostile comments from the unmarried members of the group.

Two weeks had elapsed between the last meeting of the group and today's meeting because of Thanksgiving, and it was interesting that W.T. remembered the discussion enough to come back to it because she had lost the term "climax." This was, of course, an indication of her interest in attaining it.

This was another point in the discussion when giving information was indicated, mostly because this was what the group members wanted. If they had gotten restless or bored, the leader would have opened the meeting for discussion again, by asking if

physical reaction was influenced by many factors--loving a person, being happy and secure with the person, or being angry with him, or being worried, or tired, or not feeling well, or other stresses and strains.

J. J. then repeated her question-- how could one tell a man that he did not satisfy one sexually and, again, she addressed the question to me. I said, we had heard that some members of our group thought that one should not tell a man about this, but we had also heard that these things could be discussed. It seemed to me that this at best was likely to be "a touchy subject." When I asked why I was saying this, S. C. nodded very seriously and said: "It will make him feel that he is not a man!" I said that was true, a man might think that and I added that sometimes sex relations "straighten themselves out" if one gave oneself and the partner some time to get adjusted to each other. J. J. said: "It's not more time that we need." She went on to explain in a very relaxed fashion that "He is the father of my two children. We had sex relations five times in the last three months, and it just wasn't any good!" S. C. said: "Maybe you don't love him any- more?," while W. T. asked "Is there somebody else?" J. J. said

they had any questions or if they would like to discuss some other topic.

This represented another attempt of the leader to tie in sex relations with the emotions one has for the partner--love, feeling secure, etc. Looking back, the leader realizes that she should have brought these connections out more strongly and tied in feeling secure with being married. By not doing this, she lost a valuable opportunity to relate sex to love and marriage. (When this was done later, it "fell flat" because of J. J.'s reaction.)

The leader should have mentioned counseling and psychiatric help for sexual problems, since both were available to the members of the group. For the consolation of the readers of this book-- and her own--the writer wishes to point out that hindsight is part of the leader's equip- ment--and the leader's curse also!--and that one can only hope to learn from one's mistakes how to do better in the future.

"No" to both questions.

I said to J.J., it occurred to me that perhaps something else was making for trouble in this situation. She and the young man had two children and perhaps she would like to get married to him and "You mind it because he has not asked you to marry him. If one is angry at a person, sex relations very often are unsatisfactory." J.J. said: "No, it isn't that. We both feel we are not ready for marriage." Several group members laughed, and H.M. said: "What are you waiting for? You've got two kids! Are you waiting for four?" J.J. shook her head and said: "No, we are just not ready for marriage."

I said, I wished I could be more helpful to J.J. It was true that many things could happen which affected a sex relationship. Having a child might be one of them; one's physical well being might be another, and a change in one's feelings toward the other person would also affect the way in which one experienced sex relationships. W.T. said: "If you don't feel good, you don't want him!" I said that was very true and I added that, on the other hand, sex relationships were part of love and also part of marriage and "all these relationships have their ups and downs!"

I also commented that in all personal relationships when there were difficulties, much depended on the time and on the way in which one talked about these problems with the other person. It usually helped to wait until the two persons were alone, when they had had some time together, and when both were in a

The leader had offered an explanation--that of wanting to get married, or at least of being asked by the children's father to marry him--which seemed to be a possibility in her frame of reference and in her system of values. It was apparently acceptable to some of the other group members, but it was not part of J.J.'s concern and did not seem to trouble her. Her statement about not being ready for marriage reflected an attitude which is found among some young girls from low socioeconomic background who consider having a child as less serious than getting married. This does not take into account the possible effects of such a situation on the child, or children (Williams, 1971, p. 73).

It did not seem appropriate to go beyond a statement about some of the factors which may affect sexual satisfaction in this setting, also because it was the last meeting of the group and J.J. had raised her question toward the end of the meeting. As mentioned before, the suggestion of discussing these problems with one's counselor or with the psychiatrist who was meeting with the group members, would have been indicated.

For a variety of reasons, most members of these groups had few skills in personal relationships, and this seemed like a good opportunity to stress that there are times and ways which are more suitable for the discussion of problems than others.

good mood. It never helped to
bring out these problems when one
had a quarrel about other matters,
or when one was out of sorts, or
saw that the other person was in a
bad mood. I also commented that
it would be important to discuss
this problem in a way which would
not hurt the other person. (Again,
I made these comments in greater
detail than I am recording them.)
The group members had listened,
quietly and attentively, and J.J.
looked at me very seriously and
said: "Thank you."

Since our time was more than up,
I explained the use of questionnaires
and gave them, along with pencils,
to group members. S.C. asked me
if I wanted the group members to
put their names on the questionnaires. I said "No," what I wanted
most of all to hear from them was
in what ways the meeting had been
helpful, or not helpful; how I could
make the meetings more helpful,
and what I should do differently
when I would meet with another
group of girls later on. S.C. asked
me: "You come back?" W.T. said:
"She was here before, I told you I
knew her!" W.T. then offered to
collect the questionnaires.

W.T., S.C., J.J. came up to me
to thank me and to wish me a Merry
Christmas. H.B. would not give
her questionnaire to W.T. but
handed it to me instead. She added:
"I am sorry I scribbled on the sheet."
I said that was quite all right. B.E.
and H.L. did not want to give their
questionnaires to W.T. either--who
had, by the way, not made any
attempt to read them. They too
came up to me individually to thank
me and to wish me a Merry Christmas. I ended the meeting by wishing group members a Merry Christmas and all the best for the New Year.

It is very helpful to extend
a meeting for a little while,
if one is in the midst of a
meaningful discussion.

With teen-age groups,
bringing pencils is often indicated.

Questionnaires are more
likely to be frank if they are
not signed, of course.

These individual contacts
with some group members
established with the leader
at the end of the last meeting
were an indication of their
positive relationships to her.
They may also have been an
expression of jealousy of W.T.
who had thought to offer her
help to the leader.

IX

Discussing Sex and Drugs with
Inner-City Boys
by Gregory T. Leville, Ph.D.

The family life educator who sets out to work with any group
of teen-age boys faces a challenge: the challenge of educating for
life. The family life educator who chooses to work with teen-age
boys of the inner-city faces an even greater challenge: the challenge
of making the very notions of family and life relevant and meaningful. This is the conclusion of the writer after five years of working
with hundreds of thirteen to fifteen year old boys of the inner-city.
Black, white, Puerto Rican, they lived in the present and for the
present. More often than not, they saw their families, homes and
neighborhoods as something from which to escape. Broken homes,
poverty, emotional deprivation, and learning disabilities were of the
ordinary. Daily life was mostly a constant struggle with survival
on the streets more important than good grades in school. For many
going to school itself was an enterprise fraught with physical danger.
And once there, what was school but just another "put down" really
leading to "nowhere?" Giving these boys an appreciation of healthy
family relationships and of life itself is the challenge of the family
life education leader.

While this chapter can be applied to work with groups of teen-
age boys in general, the writer has been specifically motivated in
what follows by his work with inner-city boys from environments
similar to that described above.

GOALS

The aim of family life education is to help people live better
with themselves and with others, to prepare them better to meet the
challenges of day-to-day living and to help them to cope more ade-
quately with the problems and tensions that inevitably arise.

For the ordinary teen-age boy growing up involves many things.
It means learning to understand and accept the process of maturation
and physiological development. It means learning to respect himself
and develop respect for other persons. It means learning to establish
satisfactory relationships with adults as well as with his peers of
both sexes. It means trying to eliminate unfounded fears and worries,

and developing healthy attitudes towards one's own sex and the other
sex. It means developing socially acceptable behavior. A family
life education program for a teen-age boy must aim at all of this,
and more, because people are different and each program must
respond not only to the general needs of teen-agers, but to the needs
of the specific group with which one is working. Therefore, the
family life educator must know his group in order to determine his
goals more specifically.

The majority of the boys with whom this writer worked were
"captives of the present" in the sense that their present life situations made it very difficult for them to work towards future goals.
Working towards a better life demanded of them the postponement
of immediate gratifications for future rewards. This is an extremely
difficult task for the inner-city boy, whose present existence demands
so much of his energies that the family life educator often has little
left on which he can capitalize. You might say that the inner-city
boy often lacks hope, and that one of the first tasks of the family
life educator is to instill hope, giving the boys a reason to live better
and making life itself more meaningful to them.

The boys often had confused and shaky concepts of themselves.
As boys from low income, disadvantaged areas, often from broken
homes, they had poor self-images. This was even more true of the
retarded educable boy, publicly classified as such, cruelly teased
by his nonretarded educable peers, and knowing at times that even
his parents were ashamed of what he was. More than once boys
voiced frustration and anger against teachers and parents who would
not give them a chance to explain things, answer questions, or do
things by themselves. Deep feelings of inferiority, hurt, and resentment came to the surface as the boys described themselves as "dumb
kids" and told how other kids on the school buses teased them about
going to the "dumb kids" school. Nor was it uncommon to hear them
complain about being treated as little children by their parents who
would give preference and responsibilities to the other, often younger,
children in the family.

As adolescents the boys had trouble enough with their self-
images. As disadvantaged, and sometimes even retarded, their
self-images were under even more strain. Improving their self-
images, therefore, is another goal of the family life educator. He
must work toward helping boys have more respect for themselves
as individuals and as men, and he must do this on both the intellectual
and the emotional level. In a word, he must lead the boys to not only
think better of themselves, but also to feel better about themselves.

The normal teen-age boy going through adolescence has a
nebulous sense of his masculinity. Achievement of his identity as a
male is one of the main tasks of adolescence. The fact that most of
the boys with whom the writer worked came from homes where a
masculine model or identification was either inadequate or not available, rendered the task of sexual identification even more difficult.
The quest of a clear-cut sexual identification is difficult enough for

youngsters reared in stable homes with parents who genuinely care
for them. It is much more difficult for boys from homes lacking in
structure, stability, consistency, and masculine influence. All too
often the boys with whom the writer worked lived in a predominantly
female controlled home environment, where fathers were either
absent or ineffective. This consequently tended to push them more
readily into gangs, where they could find peer models of male identification, and where they could develop and act out many of their
negative feelings toward women.

Another goal, therefore, of a family life education program is
to offer boys a model for male identification and increase their awareness of themselves as men. This is the fundamental advantage of
using a male group leader. A male leader, however, is called for
in this situation also because of the psycho-sexual development
occurring at this time. During early adolescence there is an upsurge
of sex hormonal activity with accompanying and often disturbing
sexual feelings, fantasies and desires which the presence of a female
leader--especially young and attractive--would only complicate.
The male leader represents a source of support to the boys, and not
continued supervision by and submission to women which, as said
above, is often a negative factor in the lives of these boys.

It is important to keep in mind also that the imagination which
has such an important role in the play-age child, continues to develop
during adolescence. The adolescent is very often, and rightly so,
described as overly idealistic and enthusiastic. He is often more
concerned with "what might be" or how "he wants things to be" than
with the way things are. Thus, realism is needed in working with
teen-age boys. Realism is even more important when working with
the inner-city, disadvantaged, and retarded educable boys. These
boys are often very limited by low I.Q.'s, defects in learning skills,
lack of motivation, fear of tests, and general low self-esteem. In
such boys flight into fantasy to escape the harsh realities of life, as
well as the use of projective, compensatory, and self-defeating
behavior, is not uncommon.

In trying to help such boys and lead them to better lives, one
must be careful not to ignore the realities of the situation. While
there is a great need to instill hope, there is a greater need not to
nurture false hopes by holding up before a boy goals that are impossible for him to attain, or that are attainable only with very great
effort. That would lead very likely to frustration, a sense of failure,
a greater conviction of one's own inadequacy, and, very often, a
lessened desire to even try to better oneself. A person's "not trying
so as not to fail" is far from unheard of.

Consequently, an important goal of a family life education
program for boys is to mirror reality, to keep them in touch with
it by examining in detail motivations, alternative behavior and consequence thereof. The goal is to help them learn to cope with reality
rather than to escape from it. This can increase a boy's self-esteem
and confidence to the extent that he learns to accept himself as he is,

and learns to work toward limited goals attainable by him.

GROUP MEMBERSHIP AND SIZE

"I'll put so-and-so in the group. He really needs it!" is a
common refrain of teachers, school counselors, and other persons
with whom the writer has cooperated in planning family life education programs for boys. This criterion of need alone, however, is
not sufficient for determining membership in a family life education
group. Another factor, much more important to the effectiveness
of the program, must be considered, namely: a boy's ability to
function constructively in the necessarily permissive atmosphere
conducive to group discussion and interaction. To put it bluntly,
the group must take precedence over the individual. This is not to
say that the education, the good of the individual, is not the ultimate
aim of the entire program. But it does mean that a boy who becomes
a destructive influence, who hinders group discussion and interaction, should be excluded from the program. In the area of selecting
boys for the program, this means that a boy's degree of acting out
and disruptive behavior must be considered in relation to the effect
it will have on the group process.

Some degree of acting out behavior is not uncommon in adolescent boys, and it is even less uncommon among disadvantaged and
retarded educable boys. While such behavior is to be expected and
does not rule out the method of group discussion, it does point to a
need for balance in a group. In selecting boys for a discussion
series those responsible should see to it that there is a predominance
of boys able to operate well in the discussion atmosphere. This
writer has found that a group of about ten boys can often handle one
boy given to excessive acting out, but can rarely handle more than
that, since boys who act out tend to "feed on" each other's anxiety,
consequently supporting each other's disruptive behavior, which
soon renders effective group discussion impossible.

What size group is the optimum? How many boys can a family
life educator most effectively work with at one time in a group? This
writer has found eight to ten boys an ideal number to work with at one
time, but many factors must be considered in deciding group size:
1) the group leader, his skills and his comfort with different size
groups; 2) the goals to be achieved; and 3) the composition of the
group, the personalities and problems of the boys who participate.

In working with teen-age boys it is very important for the group
leader to be himself. Boys can easily pick out a phony. For this
reason, it is necessary to consider the leader, his anxieties, his
skills, his comfort or discomfort with large or small groups. If he
is uneasy or unsure of himself with a group, the boys will pick it up,
connect with the leader's anxiety, probably become more anxious
themselves, and begin to act out.

The goals must also be kept in mind. If one is merely to impart factual knowledge, the number of boys present lessens in importance. Lectures and films can be used with large groups. However, the goals of family life education in general, and especially with groups of disadvantaged and retarded boys as described above, demand emotional involvement and aim at attitudinal change. Factual information is imparted, but the emotional involvement of the group, essential to learning for living, is far more important. For this reason the group must be kept small enough for all to be able to participate actively in the discussions and to interact with one another.

The boys in the group constitute the third criterion for determining the size of the group with which one is to work. With the boys of the inner-city, and especially with the slow learners and retarded educable, the writer encountered a high level of acting out behavior coupled with great personal needs. After experimenting with groups as large as fifteen, the writer concluded that the attainment of the goals described earlier in this chapter necessitated working with groups of about eight boys at one time. It should always be remembered that group size should be correlated with the group members' level of neediness and tendency to act out.

The desirable outcome of the adolescent stage of development is the attainment of a reasonably clear and stable identity, and of a self-satisfying sense of selfhood. To achieve this, it is crucial that the adolescent have room, freedom and autonomy, to grow into what he chooses to be. In keeping with this line of thought, a boy's participation in a family life education group should be of his own choice. This does not mean that one leaves all initiative for joining a group in the hands of the adolescent. He can well be encouraged and invited to participate, as for example, by the school counselor; but participation in the group should remain voluntary and after the program has begun, a boy should be allowed to drop out if he so wishes. Leaving this basic freedom of action in the hands of the adolescent avoids many problems of resistance and "sabotage" which one often encounters in a group of boys compelled to attend. However, within this framework there still remains room for encouraging participation and for explaining the program to a boy so that he can then make a reasonable choice. In the writer's cooperative programs with the schools, it has been standard procedure for the school counselor to talk to each prospective group member in advance and to explain the program to him.

GROUP PROCESS

Group discussion is the basic modality employed by the writer in his work with teen-age boys. This is based on the premise that people internalize knowledge and integrate it best into their lives by becoming actively involved in its acquisition. The process of group discussion also responds to the needs of the adolescent boy and the goals of family life education programs in many other ways.

Group discussion gives the adolescent boy an opportunity for self-expression, self-direction, and decision making, which responds to his process of self-actualization and search for an identity. The group gives him a chance to choose what he wants to talk about, deciding when and how he wants to talk about it. He can express himself, compare himself with his peers, learn how he affects others and is affected by them, and gradually develop a philosophy of life. He can test himself, his peers, the leader. He can increase his ability to verbalize, a particularly important factor in relation to retarded educable boys and others of limited ability. He can learn socialization.

When working with a group of teen-age boys the writer suggests three rules, which he clearly establishes from the outset of the program. The first rule is what happens in the group session is confidential. It is made very clear that the leader is not to tell anyone what goes on in the group, what this or that boy says. The writer urges the boys to do the same, to keep what happens in the group within the group, out of respect for one another. This insistence on confidentiality lends more weight to the program, gives it more importance in the boys' eyes, and consequently tends to increase their self-esteem. Urging that they not talk about what others say out of respect of these other persons works toward the same end. This is a point to reemphasize often during a program.

The second rule can be phrased: Everyone gets his chance to say what he wants. The writer makes it clear when he first meets the boys that each one may say whatever he pleases, short of attacking others, but he must give equal time to the others. Shouting or laughing another person down is not permitted. The reason again is mutual respect. The writer tries to get across the idea that each one has a right to "say his piece" and if one wants his right respected, he should respect another's. At times, however, one may have to intervene when one boy attacks another or puts another "on the spot," so to speak.

> John added that his father had told him about growing up about a month ago. William excitedly started pushing John: "Tell us what your father told you." John did not want to, but William and the others kept making fun of him and insisting that he tell. At this point I intervened and said to everyone in general: "Maybe John feels that what his dad told him is just between them, kind of confidential." John's eyes lit up when I said this, and the others seemed to accept the confidentiality explanation, since this is one of the ground rules of our meetings.

At a different meeting one boy attacked another:

> Willie, to my immediate left, leaned over and said:

"Emmet is a queer and sucks dicks." I simply
ignored the remark and called Willie's attention
back to the topic under discussion.

   At a later meeting in this same discussion series someone in
the group pointed at Emmet and said: "We got a faggot right here in
our group." This time the writer recalled the ground rules of respect
for each other, and said they could talk about homosexuality all they
wanted, but that the group meetings were not the place to attack or
make fun of one another. When ground rules are agreed upon and
adopted at the outset of a series, it is often sufficient to merely
recall them.
   The third rule is a natural conclusion of what was said above
concerning a boy's ability to function in a discussion group, namely:
whoever excessively disturbs the group will be excluded. The writer
believes it is important to clarify this right at the beginning of the
program to avoid misconceptions. It is important that the boys know
what is expected of them and what effects will follow certain kinds of
behavior, a very important principle of socialization. This rule is
also presented to the boys as required by respect for others in the
group and their right to discuss without undue disturbance. For this
reason, when a boy does disturb the group, the leader should let
the other members of the group handle the matter, if at all possible.
In a word, he should try to make constructive use of the peer group
influence. Sometimes just sitting back and waiting, will be enough,
and the other group members will handle the disturbance. Members,
usually natural leaders, will speak up and tell others to be quiet or
to get serious. At times, when a boy has been acting up too much,
the others have told him to be quiet and have urged that he be put
out of the group. Usually, however, it does not go that far, and
group pressure is enough to correct the situation.

Alfred and Walter were doing a lot of talking aside to
one another which was disturbing the discussion process. Leroy made some comments that were inaudible,
and I simply said that I could not hear him. He then
told Alfred and Walter to shut up, and Gary added
that they should "shut up or get out if you don't want
to discuss."

A legitimate question here might be: How long do the discussions
last? The writer has found that an hour's discussion is about all
that disadvantaged boys can handle. Forty-five minutes, or even
thirty minutes of good discussion, are much more valuable than an
hour and a half of tired, drawn-out discussion. Working with boys
who are intelligent, self-assured, and verbal, however, is another
matter, and discussions of one and half to two hours can be very
constructive.
   While a permissive atmosphere in which boys can speak freely

and bring up whatever is of interest or concern, is essential to effective group discussion, a considerable amount of structure is needed when working with young teen-agers, especially from the inner-city. When there is insufficient structure to initiate, focus or sustain discussion, the writer has found that the level of anxiety in the group rises to a point where the boys begin to fall back into patterns of regressive, acting out behavior: laughing, teasing, table tapping, moving around, playing with whatever happens to be handy. This does not mean that the leader should impose a structure by telling the group what they must talk about. In general when one does not know what to do or say, yet knows that something is expected, there is a tendency to become anxious. The lower the self-image and the level of self-confidence, the greater will be the propensity to become anxious in such situations. At times the group itself will furnish sufficient structure, spontaneously initiating and maintaining a constructive focus. At other times the leader will have to use certain techniques to structure the meeting. The need for this will vary and depend on many factors. The anxiety level and coping ability of the individual can vary on any given day for numerous reasons: health, family and social conditions, approaching holidays, neighborhood situations, not to mention the anxiety of the leader, which can easily communicate itself to the group members. More than one meeting has been difficult because of the proximity of holidays, and because of racial tension and violence in which the boys were caught up emotionally. In all such situations an additional measure of structure seems to be needed to maintain an atmosphere conducive to effective group process.

While discussing group process in family life education, it is important to distinguish between "dealing with feelings" and "talking about feelings." In his training of family life educators, the writer has often encountered the assumption that talking about feelings is equivalent to good group process. For some leaders getting a group to openly discuss their feelings is a goal in itself and the criterion of success. In the writer's opinion this is not necessarily true. While personal feelings can be talked about very appropriately and constructively in a family life education group, more often than not the effective family life educator will be working with a group's feelings rather than openly discussing their feelings. Bolstering a boy's self-esteem, allaying unfounded fears, encouraging initiative, reducing exaggerated feelings of guilt, instilling good feelings about sexuality, all of this an effective family life educator can accomplish without explicitly discussing the boys' personal feelings in these areas. How to do this involves a good working knowledge of personal and interpersonal dynamics as presented in other chapters of this book.

GROUP LEADER

The family life education group leader must know himself, his feelings, attitudes, prejudices, fears, and anxieties. The writer remembers meeting with a teacher prior to a group session in a school. He told the writer excitedly how a couple of boys in the group needed help, and how he had caught them with a filthy picture that morning in class. With a great deal of self-righteousness he described how he had angrily taken the picture away from the boys, told them it was filthy, and ripped it up in front of them. One must ask: what message did this teacher give the boys by the way he handled the matter? What effect did he have on them? This writer cannot help but feel that the teacher's own feelings about sex and his own uneasiness in handling sexual matters made him adopt a "panic approach" to a situation which could have been handled with much more finesse. It is hard to believe that the boys did not pick up this man's uneasiness with sex, and made up their minds not to stop looking at pornographic pictures, but simply to make sure that no teachers were around in the future when they did so. The teacher's panic reaction probably closed the door to any future healthy influence he might have had on the boys in this area. Sensing the man's uneasiness, the boys would be sure to avoid the "taboo" topic in the future.

This is the type of reaction in which the family life educator cannot afford to indulge. He must know himself and his feelings, and be able to handle them well, if he is to work effectively with boys.

The leader must know his views on issues that the boys will bring up, such as for example: masturbation, premarital sex, drug usage, birth control, abortion, homosexuality, and the like. It is not the leader's task to impose his own view or convictions on the boys, but it is his task to stand for something. The adolescent boy is going through a period of rejecting and reevaluating many ideas and values poured into him throughout his childhood. He is in the process of fighting against many of these values, in the process of casting off their yokes, often in order to later freely reaffirm and adopt many of these same values as his own. However, in order to accomplish this, the adolescent needs something to fight against, something to weigh and criticize and question. If there is no resistance to his fighting, if the important adults in his life do not stand for something that he can question and that they can defend, if they do not hold and affirm values and standards without imposing them, then the adolescent will have a much more difficult task in developing a meaningful value system of his own.

The group leader has an obligation to take a stand on important issues, and to not escape the issues by employing the technique of constantly turning all questions back to the group for consideration. This, however, does not mean that the leader should plunge right into the middle of a discussion the moment views and opinions appear that are in conflict with his own. As much as possible he should avoid taking sides during a discussion. He should rather help the boys to resolve their differences through their own efforts by leading them to explore motivations, different meanings, alternative approaches and solutions to problems, and the consequences of different opinions and courses of action.

The group leader must establish a relationship with the boys in the group. Establishing a relationship is as important in a family life education group as it is in counseling. But doing this does not mean that it is the leader's task to become part of the group as an equal among equals. He is not a teen-age boy and should not act like one, basically because the boys neither want nor expect it. They expect adults to be adults and to act like adults. While the leader should be accepting of the boys, their mannerisms and their language, there is no good reason for his adopting their language or mannerisms. An effective healthy relationship can be established without that.

This is not the place to develop a treatise on relationship, but it might help to mention a few techniques that have helped this writer in working with boys: 1) Relax and be yourself. 2) Learn their names quickly. 3) Chat with them individually before and after meetings, asking about their particular interests, hobbies and the like. 4) No matter what opinion a boy voices, remember that he deserves credit for speaking up in the group, and should be supported at least for that. 5) Never put a boy down in a group. 6) Remember what a boy says during a meeting and refer back to it when appropriate. 7) Enlist the boys' help when possible in setting up projectors, checking attendance lists, and the like. 8) Challenge them, expect something of them, especially of the retarded educable boys. They do not want to be "written off" and given no responsibility. 9) Along the same lines as above, ask for their help, as for example, getting them to suggest what you might tell parents about understanding their teenagers and getting along better with them. 10) Send personal letters to boys between meetings reminding them of the upcoming sessions. This can have great meaning to boys with poor self-images, often starving for attention. The relationship of the family life educator to his group is a dynamic one, a relationship of give and take, as the leader gradually uncovers the here-and-now concerns and interests of the group members and gently nudges them into further discussion. The group members should not be cast in a purely passive role, as if they were disciples sitting in silent awe at the feet of a master. On the contrary, they are active contributors to the content of the meetings and group process, sharing their thoughts and feelings, in constant interaction with the leader and with each other. Thus, while the leader must be prepared to furnish supportive structure, he must not do so at the expense of constructive discussion. He has to encourage a permissive atmosphere in which spontaneous discussion can flourish while providing enough structure and support to control the level of anxiety. A practical guideline might be worded: if the group is actively engaged in a constructive discussion, let it go! Family life education leaders, in their desire to educate a group, can easily get caught in the trap of subtly imposing their own train of thought on a group. The leader should contribute something, it is true, but he must be careful not to stifle the initiative of group members. If the leader must err, let it be in the direction of permissiveness.

It is important for the leader to "tune in" to his group and to know where they are. In a word, he must be able to listen well, to perceive and to respond to his group with continuous flexibility.

> I arrived about fifteen minutes early for the meeting.
> Only one boy was there. While we were sitting around
> waiting for the other group members to arrive, <u>Dave</u>
> began telling me about the gang trouble and fighting
> going on in the neighborhood. There had been two
> incidents during the past week when police had been
> summoned. As the other boys arrived for the meeting,
> I saw that they were caught up in the excitement and
> tension marking the area and were eager to talk about
> it. Consequently, I let the discussion continue on
> this topic for the entire meeting.

In the previous meeting these boys had specifically asked to talk about girls and sex in the following session. However, had the writer ignored the mood and small talk of these boys prior to the beginning of the meeting, he would have failed to respond to the boys' concerns and needs at that moment. By encouraging them to discuss the gang trouble and violence in the neighborhood, he was actually structuring the discussion, but doing so along the lines of the group's interests at that time. "Meet your group where it is, " is a useful guideline.

Flexibility, however, is a must. Sometimes shifts in focus are called for during the course of a meeting. A good discussion may already have begun. Then suddenly the unexpected, which is not a rarity when working with groups of teenage boys, occurs. It might be an outside disturbance or an inside joke. Whatever it is, the leader should be alert to its discussion potential.

On one occasion, while the writer was working with a group of young teen-age boys in a housing project, the following occurred:

> It was towards the end of the meeting and the boys were
> engaged in a discussion of dope and glue sniffing. Sud-
> denly a girl opened the door and threw a sanitary napkin
> into the room. Two or three of the boys laughed ner-
> vously. No one said or did anything more, so I asked
> what it was. <u>Harold</u> said he did not know, so I asked
> someone in the group to please tell him. This led
> <u>Jason</u> to say it was what woman use when they have
> intercourse. <u>Bill</u> then said it was not, and <u>Darrel</u>
> asked why a woman bleeds when she has intercourse.
> The remaining fifteen minuts of the meeting were
> spent discussing sex, about which the boys raised
> many questions.

Had the writer tried to ignore the incident and urged the boys to continue their discussion of glue sniffing, he would have failed to meet
them "where they were," namely thinking about girls, sanitary nap-
kins, and the mysteries of sex.

There are different opinions as to whether or not a family life
educator should answer personal questions put to him by group members. An absolute guideline cannot be given. When boys ask a family
life educator personal questions there is often a tendency to feel
"this is none of their business." Even professionals can be jealous
of their privacy. However, at times personal questions deserve
answers. The following excerpt is from a meeting at which hetero-
sexual relationships were the main topic of discussion.

> William wanted to know how to "ask a girl for pussy."
> I turned this back to the group. Alfred said he wanted
> to know how to "make" his girl friend. I suggested
> it might help them to take a look at how a husband
> and wife might ask each other for sex. Willie said
> he starts to kiss her and touch her all over. Alfred
> and Antonio took up the same idea, with much grinning
> and laughing. I wondered if they ever came right out
> and asked each other. They said you can't do that,
> and I wondered why not. There were no answers so
> I asked if they thought it was important for two people
> to be able to talk to each other and ask each other
> for things, sex included. Bill here asked me how
> I ask my wife, and I answered that sometimes we
> just hug and kiss and wind up making love to each
> other, without ever explicitly asking the other with
> words. I then added that sometimes I verbally ask
> her to love me, or let me love her.

The boys' questions were the result of sincere interest and of a
desire to learn how to better relate to girls. For this reason the
writer answered the questions and continued to focus the discussion
on honest concern and communication between men and women, ideas
which were quite foreign to nearly every boy in that group. When
situations like this arise, the leader should consider the motivation
of the question, the effects on the group of answering or not answering, and how the answer might fit in with the goals he is trying to
achieve.

DISCUSSION CONTENT

What does a family life educator talk about in a program with
teen-age boys? What are their main interests? What kind of questions do they ask?

It has already been said that the leader must "tune in" to his group and meet the members where they are. He has a responsibility to his group as regards furnishing content material and focusing discussion, but he cannot allow himself to be a slave to previously planned topics and discussion outlines. While the degree to which a leader structures a discussion will necessarily vary with the size of the group and the goals to be achieved, the general rule is that no set amount of material needs to be covered during a session. This is a corollary to the fundamental purpose of family life education, namely, the emotional involvement of the individual in the acquisition of knowledge with a view to attitudinal change. The amount of material discussed is not as important as the quality of the discussion and its impact on the lives of the boys in the group. Many a group leader has been frustrated when he has not succeeded in fully covering a carefully prepared outline. If the goal of the meeting were only an intellectual imparting of information, such feelings might be justified. But when dealing with a group of teen-age boys in a family life education program, the family life educator will avoid a great deal of frustration by remembering that reaching the boys emotionally is much more important than inundating them with factual information.

The leader must also remember that his group is a resource of knowledge. Regardless of attempts at homogeneity, not all the boys in a group will be at the same level of physical, psychological, and social development. On a given subject one boy will often know more than another, one will put in this, another that, until the group as a group pieces together a fairly complete picture. Therefore, the family life educator should approach his group as a source of knowledge, and utilize this source to the fullest, before embarking on a program of imparting knowledge, which will often cast the group members in a passive, receptive role. The leader, employing the various techniques of discussion leadership, should focus a discussion in such a way as to cull as much information as possible from the group members themselves, furnishing content material as the needs and concerns of the group, and not his own interests and needs, dictate.

Below is a portion of a discussion about sex with six thirteen-year old boys in a South Philadelphia Housing Project. Individually none had the whole picture of how a baby is born, but as a group they managed to come up with a fairly complete picture, illustrating well that the group is a primary resource of knowledge.

> After this they said they wanted to talk a bit more about sex. To get them started I said: What do you want to talk about...about girls? They said yes. I went on: Do you want to talk about what girls are like, or how babies are born, or...? Yeah, how babies are born, they said. I asked how they thought babies were born, and Ronald said that his brother had told him that when a boy puts his penis in a lady's vagina she starts squeezing it and then the sperm

starts coming out through the penis. Stanley said he
wanted to know how the baby was born. I said: Okay,
where does the baby come from? Larry hollered out:
from the vagina. Ronald said no, from a lady's breasts,
and Larry hollered out again that it comes from the
vagina. Ronald then said that it grows in the stomach.
John added that was right since the lady's stomach gets
fat when she has a baby. Paul inserted that sometimes
they have to cut the stomach open, and Stanley commented that the baby grows in the stomach for nine
months.

Bernard then cut in asking: if it is twins, do you
get both of them out of the vagina at the same time?
Ronald answered that one has to be born at a time,
like one eight seconds after the other, and he went
on to give an example of some twins he knew where
one was born one minute after the other. At this
point I summed up some of what has been said,
namely that the baby grows in the stomach for nine
months, comes out of the vagina, and that twins
come out one after the other. The boys all agreed
that this was right, and I then wondered how the baby
got in the mother's stomach. Somebody said it was
by corpuscles, and Larry said no, it was necessary
for an egg to crack open before the baby starts to
grow. I asked what he said, and he repeated that
an egg pops open and a baby starts to grow. I asked
why an egg would pop open and Stanley said: when a
man shoots sperm into the lady's vagina, that is
what breaks the egg open, and the baby starts growing,
and then in about nine months it is time for the baby
to come out of the mother.

No one boy had all the facts straight, but as a group they possessed
nearly all the needed information, and the leader's main task was
to get them to share, clarify, and integrate it.

The dominant interest of the boys with whom this writer has
worked is sex, that is, physical aspects of sexual growth, differences
between men and women, intercourse, pregnancy, veneral disease,
homosexuality. An interest in these topics overshadows all else in
meetings with boys. They want to see pictures and almost always
ask for films showing intercourse. Most of them view sex in a very
impersonal way, as something to use for what one can get out of it.
They seem totally unaware of the emotional and interpersonal dimen-
sions of sexuality. They exhibit a singular lack of awareness of the
purpose of sex in their own lives and in relationships to women, whom
they generally consider as objects to be used.

Questions about sex are by far in the majority in working with
groups of teen-age boys. Typical questions asked by the inner-city

boys, ages thirteen through fifteen, with whom the writer has worked
were:

Does a guy have to get a girl during her period in order to have a
baby?
Does a woman have eggs when she is pregnant?
How is a baby born?
How many holes does a woman have?
Is a girl still a virgin after a guy has fingered her?
What are balls for?
How do you know when a girl is dirty (i.e., has VD)?
Do girls talk about boys they have been with?
How many eggs do you need for twins?
Don't ladies try to get rid of babies when they are pregnant?
Why do women get water all over the floor when they have a baby?
Why do people kiss?
Can a guy jerk off and piss at the same time?
What happens if you cut off a man's testicles?
What does it mean when a girl has wet pants?
Can a girl get pregnant if a guy has her only once and real quick?
When does a guy start sperming?
Why do women bleed?
Why does my penis get hard even when I don't think about girls?
Why do faggots dress like women?
Why do people get circumcised?
Can people stick together like dogs?
Does masturbation cause pimples?
How do you ask a girl for pussy?
Does a girl's breasts get big when a guy pets them?
Why do some guys chew a girl out?
How come a girl gets hot when you hug her?
Does it hurt when a guy fucks a girl?
How can a girl clean out the sperm from herself?
Can you piss in a girl when you fuck her?
How does a baby eat while it is inside the mother?
How can you tell when you get VD?
Why does a guy shoot in bed at night and wake up with wet pants?
Do girls really go to men doctors and undress to be examined?

The writer has listed the above questions at length because
listening to what group members actually say is the first, indispens-
able step to truly understanding them and their needs.
While most of the questions concerning sex are markedly
impersonal, the boys will occasionally raise some questions that
develop into very profitable discussions concerning personal relationships. The following questions have been raised by groups of boys
and have developed into very worthwhile discussions.

What do you do if you get a girl pregnant?

Why do people have sex with one another?
Why don't our parents talk to us about sex?
Why do people get rid of babies?
Why do people get married?

Although an interest in sexual matters seems to overshadow
all else, other subjects are discussed in family life education programs with young teen-age boys, such as the following:

What it means to be a man.
The pros and cons of belonging to a gang.
The need for a high school education.
The boys' relationships to their parents.
The kind of people you like for friends.
The question of racial prejudice.
The boys' feelings about themselves.
How to get along with others.
Ways your family can help you grow up.
The boys' relationships to police.
What to do on a date.
The whole gamut of changes occurring during adolescence.
The entire area of drug usage.

In regard to the last mentioned topic, the writer has found the
use of drugs of all kinds to be the second most prevalent topic or
area of concern to the inner-city boy, age thirteen to fifteen, with
whom he has worked. A number of conclusions stand out in his mind.
While there are exceptions, to be sure, the use of hard drugs
does not seem to be the major problem in this age group. The boys'
involvement is with marijuana and "huffing," the inhaling of glue-like
substances and various kinds of volatile solvents. When speaking of
drugs, most of the boys viewed the use of hard drugs as "stupid and
for crazy people." "Huffing" and the use of marijuana were all right
because these made you feel good and helped you get away from your
problems. "Problems don't seem so big when you get high" was
often heard. Some boys also claimed that getting high helped them
"think out their problems better," apparently because it helped them
relax and not be so uptight.
Concerning the boys' knowledge of drugs, a great deal of ignorance about the various kinds of drugs was prevalent. However, the
great majority of the boys were well aware that getting involved with
drugs was dangerous. They had seen and often lived with the effects
of the use of hard drugs. While the dangers were evident, even the
dangers of "huffing," there always seemed to be the attitude that "it
can't happen to me. I'm too smart." In this area, as in others
pointed out earlier in this chapter, the boys were unrealistic and bore
out the need for the family life educator to mirror reality.
However, the writer does not want to leave the impression that
the family life educator should concentrate on giving boys more infor-

mation on the effects of drugs and dangers of drug usage. On the contrary, he believes that a different emphasis is needed. While readily admitting the multiple causality of drug usage, the writer has found that many boys use drugs because 1) they have nothing else to do, 2) they are forced into it by various kinds of peer pressure, and 3) they seek the pleasure that results from getting high. The writer's experience with the inner-city boy leads him to consider the above reasons, offered by boys themselves, as very realistic and worthy of attention when planning drug prevention programs. As stated at the outset of this chapter, the real challenge of working with the inner-city boy lies in making life meaningful and satisfying to him. To the extent that a family life educator can achieve this goal, to the extent that he can help boys find pleasure and satisfaction through constructive living and relating to other people, to that extent he will be engaged in realistic drug education and prevention. Self-knowledge, clarification of values, satisfying relationships, cultivating hope and realistic goal setting, and the achievement of these goals and hopes, these are the areas of greatest relevance in drug education for the inner-city boy.

In this chapter the writer has tried to share with the reader his thoughts about conducting family life education programs with groups of young teen-age boys, especially of the inner-city. Such work is demanding. Preventive as well as remedial, it requires that the family life educator possess a sound knowledge of the personal and interpersonal dynamics directly related to the boys with whom he is working, together with a sound knowledge of group process. This is not an area for the untrained to jump into with charts, films, much good will, and little more. The writer believes very strongly that the professional family life educator must always know what his goals are and how he is trying to achieve them. There is much room for different methods and techniques, but little room for a hit-and-miss approach with other people's lives.

X
Answering Children's Questions about Sex

The mothers who were the members of this group met because they had children who went to the same public school. This school was located in a stable neighborhood of row houses where most people owned their homes. It was a small school which was attended by about seven hundred children. With the exception of approximately one hundred black children, who were bussed to the school, the student population was white at the time when the group met.

CHARACTERISTICS OF GROUP MEMBERS

A "profile" based on the registration sheets which twenty six group members filled out showed that most of them had a tenth grade education, although a few had gone to the eleventh and twelfth grade. Only one mother was a college graduate. One mother had a degree in nursing, in addition to her high school diploma, and one mother of four children went to night school, encouraged by her husband, to get her high school diploma. None of the group members were divorced, or separated from their husbands, although references to husbands tended to be somewhat negative. Most of them were Catholic, and the balance were Protestant. This group did not have any Jewish members and, probably because of the distance involved for the mother of bussed children, it was a white group, although invitations to the meetings had been sent to all the mothers whose children attended the school. The husbands in these families were mostly blue collar workers; they were employed as truck drivers, in factories, and in related occupations. While no husband of a group member was out of work while the group met, the recession and lay-offs of employees in industrial plants in the area had caused economic problems for many other parents of children who went to this school. Even if a husband of a participant would have been unemployed, it is doubtful that this problem would have been discussed in the meetings because the mothers' attitudes to family life, as described below, would not have permitted this. All members of this group were very much concerned about their children and very eager to do their best for them. While many of them lacked an under-

standing of the needs and problems of growing up children, and tended
to "see things in black and white, " they were willing to explore new
approaches to the task of helping their children to grow up, although
such approaches had to be presented carefully, so as not to shock
their strongly developed sense of what was right and what was wrong.
This was based on their own experiences of growing up, which were
characterized by obedience to parents who were strict and by acceptance of the standards and values of these parents. In dynamic terms,
group members can be described as having strong Superegos, and
traditional attitudes and values. They represented the "silent
majority, " and were positively oriented toward society, church, and
school. These mothers were one of the few groups with whom the
leader met at that time who did not make any negative comments
about the school or the teachers. On the contrary, they backed the
school fully. The writer would venture a guess that most group
members were better mothers than wives and saw their most
important role as that of being a mother. It was obvious from their
references to members of their own families that they had strong
ties to their own parents, or at least felt strongly their obligations
to them. One of the mottos of family life for most group members
was "sticking together, " and "taking care of one's own" probably
came next.

The concerns of the mothers were reflected in the questions
they checked, or listed on the registration sheets. Some topics which
are usually of interest to mothers of school-age children had been
listed on these sheets, as this often stimulates group members
especially those who do not have much experience in the discussion
method to formulate their concerns. The topics were only suggested,
and ample space was provided for group members to add their own
specific questions. Discipline--Why? When? How Much? received
the largest number of checkmarks: twenty. One specific discipline
problem was listed: parental disagreement about discipline, especially
when both parents worked different shifts. How to Answer Children's
Questions -- about Sex, about Death, etc. and The Rights and Responsibilities of Parents received the next largest number of checkmarks:
fifteen; How to Live with Teen-Agers followed, with thirteen checkmarks.

The fact that the members of this group were highly motivated,
concerned about, and devoted to their children was reflected in their
attendance. Although the group met at two week intervals, because
these were the only meeting dates which the writer could offer, and
although it met in January, February, and March of a winter with a
series of snowstorms, accompanied by colds and related health problems of children and of parents, eight mothers came to all six meetings, and seven came to four meetings of the series. Attendance at
the individual meetings was 17, 19, 16, 14, 17, 17.

GOALS OF THE DISCUSSION SERIES

The goals of this discussion series were--in line with their characteristics as described above--to help the members of this group to accept some new ways of coping with their children's problems, and to wean them away, as much as possible, from their somewhat strict and narrow attitudes in child raising. If some members of this group could see that there was more than one way-- the "tried and true" but not so true anymore! way--of reacting to a child's behavior at a given point, this would hopefully result in less conflict between parents and children, and in a warmer, and more relaxed atmosphere in the homes of these families. If the group members could also see themselves as better mothers, this would increase the satisfactions which they derived from this very important role and would, in turn, make them more able to function better in relation to their children and perhaps also to their husbands.

THE RELATIONSHIPS OF GROUP MEMBERS TO THE LEADER

Most group members were able to develop very good relationships to the leader which was due, on their part, to their desire to receive help through the medium of the discussions. The leader found the group easy to work with, and interesting, because it reflected the concerns of parents who were threatened by a society in transition, with which they found it difficult to cope, and because they were very different, for instance, from the parents of acting out children, who were in conflict with society, with whom she had worked. Since the writer had usually not found it difficult to adapt her "pace of leadership" to the tempo of the group, she did not find it difficult to do this now. Furthermore, the genuine desire of most group members to be better mothers made them a rewarding group to work with.

THE DISCUSSION SERIES: ITS PLANNING AND SETTING

This series was planned because the school counselor was very much aware of and concerned about the problems in the families of many of the children who attended the school. She had very good relationships with many of these parents, whom she had been seeing because the children had problems in school, or because the parents had come to her for help with their own marital or personal problems. The counselor was instrumental in planning a first meeting with the mothers on discipline problems. Their response was very good; this had been their first experience of discussing a topic of this nature. The writer had offered leadership to the group. When the mothers wanted more discussions of this kind, the counselor encouraged them to plan a discussion series of six meetings as a next step. Because the members of this group were not experienced in such matters as planning activities and preparing publicity to mobilize a group, she helped with this part of the planning process, as much as needed, and in a tactful fashion, which did not take the initiative away from the group.

The counselor attended most of the sessions and was an active and participating member of the discussion series. She shared some experiences from her own family life--she had several children--with the group members, who appreciated this; she did not monopolize the discussions and she was not competitive with the leader. It may be that some criticism of the school might have been expressed, if she had not been present but, again, this group may not have been concerned with such matters because of their identification with society and its organizations. In any event, this was a small loss as compared with the support which her presence gave to the meetings, and to the strengthening of the relationships of some of the mothers with her, which was one of the results of the meetings also.

Since group size and group composition have been covered in the discussion of the characteristics of group members, these topics do not need to be presented again at this point.

SESSION IV

February 24, 1970: Seventeen group members attended this meeting; all of them had been present at earlier meetings. Present were Mrs. M., Mrs. S., Mrs. B., Mrs. T., Mrs. Ss., (who is small and pretty, with dark hair), Mrs. R., Mrs. G. (with her baby, as before), Mrs. Mm., Mrs. Bb., Mrs Bbb., Mrs. P., Mrs. Gg., Mrs. I., Mrs. Jt., Mrs. Mmm., Mrs. L., and Mrs. W. Group members sat in that order. The school counselor had to go to a meeting and was not present today. Mrs. W. brought messages from two group members who had the flu.

If one meets with a large group of mothers, it is often not possible to identify a group member as soon as one would like to be able to do this. It is, however, never too late to add identifying comments, because identification and individualization of group members is one of the best tools for strengthening their relaship to the leader.

While it is preferable to have mothers attend without bringing babies or preschool children to a meeting, their presence is often necessary so that the mother can come. If the leader does not get flustered, the presence of the children will not interfere with the discussion.

I offered to summarize the main points of our preceding discussion, which I did in about fifteen minutes --without interruptions--which was due, I think, to the group members'

It might have been preferable to omit the summarization but, on the other hand, this enables the members of some groups to dissociate

eagerness to get started on today's discussion. I ended with the statement that we had planned to take up today how to answer children's questions about how babies are born and related matters, and this is what we did. (Next time, group members wanted to discuss how to answer the questions of teen-agers about sex relations and related matters, how to help them to cope with problems in these areas, and also how to answer children's questions about death.)

themselves from their preceding housekeeping activities and to turn their attention to the discussion group.

Agreement on the topic to be taken up at a group's next meeting is often helpful, because it enables the members as well as the leader to organize their thinking and their questions for the meeting. (This also made it important enough for Mrs. I. to take time off for that meeting.)

Teen-agers' questions and problems in these areas are of concern to parent groups from all groups of the population, but how to answer children's questions about death seems to be more the concern of parent groups from simple educational background, of parents who are quite church oriented, but who sense that children sometimes need more than the answer "God has taken your father," for instance, to help them understand and accept death.

Mrs. R. "picked up" my statement, almost before I had finished, and said: "we should tell them everything!" Several group members (Mrs. Mm., Mrs. I., and Mrs. Mmm. were among them) nodded to indicate agreement but several others (Mrs. T. and Mrs. Tt. for instance) shook their head disapprovingly. (I might add that Mrs. I. had told the group, before the meeting started, that she had taken time off from work to attend today's meeting.)

I said, with a smile, we are on a controversial topic and would the "pros" and the "cons" perhaps give us their reasons? Nobody answered

As was to be expected, opinions on how to cope with this problem were sharply divided.

The embarrassment of group members was too great to permit such a discussion. This was also reflected in

and I noticed that Mrs. Mm.--who is probably one of the mothers in this group who is most at ease with her children--started to blush. (Her face remained red throughout the entire meeting.)

I went on to say that this was not only a very controversial topic, it was also a very difficult one for all parents to deal with, and also one on which many of the parents I had worked with, had disagreed very much. Some parents felt that children should know certain things, while others felt that they should not or that they were too young. What's more, many parents did not feel sure about how to best answer their children's questions when such questions were asked.

Again, several group members nodded to indicate that this was so but no comments were made, nor were any questions raised. I went on to say, "Very often, if one had a difficult job to do, it was helpful "to tackle it, one step at a time." How would it be if we did this together? When many more group members nodded, I said: "What is the first question children usually ask?"

Mrs. Mm.'s blushing.

It is important to recognize the underlying feeling of the group members and to allay some of their anxiety by making reference to similar feelings of other parents. Such recognition increases the ability of group members to express their doubts and fears which will enable them to deal with the problem in more realistic and more appropriate ways.

It would not have been helpful, in the writer's opinion, to press group members to raise questions at this point. The suggestion of "partializing the problem"--by tackling it one step at a time--was more helpful because it made the task of answering children's questions in these--always emotionally charged--areas more manageable and, therefore, less frightening.

The greater response of group members--although it was still nonvocal--encouraged the leader to formulate the first question one can expect from children. If the group members had not responded, she would have provided the answer and gone on to present simple questions, with simple answers, until group members would have entered the discussion. This is bound to happen, sooner or later, and the leader's anxiety if faced with a non-responsive group is often the

Again, it was Mrs. R. who replied by saying: "why does the lady have a fat stomach?" Mrs. Mm. said: "one of my friends told her little girl: 'because she swallowed a watermelon!'" I think that is wrong; I told my little girl: "she is carrying a baby," when she asked me about one of my friends who is pregnant. Mrs. Mm. agreed: "children should get this information from us."

Mrs. Mm. added that she had told her daughters "about menstruation, and about the egg and the sperm." The girls had not wanted to come into their parents' bed anymore, explaining that "the sperm might come across the sheet." (It will be good to discuss, without too much emphasis, at the next session, at what age children should stay out of the parental bed.) I said: "If children are older, they often prefer to stay in their own rooms and that is better anyhow, because it gives everybody some privacy."

Mrs. Bbb. agreed with Mrs. Mm.; turning to her she said: "This information should come from the home; if one answers a child's questions and he is satisfied, they don't ask you again." (I thought this was wishful thinking, but I did not say this, of course.)

Mrs. Ss. said: "I know that you should tell them, but it is very hard to know what to say, and it is embar-

greater problem in such a situation than the group members' initial silence.

The discussion is now under way. At this point it is best to "let the group members take over," although the leader may feel that some of the points -- "swallowing a watermelon," for instance -- could well be discussed further.

While Mrs. Mm. is more "modern" in her approach to child raising than some of the other group members, she was obviously unaware of the implications of her daughters' refusal to join their parents in bed any longer. Since this is a very desirable development, anyhow, a casual reference to the desirability of not having such visits, when children are older, was all that the leader thought indicated.

In an animated discussion, which this started to be, group members often turn to each other.

With a more sophisticated group, and one which the leader knew well, the question: "Isn't that wishful thinking?" accompanied by a smile, might have been indicated to open up the discussion of parental feelings in these matters. This approach might have scared the members of this group and made them feel inadequate.

It is important to dispel any lingering notions of a group of mothers of the type

rassing." I commented of course these things are difficult to discuss and I went on to point out that to adults, as we are, sex, and sex relations are connected with all kinds of feelings and emotions, which cause us embarrassment, but with most children, this is a very different matter. All they want is some information because they are puzzled and they want to know where babies come from, just as they want to know how come the electric light goes on if you turn on a switch? (As usual, the comments of group members and my own are recorded in the order in which they followed upon each other, but they are not recorded completely.)

I went on to say that one thing which made this more embarrassing was that the parents of our group members probably did not discuss these matters at home. Several mothers nodded and Mrs. W. replied: "this was never discussed!"

described here, that children who ask such questions are not normal or that they will be led into sexual experimentation if such information is made available to them. Since the leader had the impression that many group members might not be free and easy in their approach to their own sex life, she thought that to give recognition to such embarrassment might be helpful to them.

It is also very important to place questions about these matters on the same level as questions about how the light switch functions, again as one way of freeing the mothers to cope with such questions in a more realistic and helpful fashion.

Recording a meeting with a group of adults is much easier than recording a meeting with teen-agers, because taking notes does not arouse the group members' suspicions. The leader recorded this meeting very fully with a view to incorporating it into the present volume.

The leader might have added a comment that the parents of our group members meant well but that these matters were really not discussed at that time. Today, when children hear so much about these matters, read about them in the papers, or see TV shows which discuss sexual problems, things are different and today's parent has a different--and more difficult-- job to do. If some group members had negative feelings toward their parents, espe-

Next, I asked: "And what is the next question most children ask?," Mrs. R. said: "Why is Mommy big up there and Daddy not?" (She was pointing to her breasts.) Mrs. Mm. laughed and replied: "You could say, before they invented bottles, the baby was fed by the mother! Progress, it's wonderful!" Several mothers laughed and this joke helped to break up some of the tension which was quite apparent today.

Mrs. Bbb. shrugged her shoulders and said: "That's easy. But what do you say if a boy wants to know why he is different from his sister?" Before I could turn over her question to the group, Mrs. Mm. said: "This is where you can bring in your religion. You can say--"God is wonderful--he made people to be men and women." She went on to explain that she had arranged for Daddy to take the boys to the bathroom, and "with six of us in the family, sometimes they needed to go the bathroom when I, or the girls, were there." With considerable embarrassment, but quite proudly also, she told the group members that her children knew the terms "penis" and "vagina" when they started going to school, and the girls, of course, knew about menstruation at that time. (It may be helpful to point out, next time, that boys should have some information about the female body and its functions, and girls about the male body, if the group members can tolerate this. Bringing the book, "What to Tell Your Children about Sex"--which I promised to do next time--may make the discussion

cially because of their failure to prepare them for their roles as wives, such comments would have been helpful.

Jokes are often a way of expressing aggression, or a variety of other feelings, but they also help to relieve tension. Again, it would not have been helpful to discuss the group members' underlying feelings of tension.

Questions about the different body build and different sexual organs of men and women are usually more embarrassing than questions about where a baby is carried, or how it is born.

Mentioning God in connection with conception, or with death, is usually not a very helpful approach because this tends to confuse small children. In this particular instance, this was not the case.

Instead of thinking about what to stress next time, the leader should have recognized the excellent way in which Mrs. Mm. had handled the situation.

A discussion of the importance of boys' having some information about the female body and vice versa would, however, have been premature although the leader had a "tie-in," partly because group members were so embarrassed, and might be less embarrassed in a second meeting on this topic, but also

a little less embarrassing for group
members, and they may also find
the book helpful in the areas where
they themselves are not very knowledgeable.)

Mrs. Mmm. mentioned that her
little boy started to ask questions
when he went to kindergarten "where
they start to notice things." Mrs.
L. nodded and said: "It's too bad,
they see too much, they will be
grown up a long time!" Several
other group mothers nodded. I
said: "We certainly do not want to
'push children,' because they will
be grown up a long time, as we all
know. On the other hand, it is quite
true that children notice many things
when they are quite young, such as
the different way boys and girls are
built." I was careful to add that
questions about these matters are
perfectly natural.

When group members listened,
but did not disagree, or ask any
questions, I went on to add that "it
is important to tell the boys that
they were born that way, and will
stay that way, because they will
grow up to be men, and to tell the
girls that they too were born that
way, and will not change, and grow
up to be women." I added, with a
smile, that "the different equipment"
is often a cause of concern to little
children, and boys may be afraid
that they will change to girls, and
sometimes little girls wonder if
they lost something which their
brothers have.

because there were more
important areas to explore.

Many mothers, particularly
if they are not too happy with
their present lot as adults,
express regret about their
children's growing up too
quickly. This is also, of
course, a convenient way of
evading giving to children
answers to their embarrassing questions, or giving them
age appropriate privileges.

The leader thought it would
be important to reassure the
group members again that it
is quite usual for small children to notice body differences,
and also to ask questions about
these matters.

The silence of group mem-
bers indicated, in the leader's
opinion, their willingness to
listen to what she had to say.
If group members had dis-
agreed, or raised questions,
the leader would not have gone
on without discussing these
first.

It is very important to present what one has to say in
terms which are appropriate
to the educational level of
group members. While there
are groups which know Freudian
terminology, and would have
mentioned the castration complex, the members of this
group were not acquainted
with these terms, and their
use by the leader would have
alienated them. If one works
with a group which is aware
of such terms, the leader
may--or may not--use them,
but the presentation of mate-

Mrs. G. nodded after I had made these comments, and added: "My daughter has asked me if she will change when she grows up and be like her older brother." She had answered her that "little girls are little girls, and grow up to be women." Mrs. G. was very pleased when several group members--and I--told her that she had handled that very well. She smiled and said: "I didn't know what to say, but I figured, if I don't tell her, she will think she did wrong." This gave me an opportunity to bring to the group another concept of parent-child relationships (Pollak, 1956, pp. 131-139). I said that there are few things that one can say with certainty about one's children, but one of them is "if a child is old enough to ask a question, he is old enough to get an answer."

Mrs. Bbb. then asked what if the children will "tell an outside person about these things?" She added that "many parents" don't want their children to know. Mrs. S. suggested that one tell one's children that these are "family matters, which the children should only discuss with their parents." I said that that was a very good suggestion, because there are many things--like money matters, or looking for another job --which one could caution one's children not to discuss with people outside of one's family.

Mrs. R. then talked about how "All my work was undone" when her

rial must always be in line with the group members' level of information. "Talking down" is an insulting as is any attempt to "dazzle" the group members with one's own professional knowledge.

It was very fortunate that Mrs. G.'s experience bore out the point the leader was making.

Using concepts or developing principles of parent-child relationships with groups can be a very helpful device, particularly if a group is eager to learn, and probably in a better position to accept a learning experience, than to explore their own feelings and attitudes. This was the case here. Furthermore, learning, in the sense of improving one's education, was an undertaking which appealed to the group members, and was in line with their goals for their own children, so that it was helpful if one could tie in their discussions to educational goals and formulate some of the results of the discussions accordingly.

The concern about "what the neighbors will think of oneself as a parent" is usually quite strong among members of groups who wish to be accepted by, and be part of, their community.

The leader made the comment about "looking for another job" to let group members know that she was aware of the economic and employment problems which some of them were facing.

Hostility toward the leader is often expressed in indirect

child had to have an operation. "I had her all prepared, just like the doctor said" but one of the children on the street started jeering "the doctor will cut your foot off," and that scared the child. (I wondered silently if she, with her reference to "the doctor" as a professional person, was expressing hostility to me also? Her remark was made in a sarcastic fashion.) Mrs. T. spoke about "bad kids in the neighborhood," and what they could do to one's child. I said, it was very true that one often "has to do one's job as a parent all over" because something interferes, but it is good if a child can tell the parent about being scared, and can get reassurance from the mother of father that what the child fears, is not going to happen.

"Animals" were mentioned next by Mrs. Mm., who has twenty-three white mice at the moment, so that the children have seen the mice being born.

ways, such as a sarcastic remark about another professional person, but on the other hand, some leaders-- and certainly the writer-- are sometimes anticipating hostility where none may be present. In any event, a discussion of such hostility would have been threatening to most group members, and therefore inappropriate.

Animals are very popular, particularly with mothers who are afraid to discuss the topics with which this group was coping. It is not helpful, in the writer's experience, to discourage the use of such a crutch but mothers should be encouraged to use the birth of puppies, or mice, etc. as a starting point only, and then to go on to the discussion of how human beings are conceived and are born. Again, it would not have been helpful to discuss this at this point as criticism might have scared the group members who had such difficulties in their attempts to cope with these problems.

Mrs. S. mentioned a movie which had been shown on television --I think it was "The Birth of a Baby"--which had been very good "but you have to take the time to be there." I commented that to watch

The leader might have acknowledged here that it is often difficult for a busy mother to take time out for watching a movie, but that this would make it possible

such a movie with the children, so
that they could ask questions, or to
read a book about these matters with
them, could be very helpful and I
mentioned the book: "What to Tell
Your Children About Sex" in that
connection. (I did this because I
doubt that most members of this
group are free to discuss these matters so that a starting point such as
a movie or a book might make things
easier for them.)

Silence followed, and when I
asked: "what about the fathers--
should they discuss the boys' questions with them?" Mrs. Bbb.
laughed and said: "The men don't
know." She added that her son had
asked her: "What's a whore? I
told him--ask your father!" This
led to some joshing from other
group members: "Of course, he
would know!" I said: "Children
hear all kinds of words, like whore,
or rape, and they want to know what
they mean. What can be one's
answer?" Mrs. Mmm. suggested
"prostitute," Mrs. S.: "A woman
who gets money for having sex
relations," Mrs Mm. "rape is when
a man forces a woman to have sex
relations." I said these were excellent answers, and they show "what
we can come up with if we put our
minds to it and try to help the children." Mrs. Ss. said: "Some
women are more embarrassed than
men." When her sister-in-law
showed her a book with pictures of
how a child is born, "she hid it when
her husband came."

Mrs. R. then asked: "but isn't
the child sometimes too young to
know?" Mrs. Mm. replied "by the
time the children go to school, they
should know," and when Mrs. R.
shook her head and said: "Sometimes they are too young, and they
can't understand," I asked the group

for the children to ask spontaneous questions. Recognition of the many demands on
the time of these group members would have been helpful
and would have strengthened
their relationship to the
leader.

The leader might well have
asked another question at this
point which would have dealt
more with the mothers' role
in these matters. Moving on
to the father was premature.

The leader corrected her
mistake by bringing up the
topic of how to explain to
children what a whore is, or
what rape is, topics which are
usually of more general interest
to mothers, and also less
threatening than any discussion of these matters in connection with their husbands.

The use of "we" is another
way of reinforcing the identification of group members
with each other and with their
leader.

Again, the leader had a good
opportunity to recognize how
difficult it is to discuss these
matters, which she missed.

"Being too young to know--
or to understand," is often
mentioned as one reason why
children's questions need not
be answered. This reflects
the parent's hope that this
unpleasant task can be avoided,
or at least postponed, and

members: "What will happen if a child asks a question and does not get an answer from the parent?" Mrs. P. spoke up--it is rare for her to do that--and said: "He will get his answer someplace else and he will get it wrong." I said this was probably what would happen and used Mrs. P.'s remark to say that "it is best if the parent can answer the child's question when it is asked" and I added that "the answer can, and often should be, a very simple one, especially for a young child." A parent can also say: "I don't know, but we will look it up together," because what is important is that the child should know that he, or she, can come to the parent with his questions.

Mrs. Tt. then gave the discussion a new turn by asking: "What if they don't ask?" Questions from me and from some other group members, like Mrs. S., Mrs. Mm., Mrs. Mmm., brought out the fact that she was talking about her son, who was going to be eleven years old. Mrs. Tt. added: "Of course he has asked very simple questions, but nothing else. He knows that we prayed to God for a baby brother, or a baby sister, and how glad we were when his little brother was born!" When Mrs. Mm. asked what the "simple questions" had been, Mrs. Tt. blushed and answered, he had wanted to know "why God did not send us a baby." (She did not hear my question about what answer she had given to her son's question, or perhaps she did not wish to tell us that.) Mrs. M. said, in an encouraging fashion: "You have made a start and now it's time to tell him more!" (She did not, however, specify what "the more" should be.) Mrs. S. added: "once you start talking to him, you

should not be encouraged, or even let pass, by the leader in a discussion of these problems in child raising.

The admission that one does not have all the answers is often very difficult for parents to make, and needs to be mentioned as a perfectly acceptable statement, and one which will not necessarily undermine the parent's authority, or the child's confidence in the parent. The leader should perhaps have added a statement to that effect at this point.

How to stimulate children to raise questions about these matters is another question which is of great concern to many mothers.

Mrs. Tt. had obviously had considerable difficulty in getting pregnant or perhaps in carrying a child to full term. She was also a very religious person who saw the will of God reflected in her ability to have a second child after what had clearly been a long time of waiting for this to happen. Because of these personal problems, the leader did not comment on the confusion of children which sometimes results if religion is brought into discussion of such topics.

will be more at ease too."

Mrs. Tt. replied, in some distress: "But it is not necessary to tell him the nitty-gritty or about birth control." Her husband's brother had told his boys "about these things" and "this is not right. Children don't know and you just put ideas into their heads."

I said to group members: "Mrs. Tt. has raised a question which is troubling many parents--what should a parent do when the child does not ask any questions? This really leads to another question--at what age should children know how babies are born, even if they don't ask questions?"

Mrs. I. said she had told her son that she was not going to work today because she was going "to a sex education class" and he had answered her: "Oh, I know all about the birds and the bees!" She added, she did not think "he knows much, and he is eleven also."

Mrs. M. said: "Mrs. Pollak told us already: if a child is old enough to ask a question, he is old enough to get an answer, and we also know that if he does not ask the parent, he will ask another child when he goes to school, or he will

It was quite touching to see a well meaning mother-- as Mrs. Tt. undoubtedly was-- attempting to cope with this situation which, in the leader's opinion, mobilized many of her own fears in the area of sexual relations, was opposed to the ways in which she had been raised and to her values and her standards for "what children should know." Part of her upset was also probably a desire to protect her son from learning about matters which had been difficult for her in her own life, such as her problems in getting pregnant with her second child.

It was important to give Mrs. Tt. recognition for the important question she had raised and to reformulate it a bit so that it could be discussed in a more general manner by group members.

It was probably very encouraging for Mrs. Tt. to hear that Mrs. I. was also baffled by the problem of discussing these questions with her eleven year old son. His references to "the birds and the bees" reflected, in the leader's opinion, the indirect approach favored by many parents, and perhaps also by some teachers, to these matters.

Because many members of this group have very definite standards for acceptable behavior, it was particularly important for them to tie in being married and having children, although--and per-

hear stories from the other children." Mrs. Tt. replied: "But when they are so young, how can one make them understand that you should be married to have children?" Mrs. Mmm. said: "But many children are born to unmarried mothers." Mrs. Mm. added that her twelve year old daughter had asked her what French kissing was and "I evaded answering her. I should have answered her, but I did not know what to say!"

I said, "It is of course very difficult to have to deal with these problems, but children have a way of asking embarrassing questions, or else we wonder why they don't ask any questions, what they know, and what they don't know. Judging from what many parents have told me, and from my own experience, it seems to me that an eleven year old boy must have some idea about how babies are born, what sex relations are, but of course we don't know if he has the right information. Another question is how one can help one's children--and especially teen-agers--see the connection between love, sex, and marriage."

Mrs. Mm. "picked up" the last point, and suggested mentioning "the marriage vows; the promise to love" in such a discussion with teen-agers. Mrs. Bbb. replied "but they know about people who get a divorce," and Mrs. Tt. added: "many men live with other women" (she meant, than the one to whom they were married). She added: "I don't think my son believes that they have sex relations."

Mrs. Ss. then asked another question "But how can one tell a boy without, you know, using vulgar terms?" Mrs. Mm. described

haps because--they saw much evidence around them of different ways in which people live together.

Once more, it seemed indicated to give recognition to group members that they were coping with difficult problems, and also with problems which many parents had been facing and discussing in similar meetings. At the same time, it was necessary to discourage any idea about an eleven year old's not having any information on sex relations, conception, and related matters, because this was very unrealistic thinking, or rather hoping, on the part of Mrs. Tt.

Here, too, the unpleasant reality--of people getting divorces, or living with sex partners other than the marriage partner--intruded on the kind of world in which many group members would have preferred their children to grow up.

The last sentence was another example of Mrs. Tt.'s unrealistic thinking in regard to an eleven year old boy.

The discussion was so animated at this point that group members raised new questions before the leader had an oppor-

her two younger children having seen the movie "Born Free;" when the male lion returned to the wilderness, she had told them "he took a wife," and this "explained it when the lion family came back to show the lion cubs."

I said, once more, that I realized how embarrassing some of these questions were and perhaps children realized, without our telling them, that we were embarrassed.

Mrs. Mm. said: "I guess you are right--these questions are on their minds!" Mrs. Mmm. added: "If you go to a restaurant and they go to the washroom--look at what is scribbled on the walls." Several group members (Mrs. Bb., Mrs. M., Mrs. Bbb.) agreed that this was true with such comments as "people have no shame," "there is no decency.

I said: "It is very regrettable that children see such scribbles and hear about so many things relating to sex relations, especially if this happens when they are quite young, but the truth is that this is the case. What we need to do is to find ways of telling children about these matters in such a fashion that they will get a different understanding of sex. No one but the parent can really do this well because of the close relationship between the parents and their children."

Mrs. M. turned to Mrs. Tt. and said, very kindly: "You can lead into it--you have made a good

tunity to encourage a discussion of preceding ones. The leader thought it more important for group members to be able to raise questions now that they were ready to do that.

Mrs. Mm.'s story was another example of the length to which some mothers in this group would go in their attempts to do the right thing for their children, while also avoiding the real questions which are too embarrassing for them to answer.

It was helpful that one group member could admit that children are concerned with these questions, although it was necessary for several group members to blame other people "who have no shame" for exposing their children to situations where their curiosity would be stimulated.

The leader would have made a mistake if she had "cut through" the projection on other people, described above. It was more helpful to share the regret expressed by group members and to use the situation to stress--again, but such reinforcement has to be a repeated experience-- what the parent's job is in such a situation.

Tying in this difficult assignment with the close relationships of the parents to their children was another way of giving the mothers support and some self-confidence for this task.

Several group members were now ready to help Mrs. Tt. to cope with her problem

beginning!" Mrs. Mm. added: "If you look for an opportunity, you will find one!" Mrs. Tt. said, rather helplessly: "Oh, no, what I need is 'an in!'" (She meant, to start such a discussion.) Mrs. L. spoke up--she is another group member who does this only very rarely--and said: "Just ask him what he wants to know!" Mrs. G. turned to Mrs. Tt. and said: "Don't think he does not know something." Her son, who is also eleven, had come home and asked her what "f-u-c-k"-- she spelled it out in this fashion-- meant, and she had said: "That's a vulgar word, we don't use it. We say sex relations!" His answer had been "Oh" and when she had asked him what that meant, he had replied: "That's intercourse-- everybody knows that." Mrs. Tt. shook her head and said, she had grown up "with four boys in the family--they never asked a question and I never asked a question!" Mrs. Mmm. said, in a helpful fashion: "You did not know, and that's why it is so hard now for you--and it's the same for many of us!" Mrs. Mm. added: "We also heard some vulgar words--and we knew this was wrong."

I said: "It is very difficult for many parents to do this particular job with their children, but it is very important also." I added that "many children have also heard stories about rape, and about people who approach children, and certainly our mothers in this group have explained to them that they should not go with anybody they do not know, or accept rides or candy, or money from a stranger." Mrs. M. said: "Of course, this is for their protection. Telling them how babies are born, about menstruation--she blushed as she said this--

and were suggesting ways in which she could approach it. It had obviously been necessary to let the group members express some of their doubts, hesitancy, and feelings, before they could come to grips with one of the aspects of how to explain these matters to children. It had also been necessary that they receive the leader's support, her recognition of how difficult this task was, but also the leader's repeated assurance that the parent must provide some answers for their children's questions and some information about these matters.

Mrs. G.'s story was helpful to Mrs. Tt. because it showed that her son, of the same age as Mrs. Tt.'s son, had asked a question of this kind.

The comments of Mrs. Mmm. and Mrs. Mm. were also helpful to Mrs. Tt. because they offered her support and encouragement. They were identifying with the leader by doing this.

is also for their protection." I said that this is very true and I added that we should discuss this more when we got together again the next time. I added that <u>one thing we should also discuss when we met again, was what children needed to know beyond that God sends a baby, because while it was true that there was a mystery in conception, beyond the physical factors involved, we also wanted the children to know about these physical factors</u>.

It will be helpful to bring to the group at their next meeting some of the reasons why it is not always helpful to children, if religion and conception (or religion and death) are closely tied up with each other. This will have to be done very carefully because most group members are quite devout.

Comment: This was a very difficult topic for the members of this group, and the unusually small number of group members who participated in the discussion was the result of this embarrassment. I was truly grateful for the way in which Mrs. M., Mrs. Mm., Mrs. S., and Mrs. Mmm. contributed to the meeting, because I knew that even these group members did this only with considerable embarrassment.

Comments of this kind are useful because they incorporate the leader's evaluation of a meeting at the time it took place.

****

EXCERPT FROM SESSION V

March 10, 1970: Fourteen mothers and the school counselor attended this meeting; one of them (Mrs. D.) had not attended the earlier meetings of this discussion series. Mrs. W. brought greetings from Mrs. Mmm., Mrs. P., and Mrs. V., who had called her to let her

It is a sign of good intergroup relationships if group members who cannot attend a meeting call a group representative or a friend to let the group know about this.

know that they were sick. Mrs. D. told me that two of her children had been sick, last time, when we met.

The fourteen mothers present were Mrs. M., Mrs. S., Mrs. D., Mrs. T., Mrs. Dd., Mrs. R., Mrs. Mm., Mrs. Bb., Mrs. Gg., Mrs. Bbb., Mrs. Tt., Mrs. Ss., Mrs. L., and Mrs. Ww. Group members sat in that order. Mrs. D. is pretty and slim; she wears glasses, and she expresses herself well.

Today's discussion took up, in further detail, how to answer the questions of children--and of teen-agers--about sex relations; how one can answer children's questions about death; how one can help them to accept the death of a family mem-ber, and what experiences might prepare a child for this.

I had started the meeting by reminding group members of the topics we had wanted to take up today, adding that we could also look together at the other questions they had checked.

Before I could go any further, Mrs. Tt. spoke up and reported what had happened with her son. "You have helped me very much. I did what I should have done a long time ago. I asked him: What do you know about sex?" Her son replied: "I don't know anything, but I have heard many things." He went on to say that they had studied

Unfortunately, the leader did not find an opportunity to discuss why some children get confused, or frightened, if we bring God and religion to the topics of conception and death. She may also have been hesitant to take up this topic because--alas!-- one is not always ready to take up questions which are controversial for a group, especially if a meeting goes as well as this one did. Leaders have their quota of fears and other emotions.

Adding that "we can look together at the questions you checked off" gave group mem-bers an opportunity to take up other questions, if the addi-tional discussion of sex rela-tions, or the discussion on how to explain death, would have been too threatening for them.

This is an excellent exam-ple of how a well motivated group member can use the knowledge acquired in a dis-cussion meeting to change one of her approaches in her parent-child relationship. It may have been made easier for Mrs. Tt. to carry out her plan of doing this because

the herring gull in class, and that the teacher had explained that: "Gulls mate. The male pounces upon the female and shoots the sperm into her." Some kids said afterwards this is what happens to people, but I didn't believe them. Mrs. Tt. had replied: "That is how it happens," and her boy had not said anything else. She had, however, offered to have him look at some of the books which Mrs. I. had loaned her after the group's last meeting; "The Birth of a Baby" was among them. Her son "who has a scientific mind and wants to become a scientist" had looked at the womb, at the Fallopian tubes, and had been especially interested in the part which the father plays in conception. "It was not easy, I was embarrassed, but it was much easier than I thought it would be."

Mrs. R. replied: "And your boy probably feels better now that you told him." Mrs. Tt. said: "I feel better too!" I said that we are all very proud of Mrs. Tt. for having done a difficult job so well, and group members started to applaud Mrs. Tt. spontaneously who was very pleased with this recognition. I joined in the applause.

of her son's rather casual acceptance of the situation. It was certainly helpful that the herring gull had been a topic of study in school, because it led directly to the matter Mrs. Tt. wanted to bring up, but had this not been the case, Mrs. Tt.'s son would undoubtedly have given her another opening for this discussion.

Again, the boy's scientific mind was helpful here, but these pictures would certainly have brought forth a response from any boy in that age group.

Since Mrs. Tt. had been quite troubled about what to do in this matter at the last meeting, she was relieved at having been able to cope with this problem. If one's capacity to cope with problems is proved in such fashion, and meets with such visible success as in this situation, one's coping capacity is increased, and one's self-image as a mother is improved.

The spontaneous applause conveyed the recognition and praise of her peer group to Mrs. Tt. This, as well as the leader's recognition of her achievements in a difficult situation, were additional experiences of an Ego strengthening nature for Mrs. Tt., with, as the leader hoped, the effects described above. While the group members' recognition was not, of course, motivated

Mrs. Bbb.--who was a little jealous I thought--then said, she had also left books on the dining room table. The school counselor commented that books can be very helpful "but not by themselves, more is needed." Mrs. Bbb. said: "But you cannot say to them, 'what do you know about sex?'" Mrs. Tt. replied: "It went like this" and repeated what she had told us before. Mrs. R. added: "At dinner when the whole family is together, is a good time for this." She added that her husband had gone bowling on that evening.

by these thoughts, the leader's was.

Jealousy of group members is a very common phenomenon and it is best ignored in group meetings which do not have the aim of uncovering intra-psychic phenomena, but are planned to help them cope in a more appropriate fashion with problems of family relationships in the here and now.

Mrs. Bbb.'s comment: "But you cannot say 'what do you know about sex'" was indicative of her great embarrassment which was shared by many group members.

While one questions whether the dinner table is really the best place for a discussion of this type, it would not have been appropriate to discourage this timing. Rather, the leader chose to suggest an alternative (see next paragraph). When a task is very difficult, any attempt at solution--unless it is clearly destructive--is better than none, and should not be discouraged. It was a reflection of the embarrassment of Mrs. R. that she chose a time when her husband was absent, but this may also have reflected a hesitancy to discuss sex relations in the presence of one's husband and sexual partner. This indicated a lack of closeness and probably also problems in the marital relationship.

I said, certainly one would select a suitable time and place for such a discussion, which might be at dinner, or when one tucks a child into bed. I added that there were usually many ways of starting such

The school counselor's comment was very welcome to the leader as it reinforced a suggestion she had made. If this comment also served to remind group members of

a conversation, for instance, by talking about a member of the family, or a neighbor who was pregnant, and asking if the child had wondered what was going on, why she was getting fat. Mrs. Dd. mentioned approvingly a book "Expectant Motherhood" which one of her children had borrowed from a library. Mrs. W. said that two teachers at the school were pregnant, and the school counselor commented that this had stimulated many of the children whom she was seeing to ask questions about these matters.

the important role she had in the lives of many of their children--a role more permanent and perhaps more important than that of the leader--that was understandable and not harmful to the group's task.

We were interrupted at this point because Mr. S., the Acting Principal, brought Mrs. D. to the group. This led to some questions about how long Mr. S. was going to stay at the school, and about some new school activities he had started.

Interruptions are often unavoidable and if the leader does not get upset, they will not upset the group.

I welcomed Mrs. D., who apologized for being late; she had not known when the meeting started. I then brought the discussion back by saying we had, last week, recognized how important it was that children received some information of this kind, and that they should be encouraged by their parents to ask questions about these matters.

Since the topic we had been discussing was a very important one, the leader did not do more than tell Mrs. D. that we were glad to have her with us, before steering the discussion back to where it had been before the interruption.

Mrs. D. said that the story in the newspapers about the recent birth of quintuplets had helped: "The children ask about them." The school counselor agreed, she had told one child who asked about the quints that babies were born "because parents had intercourse." Mrs. T. got very red in the face and said: "They would giggle if you said that." Mrs. S. replied: "Giggling is a sign of embarrassment, we giggle too." Mrs. Mm. agreed and reminded us of "the jokes" which adults told and "how we all giggle."

Stories about multiple deliveries are very often a good starting point for children, and even more so for their embarrassed parents.

The leader had the impression that the school counselor was a little ahead of the group when she used the word "intercourse," but the leader did not, of course, react in any fashion to this comment. This would have been very unprofessional behavior, and also would have hurt a person who was well motivated and helpful to group members and to the leader.

Mrs. Mm. then went on to say: "There is more to tell them than just how babies are born." Mrs. Tt. said her son had mentioned during their talk: "The male gets an urge," and she had told him: "With people there is more to it than that, and you will learn about that when you are older." She then went on to tell us that she had "used the right words, penis and vagina," and when Mrs. Bbb. asked her: "But how did you get started?" Mrs. Tt. replied: "I told you; he said: 'guess what we talked about today?' and I said, I did not know and then he told me about the herring gulls and I said to him: what do you know about sex?"

Mrs. Tt. then turned to me and said; "I said word for word what you had told us." She added: "When I was finished, I told him, I don't want you to talk about this to other children. You are mature enough to know about these things, but some parents think their children are too young to know. If other children talk about sex, just listen and then come and ask me."

matters, because one does not usually giggle if reference is made to something completely unknown.

While Mrs. Tt. might well have tied in sex with love and marriage at this point, she was probably so flustered that she did not think of this. Also "you will learn this when you get older" is a very usual way of coping with children's demands, for many members of this group.

It is interesting that Mrs. Bbb., who is a very attentive group member, apparently could not believe what she had heard so that Mrs. Tt. had to repeat her story.

This is a good example of how a mother used a new technique of coping with her problem in the area of giving sex education to her son. She opened up the discussion of this topic, she gave her son some information and she handled her own concern about "what her neighbors might think of her" in a fashion that was acceptable to her and that did not confuse her son. She also kept the lines of communication open so that her son would feel free to come to her with further questions.

If Mrs. Tt. found it necessary to say "word for word" what the leader had said, this is not uncommon if group members are faced with a difficult task and do not have much experience in solving problems of parent-child relationships in a new way. Undoubtedly,

Mrs. Bbb. spoke up at that point and mentioned "wet dreams." I said that many parents are concerned about wet dreams--and just to be sure--I asked what they were. Mrs. Mm. explained this and she also said, in answer to Mrs. R.'s question, that most boys have wet dreams when they are thirteen years old and some when they are younger. Mrs. R.'s reply was: "oh dear!" and Mrs. M. said to Mrs. Tt.-- who was listening intently--: "I can hear the wheels go around!" Mrs. Tt. nodded and said: "I have something new to think about!"

I said, "What might one tell a boy if he has a wet dream?" Mrs. Mm. blushed and said: "You tell us!" I smiled and asked group members if they knew what "passing the buck" was? This led to some laughter which broke the tension. The counselor mentioned that it had been very difficult for her husband to discuss these matters with their boys, and that she had also found these discussions difficult.

I said that I was grateful to her for telling us about these experiences, and I recognized, once more, how difficult it was for parents to talk about these matters. I added that our group members deserved great credit for doing such a difficult job, and for wanting to tackle

her use of the leader's words was also due to her identification with the leader, and it was an indication of her positive relationship to her. In the difficult and emotionally charged area of family relationships, learning is best accomplished through the tool of a strong relationship with an accepting and supportive person from the helping professions.

Wet dreams are also a concern to many parent groups. It is good to make sure that everybody understands a question because some members of a group which is as inhibited as this one was might hesitate to ask.

It is interesting to note how much more interchange there was now among the group members, and how much more able some at least were to participate in the discussion.

The leader tried here to find out if group members were ready for further discussion of the topic of wet dreams, but they were not.

This was another instance of the counselor's helpful attitude in these meetings.

The leader thought that the group members who were so embarrassed might find it easier to tackle this question if it gave them an opportunity to tie in love and sex with their moral standards and values.

so many aspects of it. I then said that wet dreams were normal for boys, that a boy should get reassurance about this, and that they were only an indication that he was physically ready to have sex relations. Of course a boy of thirteen was not ready in any other way for such an experience, and such a discussion would offer the parent another opportunity to tie in sex with love and marriage, and with one's standards and moral values.

Mrs. R. then brought up masturbation, adding: "You know, playing with yourself." The counselor commented that touching oneself is pleasant, that there is nothing more to it. When Mrs. T. asked: "But what do you do to correct it?" Mrs. Bbb. replied: "You don't correct it!" The counselor added that when this happens in school, the teachers encourage a child to pick up his lessons. Mrs. Bb. added: "You can send him to the store!" Mrs. Mm. said that men in prison often had no other outlet and Mrs. L. explained that her little boy "used to move back and forth in his playpen, and the doctor said to ignore it." Mrs. D. added: "Girls masturbate too," a comment which shocked some group members, for instance, Mrs. Bb., Mrs. M., and Mrs. T. The counselor agreed, adding: "With girls it is less visible, they don't have an erection." Tight pants and riding on trains were mentioned by Mrs. D. and Mrs. Bbb., respectively. Mrs. T. who had looked more and more startled, and who had again started to blush, laughed now, obviously to hide her embarrassment. (None of the group members reacted to this, nor did I.) Mrs. Bbb. added: "If this makes you uneasy, the boys realize it,"

At this point the leader would have preferred it if the counselor would not have "jumped into the fray" but you can't have everything!

Mrs. D.'s comment went contrary to the theory that "sex is for men, women are above such things" which I thought some group members might be subscribing to.

It was again noticeable how much more animated the discussion was at this point; as group members were now able to pool their information about masturbation, some of them at least were quite knowledgeable. A leader may be tempted to think of a group of mothers such as the present one as being less well informed than they actually were, but with some support from a sympathetic professional person, they were able to enter such a discussion in a very active way, and to share their knowledge of such matters with others less well informed--or more embarrassed--group members.

and she also added "they do it in their beds at night," to which Mrs. Mm. replied: "You should not go into their bedrooms at night."

I commented that masturbation was fairly common and normal for children of all ages, that one should not get troubled about it, but that one should also not encourage it. If a child masturbated very obviously, it was quite all right to tell him: "Don't do that in the living room!" (I did not add--which I can do next time--that too much masturbation may well indicate some disturbance of the child, and should be looked into by a counselor, or by some other person from the helping professions.)

I also added that any discussion of what masturbation meant in relation to the sexual desires of teenagers would again offer an opportunity to tie in sex with love and marriage.

Mrs. D. then expressed her concern because her son looked at the pictures of nude women in Playboy Magazine; her neighbor threw the magazine in the trashcan, and he picked it up there. Mrs. W. commented that it was not necessary to do that, the corner drugstore carried Playboy and Mrs. M. added: "They don't need magazines, just look at the billboards." Mrs. Bbb. described how her son had giggled when he had seen such a magazine in his uncle's hands, but when she had suggested that she and he look at it together, her son had "sheepishly" said--"I guess not!"

When Mrs. R. asked what to do about "looking at these pictures," I said one could explain to one's children that we saw many such pictures, that they might look at them if they wished, but that one

This remark was not absolutely necessary in view of the standards for acceptable behavior of the group members. It reflected the experience of the leader with more "sophisticated" groups whose members sometimes have qualms about interfering with any masturbation for fear that this will inhibit the child sexually. A leader often longs to express a point of view--as I did here! --even if it is not in line with group concerns and group behavior.

The leader assumed that group members would not want to have such pictures in their homes, but if they could be encouraged to let their children look at these pictures in

did not want to have such pictures around in one's house, if that was the way one felt about it. Several group members nodded to indicate agreement, and Mrs. Mm. added: "Your own life will be the best example!"

I went on to say that one could use the same approach when teen-agers asked questions about sex relations outside of marriage, or about the use of drugs. One acknowledged that these things exist, but one outlined what it did to a young person if he--or she--had sex relations and might be burdened with the responsibility for a child, or for a wife and child, might have to give up the fun of being young and free of responsibility. Similarly, one could outline how self-destructive drugs were and what they could do to a young person's health and happiness. "Feeling sorry for young people who do that to themselves" was an excellent approach in discussing these matters, and it often got one's point of view across much better than telling the young people that this was wrong. Mrs. Bbb. said approvingly: "My kids often say that I am always hollering at them, but I tell them, 'I love you so I holler.'" The counselor added, many children have told her "my mother cares, she won't let me do this."

I said, we had also wanted to talk today about what we could tell children about death?" Mrs. Mm. replied: "I know what you don't tell them." She described with considerable feeling that there had been two deaths "in quick succession" in her family. Her brother had died suddenly away from home and his three year old daughter had been told that her father was staying at work. When her father did not

the privacy of their room, for instance, that would be much more helpful than a prohibition to look at them which would be unenforceable and would only increase the children's interest in seeing them.

The leader was concerned mainly with discouraging "preaching to the teen-agers," or telling them what to do and what not to do, approaches which members of this group might be inclined to use, and which rarely--if ever--meet with success.

The leader missed an opportunity to comment on the appreciation which many children have for their parents' caring for them, even if it takes the form of "hollering" or of not allowing them to do certain things, in line with the theory that the parent represents the conscience, especially for the young child, before parental authority is incorporated into the Superego (Freud, 1966, pp. 526-526).

It is quite common for parents of young children to assume that the death of a close relative need not be discussed with, or explained to them, and the stories told by Mrs. Mm. and Mrs. R. are good examples of the reactions of children in such a situation.

come home, the child "panicked" and now, if someone went to work, the little girl told them "don't go to work, you die there." She added: "Children should be told immediately if someone in the family has died." Mrs. R. asked if the neighbors had not come to the house and talked about the death, and Mrs. Mm. explained that they had come, but "they just fussed over the children, everyone felt sorry for them! Nobody told them that their father had died, and that was when they should have been told." Mrs. R. commented that her father had died when her son was four years old. "He lived with us and for a year my boy looked for him, he went through the house from top to cellar." Mrs. Tt. said, also with considerable feeling: "At first you don't know either what happened." When her parents died, she had been married for a while and "I knew they were dead but sometimes I found myself at the door, saying: 'I wish they would come!'"

Mrs. Mm. then wondered: "What about the older children-- ten, eleven, twelve? Should they go to a funeral or to a wake?" She added that the first funeral her children had attended had been a military funeral "they had not been prepared for this and they were very shaken." She had been sorry that she had taken the children but would this have been the same, if the children had been fifteen? Mrs. Ss. said she had not been prepared when her mother died; she had been fourteen and "it was very bad for me for a long time." She had taken her children to funerals at her church: "In this way they had the experience but it was removed from them because the people who

The topic of death, especially of the death of a close relative, is very emotionally charged. Since group members were more at ease with each other, and more assured of support from each other, they were ready to share some of their difficult experiences. No activity on the part of the leader was needed at this point, but such activity would have been indicated if a group member had brought out material of too personal a nature, or if a group member's defenses had broken down.

This is an example of an excellent discussion, with interaction of group members

died were strangers, and not their family." Mrs. Mm. nodded and added: "If you could take them to the funeral of a friend's parent; they would be--and you would be-- sympathetic but not actually involved." Mrs. Mm. then added: "Of course, whatever you do, sometimes it does not work out. When I have chest pains, my children are worried. They say, 'You are not going to die' to me." I said, children had all kinds of reactions to death and illness, but I thought we had agreed that they should be told that someone in the family had died, that the person would not come back and that this was, in the long run, easier for the child and for the parent because the parent would not have to pretend that a loved person was coming back, while knowing that this person was gone forever.

Mrs. T. then asked: "But how can you explain to a child that you had a stillborn child? My little girl wants to know why she does not have any brothers and sisters." Mrs. W. replied that she had explained this by saying that "God does not want us to have any more children." Mrs. Tt. added: "And every death is a very different experience, not only for each of us but also at different times. Each time we must find a way to deal with it." Mrs. Mm. agreed; she had been giving birth to her younger daughter when her mother died. "For a long time her death was not real to me. I had not been with her when she died and I had not been able to go to the funeral." She turned to me and said that attending a funeral "does make it real." Mrs. R. agreed, adding "you must talk about the dead. I say, it was nine years ago that

who discuss each other's situations and expand on them. Such a discussion leads to a widening of each group member's horizon because new approaches to a problem are brought out.

The leader missed an opportunity to discuss the anxiety of children if a parent is sick and ways to allay this anxiety.

The leader's summarization of what the group had discussed served several purposes, but one of them was the reinforcement of the learning process since repetition was one way of strengthening the acquisition of new knowledge (Hilgard, 1956, p. 233).

Group members were adding new instances here of problems in explaining death to their children and they were also expressing some of their own feelings of grief and of loss at the death of their own parents. This is, of course, better than repressing such feelings and it also enables one to understand better and to cope more helpfully with the variety of reactions which children have when they suffer similar losses. "Shielding a child from death...displays more of the anxieties and concerns of the parents...than the child's genuine capacity to manage knowledge of the existence of death. Naturally, method of explanation, timing and individual differences have to be considered" (Feifel, 1973, p. 5).

grandfather died, or today would have been his sixtieth birthday."

I was ready to terminate the meeting--our time had been up a while ago--when Mrs. Ss. said, rather plaintively: "Now I know what you don't tell children--but what do you tell them?" Mrs. Mm. said: "The truth--the person is dead, he won't come back. We loved him and we all miss him--or her!" Mrs. W. added: "I also tell them that God has given us a certain length of time here on earth."

I said: "These are all excellent suggestions; one might also add, if one thinks that a child is worried about the death of a playmate, or of another child's mother, that some children die, but that many more children live to grow up, that some mothers die but that most mothers live to be with their children for a long, long time and, besides, there is always someone 'like your Grandma' who will take care of little children."

Here again, the leader tried to cover additional situations--like the death of a playmate, or of another child's mother--which may well be part of a growing up child's experience, and may frighten the child. Since many parents --as well as other adults, including some members of the helping professions--have a tendency to avoid discussions of death as too painful and too anxiety provoking, the leader wanted to convey to the group members some reassuring as well as truthful ways of coping with these problems.

I forgot to record that I had brought a copy of "What to Tell Your Children about Sex" (paper back edition: $0.50). Group members passed it around, several wrote down the title! Comments were made on how inexpensive the book was and I was asked where it could be bought.

The counselor talked to me after the meeting, mostly about the problems which some children of group members have in school. She expressed her appreciation for the opportunity to get to know mothers

Since money is somewhat scarce for many group members, it seemed best to bring them an inexpensive publication, so that they could afford to buy it, should they wish to do so.

If the counselor's presence had inhibited the group, the leader would have had to accept her offer not to attend the meetings. She had asked earlier if she should not come,

better in the meetings, and asked me if I or the group members minded her coming to them. Should I think it better that she not come, she would stay away. I told her that her presence was helpful to the group because she shared some of her own experiences with her family so readily.

Comments: This meeting was the best this group had had so far. The participation of group members was freer, and their interaction much more active than before. Mrs. Mm. and Mrs. I shared personal experiences with death in their families; Mrs. W. and Mrs. R. became much more emotionally involved than is usual for them when this topic came up. As I look back upon the session, this greater freedom was due to three factors: 1) group members knew each other and me better now; 2) they were encouraged by the "giant step" which Mrs. Tt. had taken, and 3) they had opportunities to share their reactions to the experience of the loss of a parent or a sibling.

and the writer had encouraged her to attend, because of her close relationship to many group members, and also because she was unusually sensitive to the needs of the group and not competitive with the leader or with the group members. Experience helps a leader determine when the presence of a person who is not a member of a group, is helpful or is detrimental to the purpose of the group meeting.

While pressures of work often prevent one from "looking back at a meeting," it is very helpful to the leader whenever it can be done, especially to leaders who are experienced and pretty much "on their own" as far as their professional activities are concerned.

It is always very encouraging for the other group members if one of them has applied some of the new knowledge in her family life, and if this has worked out well, as was the case with Mrs. Tt.

Discussing the death of members of their own families offered opportunities to express grief and the writer would judge that such expressions were discouraged in other situations because of the emphasis on controlling one's feelings, which were probably part of the standards for approved behavior for many members of this group. Furthermore, death and its implications--real or fantasied--are feared by many persons from all strata of society who tend to avoid

mentioning it. "In short, fear
of death is a basic concept
because it seems to regard
Death, capitalized to indicate
a personal menace, as the
embodiment of every form of
human evil, failure, disgrace,
disaster, and corruption"
(Weisman, 1962, p. 16).

XI
Reacting to and Handling of Children's Stealing

The mothers who attended these group meetings had a different
motivation for coming than those described in the preceding chapter.
They lacked the unifying bond that attendance at the same school provides; instead, eleven schools, all located in the same school district of Philadelphia, made referrals of mothers to the group meetings.
Self-referral, which had been the motivation in the group described
earlier, was replaced here by the judgment of the professional staff
of these schools--principals, teachers, and counselors--who felt
that a mother might find help for her problems which were caused
by her child's problems in school and which, in turn, were probably
a source of the child's problems in the school setting as well.

The problems of the children, which caused concern to the
school staff, were those of acting out behavior which was disruptive
in the school situation. Acting out behavior took many forms, from
the inability to sit still, to getting into fights in and outside of the
classroom, to more serious forms of behavior, such as destruction
of property, stealing, and fire setting. Behavior of this kind is not
only a problem in the school and a handicap to learning, but it is also
likely to get the child, and later the adolescent, in trouble with the
law, the Courts, and add thereby to the normal difficulties which are
part of the growing up process.

The nature of the discussion series required some special
approaches. Since group members were not self-referred, at least
when these discussion series started, they needed much more encouragement to attend the meetings. Such encouragement was give in
various ways: When making a referral, the school personnel
described the meetings as planned to help the parent who was concerned about the child's problems in school, and this was, of course,
the purpose of these meetings. This emphasis meant that the parent
was not made to feel guilty because the child had problems; rather,
recognition was given to his desire to cope with them. The school
staff also followed up on their referrals by making telephone calls
to group members who had missed a meeting, sometimes by visiting
them when this seemed indicated. A few group members who had
relationships of long standing to their school counselors used to
share some of the content of the discussions with them, and the

school counselors' interest in the meetings and approval of them
strengthened the relationships of these group members to the leader,
in turn.

After a referral to the group had been made, and accepted by
a mother (since the meetings were scheduled for ten o'clock in the
morning, only a few fathers came, and only sporadically), the group
leader sent her an individual letter inviting her to come, with information about the dates, hours, and place of the meetings, and also
with some information about the public transportation which would
bring that person from her home to the school where the group met.
These invitations were sent out several times by the discussion
leader until it became clear that this mother did not intend to follow
through on the referral. Group members who had attended one, or
several meetings, but had missed a meeting, received individual
letters from the leader also, inviting them to come to the next meeting, with a brief summary of what had been discussed in the meeting
which the group member had missed. Here, too, the emphasis was
on giving recognition to the problems of the parents, and the letters
were very carefully worded, so as not to make the mother feel guilty
about having missed a meeting. "We missed you but I know that a
busy mother cannot always come to a meeting," was one way of
starting such a letter and, very often, this approach encouraged
mothers to attend the meetings again.

Since the discussion series--of which there were eleven, with
a total of seventy-eight meetings--were cooperative projects between
the schools which made these referrals and the Family Service of
Philadelphia, which made available the leadership of the writer, it
was essential to keep the lines of communication open between the
leader and the school personnel. This included not only the principals, teachers, and counselors of the cooperating schools, but also
the counseling supervisors and the superintendent of the School District to which these schools belonged. Such communication was
achieved primarily by the leader's sending regular reports to the
school personnel, which gave the names of those who had been present, as well as the names of those who had been absent from the
meeting, and which contained a summary of the major topics which
had been discussed at this particular session. In order to preserve
the confidentiality of the meetings, the contributions of individual
group members--the problems they brought up for discussion, the
questions they raised, the points of view they expressed--were not
identified in these reports.

CHARACTERISTICS OF GROUP MEMBERS

The families represented in these projects belonged to a low
income group and showed the characteristics of a working class
subculture. Husbands worked in semiskilled jobs with low job
security. Periods of unemployment were part of life, as were a

variety of health and family problems, often accompanied by hopelessness. One group member shrugged her shoulders and said: "If
you have the rent paid and the groceries made, you should be satisfied."

For both husbands and wives, graduation from high school was
the exception; leaving school as soon as possible to start to work
was the rule. Marriage tended to take place at a very early age and
the number of children in these families used to be quite large. For
example, at one point, eighteen families of group members had a
total of seventy-one children living at home. In these large families
many mothers leaned on the older children to take care of their
younger siblings, and these responsibilities often were assigned too
early to children whose own dependency needs had not been met.
Because of the size of these families, there was in many instances
little individualization of the children, little realization that their
needs were different and, as a result, few if any attempts to meet
these different needs of the children in a satisfactory and growth
promoting way (Minuchin et al, 1967, p. 197).

The hopelessness, combined with the demands of large families,
may have been the reasons why many members of this group showed
little, and often no interest, in their children's achievements in
school (Minuchin et al., 1967, p. 214). They did not keep in touch
with their teachers or other school personnel. These parents were
obviously unaware that to show interest in a child's achievement in
school might be meaningful to him as one sign of parental concern,
might make him feel loved and important, and might encourage any
of his strivings for better educational goals. A closer contact with
the schools would also have been a check on some of the lies which
children with poor school records often told their parents. This
lack of interest in the children's achievement in school was in line
with the lack of interest of most group members in their husbands'
work. In contrast to most middle class families--or to many immigrant families--education was not seen as one way to a better life,
and competitiveness--for better grades or for better jobs--was not
part of the personalities of many group members.

Marriage relationships were often poor, with little communication between husband and wife, who often lead separate lives (Minuchin et al, 1967, p. 24). Husbands tended to be nameless, they
were usually referred to as "he" and the content of most references
to husbands was negative and belittling. One group member, whose
husband was kind to her--she was an epileptic--was the object of
admiration, perhaps tinged with envy, on the part of most group
members; she was obviously considered as being in an exceptional
position.

It was not unusual for these families to have what one mother
called "the second crop" (of children); they were the result of a
separation of the couple, which was followed by a reconciliation and
a resumption of the marriage relationship several years later. As
these mothers described their husbands, the latter felt that they had

fulfilled their obligations if they supported their families; they did
not share the mothers' concerns and did not assume much responsibility for the raising of the children. This task was seen as "women's
work," again as presented by the mothers who resented being regarded
as housekeepers and mothers only. As they talked about their own
and their husbands' activities, one got the picture of a "woman's
world" which was separated from "the man's world," in line with
many descriptions of the life style of members of the working class.
Many group members also voiced complaints about their husbands'
drinking and being abusive. While sex relations were not discussed
by group members, the writer ventures a guess that when they took
place, they did not bring joy or happiness to the partners, and that
here again the mothers felt used and abused.

The relationships to their own families--parents, siblings,
in-laws--varied from considerable closeness, mostly with the group
members' own mothers, to open hostility, mostly to in-laws, and in
the case of one group member, to her large family of siblings, all
of whom had been raised in orphanages, while she had been raised
by her grandmother. An interesting phenomenon was the close
relationship which several group members had with their daughters
who were part of the "first crop" and who were married; they used
to see each other frequently and most married daughters were
described, with pride, as having made good marriages, living in
better neighborhoods than their parents, owning cars, etc. They
were examples of upward mobility and while this term was unknown
to the group members, they approved of its manifestations. An
example of the closeness described above was mentioned on Mother's
Day because one group member used to send flowers on that day to
her married daughter, who returned the compliment. It seems a
safe guess that most relationships which were meaningful to the
group members developed with members of the same sex, just as
their husbands seemed to prefer being with men for relaxation during
their free time. Neither is it surprising that most of the children
who had problems in school were boys, since the mothers' negative
attitudes to their husbands, and their preference for their daughters,
aroused anger and jealousy in their sons. As the fathers did not
take much interest in their children, they did not usually offer any
strengthening relationships to the boys which could have counter-
acted some of the mothers' negative attitudes.

Most group members had few social relationships in the sense
of having a circle of friends, or of being active in a variety of organizations. They had one or perhaps two close friends, and relationships to neighbors tended to be stormy. Many members of this group
got involved in their children's fights, partly because they tended to
be defensive where the children were concerned but, also, because
they enjoyed "a scrap" with a neighbor as a break in their routines
of keeping house, cleaning, cooking, and washing for their large
families.

Another characteristic of most group members was that the

areas in which they lived tended to be small and somewhat isolated
communities, although they were parts of a large city. "Going down-
town" was rare and somewhat in the nature of a venture; shopping
was done in neighborhood stores, preferably in small ones which
extended credit in periods of financial stress. Going to the five and
ten cent store in the areas where the group members lived was a
favorite way of breaking the monotony of their days. Reading or
going to the movies was not mentioned; interestingly enough, they
did not watch TV very much, perhaps because of the many hours
they spent taking care of their families. Many group members seemed
to be careful housekeepers, and one of the most frequently voiced
complaints about husbands and sometimes about children, was their
lack of appreciation for "a nice home."

GOALS OF THE DISCUSSION SERIES

The goals for these projects were related to the premise that acting out behavior of a child usually reflects, either consciously or unconsciously, the acting out behavior of the parent (Rexford, 1957, pp. 75-85;
Simcoe, 1956, pp. 443-450; Stein, 1973, pp. 347-364). Observation of
the parents' behavior in school had supported this assumption. Most
parents of the children who were in trouble because of their acting out
behavior were themselves in conflict with society and many of its institutions; they fought the schools and undermined any confidence which some
of their children might have had in them by their disparagement of its
teachers. References which the group members made to the Courts, to
the law, or to the police, were always negative (Lewis, 1966, pp. 11-16).
One member of the school personnel had given a name to this parent group:
"the screaming parents," because their complaints were very loudly
voiced and often accompanied by threats of more drastic action. Most
parents whose children showed the above-described behavior in school
did not see education as anything which would contribute to the child's
future, to his happiness, or to his success in adult life. They did not,
incidentally, fight the schools in order to have methods of teaching
changed, or other approaches used to bring the school and the students,
or the school and the community closer. Their negative attitudes
toward the schools were an end in itself.

Efforts to reach the parents in other ways, for instance, through
referrals for counseling or for psychiatric treatment--either for
their children or for themselves--had usually failed. A distrust of
these services, referrals to which may have been seen as an attack
on their judgment and as criticism of their adequacy as parents, was
in part responsible for these failures. Fear of the one-to-one relationship on which these contacts were based was also a powerful
element in preventing them from taking advantage of these resources
to cope with their problems.

Taking these factors into account, the six goals of these discussion series were as follows: First, to get the parents to use a

community service which most of them had not used before; second, to ventilate some of their negative feelings toward the schools so that they could move beyond the expression of these feelings; third, to develop a relationship with the writer as their discussion leader, which would enable them to see a person from the helping professions as interested in them, willing to listen to them, to accept their point of view where valid, but also to disagree with it when it was not helping their children; fourth, to use the permissive and accepting setting of these discussions for a slow changing of their negative attitudes toward the school, where this was harmful to their children; fifth, to use the discussions for a learning experience in the area of family relationships, of techniques of child raising, and of understanding some of the reasons why children behave in the way they do, so that the parent can help them to modify this behavior where it affects the child's chances for his future life; and sixth, to increase their feelings of self-worth, and to give them some confidence in the capacity to function in the parental role. This last goal was important because most group members had a low self-image of themselves as wives, so that they could not get much support in coping with their problems as mothers from their marital relationships. On the assumption that the referrals for individual help had been too threatening, so that most parents had not been able to accept them, or to keep up a meaningful contact for any length of time, they were now offered help in the form of group discussions which are less threatening than individual contacts because of the support which group members offer to each other, and also because it is easier for group members to set limits to how far they wish to involve themselves in a group setting than in individual contact.

The professional people who participated in these projects were aware of the difficulties to be faced in mobilizing a group of parents who had so little motivation for their participation. A few criteria were developed, so as not to "stack the cards" too much against our efforts: mothers who had had psychotic breakdowns, mothers who were mentally retarded, and mothers who had shown absolutely no interest in their children's school adjustment--who had not even come to the school to scream at the school personnel!-- were not referred to the discussions. Since the mothers were the focus of the project, no limit was set on the depth or on the nature of the children's problems.

While it is never possible to offer discussion leadership which will result in a learning experience and an experience of growth unless the group members have positive relationships to the leader, this was particularly true for this group. A strong relationship to the leader was necessary to gain their confidence, and to help them accept her as a person apart from the school system but, at the same time, concerned about their children's problems in the school. Work with this group of mothers would have been impossible if they had transferred their negative attitudes toward the school and its personnel, onto the leader. A strong relationship was also a sine qua non because of the low degree of anxiety of most of the mothers, and because of their almost total lack of insight into the contributions of their own problems to their children's problems. As the first project started, and as new mothers joined the group, the leader needed to offer to them again and again the experience of being accepted as people, of having their difficulties as parents recognized, and of being given recognition of any efforts, however feeble, that they were making to help their children, of which coming to the meetings was one.

THE DISCUSSION SERIES: ITS PLANNING AND SETTING, GROUP SIZE AND GROUP COMPOSITION

The group met in a comfortable room where one could sit around a table. The meetings which lasted an hour and a half were planned for ten o'clock, on the assumption that the children had gone to school by that time, that the mothers had had a chance to get dressed themselves, and, also, as one group member phrased it, "to catch my breath. " In most of these families, the mornings seemed to be filled with considerable noise and confusion, which was partly due to the large size of the families, but also to a lack of planning for such routine matters as breakfast, clothes to be worn, and lunch money to be available. Coffee and coffee cakes started the meetings off; and after some initial help from the leader, group members took charge of buying the supplies, making coffee and cleaning up after the meetings. A kitty--a coffee cup--was on the table and group members and the leader contributed to it to cover the cost of the refreshments. When new mothers came, the leader made some casual remark to the effect that "anyone who does not have any change should, of course, have coffee and cake all the same; having no change happens to all of us. " Since some group members were at times short of money--when husbands were out of work, or when assistance checks had not come through, or when some illness had used up their slender resources--this helped to overcome any feelings they might have of embarrassment about not being able to contribute the twenty five cents which the more affluent group members and the leader used to deposit in the coffee cup. Having coffee and cake served a variety of purposes: it enabled group members to relax, it provided some food for the body--in the morning's confusion many mothers did not find the time to prepare their own breakfasts-- and it also provided emotional support, as food so often does. Furthermore, this tied in with the mores of group members, who drank large amounts of coffee, and for whom coffee and coffee cakes were the usual form of entertaining visitors.

It is usually a better plan to have mothers attend meetings of this kind without their children, partly because this permits them to devote their full attention to the discussions, partly because many mothers are glad to be relieved of the burden of caring for their

offspring. However, it is not always possible to work out arrangements for the care of young children, and several members of this
group brought their preschool age children to the meetings, when
this was the only possible solution. The children kept busy with
toys, crayons, and games which the mothers brought along and they
enjoyed the refreshments. Group members were helpful, if a child
turned to them, and since neither they nor the leader were upset by
the children's presence--and did not pay much attention to them
either--their presence was not disruptive.

The room where the group meetings were held was located in
the school where the School District Superintendent had his office,
and group members came eventually to look upon this location as a
prestige location and to regard the conference room, where they
met, as "our room." This development took considerable time, of
course, and it was helped by the courtesy which the District Superintendent extended to the group, by welcoming them every fall, and
by apologizing to them, on the rare occasions when the conference
room was not available for the meetings. These were the only occasions when some one from the school system came to the meetings,
as neither counseling supervisors, nor principals, teachers or
counselors were ever present.

As to the size of the group, the number of mothers who were
referred was necessarily much larger than the number of mothers
who came to the meetings, and, of the latter, again some chose to
come once or twice only. This may have been due to the fact that
they did not wish to participate in such activities, or that the discussion approach was foreign to them and, furthermore, that they
did not see how it could be of help. In some instances, it may have
been that the mothers gave "lip service" to the referral, and decided
to stop coming after having attended one meeting. This is an experience which is well known to anyone who has attempted to refer someone for some form of professional help, the value of which seems
doubtful to the person who is being referred. Certainly the interaction between these particular group members and the leader may
have been another reason for their dropping out of the projects,
because it is not possible to develop positive relationships to everyone who attends one's group meetings. One interesting phenomenon
stood out, however, when the leader and some of the school personnel
looked at the "dropouts" from the projects: there was a close relationship between the investment of the referring school personnel,
and their belief in the value of these projects, and the ability of the
mothers to maintain their contacts with the group. This is again
well known and is comparable to the reactions of clients or patients
who are being transferred to another counselor or therapist. Once
a discussion group had "settled down," attendance varied from eight
to fourteen mothers at every meeting, depending on such factors as
the weather, illness of a child, or of a member of one's family,
which usually necessitated taking charge of the other household, in
addition to one's own. Extra jobs, between Thanksgiving and

Christmas, which were important because they made available some additional income, also affected attendance sometimes.

In regard to age, the group usually had a predominance of women in their thirties and forties, although some younger and some older mothers participated also. The group, which had started as a group of white mothers, accepted some black mothers later on, and did this easily, quite in contrast to some of the racial conflicts which had erupted in parts of that particular school district. It was difficult to evaluate whether this acceptance reflected the true feelings of the group members or was due to their realization that integration in the public schools was here to stay. Since the meetings were not aimed at achieving better interracial relationships, the leader did not explore this matter further. In any event, group members who had attended the meetings previously, remained in the group after black mothers were referred to it, and the number of black mothers who did not continue to attend the meetings after having started to come, was comparable to the number of white mothers who acted in the same fashion.

Group members were Catholic or Protestant by religious affiliation and, although their marital relationships were usually poor as previously described, only very few of them were divorced or separated.

REPORT ON SESSION IV OF THE FIFTH DISCUSSION SERIES

Because of the special nature of these cooperative projects, meetings were not recorded in the usual form; the reports sent to the school personnel took their place. The leader kept additional notes for her own information, the purpose of which was to identify the contributions of group members, and to cover other parts of the sessions which were not included in the reports.

SESSION IV

March 19, 1964: Eleven group members attended this session: Mrs. J., A. School; Mrs. W., B. School; Mrs. A., Mrs. B., C. School; Mrs. C., Mrs. McP., E. School; Mrs. E., Mrs. S., M. School; Mrs. Kk., Mck. School; Mrs. G., Mrs. Ss., P. School.

Absent were seven group members. (Names and schools followed.) Letters of reminder of the next meeting will be sent to the group members who were absent

Listing the names of the group members who had attended and of those who had missed the session enabled the counselors to follow through with the absent mothers, as previously described.

If a group does not meet on its regular day, or if there is a longer interval than usual between meetings, as was the case here due to Easter vaca-

today, and to those who were present also, because of the two week
interval until we meet again.

Main Topics Discussed: Stealing.
Toward the end of the meeting we
started to discuss Lying. As group
members started to leave, one
mother brought up a special problem, namely, how to handle the
wish of a younger child to sing in
the choir, when an older child is
singing there who has a more beau-
tiful voice. Group members suggested that the younger child might
be encouraged to play an instru-
ment, if possible. We will discuss
this matter more fully when we get
together again, as it is part of
Competition of Children in the
Family, and How the Parent Can
Handle It.

I started the meeting by review-
ing briefly that children's stealing
is a problem for many parents,
that children are exposed to many
temptations, in stores, etc., but
that parents must help children
learn that taking--or keeping--
what does not belong to you, is
wrong.
I added that I had been troubled
by something which had come up
last week, and that I wanted to take
this up again. I said, with a smile,

tion in the schools, letters of
reminder are helpful, partly
because many mothers from
low educational backgrounds
are not as used to entering
and keeping appointments, but
partly also as an indication
of the leader's interest in
them. Members of these projects commented often with
appreciation on the letters,
just as some teen-age group
members had done.
    As previously stated, the
leader did not always follow
through on such planning
unless it seemed imperative
to her--see next paragraph.
In most situations it is usually
preferable to let group members take the initiative, so
that they can bring up their
more immediate concerns
and problems. This group of
mothers needed a very permissive approach also because
of their negative attitudes and
ideas about the schools.
    Their acceptance of the
leader and of a school sponsored activity such as the
projects were, was a step in
the direction of developing
more positive attitudes toward
educational opportunities as a
whole.
    The review gave the leader
an opportunity to stress again,
as she had in the preceding
session, that children need to
learn these basic concepts.

It is essential to be truthful
in one's statements as a
leader, if one has not followed
through, or dealt with, an

that group members probably knew by now that I have hindsight, that is, many important things occur to me after a meeting has ended.

important point of view before. The leader has to do this as soon as the opportunity presents itself, and preferably at the next meeting of the group. The silence of the leader is usually interpreted as agreement with the comments made, and if the leader does not agree, this needs to be put into words, and stated very directly.

"Having hindsight" was one form in which the leader-- and later on, some members of projects also--presented additional material, or raised additional questions. Since one often has excellent ideas, or flashes of insight, after a meeting has ended, reporting them to the group adds to the group experience. It is also further evidence of the leader's concern about group members.

The leader took a stand, and trouble started!

The point which I then discussed was that one may not keep anything which one finds, with reference to the eight pennies which a little boy had found. Rather he should learn that anything which one finds should be turned over, e.g., to the principal or in other situations, to the police. That started a heated controversy, and from here on, the discussion was under way.

One group member said: "I must disagree with you, " explaining that she had lost her wallet, and no one returned it to her. If she should find a wallet, why should she then not keep it? When another group member suggested that she could have gone to the police station with the wallet she found, that brought out negative remarks about the police from several group members: "they keep the money;" when bikes are found "they

The example of the wallet showed the somewhat infantile quality of reasoning, the "tit for tat" approach to life's problems--and also to family relationships--which some group members had. Beyond that, it showed a faulty Superego development, and confusion about some well established concepts of right and wrong. It must be remembered that the members of this group did

sell them instead of giving them to the kids who found them."

One group member added that she had found a purse, had called the person who had lost it, and had been asked: "what did you do with the money in it?" Another group member had been accused by the driver of a taxi, in which she was going "to the clinic, I was taking my sick mother," of having opened a handbag which she found in the taxi.

Fortunately, a few group members had sounder ideas. One mother had lost her pay envelope, but had returned one she found "because I knew this person needed it more than I." Another mother had told her son that he must return a dollar bill which he found in a drugstore--he had protested violently, of course!--and when he, in turn, lost money there, the owner of the drugstore had told him that 1) it had been found and turned in, and 2) as a reward for

not belong to a part of our society which is opposed to personal property and advocates communal living. If one lives in a society which protects personal property, and if one does not disagree with this principle, it is important to live in accordance with it and to teach one's children these same concepts of right and wrong. Later in life, they may come to develop very different ideas about private property, but these will, hopefully, be based upon their judgment, their values, and a mature decision on what course their lives as adults should take.

Most members of this group were quick to take offense and attempts to explain to them some of the reasons why other people may distrust one, would not have been successful. Furthermore, they would have led the discussion away from the main topic under consideration. Any attempts of this kind would also have failed because the members of the group themselves distrusted many other people.

These mothers helped the leader, a phenomenon which occurs quite frequently, especially when some members of a group have attended several discussion series, as these three mothers had, and have begun to identify with the leader, and with the leader's points of view.

With some parent groups, the last two stories could have been used for a discussion of whether children's

being so honest, he could have the dollar he had turned in, also. A third mother's child had found a dollar, had wanted it to go skating, but had been made to return it also. The mother had then, to reward him, given him a dollar-- "out of the food money, but I can stretch it"--so that he could go skating.

I used this material to stress the importance of 1) <u>getting children to see that what does not belong to you may not be kept</u>; 2) <u>that honesty and good behavior get rewarded</u>. I added that <u>children are not born knowing these things, and that it is the parent who has to teach children what is right and what is wrong</u>. One mother made the interesting comment: "<u>The best reward is when you know they would not do anything wrong whatever people say.</u>"

good behavior should be rewarded, e.g., with a dollar bill, but this would have been contrary to what many of these mothers had been doing in their homes. Since it is better if a child is encouraged to do what is right in such fashion than if he is not taught to do this or does not have any, to him, sound reason for doing it, the leader did not start a discussion of this approach. She felt that this could wait until more basic problems of the children, of which stealing was one, had been explored.

The story of the "food money which can be stretched" (if one uses a dollar for other purposes) shows more clearly than long descriptions could, the tight financial situation which many of these families were facing. It would not have been told by a group of middle class mothers. It is important that the leader be aware of such remarks, as they are important cues to the background of group members.

The leader's contribution here was that of teaching the mothers by formulating in more general terms what some group members had said. This would, hopefully, enable the group members to cope in a more helpful fashion with additional incidents of stealing, as they occurred. If they accepted this formulation, they would have some guidelines not only for coping with their children's behavior, but also for clarifying some of their own confusion in these

areas, a confusion which
indicated their faulty Superego
development.

Stressing that the parent
has a role in teaching children
such concepts as right and
wrong, served several purposes. First, if the mothers
could see themselves in an
educational role, they would
in all probability be less
ready to condone the children's
socially unacceptable actions.
Second, since most group
members had positive relationships to the leader and
were identifying with her, they
could accept more easily a
different parental role if its
educational components were
stressed in such fashion
because she was often referred
to as "our teacher" and the
group was called "our Thurs-
day class" by its members.
The leader did not correct
such statements nor did she
attempt to explain in what
ways her approach to problems
and her goals differed from
those of a teacher. In her
opinion, this would have interfered with the relationships of
group members to her, and
confused them. She would
have started such a discussion
in a leadership training session where such clarification
would have been helpful.

This last comment made
by a mother showed, among
other things, that many members of this group were pre-
occupied with what other
people said, or thought about
them. In the leader's opinion,
this preoccupation did not
express the desire to be
accepted, but rather seemed

to anticipate negative reactions, perhaps because of their many fights with their neighbors which often provided welcome distractions also, as previously reported.

The group member who had said: "I disagree with you," asked in a voice expressing disbelief, if "everything must be returned, even the things in a boarded up house, which the children bring home?" Several group members spoke up, saying "the house belongs to somebody," "the people may want their things again," "this is stealing." Another group member voiced more contempt for "the cops" at this point because it took an hour to get police when an empty house in her area was being broken into.

This example shows again the faulty Superego development of some parents which is reflected in the actions of their children. It was fortunate that some other group members had clearer ideas about the question of ownership versus stealing.

I said, I was sorry that I have to repeat things with which some group members disagree, today, that I know that I am not going "to be very popular," but whether the house is boarded up or not, whether one's own wallet was returned or not, one may not keep that which belongs to others, and, more important, children must be taught that.

By expressing her regret, the leader attempted to prevent further antagonism on the part of the "dissenting" group members, as learning cannot occur in an atmosphere of hostility between leader and members. She also had a suspicion that some group members, who did not voice disagreement with her, were all the same considering her point of view extreme. Also, the writer, who prefers to be in harmony with most members of her group, was looking for a way of presenting her point of view which would not jeopardize this positive atmosphere too much.

While attempting to preserve this atmosphere, it was imperative however, that the writer take a stand, and do this again, to dispel any lingering doubts of group members in this important matter. It is well known that once children and, later, teen-agers are in trouble with the law, their future is likely to be bleak, and parental teaching about stealing is one way of helping children to avoid getting into trouble.

I added that one has sometimes difficult experiences, such as being asked "what did you do with the money?" and I also recognized that not every policeman, or every other human being one meets was perfect. All this did not alter the fact that children must be taught by the parent first and foremost that one must not take that which does not belong to one, and must return what one finds. I tied this in with the desire of group members to help their children grow up so that they would not be in trouble, would have a smoother and easier life than their parents--"why else would you come to our meetings here?" and I gave them recognition for the patience and the wish to do well by their children, which they brought to the task of raising their families.

It was important to accept the justified complaints of group members. Being defensive, for instance, about the police--some members of which were being accused by group members--would have been detrimental to the purposes of the meetings. Over-identification with the forces of law and order would have been just as damaging as an acceptance of stealing. This was one of the situations where effective leadership hinges on recognition of such pitfalls. If one is clear about the goals of a project--which were helping parents with the problems of acting out children-- one can avoid becoming sidetracked and involved in tangential issues, such as the ways in which the police function or do not function to the satisfaction of the community. These issues belong in the areas of citizens' action groups, community organization, and related activities.

It was equally important, however, to recognize the concern of the group members about their families, and their investment in the task of child raising. Also, coming to the meetings represented real effort and a departure from their usual way of life for many group members, and this too deserved recognition.

The group member who had

The leader's feeling was

brought a problem to the meeting last week then took over. (I had the feeling that she was also trying "to get me off the hook" in this fashion!) She said, did we remember that she had had a lot of trouble with her boys stealing money from her, and that she had told them in desperation "you know-- I am not your mother anymore-- don't you call me Mom!" She added that her boys had told her they were sorry, had offered to repay the money they had stolen and had asked if they could please call her "Mom" again. This had happened spontaneously: "I did not have to use the speech I had rehearsed on my way home from the meeting." Group members as well as I told her how glad we were that this had happened; the suggestion was also made by two group members that it would be good to let the boys repay their mother.

I was ready to "move on" in our discussion but additional situations of children's stealing were brought up by other group members who had not mentioned them previously. One mother's two children had also taken money from her, a dollar, which they had split; the younger boy had returned his share to her, but the older had not done this. She had taken the older one to the

based on the fact that this particular group member had a very positive relationship to her.

This mother had been very troubled as to whether "she had done the right thing" and group members as well as the leader had pointed out to her other ways of handling the problem.

Since many members of this group did not have much verbal facility, it was a considerable gain if they acquired in a meeting new skills in expressing themselves and in communicating with members of their families. A learning experience of this nature reinforced any learning of new approaches in child rearing, since the way in which problems in these areas are approached can be sometimes as important as the new techniques are.

The expressions of pleasure by the group members and by the leader were indicated as reinforcement of the decision of the group member to try a new approach. The leader missed an opportunity here, however, to endorse the suggestion of having the boys repay the money they had stolen.

The fact that group members continued to discuss stealing was an indication of how serious and how frequent this problem was for most of the families. It was helpful that group members who had not discussed stealing episodes previously were now free to do this.

Once more the police were

police station, but had been dis-appointed because the policeman had told her that it was not his job to talk to her boy. Several com-ments were made that the police-man had not been "nice, " that he "could have helped you, " but the mother was also told that "if he won't do it, you got to talk to your boy!" (When another group mem-ber suggested "his father should do it, " the reply was: "Oh, him!" with a shrug of the shoulders.)

Another incident was discussed in which the money a boy had earned on his paper route was taken from him by another boy. The group member wanted to know if this was stealing and group members as well as I agreed that this was indeed stealing. The mother was encour-aged to find out who had done this and report it to the parents of the child, asking that he return the money and be punished. One mother said: "If they don't do it, you have done the right thing!"

Another mother had been leaving pennies on the floor to test her child's honesty. The child took the money but told his mother he was saving the money for her. We agreed that the child should be told that money on the floor does not belong to him and that he should not take it. In another situation, when a father often loses change in his armchair, which the children return to him, they are told "for being honest, you may keep a dime." The group members who discussed this incident agreed that this was a sound idea.

mentioned in a negative fashion, but so was the group member's husband. The writer had sometimes wondered whether negative attitudes toward men in general were expressed in this fashion, in addition to the negative feelings of many group members against the police as an institution.

The group member who asked whether this was stealing was quite serious, and her question was taken up in a similar vein by the other group members, with the leader following suit, needless to say.

As the last remark indicated, some group members con-sidered it quite likely that the parents of the other child would not believe the accusa-tion and would not punish their child, but the encouragement "to do what is right, " irrespec-tive of whether other people act on this, was supportive of the goals of this discussion.

"Testing" children was an approach which many mem-bers of this group used, often with reference to similar experiences when they were being tested by their own parents. Considerable dis-trust existed among many members of these families, but this was not the main topic of the discussion and the leader did not think it indicated to take up this problem at this point.

Rewards for good behavior are discussed by many parent groups. While this method of child raising is not the most effective one, it often serves as a first approach, as in this instance, until more sophisticated approaches can be developed with a group. Getting a dime, under these circumstances, as an encouragement to being honest, was certainly a step forward, as compared to condoning a child's stealing. Again, the leader did not think it indicated to discuss these other, and preferable, approaches, because they would have been "over the heads" of most members of this group. A realistic evaluation of the stage at which the members of a mothers' group are ready for new approaches is essential if they are to benefit from the discussions and to move toward the goal of better parent-child relationships.

Next, I asked the group members if they would like to start to discuss lying; they agreed to do this, because, as one mother said: "When they steal, they have to lie to you."

The leader suggested a related topic which had been a concern to group members but had not been discussed fully before. While it is not essential to discuss topics that are related to each other, in sequence, it often happens that such a sequence develops easily. Anything which helps parents of low educational background to see the interrelatedness of events in family life, the cause and effect relationships of certain actions or feelings, is helpful since thinking in terms of concepts or in any fashion which is not concrete, is not usually part of their intellectual equipment.

The leader missed an opportunity here, however, to point

The first incident of lying was connected with a small boy's lying about his homework; he had told his teacher "the puppies chewed it up" as one of his many excuses. The mother had been surprised to hear that there had been trouble with homework for quite awhile. Another mother had been told that her boy had not been given any homework to do, which was a lie also.

I suggested that we might like to devote a whole session or more, if the group members would want us to do that, to homework, and asked if we might perhaps use the time we had left today to look at some of the reasons why children lie.

out a few of these cause and effect relationships; this could have been done casually and without urging group members to discuss them further, unless they would have done so spontaneously.

Homework was a frequent source of problems because few mothers in this group made available to their children a setting which would be conducive to doing one's homework, or encouraged them in their endeavors to get any homework done, or respected their, often feeble, efforts to learn. As previously mentioned, many members of this group did not keep in touch with the school--hence the surprise of these group members when they heard that there had been trouble with a son's homework, or that homework had been assigned, contrary to one's child's statement.

The leader took the initiative here in making this suggestion because the question of lying had not been really explored. It is sometimes necessary to direct a discussion in this fashion so that it does not become superficial. In doing this, consideration needs to be given to the degree of anxiety which such moving on to a new topic represents; if it is very great, one does well to follow the group members' leads. This was not the case in this instance, however.

The suggestion of looking at some of the reasons why children lie was made because it is always more helpful to parents--and also to members of other groups--if they are encouraged to look beyond the problems with which they are coping, at some of the causes of these problems. Any understanding of the cause and effect relationships in family relationships leads to an extended capacity to recognize similar problems, to an avoidance of situations which create such problems and to an ability to cope with them more effectively when they occur. The degree to which this understanding can be developed depends on many factors of which the motivation of group members is the most important one.

Giving attention to each child is usually a great problem for mothers of large families who, in addition, do not have much insight into the individual children's needs for such attention. The tendency in many families of members of this group was to make the older children responsible for their younger siblings, at a very early stage, mostly in order to get some relief from the burdens of keeping house for their large families.

The leader pointed out here some of the common causes of lying, and added one, misbehaving, which group members had not mentioned but which fitted in with the discussion of this particular point. To formulate in a more comprehensive manner the concerns of group members, the topic which is under consideration is helpful because it will, hopefully, encourage them to see that many prob-

"Fear" was given as one reason for children's lying, but also "wanting to get your attention." One group member had been told by her child that he did not like to be really healthy because you didn't get the parent's attention when you were well. Another mother told the group that when her child had been very sick, he had upset the rest of the family.

I could use these points to bring out the various ways in which children attempted to get their parent's attention--by lying, illness, doing what they should not be doing, "misbehaving"--and I could also recognize that it was difficult to give to each child, especially in a large family, as much attention as he needed.

lems of their children are
interrelated and often have
common causation.

It was important to give
recognition to the reality
factors--the large families of
most group members--which
contributed to this problem.
Overlooking, or glossing over,
such reality factors leads to
negative feelings toward the
leader who may be perceived
as and accused of not understanding the group members
and their concerns, or of
living in a different world, or
of not caring about them.

One group member added: "You
would like to cut yourself in little
pieces...." Another group member said that she was now closest
to her oldest child who was in
junior high school--this as the
result of a treatment contact--and
that this child had said to her:
"Now I am your pet--before that,
he was your pet!" She added that
being close had helped the oldest
child.

The comment about wanting
"to cut oneself in little pieces..."
was a touching expression of
this group member's love for
her children. The second
group member's comments
were excellent examples of
the problems of family relationships which exist in these
families, and also of the awareness of many children of these
problems. The writer missed
an opportunity here to point
out that children often know
much more than parents--and
other adults!--give them
credit for.

Under other circumstances
the leader would have given
recognition here to the help
which individual counseling
can offer, since the group
member who had made the
last comment had mentioned
that she had followed through
on a referral to a child guidance
clinic. Because that group
member was likely to get
rather argumentative when
counseling was discussed, and
gave recognition only grudg-
ingly , and with many "ifs"

and "buts", she did not do this, especially as the session was already running quite a bit over the allotted time, and some group members, whose children were expected home from school, were beginning to get up, to start clearing away cups, etc. It is usually better to terminate a meeting on a positive note, if at all possible.

A discussion of some of the ways in which children attempt to get parental attention, and of some of the methods which parents can use to satisfy some of these demands-- especially when they wish to help a child over a difficult period in his development--may be helpful, sometime later during the ongoing discussion series.

This writer has found it helpful to jot down such suggestions for future meetings as they occur. They may not be pursued, but they can serve as points of reference if a group is not sure of what it wishes to take up at a later session, or if certain topics have been exhausted, or when a discussion has moved in a direction which makes it threatening to the group members. Such reminders of topics which might be helpful to a specific group are also excellent indicators of what it has achieved, in relation to group goals, what has not been achieved, ·and of the level at which group members function.

Comments: All the group members participated; even Mrs. Ss., who used to be silent, felt free to speak up spontaneously today.

In recognition of the school staff's great investment in these cooperative projects, reporting back included information on many matters, as can be seen from the preceding presentation. Since participation of group members is not only desirable, but also often equated with possible gains of group members, the writer always included her observations about the participation of group members in her comments.

In cooperative projects, it is important to keep in mind that the cooperating organizations, and their representatives, need to get some gratification and some recognition of their endeavors and, if their point of view and sometimes their goals, differ from one's own, both should be respected and taken into account as far as this can possibly be done without detriment to the cooperative project and to its participants.

An interesting development is that some members of this group have come to regard these meetings --which they did not plan for themselves--as one place to which they can bring their problems, and to which they look for help with these problems; this is a step forward.

This development was indeed a step forward from the attitudes of distrust and resistance which many members of this group had shown when they started to meet. It had been brought about by many factors, of which the most important ones were probably the repeated experiences of belonging to the same group, with the same leader whom they had come to accept and to trust, and where they had learned to count on the support and help of the other members of the group.

The discussion showed clearly that most group members were in considerable conflict with and in opposition to the rules of society regarding private property and that they needed some help to clarify for themselves--as much as this could be done!--such concepts as stealing, what you may keep or may not keep, if you find something, before they could be encouraged to tackle the problems of stealing of their own children.

This statement pointed to the root of the problems of stealing and of other antisocial behavior which many children of group members had. It also recapitulated the premise on which the discussion series on parent-child relationships with these parents of acting out children had been based (Pollak, 1964, pp. 489-494).

****

Because of the cooperative nature of these projects, the results could be evaluated from three different points of view: that of the participants, that of the cooperating school personnel, who had close contacts with the children of the group members, and contacts of varying frequency with the group members themselves, and that of the group's leader.

The group discussion members were asked to fill out questionnaires at the end of every discussion series and most of them filled them out in great detail. Since this represented considerable effort on the part of the group members, who were not very literate, and who were certainly not used to formulating their thoughts in writing, this fact in itself was an indication of their commitment to the projects. Comments which reflected the group members' evaluation of the discussion series were: "I learned a lot about children;" "The meetings helped me to face most problems a lot calmer and more sensibly;" "Helped with the problem of stealing in the home, and correcting the child in school;" "When you sit home and think about your problems, you boil over. You come here and it gets better;" "I did not feel so completely helpless." "It makes you see that your child is not the worst, and you try some more." It was interesting that many of these comments--of which the above is only a small sample--indicated the feelings of helplessness and discouragement of many group members in the face of their children's problems, the relief which the expression of these feelings could bring, as well as the experience of learning better ways of coping with their children's problems, and perhaps also with their own problems. Undoubtedly one is better able to function if one does not "boil over," does not feel helpless, and is able to act in a calmer and more sensible fashion.

The cooperating school personnel reported many instances of better school adjustment on the part of the children of group discussion members. Some children's grades had improved; in some cases of truancy, the children's attendance had become more regular. One boy, who had been about to be expelled, had managed to stay sufficiently out of trouble to be kept in school. One family had accepted the counselor's referral to a child guidance clinic and, more important, had followed through on this referral. Another counselor, who had known the family of a group discussion member, had checked with the junior high school which the oldest boy was now attending, and had learned that he had not been in trouble there. One group member's daughter was being seen by the school counselor, and the mother was now able to let the girl handle her own affairs. This group member, as well as some others, had developed more positive relationships with the schools which their children were attending. They kept in closer touch with the schools, took more responsibility for seeing that their children came to school on time, and did their homework. One group member, who used to come to the school every week and sometimes more often, to complain about the teachers, the principal, and anybody else with whom her children might come in contact, had not done this for several months. Where these changes occurred, they were the manifestation of a more positive attitude on the part of the parent toward learning and getting an education which, in turn, affected the children's attitudes in these areas. Since irritation, annoyance, and other negative feelings have a tendency to snowball and to create their own vicious circle, any lessening of such feelings between parent and school staff was bound to make the child's adjustment in school easier also.

In some situations, counselors had noted other changes in their contacts with the group members, such as the development of friendships among them, and also greater participation in organizational activities. Some mothers had become involved with the parents' associations in their schools, or mentioned having become more active in their church groups, or in Girl Scout or YWCA groups in their area. As previously mentioned, many members of this group lived in considerable social isolation and their attempts to broaden their social activities were a step forward. Hopefully, they would learn from other people sound additional approaches to the problems of children at home and in school, and would find outlets for their energies and drives. Last, but not least, such activities would enrich their own, often drab and monotonous lives.

Several counselors commented on the physical appearance of some group members which had improved noticeably. They had started to come to the meetings as they used to come to the schools, in housedresses, which were often not very clean, or in jeans, which were torn, but as they continued to attend, they changed to pretty dresses, or to clean jeans with sweaters or blouses which matched them. Lipstick and other make-up began to be used and, as one counselor phrased it: "the stockings came up and the curlers came down." Two group members who were very obese, had started to lose weight; one of them attended a Weightwatchers Club, in the company of her married daughter. One of the mothers whose appearance had changed, had told the counselor how pleased she had been by the positive comments on her appearance which other group members had made, such as: "you're all dolled up today." The approval of other group members and of the leader had undoubtedly encouraged such changes and, since one's positive feelings about one's physical appearance affect one's self-image positively in turn, this new emphasis on one's looks was a desirable development.

The writer would like to add a comment about the importance of one's own appearance which, in her experience, should be appropriate to the group and to the goals toward which one is working. With this group, attractive but simple clothes were indicated, so that she was a step--or maybe two steps--ahead of the group members, but not "out of reach" as far as their attempts to improve their appearance were concerned.

In the leader's evaluation, those group members who attended the meetings, and who involved themselves in the discussions, had shown growth in several areas. Many of them had learned to raise questions with a view to finding answers which is, of course, quite different from raising questions with the primary purpose of creating conflict. They had also learned to discuss their questions, and any problems they were encountering, from a variety of points of view. This was a new development for those group members who had tended to see their problems in absolutes, in black and white, so to speak. This development led, in turn, to the realization that there was more than one answer to any given problem and that children, their needs, their capacities, and the opportunities they should have, varied with the individual child, and again with his age, his place in the family, and with any special events in family life, such as the birth of a sibling, or the death of a close relative. This led to some under-standing that the parental role should change to keep step with the children's growth, and that methods of child raising which "worked" some time ago, need not be effective at a later point. As the dis-cussions progressed, members of the group were less inclined to blame others for their problems, to accuse other children, other parents, teachers, and principals of getting their own children in trouble, or of "not doing their job." Instead, many members of the group became able to look at the problems which existed in their own families, such as stealing, lying, etc., and they were willing to concentrate on how they could deal with these problems. Because it is much easier to avoid responsibility for one's own failings by ranting about the shortcomings of others--a technique which does not, of course, come to grips with the underlying problems--this willing-ness of the parents showed progress, wherever it occurred.

The realization of many group members that others had similar problems offered reassurance, and lessened any anxiety and any feelings of incompetence as a parent which a group member may have felt. This also decreased the need to blame outside forces, so that psychic energy was freed to cope with the problems in parent-child relationships in a more adequate and more task-oriented fashion.

The two emotional experiences which made such learning pos-sible--when it was achieved--were the supportive relationships which the members of the group offered to each other and the experience of a relationship to an understanding and accepting leader with whom they could identify (Pollak, 1956, pp. 131-139). If the learning which was achieved, and the changes which occurred, seem to be small gains only, especially in view of the time and effort of the professional people who participated in the project, one must keep in mind that members of this parent group had many problems--emotional as well as economic and health problems--and that they had little education and few inner resources to cope with these problems. Since many group members had also been reluctant to use those community resources which were at their disposal, they had deprived themselves even more of sup-ports which might have been of help to them.

If one compares this parent group with that described in the preceding chapter, the parents of acting out children lived far more isolated and lonely lives, in regard to the geographical area to which they limited themselves, and in regard to their social relationships. Not wishing to use the community resources which were at their disposal contributed to their isolation, and made them feel that they were alone in their attempts to cope with their problems. These parents also lived in conflict--or, at least, in more open conflict-- with the institutions and organizations of their community, and their actions were usually not motivated by the forces of the Ego or the Superego. They acted upon libidinal impulses, and their children's problems reflected the personality constellation and personality problems of the parents. If the leadership offered to the parents of acting out children had to be understanding, it also had to be an Ego- supportive and Superego-supportive experience for them. This was different from the experience which the mothers described in the preceding chapter needed. The latter had led very different lives, were part of their community, identified with or at least accepting of its institutions, and were ready to use the community resources which were available to them. Most of these mothers lived under the shadow of a too powerful Superego which bound them to the les- sons learned from their strict and authoritarian parents when they were children themselves. They needed a more permissive leader- ship so that they could allow themselves to move away, at least to some degree, from the values and the teachings of their own parents, and to become more flexible without feeling guilty. This, in turn, enabled them to permit their own children to relate to them in dif- ferent ways from the relationships they had experienced themselves when they were growing up.

XII

Problems of Overprotection and of Social Relations of Physically Handicapped Children

In contrast to the mothers described in the preceding chapter, the members of this group were a natural group for more than one reason. Most important was the attendance of their children at a special school for physically handicapped children and their strong motivation which was due to the problems of having a handicapped child or, as in some instances, several handicapped children in the family. Furthermore, the discussion series which were offered to these mothers were planned because of the desire of the group members to use all forms of help which were available to them in the community, a desire which was supported by the principal of the school, as well as by the counselors on his faculty and the counseling supervisor.

This school served handicapped children only and it had the physical facilities and the special staff which the children needed-- such as ramps instead of steps, a swimming pool, physical therapists, nurses, and more counselors than one would find in regular schools. It also had a larger number of teachers who had special knowledge of the children's conditions and special skills for dealing with them in the classroom situation. Classes were, of necessity, small.

The parent group had four discussion series but, since the writer offered leadership to these mothers for the second, third, and fourth discussion series, this chapter is based on these discussion series only. They totaled eighteen meetings; with few exceptions, the groups met weekly. Three evening meetings were planned, for the third and fourth discussion series, respectively, to give the fathers opportunities to attend. The discussion series were the outcome of a single meeting for which the writer had offered leadership; they were planned with the president and with other members of the parents' group, with the school coordinator, who was also the mother of a handicapped child, and with the principal.

CHARACTERISTICS OF GROUP MEMBERS

The only common factor in the lives of these parents was the handicapped child as a member of their families. In all other ways, they differed markedly from one another; they were heterogeneous in regard to education and to social and economic backgrounds. The handicapped child, however, forged a bond between the mothers; one of its results was that the white and black members of the group accepted each other readily and related to each other very well. Although considerable interracial tension existed during the period when the group met, no reference was made to it in the discussions, nor did the attitudes of group members reflect these conflicts.

Many members of the group volunteered their services in the school and assisted the teachers, other school personnel, and the children in a variety of ways. These volunteer activities were welcome to the school, since many children needed help in getting dressed, in getting in and out of the swimming pool, and in other activities for which nonhandicapped children of the same age can assume total responsibility. In addition, these activities brought the mothers who participated in them in close contact with each other, often several times a week. As a result, they had gotten to know each other well, had developed good intragroup relationships and had become a closely knit group. Their volunteer activities also brought the mothers in close contact with the school and its personnel; the mothers knew and understood its services. This helped them in many ways, one of which was that it allayed the fears which many mothers had when their handicapped child started to come to the school, either as his first experience of school attendance, or as the result of a transfer, because the child could not hold his own any longer in a school for children who were not handicapped. They also felt, and rightly so, that they were making a contribution to their own child and to the other handicapped children, by donating their time and effort as volunteers. Last, but not least, these activities gave them opportunities to see how the professional people dealt with a child's handicap; they observed, for instance, that a child who is learning to use crutches and who has fallen, may need to learn to get up without help as a step toward the mastery of his crutches. Since many of these mothers were overprotective of their children, eager to prevent them from being hurt and from other difficult experiences, the example of the school staff was one way of counteracting their overprotectiveness.

The members of the group were identified with the school; any reference to it and to its services was always made in very positive terms. They were eager to help it, not only by volunteering their services, but also in other areas. Since most of them were experienced in organizational activities, they developed publicity materials for it such as flyers, posters, and newsletters efficiently and well. They were quick to assume and to divide among themselves responsibility for any task which was going to assist the school which their handicapped children attended, or the children themselves. They had devised a variety of ways to raise money for the school which went beyond the usual bazaars or cake sales, such as selling clothes, handbags, and other items at reduced rates, which they secured by canvassing shops and manufacturers who contributed these items.

Many group members were active in their communities, in addition to their activities on behalf of the school for handicapped children. They cherished in particular any activity which gave them opportunities to explain the condition of their handicapped children which would dispel some of the erroneous beliefs about these handi-caps. One of these, which troubled many mothers deeply, was the assumption that a crippling condition, which prevented a child from walking without crutches, or from talking, indicated also that the child must be retarded.

Each group member was, of course, different in terms of personality structure, of defenses used, of their approach to the pro-blems of the handicapped child, and to the problems which his pres-ence usually caused for the other members of their families and for the group member himself. Still, some common factors in these areas emerged. Having a handicapped child caused anxiety in most group members, which varied as to its intensity, but which was always present. The intensity seemed to depend on the number of handi-capped children, which was very understandable, but also on the age of the child. The mothers of young children appeared to be more anxious, perhaps because they had not yet had opportunities to accept the problems caused by the child's presence, and to integrate them into the fabric of their lives, as much as that can be done. This anxiety expressed itself in many forms, but the most obvious, and most frequent one, was overprotection of the handicapped child (Cohen, 1962, pp. 137-142; Kennedy, 1970, pp. 410-416). It was difficult for the group members to evaluate realistically any physical risks which the handicaps presented. In their fear of further injury, of actions which might increase the child's handicap, perhaps also in their unconscious desire to protect themselves from having to cope with more problems, more pain and anguish, and more distress than they had already, most group members did little, if anything, to encourage the child to reach out beyond what he was achieving at a given moment. While it is difficult for many parents of normal children to realize that a child is ready for new experiences and should be encouraged to try them, this was doubly difficult for most members of this group. As a result, many children of group members had not learned to develop what abilities they had to move around, to do things on their own, so that the limitations inflicted by their physical condition were rein-forced by maternal overprotection. Since it is well known that most children--and most adults--try to live up to the expectations of those around them, unless these expectations are completely unrealistic, the low expectations of these mothers, which went along with their overprotection, also negatively affected the goals which the children set for themselves and their performances in a variety of areas of functioning.

Along with overprotection went considerable permissiveness,

an inability to say no to those demands and wishes of the handicapped
child that they could fulfill. Some of this inability was, of course,
the mother's attempt to make up, to compensate to the child for his
handicap. As a result, the limits which would ordinarily be imposed
on children of that age group in these families, in the areas of clothes,
hours to be kept, behavior to be tolerated, were not imposed on many
handicapped children. Where this was the case, it affected not only
the handicapped child, but also any other children in the family, who
tended to resent this preferential treatment and who also, very often,
played on the parent's guilt about this treatment (Cohen, 1962).
Furthermore, many fathers were aware of the mothers' overprotection
and permissiveness which they usually attributed to the mothers' being
with their children for much longer periods of time than they themselves were but of which they did not approve, so that this difference
of opinion often led to marital discord.

The presence of the handicapped child caused not only anxiety,
it also caused feelings of guilt and attacks of depression (Mandelbaum
and Wheeler, 1960, pp. 360-367; Olshansky, 1962, pp. 190-193). The
anxiety was often manifest although it was not openly mentioned; the feelings of guilt were mentioned only in the context of shortchanging the other
children because of the demands of the handicapped child. Since the handicapped child was a considerable emotional as well as financial burden
for all members of the family, but, most of all, usually for the mothers
in these families, it is justified to presuppose the existence of death
wishes concerning the handicapped child in the mothers and this probably
accounted, at least in part, for the feelings of depression and guilt.
Some members of the group could talk about their state of depression,
for instance, by mentioning crying spells, especially when the children were young; other mothers had repressed the expression of these
feelings. As one group member formulated it, "you cry inside."
The feelings of guilt about their death wishes were not mentioned by
the members of the group. It would have been very inappropriate
for the leader to delve into these areas in view of the aims and goals
of the meetings, but whenever members of the group mentioned the
individual treatment experiences which many of them had had, she
recognized the magnitude of the problem which the handicapped child
presented and encouraged them to turn, or to return, to these sources
of help.

The anxiety of group members was also very apparent in the
urgency with which their questions were raised in the discussions.
It was as if they were afraid that they would not get their fair share
of the leader's interest, professional knowledge, and responses. It
was interesting that the questions were much more frequently directed
at the leader than was the case in meetings with other parent groups;
part of this may have been due not only to the group members' anxiety
and to their hopes for solutions of their problems, but also to their
considerable contacts with physicians, physical therapists, nurses
whom they asked and from whom they received the necessary instruc-
tions for the physical care of their handicapped children. This

urgency was one of the factors which the leader took into account in deciding on the approach which would be most helpful to these group members.

Along with the anxiety of group members went some often unrealistic hopes for "a miracle." As one of the group members formulated these hopes, another said: "You hope you will wake and all will be well." Whenever such thoughts were expressed, they were, of course, a denial of the problem, a way of seeking an escape from an intolerable burden. One of the tasks of leadership was to help those group members who were hoping for miracles to accept that, while medicine and science make startling advances, nobody can predict just what will be discovered to help the handicapped child, or when this may happen, so that he and his family need to cope with the problem of the handicap in terms of present medical and other resources.

As mentioned before, the bonds between the members of the group were very strong, based as they were on the shared experience of having a handicapped child. As a result, group members were quick to give support and reassurance to other group members; they did the same also with their handicapped children. While this support was helpful in most instances to the other group members, the reassurance was often not, because it was usually based on denial, on the inability to face the other person's pain, perhaps with the unconscious desire to be spared pain oneself. Another special task of leadership for this group was related to this trait. Most group members needed to be helped, as much as this was possible, to use different, more reality based approaches, since the avoidance of the reality does not strengthen the individual and certainly does not increase his, or her, coping capacity.

Because the problems which the handicapped child presented were part of the total family's situation, and were very likely to remain that permanently, they affected many relationships within the family and many areas of family life. The reactions of the other siblings and of husbands to overprotection and to permissiveness have been mentioned. Grandparents and other relatives were often described as adding to the parental problems, either by rejecting or by spoiling the handicapped child. Providing the appliances, such as crutches, wheelchairs, braces, special shoes, providing medical care often caused a heavy drain on a family's finances. The attendance of the child at a special school, chauffeuring him to any social or group activities to which another child of the same age would have gone unattended, made extra demands on the parents' time and efforts. Although most members of the group were concerned with the problems of the child's present life--whether he was of elementary school age, or a teen-ager--a few group members anticipated the need to provide for the future of the handicapped child, for the time when they themselves would not be here to care for him anymore. These problems, as well as the problems of the older handicapped person in finding a mate, were not brought out very frequently probably because they were too painful to face, perhaps because the parent hoped for a miracle but perhaps also because coping with the present required all the strength which group members had at their command.

In addition to the reactions of members of their own families, the reactions of other children to the handicapped child aroused deep concern in group members. The handicapped child did not attend the same school as the children in his neighborhood, and was usually not able to participate fully in their after school and recreational activities, facts which affected his social life and peer group relations. The attempts of the mothers as well as the attempts of their handicapped children to cope with these problems varied greatly, as did their reactions to it. Help with the handicapped child's social relationships took the form of including neighborhood children--at the expense of the parent of the handicapped child--in the latter's outings, such as shopping trips or lunches. It included providing backyard equipment, or games which the nonhandicapped children would enjoy and offers to invite the neighborhood children over so that their mothers could have a free afternoon. All these devices were well meant because their purpose was to provide the handicapped child with the company of children of his own age who lived around him. Some, however, were more effective than others, and most of these devices were effective for a certain time only. When the neighborhood children became teen-agers and sometimes earlier, they tended to withdraw from the handicapped child and to prefer the company of their own friends who attended the same schools. As a result, it was quite common for handicapped children to play with children in their neighborhood who were considerably younger, a development which most mothers resented very much. Resentment was also shown by many group members when they described their attempts to encourage the peer group relationships of their handicapped children with neighborhood children, although other group members reported these matters rather matter of factly. Many handicapped children coped with their handicap very realistically in their contacts with friends, for instance, by offering to be umpire when they played football, but other children bought candy or other goodies for the neighborhood children in what their mothers described as their attempts "to buy friendship." This was possible because handicapped children received more spending money--as well as more toys, more numerous and expensive clothes--than children of a comparable age and comparable background; needless to say, these material advantages were provided in another effort to make up to the child for his handicap, as tokens of the parent's concern and love, and perhaps as an unconscious expression of the parent's guilt, because of the unavoidable resentment which the handicapped child aroused in his parents. "Why did it happen to me?" was often reported as one reaction when the parent had first learned of the child's handicap.

From the descriptions of the group members, it was clear that any contacts of their handicapped children with nonhandicapped children required more effort on the part of the child, and of the parent also; second, these contacts were not as numerous nor as spontaneous as they would have been had the child not been handicapped; third, as the handicapped child grew up to be a teen-ager or a young adult, his social contacts with nonhandicapped young people seemed to be rare, and the social lives of the young handicapped persons were usually fairly limited. It was probably for this reason that group activities with other handicapped children were very much sought after and encouraged by the parents, many of whom also described their children, especially as they grew older, as preferring these activities to social activities with nonhandicapped young people.

Another considerable concern of group members were the reactions of other adults to the handicapped child. Most group members were acutely aware of the stares or comments of strangers. If these comments expressed sympathy as was sometimes the case, this was resented as much as were comments expressing pity or attempts to be helpful to the child. Many mothers described themselves as "stiffening" when they went into a store or a restaurant with the handicapped child; some admitted being "oversensitive" to the reactions of others. Bitterness was also expressed, quite frequently, at the reactions of friends when they first learned of the child's handicap and here, too, it did not seem to make much difference what form the reaction took. Most members of this group were so absorbed in their efforts to cope with the problems of the handicapped child that they had little strength, and little desire, left to deal with the reactions of children, or of adults, who were not members of their own families.

The numerous emotional, financial, and other demands which the handicapped child's presence created on the mothers had a variety of consequences, and it did not make much difference, incidentally, whether these demands were based on realistic factors or on unrealistic ones, such as guilt or anxiety. These demands affected the other children and provoked such reactions as their withdrawal from the handicapped sister or brother and, in a few instances, their overprotection. If any open rejection of the handicapped child by his siblings occurred, it was not mentioned in the discussions, probably because this would have been a most threatening reaction which group members handled by denying its existence. The additional demands of the handicapped child had, in all probability, considerable effect on the marital relationships of the parents also, but neither the mothers, nor the fathers, brought this problem up in the discussions.

Another result of the involvement with the handicapped child was the inability of almost all mothers to focus on some of their own needs, to have some activities which they would enjoy, and which would not center on the handicapped child. It was as if they felt that they belonged to the handicapped child, had to devote most of their love, time, and energy to his care and comfort, and what love, time, and energy were left, to the other children in the family, probably in an attempt to make up to them for what they had lost or had to bear because they had a handicapped sibling. As a result, the mothers' own dependency needs were not met and some of the depression from which most group members suffered was probably due to their self-deprivation and to their feelings of depletion. These feelings also explained, in part, the very strong relationships to the leader which many group members developed, which will be discussed later.

Contrary to some of the findings of Polansky et al (1971, pp. 643-650), the writer did not observe pseudostoicism in the group members, that is, the attitude toward the handicapped child which converts a potentially shattering liability into an asset. Neither did the mothers express any gratification at the thought that this child would probably not leave them, indicating that they saw him on a deeper level, as a defense against separation anxiety (Bowlby, 1960, pp. 89-113). The goals of the meetings which are being discussed here and the different techniques used may well account for these differences.

The fathers of the handicapped children were concerned about maternal overprotection, as previously recorded; they were also concerned about the social lives of these children and the financial problems which their special needs created. No mention was made of the effect of the handicapped child on the other siblings, or on the marital relationships, but that was probably due to the fact that the fathers did not have as many meetings as the mothers. Participation in the discussions was carried by a smaller number of fathers as compared to the participation of the mothers, but here, too, the number of meetings may have been a deciding factor. Those fathers who participated in the discussions expressed strong feelings of responsibility and commitment to the handicapped child, and they seemed to be much less anxious than the mothers were. The leader had the impression that the demands of their work, whatever its nature, along with the responsibility of being the breadwinner, had helped them to repress many of their emotions, thus enabling them to integrate the problem of the handicapped child into their lives in a more realistic fashion. One wonders if the mothers would have reacted in similar fashion if they had been employed outside of the home, but the demands of the handicapped child, as well as their own involvement with him, seemed to prevent them from considering such activities.

The concerns and problems of the mothers were reflected in the questions they wished to discuss. Overprotection, permissiveness, and social relationships of handicapped children were always at the top of their lists of questions and additional questions which group members raised were also usually related to these main topics. The material from which the writer drew many of the group characteristics presented earlier, for instance, in regard to the reactions of grandparents, friends, and strangers, was usually presented in the course of a discussion of these questions, almost in a tangential fashion, but not with requests for help with these situations.

The attendance of the mothers--which will be discussed in more detail later in this chapter--was very good, and was another evidence of their concern about their handicapped children.

GOALS OF THE DISCUSSION SERIES

The nature of the major problems with which these group members were coping determined the goals for these meetings. This
holds true for every discussion series with the purpose of offering
help with problems of family relationships; it is equally true, incidentally, that the goals, as the group members would formulate them,
might not be identical with the goals of the group's leader. It was
possible, however, to help some members of this group who were
looking for solutions of the problems which the handicapped child was
causing. In the repeated discussions of overprotection, for instance,
many group members came to realize the importance of letting the
handicapped child try out his wings; in the discussions of sibling
rivalry and of the siblings' manipulation of the parent, many mothers
recognized what had caused these phenomena, how they could deal
more helpfully with them and also avoid, to some extent, provoking
these reactions. The members of this group were also looking for
the emotional comfort of sharing the numerous problems of raising
a handicapped child, and for opportunities to express some of their
fears, anxieties, and sorrow. All these goals were sound because
they helped the group members to gain strength, and to cope better
with the demands made upon them.

Some other goals of these group members were not sound, however, and foremost among them was the desire to find ways of coping
with these problems which were unrealistic, if only they would be
less painful and would offer an escape from the burden and suffering
which the handicapped child caused them. This desire was apparent
in the efforts of many group members to avoid discussions of the
handicap, and of the possible chances for recovery with the child. It
was also apparent in some of their attempts to cope with the problems
of his social life, and certainly in their marked hesitancy to mention
any plans for a future when the parent would not be here anymore to
take care of him. This desire to find relief, if only temporary and
unrealistic relief, was also expressed in the reassurance which many
group members were quick to offer to each other, a reassurance
which was often only another attempt to avoid having to face a difficult situation. Leadership for the mothers of handicapped children
had to take into account their realistic and unrealistic, their sound
and helpful, and their not so sound and unhelpful goals, as will be
discussed below.

In the discussions of family life which were frequently out of
focus because of the emphasis on the handicapped child, it was important to help the mothers to realize that he, as well as all children,
had assets as well as liabilities, and that recognition should be given
to his abilities instead of concentrating on his handicap. Because of
the tendency of most members of this group to devote most of their
attention, time, and efforts to the handicapped child, they needed
encouragement to think of themselves also, in terms of their husbands
and their marriages and, furthermore, in terms of their own needs

as adults. In contrast to the group of mothers described in the preceding chapter, the members of this group needed help in becoming
less involved with the child who was creating a problem, in gaining
some distance, some perspective, and in concentrating more on other
members of their families, themselves, and the world around them.

THE RELATIONSHIPS OF GROUP MEMBERS TO THE LEADER

Because the leader wanted to be helpful, it was easy for her to
gain the trust of most group members, and this trust enabled them
to develop warm relationships to her. Since their problems were
great, as were the accompanying anxiety and emotional distress, they
were eager for opportunities to develop such relationships, to use
them to ventilate their feelings, to bring up their problems, and to
find some relief from them. The discharge of emotions was as
important for the members of this group as the bringing up of problems, and the finding of possible solutions of them. The group
members accepted the leader because of her professional competence;
they were aware that she had for several years offered leadership
to parents of children with hearing handicaps and to retarded teen-
agers also. They looked beyond her professional competence, however, for someone who would be strong and on whose strength they
could lean, if they wished to do this, and for someone who would
understand them but not feel sorry for them.

A positive relationship to the leader, which for many group
members had elements of identification and of transference, was
helpful to those who could develop it, partly because of their feelings
of anxiety and depression, and partly because of their unmet dependency needs. These relationships found expression in such comments
as: "You don't have any children, take us as your children," or
"we want to be good today so that you will remember us as your
good girls." The need for a strong relationship to the leader and
for the comfort it could offer was sometimes expressed through a
physical contact, such as putting one's hand on the leader's hand.
This usually happened in moments of acute distress.

SOME SPECIAL PROBLEMS OF THE LEADER FOR GROUPS OF
PARENTS OF HANDICAPPED CHILDREN

"Feeling sorry" for the members of the group would, for
instance, prevent a leader from helping group members to face some
consequences of their actions and reactions. It would permit them
to avoid difficult tasks such as how to explain to the child his handicap and his chances, if any, for its cure. It would let pass the
inappropriate reassurance--reassurance which is not based on
reality, but on the wish to avoid hurting and being hurt--which many
group members offered to each other, and it would not have helped

them to face their fears and anxieties, so as to be better able to cope with them.

Another special aspect of leadership for the mothers of handicapped children was the importance of accepting the great, and sometimes overwhelming anxiety of group members, which manifested itself, for example, in the barrage of questions which were addressed to the leader. It was also essential to permit them to express their sorrow in the meetings. Frequently, group members raised questions, or made comments, with tears in their eyes, and they made references to their distress, for instance, to crying spells, and to attacks of hopelessness. As two group members phrased it: "The sorrow of death passes, but our sorrow does not." "Our problems stay with us, day in, day out." These feelings had to be expressed freely but, again, they were not to be shared by the leader.

While it was essential to accept the problems of these mothers, it was equally essential to encourage them to go a little further, not only in their attempts to cope with these problems, but also in other areas of their lives. Many mothers needed the group's, and the leader's approval, to be more firm in setting limits for all the children in the family, and they certainly needed this approval for any attempts to free some of their time and energy to think a little of themselves, to enrich their own lives. It very often happens that some problems cannot be solved, that certain factors in the lives of group members are here to stay and that all they can do is cope more effectively, without prospect of great improvement, much less of total change in one's situation. If this is the case, the leader and the group members work toward the greatest amelioration which can be achieved in regard to these problems. Because of this limitation it is very often helpful to focus on other areas of the group members' lives which can be enriched, can bring new experiences and can contribute to their enjoyment of the present as well as to their future lives. For instance, a realignment of marital relationships, with greater investment in them, might increase the marriage partners' happiness, or would at least enable them to find some comfort and some support in the marriage relationship which would, in turn, give them greater strength to cope together with the problems of the handicapped child.

It is difficult to know when and how a leader can best intervene if the atmosphere of the group discussions is emotionally charged, as was so often the case in these meetings. Two factors made it possible to do this; they were the positive relationships of the group members to the leader and their desire for some relief, if even temporary relief, from their problems. In addition, most of them were intelligent, able to verbalize and appreciative of the leader's ability to verbalize. They went along with any attempt the leader made to formulate with them, and for them, and they adopted certain phrases she used and used them themselves in later meetings. One of them was the term "lousy kids," which the leader had used to point out the importance of not giving too much weight to some of their children's requests, to temper tantrums; in one instance in connection with sending children to their rooms if they persist in annoying a parent. This phrase had served several purposes, one of which had been to help the mothers get some perspective in regard to their children's problems, while the second had been to break the tension and to drain off some of the emotions when they threatened to over-whelm some members of the group. The acceptance by group mem-bers of this term was, of course, a sign of their identification with the writer and this became even more apparent when the group's present to the leader at their last meeting was accompanied by a card which read: Best wishes on your Retirement, from Your "Lousy Kids."

Contrary to what the writer had expected, it was not essential to be familiar with the physical condition of the handicapped children, their medication or the kind of appliances which a child had to use. Questions of this nature had been and continued to be addressed to the doctors, nurses, and physical therapists with whom the mothers were in close contact. When a question raised for discussion by a group member presupposed special information of this nature about a child, for instance, the fact that the child was unable to speak, in addition to being on crutches, this information was usually supplied by the mother who was raising the question; in the rare instances when this was not the case, the leader asked for it, and received it, in a matter-of-fact way. What was very helpful to the leader, however, was the opportunity to see the handicapped children in the school which they attended, to become aware of the variety and the degrees of these handicaps, of their effect on the child's life, on his mobility, or his ability to communicate, and also of their effect on other people. Beyond this, meeting in the school which the handicapped children attended gave considerable stimulus to the discussions and probably contributed to their spontaneity also. This meeting place had been suggested by the members of the group, and it proved to be an asset to the sessions, as well as to the leader.

The size of the group varied considerably because the evening meetings drew large numbers of fathers and of employed mothers who could not attend the regular morning meetings of the discussion series. One such evening meeting brought out fifty parents, while the morning meetings were usually attended by between ten and fifteen regular group members. About half of these group members attended three or more of the six meetings; this was good attendance for a group of this kind, partly because all but five of the group members had children who were attending other schools, partly because coming to the meetings involved considerable travel time, and because the volunteer activities of the group members at the school demanded a good bit of their time also.

The fact that this group was heterogeneous in its characteris-tics except for the existence of a handicapped child, was reflected in the information which group members had provided about them-selves. Fifty one mothers filled out registration sheets; if one

defines their social and economic background by their husbands'
occupations, these ranged from physician, librarian, cost analyst,
credit manager, sales representatives, owners of wholesale and
retail businesses, to printer, presser, sheet metal worker, packer,
handyman, and maintenance man. None of the regular group members
were employed.

Seven of the fifty one mothers had completed their college
education or had attended college; two of these seven mothers had
gone on to graduate study. Thirty group members had completed
high school; three of them had, in addition, attended business schools.
Eight mothers had attended, but not completed high school, while
one group member had not gone beyond elementary school. Five of
the registration sheets did not have any information about the educational background of group members.

The number of mothers and fathers who attended these meetings
did not correspond to the number of registration sheets; it was much
larger. This came about because the fourteen fathers who attended
one or all of the three evening meetings with the group, did not fill
out registration sheets; neither did those mothers who came to the
evening meetings only.

Ten of the fifty one group members who had filled out registration sheets were black, as were four additional group members who
had come to the evening meetings only. While no information about
religious affiliation was asked for, in the writer's opinion, about a
third of the group members were Jewish.

Following is the recording of Session IV of the Third Discussion Series with the Parents of Handicapped Children which was
devoted mainly to the topics of overprotection, overpermissiveness,
parental guilt, and the problems of social relationships of handicapped
children.

SESSION IV

October 8, 1969: Fourteen mothers
were present: Mrs. B., Mrs. Bb.,
Mrs. C., Mrs. E., Mrs. F.,
Mrs. Ff., Mrs. G., Mrs. H.,
Mrs. K., Mrs. M., Mrs. S.,
Mrs. Ss., Mrs. T., and Mrs. Tt.
All of them had attended earlier
meetings of the group.

As usual, some of the mothers
came after the meeting had started
because they had duties at the
school that morning. They did
this by slipping into the room very
quietly, so as not to disturb the
discussion.

As previously mentioned,
this was a group of mothers
who were close to each other
and who were also eager to
come to the meetings, so
that they would join the group
in an unobtrusive way.

Before I could offer to summarize what we had discussed last week, Mrs. H. started the discussion off with reference to an argument which she had had with her husband. Mrs. H. explained that she had never let her five year old daughter out of her sight. "I guess she is with me too much. I have not been to a movie since she was born." Mrs. K. replied, "But that is not right. Remember, we said last week, we should pamper ourselves and forget the lousy kids once in awhile!"

Mrs. G. shook her head and said: "you think she will be hurt if she is out of your sight. I thought so too, but I learned!" She described how her boy had been unable to walk, had been crawling, but the doctor told her to put him outside the house, which she did. "He crawled and fell and I stayed inside the house, and cried. He did not cry!" The result had been that the little boy had learned to use his crutches so that he stopped crawling and started to walk. Mrs. H. listened attentively and added, her little girl wanted to play outside when she saw the other children playing "but I don't trust her,

Mrs. H.'s description of her overinvolvement with her daughter was indicative of the tendency of many group members to concentrate on the handicapped child to the exclusion of other members of the family, and of one's own needs. It was an excellent way to start off today's discussion.

It was better to let the discussion veer toward Mrs. H.'s overinvolvement than to steer it toward the disagreement among the marriage partners which was the less immediate problem and could be taken up at a later time.

The spontaneity with which group members took up the discussion of Mrs. H.'s problem was a sign of their concern for her, but this happened also because overinvolvement was, or had been, a problem for many other group members also.

The reference to the "lousy kids" was an indication of the acceptance of and identification with the leader.

The willingness of Mrs. G. and Mrs. S. to share their earlier painful experiences with Mrs. H. was evidence of their desire to be helpful to her. It also offered release of their emotions and was, for that reason, helpful to Mrs. G. and Mrs. S. at the same time.

she may get hurt." Mrs. T.
replied "you never know what a
child can do until you let him try.
You may be doing your daughter an
injustice if you don't let her find
out what she can do--and you are
certainly doing yourself an injustice!" Mrs. S. agreed and told
Mrs. H. how difficult it had been
for her when her boy started to
play outside and she saw him fall."
He got hurt, of course, but he got
over being hurt, and he got confidence so that he could try out new
things." Mrs. H. replied she
guessed she would "try out" letting
her little girl go outside, adding
"now that I think of it, sometimes
she can do things on her own which
I did not expect, and I am surprised
by what she can do."

I said, it was easy to overpro-
tect a child or a young person but
it was much more helpful to
encourage them to do new things
and to do as much as they could
because that will make them as
independent of others as possible
and because of the feeling of
achievement which all of us had
when we had mastered a difficult
task, a feeling which very often
encouraged us to go on to try our
wings further.

This was an appropriate
point to summarize and to
add some concepts, such as
that of mastery, which often
leads to additional attempts to
achieve.

Mrs. Tt. then brought up the
problem of getting her daughter
ready for school, and her fear that
she would miss the school bus.
There was a quick discussion of
the schedule on which the bus oper-
ated and what a mother could do if
a child was not ready. Mrs. Tt.
did not have the use of a car. I
said, "may I say something" and
was told: "you may have three
minutes!" This was said with a
smile and I replied with a smile
also: "why do some children daw-
dle in the morning and what happens

The leader did not want the
discussion to turn to the topic
of bus schedules so she
brought it back to the more
important one of a parent's
taking over tasks which a
child can and should perform.

if the parent steps in and takes over? "

Replies came quickly: "they want to get your attention; they want to see if you will let them stay home." "It's easier for them if you do it." I said: "all this is very true--and where do we go from here? "

One group member said: "Remember, your job is to make them independent, " and another added: "if you step in and take over, you don't do that, and they will continue to lean on you!" Mrs. Tt. nodded and said: "my daughter loves to have me do for her. It will be better if I call her half an hour earlier and let her do as much as she can for herself." Mrs. G. agreed, she had been dressing her son every morning but one day he took the shirt away from her--"he cannot speak, you know"--and from then on he dressed himself.

Mrs. E. commented, with tears in her eyes, that coming to the school had helped her to see how much more her son could do for himself than she let him do at home. She added that her younger child might also be suffering from the same crippling disease. Group members were very supportive: "You don't know for sure;" "it may not be so;" "you don't know until you have taken him to several doctors, " were some of their comments.

One group member who was sitting next to me said, half under her breath: "Oh God." I said, we all hoped that Mrs. E. would not have two sick children, but we knew how

"Where do we go from here? " is an example of the leader's taking the group one step further, an approach which was particularly important with these mothers because of their previously mentioned tendency to avoid looking beyond a problem situation and to finding a possible solution for it.

The leader missed several opportunities here to give credit to group members for their helpful comments, and especially to Mrs. Tt. for planning a new approach to the problem of her daughter's dawdling. Looking back, it is likely that the casual reference by Mrs. G. to her son's inability to speak troubled her, and prevented her from focusing on the discussion. This is an example of how the leader's becoming overidentified with a group member, or with a group's problems, damages her effectiveness.

Reference to the learning experience which coming to the school often provided, was made previously.

Mrs. E. needed recognition of what she would bring to the situation, should it arise, beyond the reassurance which some group members

much courage she had shown in learning how to live with the older boy's problems, and she had that courage and her experience to draw on, if she should need it. Mrs. E. who was sitting at my right, put her hand on mine for a moment and said: "Thank you."

we re offering her.

Such brief physical contact often provides relief to a person who is emotionally distressed. This tool, if it may be so called, should be used very selectively only if the leader initiates the contact. If a group member does this, as was the case here, pressing the hand briefly, and then withdrawing one's own hand, is the best way to handle this situation, in the writer's experience.

I then added that we had heard so many excellent comments and suggestions for Mrs. Tt. that I just wanted to say, once more, how helpful it was to let the children-- all children--assume as much responsibility for themselves as possible, to encourage them to be independent and not to fall into the trap of "doing for them," because everyone must eventually do as much for himself, or for herself, as possible.

The discussion then turned spontaneously to the different feelings of the group members toward their children, to their guilt about this which often led to overpermissiveness and to the recognition that some children, whether handicapped or not, were aware of their parents' feelings and used this knowledge to manipulate them.

Mrs. Ff. described her older daughter as "very sensitive, she cried easily, "while the younger daughter who was the handicapped child in the family was tough and also very pretty. Mrs. Ff. had always felt that the older daughter needed more consideration. Mrs. S. added that her middle child, who was not handicapped, got left out also. Furthermore, all the chil-

This may have happened because group members wished to discuss new problems, but it may also have been a reaction to Mrs. E.'s difficulties. In any event, the leader thought it best to go along with the group's wishes in that matter.

This part of the discussion gave evidence of the considerable amount of insight which many group members had. The leader would have done well to recognize this!

dren accused her of being partial
to the oldest son. As a consequence,
she tended to give in and to be as
permissive as possible with all of
them. This created problems, of
course. Mrs. Ff. said: "I know
what you mean. If my older daughter cries, I am conscience-
stricken." Mrs. B. nodded and
said: "you always feel guilty,"
and Mrs. Bb. commented: "if we
feel guilty, we give in."

At this point, I mentioned that
many children manipulated their
parents and, turning to Mrs. Ff.,
I said, I had wondered if her older
daughter did not use her tears,
her sensitivity in that fashion.
Mrs. Ff. looked startled--but not
shocked--and replied: "I must
think about that."

It was usually easy for
most members of this group
to accept a statement, or a
question of the leader, and
they were willing to explore
them, because of their eagerness to help their children
and perhaps also because of
their good relationship to the
leader.

Mrs. T. agreed: "children
manipulate their parents and they
know our point of vulnerability."
Mrs. Ss. agreed also, adding that
she had also known which one of her
parents could be dealt with more
easily, and how. Mrs. B. said
with considerable feeling: "even
if you know they manipulate you,
you often give in. If you don't,
you hate yourself all day! If you
give in, you hate the kid all day!"
Mrs. T. said: "and if you are
conscience-stricken, you indulge
all the children!" Mrs. B. agreed:
"and then you say 'yes' to things
which you don't find acceptable at
all!" Mrs. C. added: "and if you
say 'no' to the child and hate yourself, you eat too much and you get
fat!"

This part of the discussion
shows how some group mem-
bers were willing to take the
discussion further themselves.
At this point, the leader did
not need to become active.

I commented that some resentment was part of all family relationships, that it was true that a
parent did not love each child in
the same way and that one need not
feel guilty about these reactions.

The leader's summariza-
tion served two purposes: to
use the group members' comments to formulate some
important concepts regarding
family relationships, and to

If one felt guilty, however, it was
important to cope with these feelings of guilt so that they would not
interfere with the discharge of the
parental role. I phrased this with
a smile to break the tension: "It
is better to hate the kid than to
hate yourself!" I stressed, as I
had in earlier sessions with the
group, the importance of teaching
children that certain behavior was
expected of all of us, that we must
learn to accept limits and must
also learn to accept obligations, and
that it was the parent who had to
teach this to the children. I made
my comments in greater detail
than this recording shows, and
often with reference to a statement
which a group member had made
today, or in earlier sessions. I
did not "pick up" the comment
about overeating, however, because
it was so obviously related to the
oral problems of unmet dependency
needs of some group members.

Several group members had
nodded to express agreement but
Mrs. B. commented: "it is very
difficult to teach your children
responsibility or to expect them to
do something about the house. I
don't wash dishes--they go into the
dishwasher--so how can I ask them
to do it?" Mrs. F. said, there
were other chores which children
should learn to do, and should do.
"When mine are bored, I say go
and scrub the bathroom floor for
me, and I see to it that they do it!"
She went on to reminisce that when
she was young, "my mother did
not have to say 'no' very often, we
girls knew what we could not do,
and what we were expected to do!"
Mrs. S. agreed: "the lines were
much more clearly drawn" when
she grew up, and Mrs. T. commented in a similar fashion. Mrs.

intervene at this point of the
discussion, before some group
members could discuss more
of their very personal problems, as they related to
orality and aggression. Such
a discussion would have gone
beyond the scope and purpose
of the meetings, and might
well have prevented the members who would have participated in it from continued
attendance, because too much
revelation of the self often is
embarrassing, later on.

The fact that the discus-
sion did not return to the problems of self-hate and of
obesity, was proof, in the
writer's opinion, that the group
members preferred not to
involve themselves any more
deeply, but this may also
have been due to their willingness to follow the leader's
cues.

Some casual remarks are
often valuable clues about
the social and economic
status of group members, but
they can also indicate special
concerns and questions which
are troubling them. The
reference to the dishwasher
by Mrs. B., to scrubbing
the bathroom floor by Mrs. F.,
were indications of their different financial situations.

B. returned to her earlier comment: "how can I expect the children to do what I am not doing, and
what need not be done in my house?"
Mrs. B. had a full-time maid,
which I knew because she and Mrs.
S. had talked about their household
help before one of the meetings had
started. Mrs. C. shook her head
and replied: "You don't really
mean that?" Mrs. B. replied:
"of course I do!" Mrs. S. said,
very often young people get married "and they don't have a dishwasher! It is good to be able to
run a house and to do this, one
must have learned this at home!"
Mrs. B. said, with annoyance:
"You know that the dishwasher is
only a symbol!"

I commented at this point because
I sensed the tension between Mrs.
B. and some of the other group
members--that one tended, of
course, to be overprotective of the
handicapped child, and to give in to
him too much also which in turn
led to conflicts with the other children. We had said this quite frequently, but we needed to add that
all children had to learn that they
had responsibilities and that, in
some situations, the parent had to
provide the children with experiences of this kind, often to create
them, because they would be helpful to them when they were grown
up. Holding a job, being married
and raising a family required
accepting responsibility of one kind
or another, and accepting responsibility needed to be taught and
learned.

"Creating an experience"
may be teaching children to
do dishes, even if one has a
dishwasher, or teaching them
to be able to clean a house, or
to do some simple repair jobs
on cars or appliances, in the
case of sons. It is helpful
to be able to feel that one can
cope with some of the problems
of everyday living; furthermore, these skills can become
important if one's way of life
changes or if one lives in different surroundings.

I added that I knew very well
that our parents were very good
parents and very concerned parents
but it seemed to me that "a little
more backbone" might perhaps be
helpful to them. Some other parent

Recognition that the parents
are concerned and good parents
was due to them, but they also
needed encouragement to be
less permissive.

groups I had known needed to be encouraged toward more leniency, but our group. . .

Before I could finish my sentence, Mrs. T. said: "we don't have to worry about leniency, we spoil the children." I said, that was exactly what I had been trying to say. Mrs. S. added: "we feel --how do we dare to say No? But this is not right, and it does not help the children." Mrs. Ff. agreed and said: "I can't wait to get home to try this out. I mean to be less permissive and less concerned."

Mrs. Ss. then gave the discussion a new turn by saying: "I want to ask all of you and Mrs. Pollak a question: do all handicapped children hoard their money? My daughter does." Mrs. Tt. replied: "No, this is not so. My daughter gives her money away." Mrs. S. commented: "But some handicapped children buy friendships." Mrs. E. replied, rather defensively, that "many children do that."

The leader might have encouraged Mrs. Ff. to try the new approach and also to let the group know how this had worked out.

Hoarding versus spending money was a topic which group members had not brought up previously, and it was likely to be very relevant, because of the many, often hidden meanings which money has in the lives of different people.

Mrs. E. was rather defensive at various points of the discussions in many sessions. This may have been due to the fact that both her children were considerably younger than the children of some other group members, so that she had not had much time to accept her son's handicap. Furthermore, she was trying to cope with the possibility that her second child might also be suffering from the same illness, and she might have been protecting herself from having to face additional problems. Some of Mrs. E.'s statements would probably have been challenged more directly in another meeting, but the other members of the group realized how vulnerable she was today.

Mrs. K. turned to Mrs. Ss. and

Mrs. T. who had much more

agreed with her. "My son always looks in his bankbook to make sure he has more than everyone else." Mrs. T. shook her head and said: "This is just the child, it has nothing to do with the handicap." Mrs. S. disagreed with her: "It has something to do with the handicap" and she went on to describe her son as "very anxious to be part of the group on the block where we live. He keeps his money locked away, and he carries the key to the box around his neck. He goes to the drugstore almost every day to buy candy for the children on the block. I know he is buying friends." Mrs. Tt. sighed: "my daughter buys candy and she gives the other children the candy, and money also. She is like your boy." Mrs. E. said, in a supportive fashion: "but both children have friends. This worked for them." Mrs. F. disagreed: "this does not work out--it cannot work out. It is buying friendship--if you buy it, it will not last."

Mrs. S. said, with a sigh: "I guess they follow our example." She went on to describe that when she and her husband take their son bowling, they usually "treat another boy on the block. This creates a little friendship for our boy." Mrs. F. replied: "that is different. We often invite other children to go with us. But the other, the buying of friendships by the children with candy, or with money--I just don't believe in it. Do you think these friendships will stick?" Mrs. Ss. replied: "perhaps not, but for a while the child has a friend." Mrs. Tt. disagreed: "it will be harder for them if the other kids go their own way later on."

Mrs. S. commented: "we buy not only with money." She

insight than Mrs. E., and also many more years of experience in living with a handicapped child, was also sometimes hesitant to recognize the impact of the handicap on the actions and reactions of the child.

This was a very helpful statement by Mrs. S. The leader was tempted to explore the question of the parental example further, but she thought it would be more helpful if the group members continued to share their experiences, their reactions, and their very different approaches to the problems of helping children to have friends.

This part of the discussion showed how anxious several

described how she invited the neighborhood children for lunch very often so that their mothers would have some free time and her child some other children around. Mrs. B. added with bitterness: "my traditional Saturdays are spent babysitting for all the mothers in the neighborhood so that my daughter will have some company." Mrs. E. replied "you make it attractive for the children to come to your house," and Mrs. F. added: "what you do is different. Many mothers appreciate it when you invite their children for lunch, or to go to a movie. That's not buying friendship, or anything else!"

Mrs. T. said that her son's only friends are those with whom he attended school here. Most of them lived quite a distance away and she had to drive her son if he was to see them. "Even then, it's not reciprocal!" She added that her son was "a loner, but then he does not have a very nice personality-- he would not have had friends anyhow." Mrs. E., who is more naive than several other members of the group, said in a horrified tone: "how can you say that about your son? He is such a nice boy!" Mrs. T. shrugged her shoulders and said: "He always knows everything better than anyone else, and the other children know it!"

I said, two thoughts came to my mind and I would like to share them with the group. One is that we should remember that some children, and some adults also, had less desire than others for friendships, or for social relationships, and were quite satisfied, and often happier, by themselves, or in the company of a few people only.

group members were to provide their children with social contacts in the neighborhood. It also showed, as was to be expected, that some mothers, such as, Mrs. F., and Mrs. Tt., handled the situation much more objectively than, for instance, Mrs. S., Mrs. Ss. or Mrs. B. Here too the reactions were different, with Mrs. B. showing considerable resentment at the demands made on her (an attitude which characterized her throughout the discussions), while Mrs. Ss. revealed her anguish at her sons' problems. This was also consistent throughout the meetings.

This is an important concept to bring to some parent groups, and not only to the parents of handicapped children. Many parents are very much concerned about their children's popularity, mostly because of their own problems in a variety of areas, and little allowance is often made for the different needs of children, and of young people, for social relationships.

The other point I would like to make was that <u>a parent's inviting other children to come along to the zoo, or to a movie, or to go bowling with one's own child was different from such activities as the child's buying candy or giving money to other children for the purpose of making or of keeping friends</u>. Here also I made my comments in greater detail than recorded.

Mrs. K. said, approvingly: "I have taken other kids with us, not only M's friends. (M. is the child who is handicapped.) Some people, they have only one or two kids, they worry about taking another kid along, but I have nine kids and one or two more, that's nothing!" Mrs. S. smiled at Mrs. K. and said: "we could all learn from you!"

I was ready to move the discussion on but Mrs. E. said: "can we talk more about buying friendship?" I said, certainly we could. Mrs. S. followed through by saying: "My son buys friendship with his candy and with his money." Mrs. Ss. turned to her and said, her daughter had come home from school with a pocketful of candy. "She told me your son had given it to her." Mrs. F. repeated her question: "If you buy friendship--will you have it for long?" Mrs. E. shook her head and replied: "but this is sharing--children should share!" Mrs. T. turned to Mrs. E. and asked: "Lillian, <u>is</u> it sharing?" Mrs. E. was getting quite restless, which indicated that she was troubled, as I knew from my previous observations, and so I said, <u>perhaps this was one of the situations where we had</u>

Mrs. K. and Mrs. S. were also two group members who came from very different economic and social backgrounds. This little exchange showed how little this mattered, because of the overriding concern of group members regarding their handicapped children.

Mrs. E.'s request showed that the problem of the children's attempts to make and to keep friends troubled her. Since it was also obviously of great interest to most of the group members, it was sound to return to this topic once more.

Because of Mrs. E.'s increasing anxiety, intervention was indicated here, in the leader's opinion.

to look not only at what someone
else, or we, did, but also at why
we did something. Sharing candy,
if one wanted a friend to have some,
was good, but sharing candy to buy
friendship was different. Of course,
we did not always know what was
behind the action, but sometimes
"we have a pretty good guess, "
based on our knowledge of the persons involved, and on our knowledge
of the situation.

Mrs. S. nodded, and added:
"Lillian, it's the motive that
counts." Mrs. E. shook her head
and replied: "I am sure the children want to share what they have!"
No one replied to her comment;
rather, Mrs. Tt. said: "sometimes, you don't have the money to
reciprocate. Maybe that's why
some mothers don't do it." Mrs.
K. replied: "you don't have to
spend any money to reciprocate.
If you invite the other children to
your house, that is enough." Mrs.
F. agreed and described how she
had invited her handicapped son's
friend. "He enjoyed being with us
--we are so many, and he is an
only child. He said Grace with us,
he ate what we ate, and when I
asked him to come again, he was
so pleased!" I commented, there
were many ways of reciprocating,
i.e., of placing invitations or
treats for children on a give and
take basis, and not all of them
needed to be a financial burden.

Mrs. K. said, with some emotion: "so often, we are afraid the
child will be hurt." Mrs. T.
agreed and added: "we say, be
careful, don't fall--and then the
other children don't want to play
with our child!"

Mrs. E. spoke of her delight
when she had met a friend recently,
with whom she had gone to college.

Group members were
sensitive to Mrs. E.'s
anxiety also, and accepted
her inability to see the children's actions as anything
else but the desirable wish to
share one's belongings with
others.

It was important to recognize that the financial investment in social relationships
need not be great, and is not
what determines the amount
or the quality of social relationships which children--or
adults--have.

The leader might have used
this opportunity for another
comment on the drawbacks of
overprotecting the handicapped
child.

This reaction of group
members to Mrs. E. reflected
their concern for her. They

That friend's son was of the same age as her handicapped boy, and she had invited him to come for lunch, with his mother. "The two boys got along very well, and now my son has another friend!" Group members reacted very positively to her story. Mrs. F. said, in a supportive fashion: "with your two children, things are a little more difficult for you, but weren't you smart to arrange this lunch? We are such a large family, there is always company, because the other children bring their friends home." Mrs. S. agreed with Mrs. F.; because of the difference in age of her children "the youngest is like an only child. That is why we are so glad if other children come with us when we go bowling, or go to the zoo!" She then turned to Mrs. E. and said, with warmth: "You have done so well! I am sure you will find other ways to help your son to have more friends." Mrs. E. smiled; she was obviously very pleased by the recognition she received from group members. I said, Mrs. E.'s story showed how sometimes a parent could help his child to meet new children, and to develop new friendships, and that this could be done in a casual way. If the parent could get some enjoyment at the same time, so much the better.

Mrs. T. added: "and Lillian you were not obvious about it!" Mrs. E. replied: "I will try again. I guess my trouble is that I am always afraid for my son!" She described how Johnny, who lived on the same street, had come over to ask her son to play pool with him, and her son had won. "I was afraid to let him in--I did not think my son could play pool!" She added some positive comments about the

were probably also relieved to have an opportunity to be positive about her contribution since they had challenged her on her statements on sharing earlier in the discussion.

This part of the discussion shows how the support, encouragement, and recognition by the group members and by the leader can help a group member to mobilize herself and to try new and better approaches to a problem with which she is coping. It also shows that while Mrs. E. could admit that she had been overprotective of her son, she

meetings which had helped her to realize that her son could do more than she thought he was capable of. "I am still afraid for him, but I will try to let him do more!" She was speaking to me, and I said that was an excellent decision and would give her son <u>more freedom to experiment and to find out what he could so, if he tried. Knowing that a parent "backs you up," was very encouraging to a child</u>. Mrs. F. said: "sometimes the kids surprise you with what they can do!" and Mrs. C. added: "as the children get older, we have to leave them alone more and more. They have to learn to make their own decisions and that goes for all children, the handicapped ones and the normal ones too!"

Mrs. K. then returned to the problem of reciprocity. She said to Mrs. T. "you mentioned it's not reciprocal, your driving your boy so he can see his friends. It's not only that. What can one do if the other children don't invite your child?" Mrs. E. suggested talking to the parents of the other children "they would not want your child to be hurt." Mrs. B. replied: "<u>You</u> would not want this to happen." Mrs. F. shook her head and said: "that does not work. You have to let the children decide whom they want to invite. That goes for your own and for the others." I said, I had been wondering about something. <u>It happened to all of us, that we invited somebody, but this person did not invite us back. Everybody had the right to decide with whom he, or she, wanted to have social relationships</u>. Mrs. S. nodded and commented: "Of course, this happens. But when it happens to our children--here we go again, being overprotective!"

could not accept the possibility that some handicapped children might be buying friendships. She would, of course, have been even less able to face some of the reasons why they might be doing this.

I was getting ready to terminate the meeting, but Mrs. M., who had come late, she was one of today's volunteers, spoke up now. Her son loved sports and had many friends "because they like to use our equipment. They take care that he won't hurt himself, but they all play together." Mrs. F. described her handicapped son's birthday party; he had invited his friends who liked to dance, "of course, he can't dance, but he put on the records, served the refreshments--he was a real nice host!-- and he had a good time." Mrs. G. described that her son had been playing with some children who were new to the neighborhood, and when he fell, he cried. "The other children were frightened, but I went out and explained to them that he cannot talk. The children calmed down, helped him to get up and they continued to play together." I commented, these were excellent examples of ways in which a parent could help his children to have friends--by providing facilities which all children would enjoy, by encouraging one's child to concentrate on the activities in which he could engage and which would give him pleasure, and also by acting as an intermediary, if the other children did not understand about one's child's handicap. Many children--and many adults-- were frightened by a handicap, but if the parent explained what it was, and explained also what the child could do, this usually was helpful in the development of the child's social relationships. "Keeping the door open" for social contacts, and welcoming other people--children or adults--to our homes usually resulted in a richer social life.

It was appropriate to give recognition to Mrs. G.'s helpful handling of that incident.

Fear of the handicapped child, which may be a fear of hurting him, or an unconscious fear of being hurt oneself, or which may be based on other intrapsychic phenomena would have been a helpful topic to explore further if it had come up at an earlier point of the meeting. At this time, it was more important to end the meeting on a positive note. This is usually helpful unless one wishes to stir up some emotions, such as anxiety in group members, which was not the leader's purpose.

XIII
Coping with Sexual Needs after Divorce or Death of Spouse

The meeting which will be presented now differs in many ways from the meetings with adults which have been discussed in the three preceding chapters. First, the emphasis of the discussions was not on parent-child relationships, but on the adults' problems as related to their experiences in attempting to reconstruct their lives in ways which included often, but not always, their plans for remarriage. Second, perhaps because many members of the group attended a considerable number of the discussion series, but also for other reasons, these meetings focused more closely on the attitudes and emotions of group members than had been the case in the meetings presented previously. Third, the members of these groups took much more initiative and much more responsibility for planning and organizing the discussion series of which this meeting was a part. These differences are discussed in more detail below.

The discussion series, for which the members of this group liked to use the title "seminar," were offered to the separated, divorced, and widowed members of the Single Parents Society of Philadelphia, which was the local equivalent of the national organization called, "Parents Without Partners." The writer offered leadership for two seminars a year, usually in January and February and in April and May. The group met weekly; it had evening meetings because all group members were employed. It met in the Board Room of the agency, because this was fairly accessible for many group members and because the agency's location provided a safe meeting place. Each seminar had eight meetings; a total of twenty seminars were offered to the group. The writer was the leader for all the seminars.

The relationship of the seminar group to the Single Parent Society consisted in the main in their being members of the latter association. One member, and sometimes two, of a seminar chaired it. Their responsibilities were to decide, with the help of a committee of group members and of the leader, what the main focus of the next seminar would be. Next, they developed some publicity for it, which was published in the monthly newsletter of the Single Parent Society. Inquiries by prospective group members were addressed to and answered by the chairpersons. If somebody was interested in participating in a seminar, his or her name was passed on to the leader, who followed through with a letter giving additional information about it. The chairpersons were also in charge of collecting the fees from group members, and they stood by in emergencies, such as a sudden snowstorm, to call the seminar members if a meeting needed to be canceled. Because the Single Parent Society endorsed the seminars, the leader sent a brief report after each seminar had ended to the organization which covered registration and attendance figures, a summary of topics discussed, and the suggestions of group members for topics of the next seminar. This report was sent to the president of the Society who shared it with the Board of Directors.

CHARACTERISTICS OF GROUP MEMBERS

Twenty to twenty five persons registered for every seminar; about one-half of them had usually attended one, or several previous seminars. A "profile" of seminar members, drawn from the information provided on their registration sheets, shows that there were more women than men in the seminars, that most group members were in their forties, although some were in their thirties, and a few in their fifties, and that many more seminar members were divorced than widowed or separated. Group members were middle class by education and occupation; many of them had completed, or attended college, and they were employed as teachers, secretaries, bookkeepers, salesmen, engineers; two members of the group sold real estate, one owned a beauty shop, one worked for a public welfare agency, and another was a psychologist. The seminars were offered to members of all racial and religious groups; it had only two black members, however, who attended several seminars and who also acted as seminar chairpersons. There was usually a slight preponderance of Jewish participants.

If one looks at the predominant problems of group members, an imbalance of interpersonal relationship--be they to their children, friends, or members of the opposite sex--was usually very noticeable. The problems of parents without partners with their children had been explored in earlier seminars, and it had been the decision of group members to turn to their own problems in the later seminars, of which the meeting described below was a part. This decision notwithstanding, some references were made to parent-child problems also in these later seminars, mostly by members who had joined the group more recently. As could be expected, most seminar members felt some confusion about their responsibilities to their children, and attempted to add to their own parental role that of the missing parent. This was especially likely to happen when death had broken up the family, but many divorced parents felt the same compulsion to accept a role which was not theirs by family composition, nor by sex. Much of this was due to feelings of guilt about the divorce; if the group member was widowed, it was due to the desire to compensate

for the death of the other parent. These attempts resulted in the
usual reactions of children in such situations, such as increased
demands on parents who were overindulgent; aggression and hostility
followed by guilt, because the ties between parents and children were
too close, and deeper conflicts especially in the case of adolescent
sons whose mothers were unconsciously, and sometimes not so
unconsciously, seductive. The overinvolvement of parents also
prevented, or at least postponed, the movement toward independence
from primary family ties which all young people must make to become
adults in their own right.

Relationships to friends were frequently distorted, and this
applied to married friends as well as to other parents without partners of the same sex. Mostly because of the loneliness from which
many group members were suffering, but also for other reasons
which were related to unmet dependency needs, or to aggressiveness,
demands were often made on one's friends which were out of proportion to what the relationship could offer and which, therefore, led in
many instances to unpleasantness and to its termination. In other
situations, where the internal problems were of a different nature,
many group members permitted themselves to become involved in
exploitative relationships, a term which they had coined and which
appealed to them. In these relationships, they were used by other
people who would, for instance, come at all times of the day or night,
but would never invite the group members to their house. Such people
would telephone routinely at all hours to discuss their problems but
did not wish to listen to anything the group members might want to
bring up which was troubling them at that time. They would cancel
social engagements if more promising opportunities came up.

It was true, however, that many group members had not
adjusted to, and had perhaps not even realized, some of the problems
in social relationships which losing a marriage partner tends to
bring. For instance, some women had not taken into account the fear
of competition which they might arouse in some of their married
women friends; a few even seemed to wish to provoke these fears.
All these group members were greatly surprised, however, when the
relationships were terminated. One very attractive young woman
was quite taken aback when group members suggested that she should
avoid going to visit her married friends at a time when the wife was
working, although the wife had professed to find nothing unusual in
this procedure. Whether the visitor was motivated by seductiveness,
or by a desire for revenge, or by masochistic impulses, was not
clear but what was clear was that such an approach to married friends
was bound to lead to conflicts, and eventually to social isolation. The
group members who discussed this particular problem were quite
astute, incidentally, in pinpointing the personal and marital problems
of a wife who would acquiesce to such a situation.

The social relationships of many group members suffered also
from what the writer has defined previously as a lack of social skills
in discussing the problems of teen-agers. Of course, this took dif-

ferent forms for the seminar members, because they were adults
and the problems which these lacks of social skills reflected were
due to unmet dependency needs and, in some instances, to aggressiveness rather than to lack of education. As could be expected
from persons in their age group, the women in the group had more
difficulty than the men in coping with such questions as how to enter-
tain one's married friends. They often did not know who should pay
the bill, if they had invited a group of friends which included men to
a restaurant, or how to plan for one's leaving a party, without putting the host or hostess to the trouble of providing an escort.

Many group members found it also troubling to go out alone,
for instance to a theater, or to a movie, and again this applied more
to the women than to the men. One of the gains of attendance at the
seminars was that some friendships developed which encouraged the
more timid group members to move out more into the world around
them. This was one way of combating the loneliness and isolation
of many group members, but it was also a way of exposing them to
new experiences which, in turn, enrich a person's life and contribute
to make him, or her, a more interesting partner in social and other
relationships.

The relationships of group members with members of the other
sex were, as could be expected, of great concern to them, and were
in most instances very difficult. Again, this was more true of the
women than of the men in the group and this was not related to the
fact that there were fewer men than women in the group. For a
variety of external and of personal reasons, women seemed to react
more acutely to the loss of the marriage partner, and this more
intense reaction in some subtle way affected their relationships to
most men. Women were more anxious than men to meet dating partners, and they went to great lengths to do this. Their anxiety did
not further their goal, because it was usually apparent to the men
whom they managed to meet. Anxiety never fosters the development
of a relationship because it tends to make the other persons anxious
also, or hesitant to commit themselves, or at least to commit themselves at the rapid pace which anxious persons usually set. Women
were also usually more openly hostile in their comments about the
men they were meeting, or had met, generally in connection with the
discussion of requests for sex relations which were made during
early or first dates. Most women who were members of this group
would not consider having sex relations at such an early stage but,
on the other hand, they were incensed when their dating partners
exercised their prerogative of terminating relationships which were
not offering them what they expected.

Expectations of a partner for a second marriage were usually
quite unrealistic, focused on what the future marriage partner would
contribute to one's life, but with little emphasis on what one was
bringing to the situation oneself in terms of assets and of liabilities.
One group member, who had teen-age children, was startled to hear
that a second husband might be assuming heavy responsibilities by

marrying her. It had not occurred to her that he would probably
have to provide for the children, if their father would be unable or
unwilling to do this, and if he was attached to the children's mother,
and perhaps also to the children themselves.

Needless to say, some members of the group were more realistic in their expectations, and their contributions helped to clarify
some of the misconceptions of other group members. It was also
very helpful when former seminar members who had remarried
returned to the seminar for a meeting or two to share their experiences in their new lives. In one instance, two seminar members
who had known each other for a long time had married each other
and they related some of the gratifications, and some of the problems,
of their new life together, to some of the topics which they had discussed in the group before the marriage. Since both seminar members had attended a number of seminars, they were able to stress
the necessity of giving oneself time before one makes any important
decisions about one's life, of exploring the various possibilities one
has from a variety of angles, and of learning as much about oneself,
one's assets and liabilities, one's needs and one's problems as one
can, so that a second marriage can be successful.

Relationships to members of the other sex which were based
on friendship only were also mentioned by a few group members, both
men and women, and were described as satisfying the need for closeness with other people, but also the need for a point of view which
was different because of the other person's sex. These relationships
were the exception, and not the rule, however.

If one looks at the deeper problems which were affecting many
members of these seminars, the feeling of being different and set
apart from married friends was one, and to it was added the feeling
of failure, if the group member was divorced or separated. The
loneliness which was previously mentioned often resulted in feelings
of depression, although loneliness was not the only cause of these
feelings. Anger--at the marriage partner from whom one was
separated or divorced, or at the marriage partner who had died,
because this death was often experienced as abandonment--was another
source of these feelings. In addition, many women who had thought
of themselves primarily as wives, experienced a loss of identity
when this function ceased. This, too, led to depression; as one
group member phrased it: "I never wanted to be anything but a wife
and mother. I cried and cried every night for a year after we were
divorced, until I adjusted to my new life."

As could be expected, the previous marriage partners of
seminar members were mentioned on many occasions, and in connection with many different problems. An interesting phenomenon
could be observed in the discussions of former marriage partners;
the statements varied, depending on whether divorce or separation or
death were the factors which had led to the termination of the relationship. In the former situations, the previous marriage partners
were usually presented in a more negative fashion, as time went on,

perhaps because the group member needed to convince himself, or herself, that the termination had been really necessary, since it had often been a step for which the group member had exerted some decisive influence and about which most group members had been, and perhaps continued to be, ambivalent. When death was the cause of the marriage's ending, the partner who had died was usually idealized more and more as time went on. Needless to say, neither attitude was helpful, the first one because it increased the bitterness of group members, the second one because the deceased became an impossible model with whom the widowed person tended to compare a potential second marriage partner. Both attitudes were detrimental to the development of the children from these unions. A divorced mother's negative attitude toward the living father made the children's relationship to the father, and sometimes also their relationship to the mother more difficult (Harris, 1972, p. 14; Klatskin, 1972, p. 193; Steinzor, 1969, pp. 26, 35, 157). Where a mother was widowed, growing up children especially had greater problems in breaking the ties to the memory of a father who was presented in such positive terms.

Many group members whose marriages had ended fairly recently, but also some whose marriages had ended several years ago were still involved emotionally with them. This involvement went way beyond the natural concern with one's past since of course one cannot, and should not, attempt to erase the experience of having lived with another human being from one's own life, even if that were humanly possible. The failure to accept and to adjust to the reality of the termination of the marriage meant that the group member who had not achieved this was thinking in terms of the past rather than in terms of the present. This interfered with making appropriate plans for the situation in which this group member was living now, with the enjoyment of what it had to offer, and necessarily also with plans for a future which could offer opportunities for a fuller life.

In addition to the hostility which some women expressed when they were discussing their current or past dating partners, many seminar members--both men and women--were quite hostile to all members of the other sex. This hostility was often expressed very openly and sometimes directed at another member of the group who often seemed to be quite innocent in that particular instance and to serve only as a convenient peg on which to hang one's hostility. It was interesting that the group members who were widowed were less hostile than the ones who were divorced and one can probably assume that the breakup of the previous marriage may have been caused, in part at least, by this hostility.

Many group members were anxious in other areas also than in that of meeting suitable dating, love, and marriage partners. The divorced or separated parents often showed considerable anxiety when they discussed their previous marriages, a reaction which the widowed parents did not seem to have. Both kinds of group members expressed anxiety, however, when they were discussing the double burden, the

new problems which they had to face now that they had lost the marriage partner. Going to work was for many women a new experience
and one which many, but not all, found difficult. Their concern for
their children was another cause for anxiety, and it led many group
members to frantic attempts to replace the missing parent, attempts
which were, of course, bound to fail. As mentioned previously, the
problems of seminar members in their relationships to their children
had been the main topics of many earlier discussion series, and some
group members had acquired a more realistic and more helpful
approach to these problems. One group member--a man in his fifties who had been widowed while his children were in their teens--
expressed this as follows: "I learned that I had to try to do what a
mother would have done, but I did not have--and what's more, I
should not!--have to try to be a mother. I feel secure about my
role--I am a man and I am their father!" Such a comment would be
less likely to be made by younger group members today, in view of
the different attitudes which many of them have toward the inter-
changeability of the parental roles.

Anxiety was also often experienced, but not openly expressed,
in regard to the future, by some seminar members, particularly by
the women among them, who were troubled at the thought that they
might not get married again. This might happen, of course (Bernard,
1956, p. 44; Glick, 1957, pp. 135-136; Goode, 1956, p. 277; Jacobson,
1959, p. 75). This anxiety was not openly expressed, in the leader's
opinion, because to do this would have been to admit failure, which
in the case of divorced or separated group members, would have
been a second failure. It came to the fore, however, in many references to their present lives and to its problems. Again, it was helpful that other seminar members dealt more realistically with this
possibility, and that some seminar members had also decided that
married life was not included in their plans for their future, by their
own choice.

While group members disagreed with each other frequently,
the discussions were characterized by the warm feelings which most
of them had for each other, by their desire to be supportive of anyone who was troubled or upset, and also by considerable sensitivity
to each others' vulnerable points. The experience of having lost a
marriage partner was the unifying bond for the members of this
group, as the experience of having a handicapped child had been the
unifying bond for the parents described in the preceding chapter. In
both situations, an unusual number of group members had had therapeutic experiences, had, or were being seen by psychiatrists, and
these contacts had given to many of them insight and sensitivity to
the inner conflicts and personality problems of others. Although the
members of the group showed considerable difference in regard to
age, intelligence, and, sometimes also in the degree of sophistica-
tion with which they approached life and its complexities, usually
these differences were accepted in a matter of fact fashion.

Another factor which was characteristic of most members of

these seminars was their readiness to involve themselves deeply into the discussions, and to look at some of their past and present experiences in terms of the underlying attitudes and feelings which had made these experiences successful, or unsuccessful. Although group members tried to avoid exposure in these discussions, as was appropriate for the goals and setting of these meetings, they let down many barriers. As a result, feelings of closeness and intimacy developed in the group. It also led, for some group members at least, to learning experiences in the area of their own emotions, and to some understanding of how these emotions had affected their family and social relationships and were continuing to do this. Insight into oneself often enables one to change certain approaches to other people and, while acquiring insight need not always be followed by such change, especially if the person lacks the strength to act upon the newly found insight, it is a prerequisite for such change. Inasmuch as some group members acquired such insight, they also felt increasingly comfortable with themselves and this, too, was no mean gain when it happened. One group member expressed this as follows: "I used to start to perspire when someone mentioned getting married again. Now I know that the close relationship of marriage is not for me, and I can listen to someone else's talking about this without getting upset."

Whenever learning on such a level happened, it came about as a result of repeated exposure to seminar discussions. This was the most important consequence of the fact that most group members attended the seminars for several years. It should be mentioned in this context that some persons developed an interesting pattern of attending three or four seminars, followed by an absence of a year or two, after which interval they returned to the group for additional meetings. Since new group members used to join the discussions almost every time a seminar started, the discussions of topics and problems which were basically the same, were enriched by the contributions of the new members, who brought out new facets of these problems.

As could be expected, the attendance of those group members whose needs the seminars met, was very good. Twelve to fifteen group members were usually present at every meeting, and sometimes attendance was higher. The higher attendance was not always an asset, because the smaller group provided a more favorable climate for the topics under discussion and for the rapid interaction of group members.

GOALS OF THE SEMINARS

The goals for this group were to gain a better and deeper understanding of oneself and of the other persons who were part of the lives of its members. The earlier seminars had been devoted to such learning about oneself in one's role as a father or a mother,

about one's relationships to one's children, and about their relationships and reactions to the parent who was part of their life situation
as well as to the missing parent. The later seminars had another
focus, which was on the group members themselves in their relations to other adults of the same and of the opposite sex. This was
a sound plan, in the leader's opinion, partly because she was aware
of the problems in intrapersonal relationships which the majority of
the divorced and separated group members had and of the difficulties
which all group members, whether divorced or widowed, had in
making a sound choice of a partner for a second marriage or, as the
case might be, in making a satisfactory adjustment to life without a
marriage partner. Any better understanding of one's own basic
needs as a person, as a woman or as a man, as a partner in dating,
love and/or sex relationships, as a partner in a marriage relationship and as a partner in friendship and other social relationships,
was likely to improve the chances of group members for more satisfactory experiences in these important areas of their lives. A better understanding of the other persons who were part of these
relationships would lead to more realistic evaluations of what they
could contribute to one's own life so that decisions to involve oneself
in a relationship, or to terminate an ongoing relationship, might be
made with more clarity. Such decisions would then be based more
on thought processes than on the often confused emotions and deeply
felt unmet needs of the participants in the relationships. If, along
with this, some group members could experience in the sharing of
problems some release from loneliness, bitterness, and other negative feelings, they would be enabled to cope more effectively with
the unavoidable adjustments which a formerly married person has
to make to a life situation of which the spouse is no longer a part.

Similarly, some clarification of the different meaning which
sex relations can have for different people might help them to cope
better with the problems which many seminar members were facing
in that area, and might prevent them from experiencing the disappointment and hurt which follow unrealistic expectations of such relationships
(Pollak, 1970, 11. 79-85). We tend to forget that many adults who are
realistic and competent in many areas of their lives, are unrealistic
and fumbling in their efforts to cope with sexual experiences, and
naive in their expectations and fantasies about them. It came as
a surprise to some--again, not to all--group members that sexual relations can be an expression of hatred as well as of love,
or of a desire to control, or to humiliate, or of the wish to find or
to give reasurance, reassurance of oneself as a human being, or of
oneself as a man or as a woman. They can be "a way of passing the
time which is more interesting than watching TV," as one group
member said, and they can be a way of expressing and satisfying
one's physical desire for another person without including love. It
was important for some members of the group to hear from others
that sexual relations need not involve positive feelings for the partner, beyond the physical component of the relationship, and that

some persons even prefer to have sexual relations which do not carry
any emotional involvement, nor any commitment to the other person.
"It's like taking an aspirin," as another group member said, a statement which led group members to coin the phrase "clinical sex" for
these types of relationships.

In the discussions of these topics the leader stressed the importance of finding out, as much as this is possible, what kind of experience one expects from sex relationships, and what the possible partner
expects so that decisions about having--or about not having--sex
relations will be based more on some realistic understanding of what
they can offer to oneself, and less on one's hopes and fantasies. If
one's system of values, or one's religious beliefs do not permit one
to have sex relations outside of marriage--much less the type of sex
relations defined as "clinical sex,"--such factors must be taken into
account when one makes a decision in this important area of one's
personal life. The leader also stressed, however, that one may not
assume that one's personal beliefs are binding for, or even acceptable
to other people, and much less may one presume to define the limits
of any relationship with the expectation that the other person must
accept these limits. The principle of mutuality applies to any relationship which involves two persons, and it requires that both of them
have some say about its contents, its meaning for each of them, and
the depth of their involvement in it.

THE RELATIONSHIPS OF GROUP MEMBERS TO THE LEADER

The seminar members were another group which related well
to the leader; this was due, in part, to the problems with which they
were coping and for which they were seeking solutions. It was also
due to their loneliness and to their need for relationships which would
support and strengthen them in their struggles with outer and inner
conflicts. As previously mentioned, many group members found this
support in their contacts with other group members also.

In addition to this support, the leader contributed to the discussions by clarifying the misconceptions which many of the group
members had, and by encouraging the discussions to move into the
area of attitudes and feelings whenever this was appropriate and
would be helpful to the group members. It was often a fine line
which separated the appropriate from that which was not appropriate
for a particular topic, or more important, for a particular group
member to share with the others. In the various discussions of sex
relations outside of marriage, for instance, no group member ever
shared personal experiences of this kind, beyond the previously mentioned requests for sexual intercourse which many women had resented,
or had perhaps pretended to resent. It would have been naive to
assume that no member of this group of persons who had been married, and most of whom were eager for relationships with members
of the other sex, had not had sex relations since the marriage had

ended, but these personal experiences were not the focus of the
meetings. Rather, the focus was on some clarification of the fact
that sexual relations have very different meaning for some people,
and on the importance of finding out what their meaning is for oneself
and for the possible partner, as well as what is acceptable to oneself,
and what is not.

In the discussions of previous marriages which had ended in
divorce or separation, most group members talked freely about their
reactions to and feelings about the ending of the marriage, and about
the adjustments they had had to make to the new situation. They did
not, however, discuss in much detail, if at all, some of the intrapersonal conflicts which had caused the termination of the marriage.

Similarly, some of the group members who were being seen by
psychiatrists, or who had had such treatment experiences in the past,
shared some of the understanding of themselves which they had gained
in this fashion with other seminar members, but without disclosure
of the causes of their problems, nor of the methods and approaches
through which they had gained this understanding. These limits were
adhered to scrupulously by the group members, and they were self-
imposed controls since the leader had never discussed such limits
with the group. What the leader had done, was to stress the purpose
of the meetings as learning about oneself and about others, and she
did this whenever it became necessary, for instance when new group
members were confused by the format of the meetings, their lack of
a fixed agenda, or the absence of lectures. The ability of the members of a group to function, and to function well, within certain
boundaries which are imposed by the purpose and the methods used,
is another indication of their good relations to and identification with
the leader. Needless to say, not all the persons who came to the
meetings were satisfied with these limits, or with the free flowing
and unstructured discussions. Some were probably threatened by
the problems which were brought out, which they had to face, and
some might also have disliked the leader. Withdrawal from attendance was the form in which these group members handled these
matters, and the leader did not encourage them to come back. This
was different from the approach used with the parents of acting out
children which was described in an earlier chapter.

As could be expected, some members of these seminars who
had not had any individual treatment experiences were in considerable
emotional distress, and the leader had opportunities to refer them
to appropriate resources for counseling or for psychotherapy. All
the seminar members to whom this was suggested followed through
on these referrals and this was probably also due, at least in part,
to their good relationships with the leader. Conversely, some psychi-
trists who were aware of the seminars, referred patients for attendance and this, too, worked out well.

The positive relationship which most group members who
remained in the group developed to the leader made it easy for her
to protect any group member whose youth or whose naivete exposed

her, or him.   This happened a few times only, but whenever one member of this group was under attack, or was being ridiculed, intervention by the leader was indicated, in view of the limitations of
self-exploration and self-exposure which the discussions had.

SOME SPECIAL PROBLEMS OF THE LEADER FOR GROUPS OF PARENTS WITHOUT PARTNERS

In this leader's experience, the main problem was to offer a
warm and supportive relationship to the members of the group, while
maintaining its character as a professional relationship. Because
the seminar members were more interesting and ready to engage
themselves on a deeper level than the members of some other parent
groups, but perhaps also because the leader responded to and was
intrigued by these factors, the temptation to get involved on a more
personal level was considerable. The meetings did not lack in
opportunities to do this either. For instance, the leader was told,
whenever a seminar had started, that most group members went out
for coffee, after each meeting, and spent another hour or so continuing the discussions. Again, whenever a new seminar started
and when group members introduced themselves, they usually added:
"call me..." (giving their first name). Because the leader had
decided that any closer involvement on her part would not be helpful
to the seminar members, she had worked out specific methods of
handling such incidents. For instance, when she was told about the
postsession discussions, she expressed her pleasure that seminar
members enjoyed being with each other. Similarly, when she
addressed group members, she always used their last names. It is
interesting that all the members of the seminars "got the message"
because if the statement about the postsession discussions contained
a veiled inquiry about the leader's joining the group, no direct invitation was ever extended to her. On one occasion when a group member had joined the seminar at one of its later meetings and wanted to
know "how do we call each other here?", she was told in a kindly
fashion: "we call each other by our first names, but Mrs. Pollak
calls us by our last names, of course." This statement was not
challenged by the new group member, nor was the leader ever asked
by anyone to call the group members by their first names. If this
had happened, she would have explained that she prefers to call
adults by their last names in a professional relationship.
The leader had clarified what limits to set to her relationship
to group members by determining what their major problems were
and how she could best help them. These are, of course, always
the criteria for such a decision, along with some insight into one's
own personality, and its professional assets and liabilities. While
the seminar members had unmet dependency needs, which the members of other adult groups had had also, these needs were combined
with strong elements of aggression, and were related more to inner

conflicts and to personality disturbance than to the conflicts which, for instance, the presence of a handicapped child brings. The outer circumstances of the lives of the seminar members made it important to encourage them to be independent and to help them to develop their potential and their opportunities for making new lives for themselves. For that reason, leadership had to be more geared to encouraging independence of thought and of action than to meeting the dependency needs and needs for closer and supporting relationships of the group members. Contributing to that goal for at least some of the members would be more helpful to them than to meet the needs for closeness which could be met more appropriately by other persons.

The leader thought also that clarifying confusion, encouraging self-knowledge, understanding of others, independence of thought and of action, trying out new solutions, and finding new ways of shaping one's life should be goals of leadership because the seminar members had opportunities for doing this, which were denied to the parents of handicapped children. The latters' problems could be helped to a certain degree but there was less likelihood of basic change in the reality situation of the handicapped child and of his family than might be within reach of a divorced or widowed person, if that person could be helped to use more constructively his or her opportunities for a more satisfying present or future life.

Another problem of leadership was to be found in the fact that many seminar members had had therapeutic experiences, were familiar with psychological and psychiatric terminology, and sometimes used it in the meetings. This was acceptable, if it was used to clarify a point under discussion, or as a short-cut which implied, of course, that all members of the group were familiar with it, a fact which had to be ascertained by the leader. Very often, however, such statements were either made to impress the less well informed group members--and perhaps also the leader--or even more often to cut short further exploration of the point under discussion. When such exploration needed to be continued because it was indicated in view of the goals of this discussion, the leader's responsibility was to see to it that this happened. When the members of one's group use such terminology, one may sometimes feel challenged to prove that one is as cognizant of it as the learned group member is; while this is an understandable reaction, it is one that needs to be curbed. One's professional competence--or the lack of it--becomes quite apparent to group members as one works with them. This tendency to use psychological or psychiatric terms was another characteristic of this group; although many parents of handicapped children had also had therapeutic experiences, they referred to them in the meetings with the leader very occasionally only, if at all, nor did they use psychological or psychiatric terminology.

Because many seminar members were well educated, well read, and familiar with programs for continued education, and perhaps also for more personal reasons, suggestions were made a few times of using a different method in the meetings, which would be more in line with formal education. One such suggestion was to assign a question to a member so that he or she could report to the group on his findings at the next meeting; another was of using personality tests, to be administered by oneself or by the group members to each other. These suggestions were usually made by persons who had joined the group fairly recently, and the leader might have acted upon them, if they had not been contrary to the purpose of the seminars, and also contrary to the wishes of the other group members. Since a meeting at which a person reports on his readings on a specific question is much easier to lead than a very rapid and free-wheeling discussion of personal problems, the leader was a little tempted sometimes to follow through on them, but her better judgment prevailed.

Following is the report on a meeting which is taken from the Eighteenth Seminar of the group.

SESSION V

February 6, 1967: Eighteen seminar members attended this meeting. One of them (Mrs. U.) was new to the group; she was a friend of Mrs. G., and would like to join the seminar for its last three sessions. In addition to these two group members, those present today were Mrs. B., Mr. C., Mrs. Cc., Mrs. Ccc., Mr. D., Mrs. Dd., Mrs. E., Mrs. Gg., Mrs. H., Mrs. Hh., Mr. J., Mrs. L., Mrs. M., Mrs. Mm., Mr. P., and Mrs. R.

Nine of the eighteen group members had attended previous seminars: Mrs. B., Mrs. Cc., Mrs. Ccc., Mr. J., Mrs. Hh., Mrs. L., Mrs. M., Mr. P., and Mrs. R.

Five of the eighteen group members were widowed: Mrs. G., Mrs. H., Mr. P., Mrs. R., and Mrs. U.

Two group members were separated: Mrs. D. and Mrs. L.

Mr. J. had been widowed, had married again, and the second marriage had ended in divorce.

The other ten group members were divorced.

The group was a racial and religious mix.

I summarized, in about ten minutes what we had discussed last week in regard to the different problems which divorced and widowed persons were facing and in regard to the common problems they were facing. Another point I brought out in this summarization was the importance of not frittering

"The kids are with us" was a joke used by group members if someone started a discussion of problems with children. Since the demands on the parent's time and love had been brought up, this had been relevant to the question of the importance of having

away today for an uncertain future, but of finding the time and money and making the effort to do some of the things one enjoyed. I added that "the kids had been with us," last week and we had agreed that the single parent should not feel that he, or she, owed it to the children to spend all the time with them, partly because this was often not at all what the children wanted but also because it left the parent to face an empty life, once they were grown up.

enjoyable activities and a life of one's own.

I added that we had not talked very much about the ways in which one could make one's life interesting and rich in the present without planning for marriage at this point, and I asked if group members would like to discuss this today. No comments came, so I said, I guessed, that was not what the group members wanted, and I read to them a summary of the questions they had raised for discussion and asked what they would like to take up today. Mrs. Hh. took the initiative, suggesting we should discuss Sex Relations Outside of Marriage and this topic took up our session tonight. (Mrs. Hh. was much more relaxed in the ongoing seminar. Her stuttering was hardly noticeable and she spoke up much more frequently than she used to do.)

The sequence which seemed appropriate to the leader did not reflect the wishes of the group members, as their silence made clear.

Mrs. Hh. was one of the group members who had accepted a referral for individual therapy.

While group members had nodded when Mrs. Hh. made this suggestion, no one spoke up. I smiled and said--perhaps we should start by asking: "why do people have sex relations?" From this point on the discussion was under way. Comments made were "sex fills a need" (Mrs. R.), "It is normal and natural to have sex relations" (Mrs. H.), "sex relations are a sharing of love and of feeling" (Mr. J.). Mrs. M. said with what I thought,

If a group seems hesitant, the leader's smile is reassuring.

Discussions usually started very quickly with this group.

Mrs. M. was a very contributive group member who had also been very helpful in planning seminars, but her attitudes toward men were always negative. The leader had referred her for individual counseling at her request

because I knew her well, was "a dig at men" that "for many people, sex is a way of making a conquest." Mrs. Mm. commented that very often sex relations are "one way of seeking closeness." Mrs. Hh. who reacted to Mrs. M.'s comment, in my opinion, said: "To have sex relations proves to a woman that she is desirable." Mr. P. shook his head and said in his usual gentle way: "there are many other ways in which people can find reassurance and love."

Mrs. Mm. said: "a new person may wonder if your marriage went wrong because of problems with sex, and you may want to prove that this was not the reason for the marital failure." Mrs. G. said, almost explosively: "No, love is the best reason!" Mrs. Gg. added, with considerable feeling: "the desire for closeness--all of us have lost a marriage partner!" This was one of the few comments she made today. Both she and Mrs. L. are usually very quiet in the meetings but I thought they were unusually quiet today. I had the impression that the discussion of sex relations was quite difficult and also probably quite strange for them. I said to Mrs. Gg. that this was an excellent comment, and I added that everyone who had lost a husband or a wife knew the loneliness and the suffering which followed such a loss, and the difficulties which readjusting to a life without the marriage partner brought.

because Mrs. M. had a variety of other problems also.

Mr. P. was one of the older members of the group who had had a very tragic life. This, and his kindness, had endeared him to many of the other seminar members, who rarely questioned his comments, and took every opportunity to make him feel welcome, to invite him to their coffee hour, etc. He was very lonely and appreciated their interest.

The leader might well have reacted to Mrs. Mm.'s comment by bringing out that sex relations with one partner tend to be different from sex relations with another partner.

The desire of group members to limit their participation should be respected, in meetings of this nature, which are not therapeutic in intent. One can find many persons in groups and outside of groups who are in their forties, as these two group members happened to be, and to whom a discussion of sex relations is a strange phenomenon. While it may well be that this reflects some difficulties in the area of sex relations, it may also reflect the person's code for acceptable behavior, value system, and a way of life which is comfortable for them, and interference with these matters is not indicated.

Mrs. U. was another group member who was very quiet, but this was probably due to the fact that this was her first meeting with the group. She listened with interest; she kept turning her head toward the person who was speaking at the moment, which is always a sign of a group member's desire to follow the discussion. In the leader's opinion, she was less threatened by the topic than Mrs. Gg. and Mrs. L. were, and her participation in later meetings bore this out.

The leader might have picked up conformity in connection with having extra-marital sex relations, but since Mr. Dd. had a tendency to be "flip"--probably as a defense--it did not seem indicated to react to his comment. Fortunately, Mrs. Cc. did this, anyhow.

Mr. Dd. said, somewhat sarcastically, "conformity--everybody is doing it!" Mrs. E. added "sex is sometimes revenge," while Mrs. Cc. said "closeness, as B. (she used Mrs. Gg.'s first name) said. Sex is part of being close to another human being." She turned to Mr. Dd. and added: "conformity would not be enough reason for many of us to do, or not to do something!" He shrugged his shoulders, but did not reply.

Mr. D. then gave the discussion a new turn by saying: "perhaps we should look at some of the reasons why some people refuse to have sex relations outside of marriage." I said, that was a very good suggestion, and added that as often as we had discussed the general topic of sex relations outside of marriage, this particular question had not been raised before. I turned over Mr. D.'s question to group members, and answers came quickly. Mrs. Cc. mentioned "one's morals," Mrs. H. "fear of pregnancy," Mr. J. "fear of too much involvement," to which Mrs. G. reacted by adding "fear of rejection also!" Mr. D. mentioned "religious reasons," and it was at this point that Mrs. G. reminded us of our discussion of "clinical sex" in earlier seminars. She added: "I fought the idea--but I think it belongs here!"

If a new group member-- or a shy group member-- raises a question which is relevant, as Mr. D. did, such recognition usually encourages these group members to participate more freely.

The discussions of "clinical sex" had been heated, partly because such relations were unacceptable to some group members, but also because this was one question on which most women in the group disagreed with the men. The leader's goal had been to make group members aware of the fact that such relationships existed and could be satisfactory. Mrs. G. had been one of the group members who had rejected the concept at first; her bringing it up at this later point showed progress since she was now able to introduce it into the discussion. This was one example of a group member's learning as a result of her participation in the seminars.

The leader should have given credit to Mrs. G. for introducing this concept, but failed to do this. The very rapid interchange of comments was probably responsible for this failure, but this does not absolve the leader.

Since several group members whose first seminar this was looked puzzled, I explained what we had defined as "clinical sex," with some examples. Mr. D. had nodded several times, but said: "such clinical sex would be meaningless." Mr. J. disagreed, pointing out that "people seek satisfaction in different ways." Mrs. Cc. added "clinical sex might be satisfactory to the person who looks at sex in this way, that is as an experience without emotional involvement. But what about the other person?" Her question which she raised with considerable feeling, led to a discussion of whether one could tell what a sexual experience meant to one's partner.

Mrs. Ccc. said that many persons misrepresented themselves in other areas of their lives and could do this also in their approach to a possible sexual partner. Mr. Dd. doubted that you could misrepresent yourself in that area, to which Mr. J. replied: "oh sure, one could do that. One would only have to express feelings for the other person which one does not have." Mrs. Cc. commented that this was what she had meant, adding that many people are "consummate actors;" this applied to many areas of their relationships to others and how would one know ahead of time what to expect from such a person. She added: "perhaps you will only know after you have had the experience, and then you will be hurt." This started another discussion off.

Mr. D. replied that one would know ahead of time. "We know ourselves and, very often, we also know the other person, what they need or want." Mrs. Hh. thought that one could tell what the sex experience meant "because we have been married." She added, sometimes "the other partner wanted sex relations and if one did not feel like it, one played the part!" Mrs. G. added: "and before it comes to that part--now that I am older, I know a line when I hear one!" Mr. J. agreed with Mrs. Hh. and with Mrs. G. that "persons who had been married are more experienced and can usually spot a phony more easily!"

When no more comments came, I said, it was quite true that when a relationship was starting, one might not know what the other person was seeking from this relationship, and one might not know either

It was important that the leader formulate some of the often diffuse comments at this point, partly for clarification, and partly to "take the discussion a step further."

how far the other person was willing
to commit himself, or herself.

It was also true that the person
who wished to develop a relationship
would use the approach to the partner which was most likely to succeed, and that might, or might not,
include the misrepresentation which
had been mentioned. Certainly
everybody could be fooled, and one
was likely to be hurt if that happened. Being hurt was unfortunately,
a price which one had to pay sometimes, if one explored new situations, or moved into new relationships but, again, this was less
likely to happen if one attempted to
evaluate the situation and the people involved, and if one's actions
and decisions were based more on
the reality, and less on one's
wishful thinking.

Mr. Dd. said, with a smile:
"there is a barter system between
men and women, and if one offers
what the other wants, that should
be acceptable to both!" Mrs. Cc.
said with considerable impatience:
"We know that men and women
want something from each other.
That is not what we are talking about
now--we are talking about the situation where one person wants more
than the other can give, or wishes
to give. We agreed that we may
not realize this until we have
become involved with the person,
emotionally and sexually, and that
we will be hurt when we have such
an experience. I think it is very
important that we realize, as single
parents, that there are people who
are hesitant to commit themselves,
and that our willingness to involve
ourselves will not change that!"
Mrs. Cc. looked startled when she
had finished and added: "I cannot
remember having said so much
ever before in a meeting!" Mr. D.

Since the leader had decided
that the members of these
seminars would be helped best
by being encouraged to make
new and richer lives for themselves wherever possible, it
was important to stress that
pain often accompanied growth.

Because the lack of know-
ledge about oneself and about
other people was often accompanied by "wishful thinking,"
leader stressed the importance
of a realistic approach to
people and to situations, on
many occasions.

Mrs. Cc. had spoken with
great feeling, which may have
been caused by a personal
experience of the nature to
which she was making reference.
She did not put this into words,
and the other group members
respected the limits of self-
revelation which she had
drawn. The leader's assumption that Mrs. Cc. was referring to a personal experience
was based on her extensive
contact with Mrs. Cc. and on
her evaluation of Mrs. Cc. as
a woman and as a person.

Another clue was the length
of Mrs. Cc.'s statement,
because her comments, which
were frequent and helpful,
were always brief and very
rarely accompanied by a display of emotion.

The recognition of her con-
bution by some group members
and by the leader was indicated,
partly because her statement

replied: "you said it for all of us!" Several group members nodded to indicate agreement, and I said to Mrs. Cc. we were all indebted to her for such a clear and helpful statement.

I then asked if I might return to a question which was raised earlier tonight. When I was told to "go ahead" I said while we agreed that one might be fooled--or might wish to fool oneself--about the extent of the other person's commitment to a relationship, I doubted that one could remain unaware of this after having had sex relations, unless one wished to close one's eyes in this matter. If one became aware of the sexual partner's involvement, or lack of involvement in the relationship, one would then have to decide whether one wished to continue the relationship on these terms, or did not wish to continue it.

Mrs. E. spoke up in some agitation and said: "but there should be a commitment between two people. How often can one go through these revolting experiences, through these disappointments in the next twenty years?" Mr. D. said "we must keep in mind that many of us are hesitant to involve ourselves in new relationships--we are the non-involved people." Mrs. Ccc. said: "I am older than many of you and I have learned to accept persons on their own terms. Sometimes, a relationship with people who just want to have a good time together is much easier, and I am on such terms with some of my male friends." Mrs. E. was shocked and said: "I expect a man to honor his courtship." Mrs. Cc. said: "what courtship? He just wants to see a movie with you!" Mr. J. agreed; very often he asked a

was helpful to the discussion, and partly because it offered to Mrs. Cc. reassurance and support in relation to her difficult experience in that area.

The leader had the feeling that the question of whether one could tell what a sexual experience meant to the partner, had been "left dangling," and it seemed important to clarify it, along with the possible choices one had in such a situation.

Mrs. Ccc. was obviously trying to help Mrs. E. who was distressed and also younger and more naive than some of the other members of this group.

Mrs. Cc.'s reaction was quite different; she was annoyed at Mrs. E.'s persistence.

woman he knew to go to a movie or
to a party with him "but I do not
intend to court her. Would you
refuse to go out with a man on that
basis?" Mrs. E. said that this had
never happened to her. Mrs. G.
turned to her and said: "perhaps
you expect more from the relationship than the other person is willing
to put into it." Mrs. M. asked,
with a smile: "do the men who
take you out tell you they want to
court you?" Mrs. E. said, "of
course not," and Mr. D. said, very
kindly: "Do not tease her, you
know very well that no man would
use those words!"

Since Mrs. E. was obviously
baffled and troubled, I said: "all
of us who have been getting together many times should keep in
mind that much of what we say in
our meetings is new and often puzzling to our new friends. What
Mrs. E. has expressed, if I understand her well, is her disappointment if relationships do not develop
as she had hoped they would. The
only 'cures' for such situations
seem to be 'going slowly,' that is,
giving oneself time, if one moves
into a new relationship and next,
attempting to understand the other
person, his expectations of the
relationship and his willingness to
involve himself in it. One cannot
take for granted that the partner in
a love or sex relationship must be
committed to the same extent to
which one is, and one always has
the choice of continuing a relationship, or of terminating it."

The leader thought it appropriate to intervene at this point,
partly because Mrs. E. needed
support, but also because she
would probably accept the
leader's statement, as backed
by professional knowledge,
more readily than the contributions of the other group members,
who were really saying the same
thing.

If some of the leader's statements were repetitive, this was
due to the difficult question
which was under discussion, and
to the fact that the statements
were so new to some group
members, and so little to
their taste too!

I was ready to move the discussion, but Mrs. E. said, very
plaintively: "but I still don't know--
how often can one get entangled in
such relationships?" Mrs. Cc.
answered: "that will depend on how
long it is also possible to have rela-

This statement bears out
some of the assumptions
made above about Mrs. Cc.'s
personal experiences.

tionships which do not lead to marriage, and to enjoy them. "Mrs. E. replied: "but that would get you into a total emotional mess!" Mrs. G. replied: "No, we said we should not do anything if we are not comfortable with it. Do you remember Mrs. N.'s problem a few weeks ago? We agreed that just because A can do something and be comfortable with it, does not mean that B must be able to do the same comfortably also!"

Mr. J. said: "we should not forget that our feelings can change too. One year from now, we may handle a similar situation very differently." Mrs. M. replied with some contempt: "teen-agers do that, we are adults." Mrs. G. disagreed with her, pointing to "the change in my emotions and attitudes" which she is undergoing now, and which she attributed to "what I have learned in our meetings." Several other group members made similar comments about the meetings.

I said, it was good to hear that our meetings had been helpful, and I added that certainly no one should do what did not feel right for him or for her, as we brought out when Mrs. N. shared her concern with the group. I added, it was true that many of us thought differently about certain matters than we did at another point in our lives, and a realistic appraisal of a situation by an adult which resulted in a changed decision, was different from the shifting moods of teen-agers. At different stages in one's life, or at different stages in a relationship to another person, one should feel free to reverse an earlier decision, if that was the thing to do.

Mrs. E. then asked if she could

It happens quite frequently that a positive comment about a learning experience leads to additional comments of this kind, perhaps because this stimulates the other group members to express their appreciation, perhaps also because of some unconscious jealousy toward the group member who took the initiative, and because of the wish "not to be outdone."

Mrs. N.'s problem had been that a young man, who lived abroad, had asked her to visit him and had offered to send her the fare. While some of her friends had seen nothing wrong in accepting this offer, she had been very troubled, and unable to make her decision without bringing it to the group.

The leader felt that she should stress the difference between teen-agers and adults in the area of decision making, as well as the right of adults to change their minds in line with the goals for this group, as previously described.

The group members who

raise another question. "You know much more than I, and I want to learn." She was encouraged to do this by several group members who reminded Mrs. E. that they had met many times and, again, positive comments were made about the sessions.

I said, with a smile, this was the night "when the seminar gets bouquets" and asked Mrs. E. what was on her mind. She wanted to know if she was "wrong" when she was so troubled if she was expected "to become entangled" after three dates. Mr. J. replied: "if that is the way you feel, it is not wrong." Mrs. M. added: "you know, some women use sex as a bait to get dates and that is why many men expect you to become entangled with them." Mrs. Ccc. replied: "men use dinner and going to the theatre as a bait also." Mrs. G. said: "I disagree. Some men play the game very differently. They create the desire in the woman!"

I commented that I would like to make something clear "just in case I need to do this, and perhaps this is not necessary." It might not be the food or the setting which created the desire--rather, it might be being admired, being important, being wanted which created the desire. Mrs. Cc. added: "and the desire may be here before the date. We make it sound as if women had something that men wanted, but that men don't have anything that women want!"

Mrs. B., who as I knew from her previous participation, was both naive and had bitter feelings about the male sex, then spoke up with vehemence. "A man may pretend: I love you but you cannot trust him until he has signed!" When I asked her what she meant,

responded to Mrs. E.'s question were supportive and also patient with her. Her real desire to learn as well as her youth and a certain childlike quality may have been the reasons for these reactions.

Mrs. E. may well have been troubled by such requests for sexual relationships because of her desire to agree, a desire with which her upbringing or her problems in this, or in other areas, may have been in conflict. She did not elaborate and her question was discussed by some other group members without probing into the matter further. This was another instance where the limits as drawn by a group member were observed by the other participants in the discussion.

she said: "signed that he will marry you. You should not submit to a man before he marries you!" She got red when she made that remark.

Mrs. Cc. said: "now, now." Mr. J., Mrs. G., and Mrs. Ccc. spoke up simultaneously; what they were saying was a protest against Mrs. B.'s statement. She was getting ready to reply and she was also getting more and more annoyed, and I said, perhaps I could be helpful at this point. We should keep in mind, first of all, that marriage was a meaningless formality only, unless one wished to be married to that particular person and wished to share their life because one loved him, or her. Next, one should not look at sex as "submitting to a man," because women as well as men had sexual drives and sought sexual satisfaction. For many people sexual relations had to be part of love relations to give them happiness or fulfillment, but for some other people this was not necessary. The decision to have sex relations outside of marriage was a personal one and people would vary greatly in the stand they took. Last, we should also remember that we had said many times that "sex is a cheap commodity," which means that it was possible for almost any man or any woman to find a sexual partner. I elaborated on these points somewhat, and I tried to make them with "a light touch."

Mrs. Hh. said: "I remember that we talked about this in earlier seminars. It is a myth that men have to try hard to get sex relations. Sex is a cheap commodity--and it is available to everyone." Mr. C. made one of his rare comments: "Would this be what we called 'clinical sex?'" Mrs. Cc. replied:

Because Mrs. B. was upset and also because the leader knew that she was unlikely to change her negative evaluation of men as a result of any reactions to her statement, the leader thought it more important to reformulate for the total group some fundamental concepts of relationships between the sexes. She also suspected that some of the less outspoken members of the group might perhaps not disagree very much with Mrs. B's point of view. While Mrs. B. did not reply to the leader's comments, she was obviously annoyed by them. But this is an example of a situation when the feelings of one group member must be disregarded in order to be helpful to the other group members.

This was an exchange between two group members of different degrees of intelligence and of life experience, and the fact that one felt free to ask, and that the other replied in a kindly fashion, showed the acceptance and good relationship of group

"It can be clinical sex, but it can also be the kind of relationship between a man and a woman who like each other and who also have sexual relationships." Mr. C. nodded and said: "Thank you."

Since our time was up, I said that we had covered a lot of ground tonight, and asked if I might bring out a last thought which applied to the area of sexual relationships. When I was told that I should, I developed the concept that a person might control what he or she did but could not control what the other person should do in that situation. I outlined this more fully than I am recording it, and this started another discussion.

Mr. J. said: "your fantasies about the other person will interfere." Mrs. G. commented: "what you said, Mrs. Pollak, is a hard lesson to learn." Mrs. Ccc. added: "that is true. Most persons cannot accept this, and I was one of them, until we talked about this in our previous seminars." Mr. C. said a little plaintively: "but your feelings would affect the other person." Mrs. Hh. replied: "you mean, you hope that they would affect the other person in the way in which you would like them to change?" Mr. D. said: "that is what we have been talking about. If one hopes for a change of heart, because one is more involved than the partner, that may happen, but it need not happen." Mrs. M. asked: "how detached can you be? It is difficult to terminate a relationship." Mr. J. turned to her and said: "You told me the other day that you were becoming more detached. All of us need to become more detached, more objective."

I said, I would like to apologize because I had not made clear what I was trying to bring out, which was members.

Expecting more than one is ready to give seemed to be an approach to relations to other people which was common to many group members. Since this leads to disappointment and conflict, the leader seized the opportunity to spell out this concept.

that the other person might well
and, furthermore, had a right to
react in specific ways if one limited
a relationship, for instance, if one
did not wish to include sex relationships. One could not have it both
ways in the give and take of relations to others, that was, one could
not limit what one offered and was
ready to give, and then expect the
partner to offer and to give more.
Also, if a love relationship, or a
dating relationship did not meet
the needs of and was not satisfactory
to the other person, one could not
expect that person to remain tied
to such a relationship, just as one
was not tied to it, oneself, under
such conditions.

I terminated the meeting at this
point while group members straigh-
tened out the Board Room, emptied
ashtrays, etc., as they usually did.

Since the Board Room was
often used the next morning,
group members had accepted
these responsibilities, which
the leader discussed, whenever a seminar started.

XIV
Realistic and Unrealistic Expectations of Adult Sons and Daughters

Since there is great concern about ways to reach people who could use help with their problems, but who are not activated enough to seek such help, the meetings described in this chapter should be of interest to many professional and paraprofessional persons who are faced with this challenge. The retired persons who were exposed to the discussion of problems with adult children were not motivated in the sense that they had requested such help. They came to a Recreation Center to play cards, or to attend social affairs, such as parties, or to an occasional movie showing. The Center gave them an opportunity to leave their homes, which had few amenities and were sometimes only rented rooms. They took the discussions described below "in their stride," much as they would have taken any other program there. The attitudes of most of the persons who came to the Recreation Center were, at best, passive and tolerant of their exposure to this experience; they would certainly not have traveled any distance nor gone to an unfamiliar setting to seek it as did the participants in the discussion series described in the next chapter. This was known to the Director of the Center and to the writer, both of whom agreed to take a chance with the group. Their decision was sound because a number of group members could be involved in a meaningful discussion at the group's second meeting. How this came about is described in this chapter.

CHARACTERISTICS OF GROUP MEMBERS

Without exception, the members of this group were lower class by economic, educational, and social standards. They lived on Social Security primarily; a few more fortunate people had small pensions to supplement it. Most of the men had been factory workers and a majority of the women had been similarly employed during a large part of their adult lives. Education was limited to grammar school; only a very few had attended high school, and no one had graduated from it.

The members of this group lived in close proximity to the Recreation Center, in a part of Philadelphia where many factories were located. Home and place of employment had always been very

253

close and they were attached to their immediate neighborhood. One
man had preferred to have repairs made to his home, which amounted
to almost its total value, rather than to move. The group members
were hesitant to go to other parts of the city, except when this was
absolutely necessary. This hesitancy was not due so much to fears
of being mugged, which so many old--and younger--persons have in
these days of increasing crime; rather, it was based on the experience
of their earlier lives, which had centered around this geographical
area.

For the foreign born group members, this timidity was probably due to the well known desire of persons with little knowledge of
English and with little education to cling to a part of the town where
they find people of similar background. The American born group
members, who were mostly of Polish or German origin, may have
been motivated by a preference for surroundings with which one is
familiar, a preference which many members of low socioeconomic
background share. The habit of staying close to home may have been
reinforced, in the past, by the longer work week which gave little
opportunity for leisure and for the exploration of what the city outside of one's immediate neighborhood might have to offer. Financial
considerations may also have played a part here, because most group
members had raised large families on small incomes, so that expenses
for carfare might have been another deterrent for such ventures in
earlier years.

Group members were about half Protestants and half Catholics.
Because more members of minority groups had moved into the area
in recent years, a number of them were black. Puerto Ricans did
not attend the Center's programs for older people, however, probably
because these families were usually much younger. Most persons
who came to the meetings were in their eighties; the average age of
participants was seventy two. The sixty and seventy year olds were
often referred to by their seniors as "the youngsters." The living
arrangements of group members reflected their economic situation.
Owning one's home was a considerable achievement and was always
mentioned with pride. In the past, group members had done various
things to make this possible, such as taking boarders, and keeping
up the mortgage payments was the most frequently given reason for
a wife's having gone to work. One way of making ends meet now,
which many widowed and single women in the group mentioned, was
to rent rooms in their homes. This seemed to serve a twofold purpose in some instances; in addition to making it possible to keep one's
home, it was also a way of meeting men with a view to marriage.
Again in contrast with the retired persons described in the next
chapter, marriage or remarriage were possibilities which some participants in this meeting were willing to consider, or at least to
discuss.

The concerns of the members of this group were very limited,
however. They did not include some of the problems with which almost
all retired persons cope, such as the loss of old friends and the

importance of making new friends, ways of meeting people, coping
with loneliness, finding new and interesting activities. These topics
were of prime concern for the members of the group which is presented in the following chapter; they were taken up again and again,
and from all angles in many of their meetings. The writer can only
speculate on the reason for the lack of interest in these areas of
adjustment to the later years of the Recreation Center group. It is
in line with many of the characteristics of the group which are outlined below, such as timidity, resistance to change, a rigid approach
to life in general, which makes it difficult for many older people to
"adapt to new roles or to modify roles to new requirements and
situations" (Streib and Schneider, 1961, p. 169). This lack of interest
was probably due, most of all, however, to the overwhelming concern
of the married group members with their relationships to their adult
children and grandchildren, which were always described as unsatisfactory. The frustration which the group members were experiencing
in these areas was the reason why they returned to these topics so
often, and why they were brought up in many cases without any connection with the question with which the group was attempting to deal
at a given moment. Their disappointment was reflected in such comments as: "you work all your life to raise them and what do you get, "
"they live in the same town, and they don't come to see you, " "Thank
God for Social Security--you don't depend on your children, " "they
don't show you respect, " "they don't care what happens to you. "
(During these discussions, many group members who did not have
any children "chimed in" with negative comments about young people
in general.) One man commented: "I keep them guessing;" he explained
that his children do not know how much money he has, nor whether
he owns his home "clear. " He implied that in this fashion, self-
interest motivated them to pay him some attention and to visit him
occasionally. Denial accompanied some of the group members'
statements about their children; it came out in such comments as:
"I wouldn't want to visit them" (although that group member's earlier
references to his children had made it clear that he was longing to
be asked to do that) and "once a week is enough. " In the latter
instance, the woman who made this statement had described enviously
a close relationship which one of her neighbors has with her grandchildren: "they are in and out of the house all the time. " She had
added quickly that this would be "too much mess for me. "

 While some members of the group would have welcomed closer
relationships to their children, living with them--either in one's own
home, or in the children's home--was a way of life to which they
reacted negatively only, and often with considerable fear. Examples
were given of such arrangements which had not worked out; invariably,
the aged parent had been the victim, and the adult children were to
blame. One man described the sad fate of a parent who had given
his house to his daughter and son-in-law; when the daughter died, the
son-in-law said to his new wife: "Throw the old man out!" A woman
described the struggles of a friend who went to live with her daughter

"two women in the house are two bosses--it doesn't work." Comments were made that "old and young don't belong together;" "the children don't want you;" "the young ones are out for what they can get." It was significant that personal experiences of this kind were not mentioned; the examples group members gave were always of what had happened to a friend or to a former neighbor. In the writer's opinion, the mores of group members encouraged "keeping your troubles to yourself, " especially if these troubles involved members of one's own family. It is well known that children of low socio-economic background are taught to be "close-mouthed" about family matters. According to these mores, however, generalized statements about children may be made, as long as personal experiences are excluded from the discussions.

Many group members were apprehensive about becoming dependent on their children, either because of loss of income, or because of ill health and increasing infirmities. The latter fear is, of course, one which many older persons from all walks of life share. They worried about rising prices, which was realistic, but they were also troubled about less realistic possibilities, such as not receiving Social Security benefits or pensions because the funds available for these payments would be exhausted. These fears were understandable, even if unrealistic, because the group members had lived through the depression, had seen banks fail, and had little trust in the reliability of the provisions made for their financial security.

Statements about children who supported their aged parents today were again made without any reference to one's own family, but the younger generation was always described as reluctant or even refusing to assume such responsibilities. It was evident that those group members who mentioned such situations distrusted the willingness of adult children to be of help to parents in need of financial assistance or of physical care. The distrust of one's children's willingness to be of help to aged parents was often compared to the obligations which many group members had assumed toward their own parents. One man mentioned having supported his mother for twenty six years; she lived with him and his wife, "today, young people would not do that!" Other group members gave similar examples; often comments were added: "we had respect for our parents, " "they worked hard to raise us and we owed them a home." The acceptance of such obligations was undoubtedly due to the feeling of moral obligation of group members, but it was also due to the lack of financial provisions for the preceding generations, when Social Security did not exist, and pensions for former blue collar workers were a rare exception. Another factor which reinforced this feeling was the stigma attached to the poorhouse, which might otherwise have been the last resource for the old people, as well as the religious teachings which favored the discharge of filial obligations.

Marital relationships were not discussed as openly as relationships to adult children, probably because the married couples in the group did not wish to do this in the presence of the marriage partner.

When reference was made to marriage, it showed that not only husbands, but wives as well, believed in a distribution of roles, in which activities such as cleaning, cooking, washing dishes, and shopping were the woman's job. The wives who mentioned their husbands' retirement in connection with their daily tasks did not encourage the assistance of the latter with these chores; they were jealous of their prerogatives of running the house and of their position in the home and family. Comments about any help from husbands were guarded and often derogatory. One man, on the other hand, commented that if his wife asks him what he wants for dinner, he replies: "that's your job, not mine." Some husbands also conveyed the feeling that their wives did not welcome their presence at home; remarks about attendance at the Center such as: "you like to get out, you are under foot sometimes" bore this out.

Neither husbands nor wives discussed marriage in terms of an emotionally meaningful relationship. The tangible components of marriage--a clean home, good meals, some financial security, especially if the wife was working also--were foremost in the minds of group members. Not expressed but probably also seen as advantages of marriage were the opportunity for regular sexual relationships. Cultural factors were reflected in this approach to marriage, since many older persons from low economic and social background, especially those born abroad, tend to see marriage more in these terms than as a way of satisfying one's needs for love and for close ties to a member of the other sex.

Similar attitudes about marriage were expressed by some of the unmarried or widowed women in the group who were renting rooms to "gentlemen," as they stressed, to make ends meet. They mentioned that their neighbors and friends joked about their roomers, and talked about their being boy friends, or possible future husbands. When these group members indicated that they might consider getting married, they never made reference to companionship, or to not being lonely anymore, much less to love. Rather, marriage was seen as being of financial advantage: "he has a pension," "with two incomes you live better."

Distrust was a group characteristic which was apparent also in other areas of life than in regard to one's income. Distrust of people with education was expressed very openly; the latter were perceived as different, not really interested in the problems of "people like us" and they were sometimes also accused of taking unfair advantage of group members. This distrust may have had its roots in their earlier experiences when they felt--and in some cases may have been--at a disadvantage in their dealings with landlords, lawyers, banks, etc., especially if a language barrier existed, or if the American way of doing things differed from that of their home country. A low self-image may also have been responsible for that negative attitude toward people whom the group members considered to be better off in some way--be it by education, or by income, or by still being a member of the employed part of the population.

Although the members of the group would probably not have put this into words, much less used these particular words, they were aware that "traditional values surround work... and that a job bestows social identification" (Ohrbach, 1963, p. 392).

The onset of senility, and some brain damage which may occur in the later years, are other causes for some of the distrust and suspicion which are personality characteristics of many older people.

The fact that many immigrants find it more difficult to adjust to old age, because of "the remoteness of their families and family identifications and the foreignness of their values and mores in many spheres" (Yarrow, 1963, p. 211) may also have found expression in the distrust of many group members. The different values and mores were certainly in part the cause of their problems with their adult children, who had grown up in this country.

While distrust of others existed, it did not take the form of interracial conflict. This may have been due to the fact that such conflict had not been part of the warp and woof of life during the active years of the group members, although conflicts between nationality groups had existed at that time. The writer is inclined to think that being old and being poor, or at least having to live on very limited budgets, united the members of this group, and was of greater importance to them than racial identity and racial strife are to many younger segments of the population.

Another characteristic of the group was their tendency to dwell on the past, and this too was to be expected. The past was not described so much as a better time, for instance, with more income, but rather in terms of achievement, of what they had done on their jobs, rising early and working late hours. They took pride in having worked hard and compared this very often to the "soft life" of people who are doing the same kind of work today.

The past was also discussed in terms of the ways in which they had taken care of their aged parents, as previously mentioned. The parents were sometimes described, condescendingly, as having "leaned on their children--it must be terrible to be dependent on one's children," and also as having been "old fashioned." "My mother wore an old wrapper around the house all the time. She wore her hair in a bun--she was old when she was forty." The woman who said this pointed to her hairdo with pride and added: "I never let myself go!"

This pride in one's appearance was another characteristic of most members of this group. Men and women were neatly dressed; the latter made some attempts to follow the fashion trends, as far as their limited means permitted. Particular attention was paid by many women to their hairdos; they preferred tight permanent waves and somewhat rigid sets, which were often admired by the other women. The use of cosmetics, however, was limited to face powder; only two or three of the more daring women wore a bit of lipstick.

The timidity which was described previously as one reason why group members clung to their neighborhood was apparent in other areas of their lives also. Most of them were hesitant about trying anything new, for instance as far as foods or food preparation were concerned. The attachment to foods with which one has long been familiar has, of course, dynamic reasons; to the members of this group, it represented the security of earlier life experiences, when they had not been threatened by age, by retirement, by their children's behavior, and by the changing mores of the world around them.

Almost all the members of this group were equally hesitant in regard to trying out new activities in retirement. Hobbies had not been part of their earlier lives; they had spent long hours earning a modest living and had not had much leisure in the past. Furthermore, the emphasis on using one's free time to develop one's talents, for one's self-enrichment and own satisfaction did not exist when they were young. During their working years, going to taprooms, playing cards, and attending the meetings of the ethnic organizations or labor unions to which they belonged were the usual pastimes for men from the lower socioeconomic class. Now that they were retired, they continued with most of these activities, but they did not add new ones. While some group members had skills that they could have adapted for use at this stage of their lives--something which many members of the group of retired persons described in the next chapter had done--this takes imagination as well as courage and it seemed beyond their capacity.

Timidity was often accompanied by resistance to change which led to a rigid approach to many problems. Group members were given to pragmatic statements such as: "young and old don't get along," "we're too old to change," "everything would be all right if we had more money." The latter statement was also an expression of their feelings and fantasies about money, which are described below. The writer's attempts to get group members to discuss these points of view were not very successful, probably because the discussion of abstract issues was new to them and threatening, like everything that was unfamiliar, and also because some group members were not sure that "talking does any good," as one of them phrased it.

Not only were most members of the group hesitant in developing new interests and resistant to exposing themselves to new points of view, they were also less interested in some of their earlier activities. For instance, when they mentioned having gone to meetings of their unions, this seemed to be more a matter of habit than of involvement, although many group members had been strongly identified with the labor movement during their working years. Similarly, the news of the day, or any political issues, seemed to be of little interest; any reference to the political scene was made only in connection with Social Security, that is, with reference to "the politicians" who did not see to it that payments were high enough.

When religion was mentioned, it became apparent that many group members had strong ties to their churches. In some cases, however, the writer had the impression that the religious faith did not seem as meaningful as the identification with a specific church

in which they worshiped for many years, and with the priest or pastor
with whom they had had contacts during that time, who had baptized,
and often also married, their children. Such a more personalized
relationship was in line with the tendency of many members of this
group to concentrate on the concrete and tangible rather than on concepts, ideas and beliefs, a tendency which was mentioned previously.
In any event, the outward forms of worship--for instance, church
attendance--were important to them and were observed, and so were
holidays, such as Christmas or Easter. Incidentally, the observance
of holidays was not due to the fact that they were the occasion for
family reunions. Because the relationships of most group members
to their adult children were unsatisfactory, references to such reunions
were usually negative ones, with such comments as: "you are left
with the dishes, " "it's better to be by yourself, " "we're too old for
all that noise. "

The question which preyed on the minds of most group members almost as much as the relationships with their families was that
of money. They brought it up in many, again often farfetched, connections; they also tended to see a larger income as the answer to all
their problems, often also to their problems with their children and
grandchildren. Money seemed to them the key to a life where they
would receive not only the tangible benefits which it can buy, but also
the respect and the attention of those around them. Some of their concern with money was due to their marginal income; a great part of
their efforts went into making ends meet. Next, an income of their
own represented independence to them, independence from their
families, if they had any, and independence in the sense of not having
to go into a home. They equated the latter with "the poorhouse, " with
all the stigma which had been attached to living there when they had
been young. Last but not least, if one has very little of anything,
this possession usually seems doubly precious, and its possible loss
doubly threatening. Whether the attitudes of their children would
have been different if the group members had had more money, is a
moot question, but parents who are old and who have a marginal
income are more likely to become a liability to their adult children
than parents who are well off and who have more funds available for
medical or other emergencies. Certainly many members of the group
must have thought along similar lines, because they had approved of
the group member who had said: "I keep them guessing" and had
admired his shrewdness very much.

GOALS OF THE DISCUSSION SERIES

The Director of the Center, who was very familiar with the
group members, and the writer agreed that the lack of motivation of
most of them, along with their personality traits, made it unlikely
that much learning--much less any change in depth--would occur.
An exposure to new ideas, however, should be attempted because

many of the Center's users were dissatisfied with their relationships
to their adult children, a state of affairs which brought them unhap-
piness and robbed them of the enjoyment of some of the assets which
the later years can bring. Since they had few interests and led con-
stricted lives, they tended to dwell on their family relationships and
on their real or imaginary grievances without attempting to find solutions to these problems.

With this situation in mind, we planned to give to group members
opportunities to ventilate their negative feelings about their families,
while "taking them a step" beyond this, for instance, by comparing
their own experiences as young adults to those of their adult children.
Additional goals were to help them to get a better understanding of
the point of view of the younger generation, to explore better ways
of relating to them, and to lead them to see how their own attitudes
and expectations of these relations contributed to their problems with
their adult children.

The two meetings which are analyzed in the present chapter
will demonstrate that group members were exposed to some new ideas,
such as that of change and its effects as an important factor in their
own and their children's life situations, and some of them accepted
this. The ventilation of negative feelings occurred very readily, as
could be expected, and some group members were helped to understand the point of view and the attitudes of their adult children better,
by comparing them to their own experiences with their parents, when
they were growing up. The goal of leading the group to an awareness
of the role which their own attitudes and expectations played in the
creation of their problems with their adult sons and daughters, however, could not be attained.

THE RELATIONSHIP OF GROUP MEMBERS TO THE LEADER

The members of this group related very guardedly to the leader.
Several factors accounted for this: One was their lack of motivation,
since people who are well motivated are more likely to relate to the
professional person who is offering help with their problems; the other
was the general distrust of people with more education than they had,
who came from a different background and whom they looked upon as
being unable to understand them. Needless to say, this was also an
expression of their hostility toward, and envy of, people whom they
considered to be better off. Furthermore, male and female were
sharply divided in the world of group members and male supremacy
had been part and parcel of their beliefs and their mores throughout
their lives, so that the writer's being a woman was probably another
reason why many group members found it difficult to accept her.
Contrary to many other difficulties of working with this group which
the Director of the Center and the leader had anticipated, they had
not taken into consideration the sex of the leader, first, because
many group members had accepted nurses and other female staff

members of the Center in individual contacts, and, second, because
the writer had offered leadership to groups of retired persons from
similar backgrounds before without experiencing this problem. In
regard to the first point, one can only speculate that the group situation reinforced any bias against a woman's taking leadership, or at
least made it less admissible to accept what she had to offer and to
suggest. As regards her earlier and more successful experiences,
the leader may well have been too aware of the problems which this
group presented, and this sometimes prevents one from doing one's
professional best. Last but not least, the author functioned best in
a positive atmosphere, that is, in a situation when most group members accepted her and her professional contribution, and related
positively to her so that her leadership of the Center group may not
have been as helpful as it might have been. The interaction between
leader and group members is affected by many subtle, often unconscious, factors and the leader's inner questions about what he, or
she, has to offer to a specific group with its accompanying fear of
failure are very relevant in that connection.

SOME SPECIAL PROBLEMS OF THE LEADER FOR GROUPS OF RETIRED PERSONS FROM LOW SOCIOECONOMIC BACKGROUND

While a leader must always adapt his techniques to a specific
group, this is even more important with a group such as the one
described above. This adaptation required going slowly in exposing
the group to new ideas, because they were not receptive to and often
suspicious of them. It also made it necessary to let pass some
statements which group members made because they would have been
alienated if they had felt challenged in too many of their thought and
behavior patterns.

Going slowly had to be coupled with a more directive approach
than the one which the leader had used in the work with other groups,
such as the parents of physically handicapped children, for instance.
Many old people have a tendency to let their thoughts wander and do
not make efforts to concentrate on the topic under discussion, especially if such concentration might lead to some unpleasant discovery
about oneself, as may happen if one examines the relationships one
has to one's adult children. Impairment of memory in the aged often
accounts for these wanderings also, so that "bringing back" the discussion is more essential with some groups of older people than it
is with many other groups. Many older people also have a shorter
attention span than in earlier years and, for all these reasons, the
work with groups of aged people usually requires more refocusing,
more formulation, and often also more repetition of what has been
brought out in the discussion.

Other potential problems in the work with older persons are
the sometimes conscious, but more often unconscious, feelings of
the group leader. Old age and the aging process arouse a variety of

reactions not only in the old persons, but also in those around them and it is essential that the professional person who offers help to older people do not reject or be threatened by them. A negative attitude to aged persons is often the result of conflicts which the helping person experienced with his own parents or with which he is still coping now. Should this be the case, an awareness of these problems is essential in order that they may be understood, controlled, and, most important, kept out of one's professional work.

It is equally essential that the helping person be not swayed by any positive feelings for or identification with the younger generation, as represented by the adult children of the group members, or their grandchildren. Because the participants were acutely aware of the generation gap, although they did not use this term, such an identification would have reinforced their negative attitudes toward younger people in general, and would have acted adversely upon any relationship to the leader which might be developing. What the members of this group needed most was the feeling of being understood in a world which most of them could not understand anymore. If, along with such understanding, some positive feelings for them could be conveyed, that would be the most helpful experience which could be offered to them.

Last, but not least, the leader had to take into account the group members' negative attitudes toward educated people. The language used needed to be simple, and the words familiar ones. While some people with little education can accept it, if they do not know some of the words used by the leader, provided they are explained in an easy and not condescending fashion, most members of the Center group would have seen this matter in a very different light, namely as additional proof of the leader's lack of understanding of them and of their problems.

THE DISCUSSION SERIES: ITS PLANNING AND SETTING, GROUP SIZE AND GROUP COMPOSITION

The principle of involving the members of a group into the planning process is excellent, and some of the most productive group activities are its result. This was not feasible with the Recreation Center group, however, because their own plans were invariably limited to social occasions, such as parties and, even there, group members did not show much initiative or much imagination. In line with their general attitudes, they preferred the well known to any experimentation. If they had been asked whether they would like to have some group discussions, for instance, on getting older and what that means for a person, they would, in the judgment of the Center staff, have reacted negatively and expressed preference for their accustomed recreational activities. Hindsight--which is always valuable although it can only be applied to the future and does not obliterate past mistakes--tells the writer that an initial approach related to financial problems, perhaps with someone from the Social Security office as a speaker, might have yielded better results in the long run. Because of their concern about their finances, the group members would probably have come to a meeting of this nature eagerly, and their interest could then have been used to plan additional meetings on other topics later on. Since this book reports on what took place, however, and not on what one wishes one had done, it must be stated that planning for the discussion series was done by the professional staff of the Recreation Center and by the writer, without the help of those who would attend the meeting.

The Center staff briefed the leader on the background and the problems of the persons who were likely to come to the meetings. They would be only a part of the population served since a number of the Center's users were known to come only for one or two activities, which might be to play cards, for some men, and to sew and to have coffee, for some women. This briefing was helpful, since the usual procedure of having group members fill out registration sheets could not be followed, mostly because the written word, and sometimes also the spoken word, were not always used with ease by the group members. Having to fill out forms of any kind was a procedure which many of them disliked and distrusted. The possible topics which group members might wish to take up were culled from the description of group members and of their problems which the professional staff shared with the leader.

Next, it seemed that a special approach might help to mobilize the group, or at least to attract them to a meeting. Movies had been shown at the Center several times, usually travelogues or movies dealing with food preparation; these programs had attracted a fairly large group. On the principle that one could expect considerable attrition of the Recreation Center group, as the meetings progressed, because of the members' lack of initial motivation, anything which would bring out a large group at the beginning of the series was well worth trying. It was decided, therefore, to show a movie at the group's first meeting.

Beyond securing a good sized group, part of which would hopefully come to later meetings also, the movie had a second purpose, namely, to set the stage, so to speak, for the discussions which were to follow. For that reason, it had to present some phase in the lives of older people, and preferably of older people from the same socio-economic background as the group members. It should do this in a realistic but nonthreatening way, while at the same time stimulating their thinking and their reactions. The common background would facilitate the identification of the audience with the persons and problems presented in the movie. While it is true that family relationship problems are universal, and are not restricted to persons of comparable background, it is easier for people with little imagination, such as the members of the Recreation Center group were, to make a connection between what they see and themselves, if they are faced with people and situations which are part of their own life experience.

The selection of a movie for a group always requires careful attention, and the professional people who were planning this meeting devoted considerable time to it. They pooled their knowledge of available movies, and decided to use "Three Grandmothers." This movie shows how three women handle the problems of the later years differently, partly because they live in and adjust to three different countries and cultures--Canada, Brazil, and Nigeria--and partly because they bring to these problems different approaches and different solutions.

The setting selected was the meeting room of the Center, because it was large enough to accommodate about seventy five people, that being the number of persons who usually came to a movie showing. A smaller room was reserved for the later meeting of the group which we did not expect to exceed twenty, so that people would be sitting close together and would not feel lost in a large and half empty room. Refreshments were not included in the plans for the meetings, partly because the meeting time followed lunch and partly because group members tended to get quite involved in the serving and the consuming of coffee and cake, with the consequence that this interrupted and often put an end to anything they happened to have been doing before.

One o'clock was chosen as the starting time because most group members preferred to come to the Center during the early afternoon, so that one to three, or one to four o'clock was the time of peak attendance. Meetings were scheduled for an hour, but would last longer, depending on the group members' response. The Center staff, who were quite experienced in preparing announcements of their various activities, offered to prepare some publicity for the meetings with the writer. Here, too, the emphasis was on conforming to patterns with which group members were familiar, and which were, therefore, likely to appeal to them.

About two thirds of the total population which the Center served were married couples, or widows and widowers; the balance were mostly women who had never been married. Additional information on the composition of the group in regard to economic and social background was given previously in this chapter.

Following is the record of two meetings with the Recreation Center group.

SESSION I

Record	Comments
April 8, 1970: Present were approximately thirty five group members; there was a slight preponderance of women in the group.	Sitting in the back of the room makes the presence of staff members less obtrusive while permitting them to

Also present were the Director of the Center, and three of his staff members. After introducing me, the Director joined his staff in the back of the room. They did not participate in the discussion as previously decided.

After my introduction, I said to the members of the group that I had been looking forward to our meeting, that we would see a movie which I hoped they would find interesting. It shows how some older people in different lands get along in later years, and when the movie is over, we can discuss what we have seen, or look at the ways in which life in this country is different from what we have seen, or whatever else the members of our group would like to talk about.

I added that I knew that they had enjoyed movies at other meetings. Many groups of retired persons with whom I had met had liked "Three Grandmothers," and the movie had started off some good discussions.

Next, I asked if we might have the movie and sat down in the first row.

The movie showing lasted half an hour; group members watched it in silence. When it was over, I stood up, turned to the group, and asked if any one had a question, or would like to say something? One woman said: "it was nice." I replied that I was glad that she had liked it and asked, what had she liked particularly, to which she did not reply. Nobody else spoke up.

observe and to feel included in the activity. Verbal participation, however, would not have been helpful to the leader's function, and might have distracted the group members also.

It is important to draw the attention of the audience to some major points of a movie which must, of course, be related to their major concerns or at least to their interests. Since many group members were foreign born, and all were very much aware of their cultural background, the life of older people in different countries was related to their own experiences.

Any reference to a group's past programs shows that the leader took some trouble in planning the present activity and is appreciated by its members. Sitting in the back might have been more convenient for the leader but she would have been less visibly part of the group had she done this.

In planning the meeting, it had been decided that it would be best to lead this discussion standing up as this would enable the group members to see and also to hear the leader better.

The woman who said: "it was nice" was only being polite, since she had nothing to add to her remark.

It happens sometimes that

a movie, or a play, or the leader's presentation of some material, is received in silence. This can imply many things such as inappropriateness or irrelevance of the materials, a language difficulty, hesitance of group members to involve themselves, unfamiliarity with the group discussion approach, or hostility. Most leaders assume that the latter is at work, but this need not be so. Whatever the reasons, it is important that the leader break this silence and help the group members to become involved in discussion.

I asked if group members would like to hear what occurred to me as I was watching the movie, and went on to outline some of the special points which the part about the Canadian grandmother makes, such as living by yourself, but remaining a part of your children's lives; inviting children and grandchildren; offering "special treats" to grandchildren, such as taking them on an outing; maintaining one's own interests such as going bowling with friends or playing the organ in church. My presentation lasted fifteen minutes; I had stopped at various points, asking if someone wished to say something, and when no one spoke up, if what I was saying was what the group members wanted to hear. The only reaction was that a man who sat in front told me to "go on," which I did.

It was clear that the members of this group needed much encouragement from the leader before they could participate, and these two questions--does anyone wish to say something? Is what I am saying what you want to hear, or shall I discuss something else?--convey such encouragement.

It is unlikely that group members would say "no" to this question, which makes it a good way to handle a silent audience.

As I was stopping again, the woman who had said: "it was nice" in regard to the movie spoke up, and this got the discussion underway. About fifteen persons participated.

Her contribution may well have been another expression of politeness and of her wish to "get the leader off the hook" but it started the discussion off, which indicated that the group members were now ready for it.

The first comment endorsed "living alone;" the reason given in answer to my question was: "you can come and go as you please." Another woman added: "if you live with your children, they want to know where you are going and what you are doing." A man said: "if you live alone, you are independent." Several other group members joined the discussion now, and their comments centered on their contacts with their children. One old man said: "it is time for the children to give to us;" a very old woman spoke with bitterness about "what the children should do for you, you have worked many years to raise them;" another man said: "you have to know when to get out;" he does this when his grandson, who is five, pulls a gun on him and his daughter says: "He is only a baby, don't mind him." He leaves, "if you say something, you only get in trouble."

One group member made reference to the Brazilian grandmother shown in the movie, and spoke about "the respect which children showed to their parents in the old country;" she made this comment with envy. A man replied to this by pointing out that "this was true for all of us over here too. We honored our parents." Another man added: "young people today, they don't do what they said they were going to do."

I commented, many older persons with whom I have met, have said what we have heard today-- namely that their grown up children don't seem to care very much about them, that they don't respect them very much, and that they raise their children very differently from the way in which they were raised. I added that I also know many peo-

The leader asked this question because no one followed up on the statement: "you should live by yourself."

Any one of these comments could have been selected by the leader for further exploration, but if a group gets going which found it difficult to get started, it is best not to interrupt the discussion. The leader does better to remember these comments for a later follow-up.

The leader recognized the concerns of group members at this point for several reasons. One was that she wished to help them to focus on the areas of their relationships to their children and grandchildren, a second that this gave her an opportunity to generalize these concerns, a third that she could

ple in their thirties and forties and they, in turn, complain that their parents don't understand them, and are hard to get along with. Would it help us here, if we tried to figure out what makes it difficult for the members of our group to understand their children and, perhaps, other young people also? Since I know from working with the younger people what bothers them, I could perhaps be a bridge and help our friends here to understand the younger generation a little better? (I made these comments in more detail but this was the gist of my statement.)

The man who had spoken about "honoring our parents" shrugged his shoulders and said: "talking don't help." He got up and left. This seemed to shock some of the group members; one of them said to me: "don't mind him," and the man's neighbor added: "he don't listen to nobody, he's stubborn." I said, it was all right if someone left because he did not think that talking about something would help. The woman who had said: "don't mind him" replied "maybe he won't listen, but if you come back, I want to hear what you can tell us." Several other group members nodded, and I said, I will certainly be back next week, and we can then try to find out, together, why it is sometimes difficult for old and young in a family to get along with each other. I added, there are many other things we can talk about also. "We can discuss whatever is on your minds, all it needs is that the question be brought up in the group."

Several group members had started to get up--one with the explanation that she had to see to the refreshments--and I terminated

now mention to the group members that their children--or the generation to which the latter belonged--found it equally difficult to understand them. She hoped that this would take them a step further, beyond complaining about their children and awaken their interest in understanding the younger generation. Last, but not least, the time for the meeting was almost up and it was important to end it with something constructive and thought provoking.

This reaction was unusual, since members of groups with more education usually express their dissatisfaction less openly. The irritability of many old people may have accounted for this abrupt departure, as well as some of the previously mentioned dislike for a woman in a leadership position.

The reaction was helpful, however, since it mobilized other group members to "rally" around the leader. This happened because they wanted to reassure her, perhaps also because they dislike the negative group member, or because they wished to become "teacher's pet," but whatever their reasons were, the results were desirable in that they strengthened the motivation of some group members to attend another meeting.

This formulation was a briefer repetion of what the leader had said previously. Such brief statements are easy

the meeting by saying that I was looking forward to meeting them next week.

The Director of the Center and I had a brief conference after the meeting. He offered to post an additional notice about next week's meeting which we agreed would be a helpful reminder. He was pleased with the participation of the group members and I told him that I shared these feelings.

to remember, and therefore helpful to old people, whose attention span tends to be short, and who also often suffer from loss or partial loss of memory.

The last sentence was made to encourage group members to think beyond their problems of family relationships for topics for further discussion.

Notices on bulletin boards in strategic locations listed the week's activities at the Center, in addition to flyers or newsletters which were sent to the homes of its members.

SESSION II

April 15, 1970: Fourteen group members attended this meeting; two of them were men. Also present were two staff members of the Center, who sat in the back of the room. The Director of the Center was out of town. We met in the large room where we had had our first meeting; no smaller room was available.

I welcomed back the members of the group, said it was nice that so many "of our friends" were free to come and asked if everybody had been here last week. Two women said that they had not been able "to make it" last week. I said, since I had not met them, I would like to introduce myself which I did. (I

The larger proportion of women present today was in line with the cultural traditions of the group, which assigned going to meetings--except for union or other organizational meetings--to women. The man who had said: "talking don't help" had probably reflected the opinion of some other men who had been present, although they had been too polite to put this into words.

A smaller room would have been preferable, as it would have given an opportunity for more informal seating.

The leader was attempting here to convey to group members her acceptance of and interest in them. The offer to summarize last week's discussion--couched in the term "bring back"--was made with the same intent, but it also served several other purposes:

gave only my name and the name of the agency.) Next, I asked if the members of the group would like to introduce themselves: "many people come to the Center and perhaps you have not all met before." Group members did this, although some spoke very softly, so that I could not catch their names.

No one added anything or made any comment, and I went on to ask if I should "bring back" to the group, briefly, what we had discussed last week; several group members nodded, and one woman said: "that will be a nice was of starting."

My summarization lasted about fifteen minutes; I interrupted it when a group member asked a question and, from here on, the discussion was under way. About half the group members spoke up.

I stressed in my presentation that it was often very difficult for older people to understand the ways of their grown up children, because many young people lived very differently from the way in which their parents lived. They had different ideas about marriage, or about how to raise children. They also might talk very informally to their parents, and it might seem as if they did not respect them. Much of this might hurt the older people, particularly if they felt they deserved better from their children, because they acted so differently toward their own parents. (I said all this in more detail, of course.)

I added that as I was getting ready for our meeting, I had been thinking back myself, and I wondered--was it new that old and young lived differently, did things differently, or was that true when our friends here were young themselves? It was at this point that the group members spoke up.

refreshing the memory of group members, helping the new group members to move into the group, and stressing those aspects of last week's discussion which were most closely related to the problems of group members.

Stressing the different ways in which younger people today live served several purposes also: first, it was recognition of a factual development, second, it generalized the problem which an individual group member had, and third, generalization usually enables people to face their problems in a calmer and more objective fashion.

Few approaches are as helpful in working with older people on their problems of family relationships with their adult children as the exploration of the older generation's conflicts with their own parents. One can take for granted that such conflicts existed, although

One woman, Miss N., said: "it was different for our parents. They had no Social Security, we had to take care of them." Another, Mrs. L., added: "my parents lived with me when they were old. They were my responsibility." Mr. C. added: "we did our duty-- the young ones today, they don't want you around." (He stressed "we".) Another group member said: "they don't like what you say, and they don't like what you do."

Mrs. A., the group member who had encouraged me to start the meeting off, replied: "well, they have their own ways," and Mrs. McC., who, as I learned later, was her sister with whom she lives, added: "we must remember they were brought up in different times." I said, I was glad that one of our friends here had mentioned "different times"--had times been different when they were young? Mrs. L. replied: "do you mean, was it different for us from what it had been for our parents?" I said, that was what I was trying to say, and thanked her "for making it clear."

Mrs. McC. said: "my parents did not want me to go out like my friends did." Mrs. A. turned to her and said: "remember how they did not want you to marry Jim because he liked his glass of beer?" She explained to the group that "he made a wonderful husband, but our parents, they were set against any kind of drinking, even a glass of beer." Mr. C. turned to the sisters and asked: "but did you tell your parents off--like the young ones do today?" Mrs. Mcc. said: "well, I did marry Jim!" She added, quickly: "of course, I would not have spoken to them as young people speak to their parents

they may have been conveniently forgotten. If older people remember that their own parents were difficult to live with, because they were different, they usually are more ready to accept the different ways of their own adult children.

In similar fashion, it is very helpful if older people can discuss how they have grown up in a world which was different from that in which their own parents had grown up, and can recognize that this had created problems for them also. The similarity of their own experiences with that of their adult children often becomes clear in such discussions, at least to some group members.

Additional advantages of such discussions are the opportunities to reminisce, which older people enjoy, to ventilate their emotions, if they wish to do that, and also to put the past into perspective because many older people tend to see it through rose-colored glasses in contrast to the unsatisfactory present.

It was necessary to recognice that young people today often express less respect and talk in a more casual fashion to their elders, because this is true, and is also a frequent cause of conflict. The leader

today." I said it was very helpful that we had heard about Mrs. A.'s and Mrs. McC.'s parents, and their attitudes about drinking, because it shows that <u>parents and children disagreed also when our group members were growing up. I would agree that "most of us" would not have spoken up as bluntly as young people do today, but the fact remains--there was disagreement between the generations in earlier times also. Why was that so?</u>

Comments came quickly. "They looked at things differently;" "they did not want us to do things they had not done;" "the times had changed, and they did not go along with these changes;" "they could not understand them--how could they go along with something they did not understand?" (The last comment came from Mrs. A.)

I said, <u>we have heard some words which are very important when we try to find out why old and young don't agree. The words are "change" and "if you don't understand the change you cannot go along with it."</u> Perhaps that applies to us also, <u>and perhaps we should look together at some of the changes which are facing the younger generation today.</u>

Miss N. said: "Some things are wrong," and went on to talk about her nephew whose parents are in a home for the aged. "His father was my brother-in-law, his mother, who was my sister, died when he was just a kid." She had argued with her nephew that he "is not doing right by them," when his parents moved into that home. Several group members reacted to Miss N.'s story with questions: Were the parents ill, did they need special care? (yes); Had they lived

did not wish to dwell on this point, however, because this belonged in a discussion with adult children who could change their casual approach, if they wished, while the members of this group could do little, if anything, to remedy this situation.

The leader was glad that she could give credit to group members for their contributions at that point. This can only be done, however, if such credit is due, because dishonest praise is usually recognized as such and antagonizes rather than pleases the people to whom it is being offered.

Since going into a home is never very far from the thoughts of older people, especially if they do not have many financial resources, Miss N.'s story was bound to get a response from the other group members.

Food is, of course, very important to many older people, partly because it is often one of the few remaining pleasures but also because being fed meets emotional needs for

with their son before going to the home? (yes); Who was paying for the parents in the home? (Social Security, and the son contributed something also). Did they like it at the home? Miss N. did not know that, but she knew the name of the home, and Mr. B., the other man present, told the group that he had a friend in that home, that the latter liked the place, which looked cheerful, and where "he gets good food three times a day." He added that he would not mind going there "if I get sick." He also admonished Miss N. "not to make any judgments;" he meant, not to judge a place she had not been to.

Miss N. grew defensive and replied that she knew what she was talking about, adding "I'm no fool!" She was obviously very annoyed also at that point.

Before Mr. B. could answer-- he was all set to do this--I said, I would like to "pick up" many important things we had heard. First of all, we have one change here--Social Security is now part of our lives, and it makes it possible to finance different arrangements for one's old age. We also have something else that has changed: "going to a home" is not looked upon in the same way, as "going to the poorhouse was," in past years. Third, we have a change in the physical condition of the parents, and such a change may make it necessary to use the greater facilities for care, which a home usually offers. (I made these comments also in greater detail than recorded.)

Mrs. K., a frail looking little woman who had only listened so far, spoke up at that point. She said: "No home for me. I want to be

love and care. It is the first encounter with love for everybody as mentioned previously. Mr. B. was obviously reacting to the description of the home mostly in terms of the possibility of his needing such a place sometime in the future.

Irritability is a well known character trait of many elderly people.

"Going to the poorhouse" was something which was dreaded by members of the socioeconomic class to which the Center group belonged. It was dreaded not only because of the quality of the care offered there, but because of the stigma attached to ending one's life in this fashion. This implied being unwanted as well as having failed to make provisions for one's old age, and such improvidence was contrary to the ideals of being self-sufficient and independent to which many members of this group subscribed.

It was interesting that being independent got this animated and detailed response from Mrs. K. While many

independent." She went on to describe her living arrangements; she rents two rooms, and her roomers know that they are supposed to take out the garbage, to put up the storm windows, and to shop for her when the weather is bad. "I charge less rent and I look after them when they are sick." Mrs. A. replied admiringly: "You have it all worked out," adding that she and her sister "have always said that we will live together later on, and we do that now. We don't want to live with our children. We want to be independent like you."

I said, <u>many older people with whom I have been meeting want to be independent, and often they have worked out very good plans for doing that</u> "like our friends here."

Mrs. K. now gave her name and added "I don't know many people here." Several other group members told her it was nice to meet her and introduced themselves to her. I said, <u>what is it that attracts so many of us to a life of independence</u>? Mr. C. said: "you can do as you please--get up early or late, come home when you want to." Mrs. L. added: "sometimes you want to be by yourself with no one to bother you." Mrs. K. said: "My husband and I, we worked hard. We raised our children, and we bought our home. Now that he is gone, I don't want to be a burden to anyone; I want to live like I always lived, in my own home, with my own things." Miss N. commented: "the young ones, they make you throw out your things when you move in with them." Mrs. A. replied: "I guess what we have is old fashioned to them. But we are used to what we have, just as they are used to what they have."

I commented, we have heard

older people regress, in terms of becoming more dependent on others, she represented the other group of older people who struggle to maintain themselves independently, often against heavy odds. One can only speculate as to what accounts for these opposite approaches to the problem of aging, but it is an indication of Ego strength if one remains independent wherever and as long as this is realistically feasible.

The desire not to be a burden is often expressed, and it sometimes covers up a wish to have someone take care of one. The wish to live with one's own belongings is one which older people express very frequently. Separation from one's bed or one's favorite chair, for instance, is one of the most often voiced complaints of residents of old age homes, if they could not take these items with them.

Mrs. A. was one of the group members who showed some understanding of the reactions of young people to older persons. She was different from Miss N. and Mr. C. who were more negative toward the younger generation.

The economic and emotional

some excellent reasons why some
older people want to be independent,
and want to live by themselves:
the freedom to come and go as you
please, the opportunity to be by
oneself if one feels like it, living
as one used to live in one's own
home among one's own belongings.
I added, how had it been when our
group members were young--had
they enjoyed becoming independent?
Several of the women present nodded: Miss N. said: "that first pay-
check--that was great. Of course
I gave most of it to my father, I
was living at home, but I had some
money of my own now." Mrs. A.
talked about what she had bought
"with the money I had left. I bought
a box of candy, and I ate it, one
piece at a time. It lasted months.
I had never had a whole box of
candy before." Mrs. McC. mentioned the dress she bought "it was
one Jim and I picked out together."
Mr. B. said with some bitterness:
"my father took the money I earned.
If I wanted anything, I had to work
without his knowing it. My mother
covered up for me, but after a while,
I went on my own."

Mrs. K. then said: "you did
what your parents told you to do,
when you were young. If I didn't
mind my father..." (she made a
gesture, indicating he would have
hit her). Several group members
agreed: this is what would have
happened to them also. Mr. C.
added: "that's what's wrong with
the young ones today--nobody gives
them a good licking."

I said, we knew that one minded
one's parents when we were young.
One was told what to do, when to be
home, how much money one could
keep of one's earnings, and if the
parents objected to drinking, as we
heard from Mrs. McC. today, one

deprivation of some group
members was revealed in the
stories which Mrs. A. and
Mr. B. told. The latter also
showed the patriarchal and
authoritarian structure of the
family in which he had been
raised. Other members of
the group could probably have
told similar stories (Leslie,
1967, pp. 300-303).

Physical punishment was,
of course, part and parcel of
child raising methods at the
time when the members of this
group were growing up. Auto-
matic obedience was expected
(Miller and Riessman, 1964,
p. 31).

The leader interrupted the
discussion at this point so that
it would not turn to the topic of
the different--and, of course,
"poorer!"--methods of raising
children today. If she had had
a deeper relationship, she

did not drink either. Did things change when our group members got married, or when they went on their own, as Mr. B. did?

Mrs. McC. said, approvingly: "You remember our names." She went on to describe how she and her husband had both worked when they were married "until the children came." She added, with pride, that her children had gone to high school "so that they could get better jobs than we had." Her parents had not approved "but we did not want the children to have to work in a factory. There are times when you must do what you think is right." I said, with a smile: "and what about Jim's beer?" Mrs. McC. laughed and said: "oh, he had his beer when he wanted it." She added quickly: "of course, we did not have hard liquor in the house." Mr. B. asked in a truculent voice: "what's wrong with it, if you don't abuse it?" Before we could get into a discussion of hard liquor, I said, many people do not drink because their religion forbids it, or because they don't like it, and that is quite all right also, of course. I have been wondering if life changed for anyone else in the group when a person got married or left home.

Miss N. said: "I didn't leave home, I didn't get married." She turned to Mr. B. and said "you could do that, you were a man." She tossed her head and added: "not that I didn't get asked." Mr. C. turned to her and replied: "You could get married right now." Several of the married women present concurred with Mr. C. (Fortunately, Mr. B. did not reply, and no argument started between them.)

might have explored with them some of their reactions to their parents' attitudes to them when they had been young.

The recognition of a group member's individuality and uniqueness, which is implied in remembering the name of that person, is particularly important in the work with older people whose self-image is low and who often feel that they are being "lumped together" and devaluated because of their age.

Mrs. McC.'s comments showed that she wanted a better life for her children, wanted them to move up in the world, a goal of many blue collar workers of her generation. The leader should have recognized her efforts.

Since many older people have a tendency to lose the focus of a discussion, and are easily distracted from it, it is often necessary to see to it that they do not stray too much from the main topic of the meeting at any given point, which is what the leader was doing here.

Miss N.'s story reflects the different expectations of behavior for men and for women which were part of the mores at the time when she was young. She also showed some antagonism to Mr. B. because of his earlier remarks in connection with her story about her nephew.

These group members rallied to the support of Miss N., probably because they were also antagonistic to men,

Miss N. was pleased by these remarks and went on to say that when her parents "passed away," she sold their house and bought a smaller one "in the same neighborhood." She lived by herself and she still does. "I do as I like--no one can tell me what to do." I said, wasn't that nice, and Mrs. McC. said, very thoughtfully: "you know, when you got married, you could do things your way. You had your husband to mind, of course, but that was different from your parents telling you what to do." Mrs. K. replied: "of course it was different. They were old fashioned." Like the lady said--she pointed to Mrs. McC.--"you couldn't go out like your girl friends. My parents did not mind a glass of beer but they were strict about what we girls wore, and the boys could not smoke. I bought the first dress I liked after I was married."

Mrs. A. added: "of course, life wasn't easy, what with the children to raise and not much money. But my sister and I, we were never sorry we got married."

I said, wasn't it nice to hear some of our friends speak so warmly about their marriages? And, isn't it interesting that what made married life pleasant was partly the freedom to do what one wanted, to live one's own life, not to be bossed around anymore even when one is grown up and earns one's own money?

Mrs. A. laughed, as I paused, and said: "you have one boss--not

but also because she had not been as fortunate as they had been in getting married. A belittling attitude toward unmarried women was also part of the mores when the members of this group had been young.

The use of "passing away" if one speaks of death or dying, was another instance of group mores.

This was an example of the attachment of group members to the area in which they had been born and raised.

The leader missed an opportunity here to point out that marriage brought independence to the group members, but also new ties of affection to a husband or to a wife, to one's children. This could have been tied in with ways of including three generations in these interrelationships for the gain and enrichment of all concerned.

Mrs. A.'s comments offered a second opportunity to make the points listed above.

Mrs. A. could have been given "a little pat on the back"

two." She added, it had been hard for her parents "to see us live differently, and to see us raise our children differently. My girls were good girls and I raised them strict, but I listened when they told me something or asked me for something. If I had to say "no," I told them why. My parents didn't do that. You asked them and they said 'no,' and that was it." Mrs. McC. replied and I saw that she was getting defensive: "They meant well." I said, of course the parents meant well. It was just that they had grown up in a different world, and had different ideas about how to raise children, and about what young people should do, or should not do. They had the last word and they had full authority over their children, as long as they lived at home. All this had been right for them, because it was the way they had been raised, but it had been difficult for our group members who grew up in a different world. Could not the same be said for the children of our friends here? They too had grown up in a different world, hadn't they?

Mrs. K. said: "they want to be independent, just as we wanted to be independent, when we were grown up. We can't hold them back--and we shouldn't try!" She added that when her children and grandchildren visit her "I am glad. I don't complain that it's been a long time since their last visit. When they ask me, I give advice-- if they don't, I keep my mouth shut." Mrs. McC. replied: "you get along well with them, I'm sure, but it's hard not to say something when you think they are making a mistake." She turned to me and said: "what should you do if they make a mistake?" Before I could

for her excellent description of her family life, as well as for the methods she had used in raising her daughters. Another missed opportunity! The leader was too intent on pursuing the main question under discussion, and this prevented her from making full use of other interesting and meaningful points which some group members brought up.

The leader's recognition that the parents of the group members had meant well was appropriate, because sometimes group members who get defensive "close ranks," and that ends a discussion which could otherwise be helpful to them.

This was a direct attempt to relate the experience of the group members when they were growing up to the experience of their own adult children.

Mrs. K.'s remark showed that she went along with this attempt.

Mrs. McC. found this more difficult, as her comments show. Her question to the leader: "what should you do if they make a mistake?" was not asked in an aggressive fashion, by the way. Rather, she was bewildered and wanted help.

Although Miss N.'s point of view was not as helpful as that of other members of the group, her contributions were welcome to the leader as they kept the discussion moving.

answer, Miss N. spoke up and said: "that's how you learn." She went on to describe an experience she had had, when she had "trusted someone" who was "not to be trusted" and that taught her to be more careful. (I had the impression that she was talking about an experience with a man when she said this.) Mrs. K. said: "many people are not what they say they are!"

Before the discussion could get off onto the need to be careful in one's social relationships, I said, I was sorry that Miss N. had been disappointed in someone she had trusted, but as she said, "one learns by making mistakes." It may be difficult to stand by and to watch a son or a daughter make a mistake with their children or with their jobs but it does not help if one gets into an argument with them. And sometimes it turns out that they were right.

Mrs. A. said: "and they'll be thankful if you don't say: "I told you so!" My mother used to say that--I got mad when she did that." A woman who had not spoken up before and whose name I had not caught said: "they don't like it if you are right." Miss N. added: "if you say too much, they will tell you to mind your own business." Mrs. McC. replied: "but they are your children. It is not right for them to tell you off!" Mr. C. said: "the young ones, they don't care how they speak to you."

Since it was getting late, I said that our time was almost up, that I knew that the group members were ready to have coffee now as usual, and that I would only like to say something before they left, if that was all right with everybody? I was told to go on and I said, we

Since even well meaning attempts to prevent the younger generation from making mistakes tend to backfire, the leader wanted to encourage group members not to interfere in such situations.

This summary was based on the contributions of the group members, contributions which were made mostly as a result of the writer's asking "leading questions." This is a good technique to use with a group like the Center group,

talked about many things today and the most important one was probably that it had been difficult for most of our friends here to grow up, because this usually meant that they thought differently and acted differently from the way in which their parents had thought and acted. This was a disappointment to their parents but it was a necessary step for our group members who wanted to live their own lives and to be on their own. They wanted to marry whom they liked, they wanted to raise their children for the world in which they were living, and if they made mistakes, they wanted the right to make these mistakes. I turned to Mrs. McC. and said, everyone makes mistakes, and the kindest thing we can do is to overlook what happened. None of us want to be reminded of something we had not done well, and the same went for the young people about whom we were talking. They were not so different from us--the young people wanted to do the same things our friends here had done-- they wanted to be independent, to have the kind of marriages they liked, and to raise their children in the ways which they liked. It was true that one often knows better if one is older and has lived longer than one's children, but one must let them go their own way. (I made these points in greater detail than I am recording them.)

Mrs. A. said: "they will respect you more if you do." I said, I appreciated her saying this and I added: "they will also love you more, if they don't have to argue with you." Mrs. K. said: "you will be more welcome and you can see your grandchildren more often."

Several other group members nodded, and I said, that is so true,

which is not used to the discussion method, much less to drawing conclusions from material presented or to formulating concepts.

Encouraging older people to be interested in what goes

and <u>even if one does not have grand-</u>
<u>children, I am sure everyone knows</u>
<u>young people, and if one does not</u>
<u>get too worried about their "out-</u>
landish" <u>clothes and strange ways,</u>
<u>they can be very interesting and</u>
<u>they are one way of keeping in</u>
<u>touch with what goes on in the world</u>
<u>in which we live today</u>.

Several group members nodded,
while others did not look very con-
vinced, of course. Since some were
also getting up and were obviously
ready to leave, I said, I had enjoyed
meeting with them and was looking
forward to seeing them next week.

on around them is one way of
combatting the tendency to
withdrawal and disengagement
which is often a characteristic
of the aged.

XV
Enriching One's Life in Retirement

Age was the common denominator of this group, as it has been
that of the group described in the previous chapter. The age factor
was taken into account in various ways in the planning of ten discussion series. The flyers and posters which publicized these series
made reference to retirement and to the later years. The books
which were displayed at the meetings were selected for their appeal
to older persons. Outside speakers invited by the group's regular
leader were people who could discuss topics of interest to older persons, such as Social Security payments and regulations, employment
opportunities for older persons, hobbies which they might enjoy, and
good grooming and appropriate clothing for them.

The emphasis on the concerns and problems of older people was
effective because the participants were older persons only, with the
exception of a few persons who were working with older people and
who came to a meeting with the leader's permission. The other
exception was a graduate student who was working for a Master of
Social Service degree. She attended one discussion series because
she was interested in the problems of the aged and wrote a term
paper on her contacts with the group members.

The discussion series were sponsored by the Free Library of
Philadelphia and the groups met in one of the library branches. The
writer was the group's leader for the last eight of these discussion
series which totaled sixty four meetings. The discussion series were
planned with some representatives of the Free Library's administrative staff, with the librarian in whose branch the group met, and
with a Planning Committee of group members. This Committee consisted of about six persons, who had attended one and often several
discussion series. They were familiar with the group members'
interests and willing to help the librarian with some of the activities
connected with the distribution of publicity materials such as the
mailing of announcements and soliciting the permission of banks and
stores in the area to display posters.

The group met weekly in the early afternoon because group
members were entitled to lower carfare on public transportation at
that time, and also because many preferred to be home before dark
because of their concerns about being mugged, etc. Some group

members came from considerable distances and this too suggested the scheduling for the early afternoon. Again, taking into
account the preference of older people, this time for avoiding bad
weather, rain, snow, and icy streets with their physical hazards, the
discussion series were planned for the early fall. They started at
the end of September, so that they ended before Thanksgiving.
Another factor which made this desirable was that many older people went to spend that holiday with their families so that a later
start would have affected their ability to attend the meetings.

The library branch in which the discussion series were held
had been selected from among many others for a variety of reasons.
It was located in Center City within walking distance of many apartment houses which were increasingly attracting older people as
tenants. Some of these apartment houses were newly built and had
high rents, and the group members who lived in them were comfortably off financially. Other members of these groups with modest
or even with limited means were also living in the vicinity of this
library because many former one family dwellings, which had been
owned by wealthy people, had been converted into apartments as a
result of the move to the suburbs of their original owners. Also, a
union had built an apartment house, where rents were low, in the
neighborhood. Not in walking distance but in easy commuting distance by public transportation, were several public Housing Projects,
from which members of the group were also drawn. This library
was also selected because the librarian was very much interested in
offering a worthwhile and interesting activity to the many older persons who came, partly to borrow books, but also partly to sit there
because they had no other place to go. Another less important reason was the proximity to the writer's office. This reason is worth
mentioning because planning of any professional service must take
into account not only the needs of those to be served, but also the
existing resources on which one can draw, and such factors as travel
time.

CHARACTERISTICS OF GROUP MEMBERS

As could be expected, the persons who attended these discussion series had in common the problems of adjusting to the later
years. Most members of these groups were in their sixties, although
some were in their seventies, and a few were in their eighties.
Two members of these groups were in their fifties, but they had had
to retire early because of health problems. The persons who came
to an occasional meeting because of their professional interest in
working with older people were much younger. Since attendance at
the meetings was usually fairly large--and also fairly fluid for reasons which will be discussed later--the presence of these "outsiders"
did not interfere with the discussions.

In the discussion series from which the meeting presented here is taken, fifty four registration sheets were filled out by group members. They furnished some interesting information on group composition, although it was far from complete. This was due to the fact that some persons who attended the meetings did not fill out registration sheets, for a variety of reasons. Some had poor eyesight, a few were hesitant about giving any kind of information about themselves, apparently in the fear that they would be approached for other purposes, solicited for contributions, etc. Some group members who spoke English with an accent did not seem to trust their ability to write in English. Offers of help with these problems were usually refused, and the leader thought it best not to insist, because encouraging group members to attend the meetings and to use the professional service which she was offering was more important than to get additional information on group members. In addition, some of the group members who filled out registration sheets without difficulty often left spaces blank, especially those which dealt with age, or with living arrangements. This may have been due to a hesitancy to give this information or to the short attention span of many older persons; here, too, the leader did not insist upon the completion of registration sheets.

Eleven of the fifty four group members were men; seventeen of the forty three women had not been married. Thirty three group members listed themselves as living by themselves; six of them were men. The other twenty one group members lived mostly with spouses and, in a few instances, with siblings or with friends. The leader had the impression that some of the latter living arrangements were made because of the need to be close to someone which many older persons have. One group member expressed this by adding to her reply: "I live in the same apartment house as my sister. I like the feeling of having her close by, but we do not see each other every day, or even very often, only when we want to." In some other instances, such living arrangements with siblings or friends were a substitution for the death of a spouse.

Living in an apartment was preferred to living in a house; forty group members lived in apartments; again, six of them were men. All but two group members lived in the city. These findings were in line with the often observed changes in living arrangements, from one's house to an apartment which many older people make, once their children are grown up. They do this because they do not need so much space any more; because the task of keeping a house and perhaps a garden in good condition is getting too much for them, and very often they seem eager for the contacts with other tenants in these apartment buildings, many of whom tend to be in their own age group. Living in the city also makes it possible for older people to go to movies, concerts, theaters, and to the meetings of organizations to which they belong, without the expense, strain, and time spent on commuting.

The majority of group members had attended or completed high school and some group members had gone beyond that and had attended

or completed college. Three members of the group had taken graduate
courses in their chosen field.

The previous occupations of the participants varied considerably;
several had been employed as school teachers, bookkeepers, secretaries, nurses, and salesladies, but the group also had among its
members a retired executive of a large firm, a former public accoun-
tant, a retired personnel manager, two persons who used to teach on
the college level, as well as several retired weavers and tailors,
two former railroad workers, a retired carpenter, a former dress-
maker, and a retired furrier. As could be expected, many married
or widowed women in the group listed their former occupation as
"housewives," often with the comment "same" in reference to their
present activities. With the exception of one person who had retired
early, and who continued to work part-time as a pharmacist, the
members of this group were not gainfully employed, although some
of them were interested in finding part-time work.

In line with their different social and educational background--
and one may presume, their different financial situations--the
appearance of group members varied greatly. Many women were
well dressed and used cosmetics; others wore simple clothes and did
not have much variety in their apparel. The men's appearance ranged
from well cut and well kept business suits to old, but clean, work
clothes which they evidently wished to put to use as long as possible.
Most group members were American born, but a number of them were
not and spoke with an accent. The latter usually belonged to some
organizations for retired workers of certain trades, which were
located in the area; they were among the most faithful group members
who often brought relatives and friends to the meetings. As had been
the case with the parents of handicapped children, the common problems of aging and of the adjustment which aging brings unified the
group and bridged any difference in educational, social or financial
background of its members. The group members who seemed to be
better off financially listened with concern when those who were less
fortunate discussed the problems of making ends meet on a reduced
income. They also were careful to point out that they shared some
problems with the others in the group, for instance, in the areas of
family relationships or of social isolation.

Only a small proportion of the group members had physical
disabilities: one woman's speech was slurred, probably as the
result of a stroke; two group members used canes, two had poor
eyesight, one a hearing loss combined with a speech impediment,
and another a deformity of the spine. Four group members were
black; the location of the library may account for this small number.
Since many other group members traveled considerable distances to
attend the meetings, however, other factors--perhaps the expense
for carfare--may have been at work. The leader had the impression
that the black group members were mostly living on Social Security
with little extra money to spend. They came very regularly and were
accepted and made welcome by the other group members and attended

these discussion series for several years.

While it is, of course, not possible to give a description of the group which will fit every member, some common characteristics emerged as the meetings went on. Loneliness, often accompanied by depression and anxiety, feelings of not being needed and of not having anything to contribute which sometimes led to further isolation from other people, and a low self-image, were found very frequently. A tendency on the part of some less affluent group members to project their problems on their financial situation, was also evident, while the actual situation often showed that it was less "what a person had, " than "how one used what one had" which was the decisive factor in coping with these, as well as with most other problems.

As could be expected, illness and the prospect of physical disability were very threatening to many group members, especially--but not exclusively--to those who were living alone. The eagerness with which questions regarding health problems were raised when a physician had met with the group, as well as the response when questions about diet and exercise were discussed, were indications of these very understandable concerns. It was interesting that the mechanism of denial was the one which several group members used when they gave glowing descriptions of the loving care which friends had received in nursing homes. Since these group members as well as their friends happened to be living primarily on Social Security, the writer had her doubts about the accuracy of the description, but she respected the need to present something which group members might have to face, in positive terms. It was much more helpful that one group member mentioned using a professional service, such as counseling, if one should be faced with having to make such a decision, and the leader encouraged this approach to the problem.

The mutually supportive relationships which most members of the group developed to each other and which will be discussed more fully later on, were so much in evidence that they can well be regarded as another characteristic of this group. On the other hand, their relationships to their adult children and to their grandchildren were not enough of a concern to be classified in this fashion, although they were of course brought up in some meetings. Similarly, remarriage and marriage, which are often solutions to the problems of loneliness of many older people, were not concerns of group members. When the leader brought up these topics, their response made it clear that they did not include these steps in their plans for the future.

Another characteristic which is often attributed to older people, namely that of paying little attention to one's appearance, of being slovenly, and sometimes bizarre, was not in evidence for the members of this group either. Once or twice an old person "dropped in" who presented such an appearance, but although the leader made every new group member welcome and took a few minutes at the beginning of every meeting "to bring our new friends up to date, " these persons never came back. The writer ventures a guess that they were marginally adjusted older persons, who had withdrawn into a shell, except for an occasional foray into the outside world.

Although the numbers of men and women in these discussions series were too small to be a significant sample, a comparison of their concerns, interests, and attitudes showed that the women, especially those who were or had been married, found retirement easier than men. "Role continuity--housekeeping, interacting with relatives, going to church and participating in various other kinds of formal and informal relationships"--was not interrupted by the new way of life (Bock and Webber, 1972, p. 29; Lidz, 1968, p. 478).

The relationships of the married group members to their adult children and to their grandchildren were brought up, but only occasionally, quite in contrast to the group described in the preceding chapter, which was very much concerned and very disappointed with their relationships to these members of their families. The expectations of that group may have been greater, perhaps based on their own background as children of immigrant families, perhaps due to lacking understanding of the changing mores of today's world, and last, but not least, to their life styles, which offered them fewer outlets and fewer satisfactions for their emotional needs in such forms as social contacts and organizational activities (Loether, 1964, p. 525).

On those rare occasions when relationships to adult sons and daughters were discussed in the group presented here, it was felt that children owe their aged parents love and respect. Financial obligations were not mentioned. Perhaps those group members who received such support were hesitant to admit that they were financially dependent on their children. At any rate a considerable number of group members seemed well off, and were obviously not in need of such support. Care, in terms of physical care, was discussed often with considerable vehemence. Some group members thought that adult children should offer such care if one is incapacitated while others were opposed to such a solution to this problem. It was interesting that most group members made reference to the--positive or negative--experiences of their friends in these discussions, again probably because they were hesitant to reveal too much of their own situation.

Friendships, mostly how to make new friends in the later years, and how to meet people, were a greater concern to most members of these groups. These questions were discussed again and again, and with considerable involvement. They usually came up in connection with the group members' concerns about how to have a full life, that is, how to involve themselves in new relationships with people, and how to develop new interests and activities so that their newly acquired leisure would be fruitful and rewarding. Activities were discussed in broader terms than the often highly touted hobbies which are supposed to fill the lives of people after retirement, although those members of the group who enjoyed hobbies and who reported on them, were listened to with interest. In these discussions the different social, educational, and occupational backgrounds of the group members were very apparent; when volunteer activities came up, one man explained how he made available his administrative experience to small businessmen, while another told the group that he did carpentry work for a children's home. One woman in the group worked in the thrift shop of a hospital; another who had taught crafts when she was employed, did this now in a summer camp for deprived teenagers, and a third helped to take care of children in a day care center. The meeting which is presented in this chapter will show in more detail the concerns of most group members about how to enrich, and to use constructively, their later years, and the different approaches and the solutions which some found to this question which is one of the major problems of aging. This has been very well formulated by Lidz:

> Satisfaction after retirement concerns more than finding ways of filling days, and it involves a general attitude toward the end of life. For some it is not just a period of decline and waiting, even though they recognize their waning abilities and increasing limitations. It is still a period of growth when the experience and wisdom they have accumulated can be used and there is time to contemplate, observe, and join the many strands together (Lidz, 1968, p. 479).

The younger generation--relatives as well as those who were not related--was mentioned many times by group members and in a variety of contexts, and this interest can well be regarded as another characteristic of this group. The attitudes toward young people, however, varied considerably and ranged from involvement with them, acceptance of them, to censure and rejection. In the discussions of this topic, it was clear that older people who had a lively curiosity about the mores of the young, and an "open mind" along with a genuine interest in them, were accepted by them in return. As could also be expected, those group members who were negative and authoritarian in their approach to the young generation, who accused them of "expecting too much," of "getting married too young," etc. did not find such acceptance. Some of the latter group members mentioned how differently they had acted when they were young; again, this seemed to be more true for the less affluent and also for the foreign born members. The writer thought it likely that considerable envy of the younger generation might be covered up by this disapproval, and that the different mores of today might be threatening to the older group members and might undermine their confidence in their own way of life. This was not expressed openly and the leader did not think it appropriate to explore the meaning of these attitudes.

"The need to be with one's own kind," that is, with other older people, was a common characteristic of all members of this group. It was found in those who liked young people, members of their own families, or young friends and acquaintances, as well as in those who were not close to the younger generation. This was very understand-

able, because age is a common bond for many people, and not only
for older persons. One's concerns, interests, role in life, and problems are usually closely related to the age factor, and tend to change
with age. The members of this group received support from being
with other older people; they felt that they could share their concerns
and their problems with them and would be understood. In the writer's
opinion, the suggestions which group members offered to each other,
when specific questions were raised, were more readily accepted
because they came from their peers. While there were considerable
differences in the age of individual group members, these were never
brought out during the meetings. What group members stressed was
the common experience of having arrived at the later years, with their
role changes, such as retirement for those who had been employed,
or having raised their families for those who had children, or being
widowed if one had been married; with their physical problems, or at
least with their diminished physical capacity and diminishing vitality,
and with the problems of using their later years constructively and
with happiness for themselves. While the age of a person is certainly
not a decisive factor in his or her professional work, the writer had
the impression that it was helpful to the members of this group that
she had been in her fifties when she started to offer leadership to
them. She often used "we" in her remarks, and many group members
commented approvingly.

The attendance of group members at these meetings was more
fluid than that of other adult groups, such as parent groups. Bad
weather, rain or early snow, tended to keep group members at home
because of their concerns about catching colds or slipping on the pave-
ment. Unexpected visits from relatives had the same effect; this
was understandable because many group members were very eager
for these visits, especially if they were made by married children,
by grandchildren, or by siblings who did not live close by. Illness
itself took a greater toll from the members of this group than from
members of younger groups. Furthermore, and this presents a
special difficulty for many older persons in general, leaving home is
often more of an effort physically as well as emotionally for them
than for younger people. It means leaving an environment soothing
to a tired body, one has to mobilize oneself, to put down an interesting
book one is reading, or to turn off the television set if one is watching
an interesting program. Last but not least, many older people tend
to be forgetful and when the demands of employment or of taking care
of a family have ceased, schedules are more difficult to keep because
one day of the week tends to be very much like the other.

If one makes allowance for these factors, attendance was very
good. In the discussion series from which the meeting which is presented in this chapter was taken, attendance at the eight meetings
was 24, 20, 17, 20, 20, 16, 23, 19. Two group members attended
eight meetings and seven meetings, respectively; five group members attended six and five meetings, respectively; three group members attended four meetings; and five group members attended three

meetings. Nine group members attended two meetings, while twenty three persons attended one meeting only. The latter came mostly to one of the three meetings at which movies were being shown; these movies were publicized and attracted many regular users of the library as well as other people who had happened to see the publicity and who dropped in to watch the movie. In many instances, these persons left as soon as the movie had been shown and did not remain for the discussion of the movie which followed. A number of the persons who came to one meeting only were also the apparently marginally adjusted older persons who have been described previously.

GOALS OF THE DISCUSSION SERIES

The goals of the series were necessarily related to the main characteristics of group members. Becoming part of the group was seen as one way of relieving loneliness; the opportunity to voice one's problems and to share them with others would, hopefully, reduce some of the anxiety and depression which so many older people experience. In addition, this would also counteract the feeling of not having anything to contribute any more for those group members who offered suggestions for coping with these problems. Every effort was made to encourage the participants to get to know each other, and this was successful with many members of these groups. They started to stay after the meetings, talking to each other, and some group members also went out with each other for coffee after the meetings. In the repeated discussions of how to meet people and how to make new friends--a topic which is great concern to older people who as a rule lose many friends through death or through illness--the meetings were always mentioned as one way of making new friends.

The decrease in anxiety which group members might have felt was expressed by one participant who stated on his questionnaire, in reply to the inquiry as to whether the meetings had been helpful to him: "They instilled in me a bit of hope for the future, which looked barren and bleak for a long time." Another answered: "Directing my attention in many new ways--raising my spirits and encouraging me." The leader did not know who these group members were, but welcomed these statements. Any experience which draws the attention of an older person so that it gets channeled into new ways, is a positive one, in view of the tendency of many people to withdraw from their environment in their later years, a tendency which usually leads to isolation, stagnation, and a lessening of the person's capacity to cope with the problems which life brings to everyone.

Relieving the feeling of not having anything to contribute, of being useless was another goal, not only because such feelings are damaging to the self, but also because they are unrealistic most of the time. When group members discussed their activities in the later years, it was quite apparent that many of them offered a great deal to others in their relationships and in their interaction with members

of their families, with their friends, and to the community organizations in which they were active. Here, too, the exchange of experiences in these areas of their lives made other group members who
were less involved with such relationships and such activities aware
that such outlets for their abilities and for their energy existed and,
more so, that they were welcome when they mobilized themselves to
try these new approaches. A striking example of this happened when
one group member reported on her contacts with an employment agency
which specialized in placing retired persons in suitable jobs. Most
of them were part-time so that older persons would not find employment too strenuous and so that their Social Security incomes would
not be jeopardized. This agency gave tests to prospective applicants
for employment, and these tests had been frightening to the group
member who reported on her experience, as they were to many others
in the group. As things turned out, they led to her finding employment in a field which was different from that of her former endeavors.
Her example encouraged several other group members to get in touch
with the same agency, and their pride was great when they too could
report on having passed the tests. Incidentally, the desire to work
in a different area from that in which one had been employed during
one's earlier years, was one which was expressed quite as frequently
as was the wish to use one's previous competence and previous skills
in one's later years. Perhaps the old adage that "change is the spice
of life" applied here, but the writer ventures a guess that the persons
who had been successful in and satisfied with their work before, might
be inclined to continue it now, either on a part-time or on a voluntary
basis. It was interesting that those group members who were interested
in finding employment, wanted it to be part-time and preferred by
far employment which was temporary by definition, such as helping
out while someone was on vacation, or taking care of a house, or of
animals and plants while the owners were away. They stated very
clearly that they wished to be free of any commitment which would be
permanent, that they did not want the work primarily for the income
to be derived thereof, although it would be welcome, but that the work
should "bring a little variety into my life, " as one group member
expressed it.

Since activity brings people in contact with others, exposes
them to new ideas, and is a well known antidote for depression, one
of the goals of these discussion series was to make group members
aware of the variety of activities in which they could engage. This
was done through the medium of the discussions, but also by inviting
to the meeting other persons who had special expertise, for instance,
the director of a workshop which sold the products of older persons,
a well known horticulturist, and several persons who taught arts and
crafts in a variety of settings. Many group members reacted with
considerable interest to the presentations of these outside persons,
although the writer cannot give examples of any follow-through in
this instance.

Volunteer work, of which one thinks at once when meaningful

activities for the later years are mentioned and which was also presented to the group by an invited speaker, met with varied responses in the different discussion series. Some members of the groups were volunteering their services in a variety of settings, as previously described, and talked very positively about it, while a few others described their experiences in negative terms. From the writer's knowledge of the latter, they seemed to belong to the group of people whose expectations are high but who do not wish to give much of themselves. In any event, this disagreement about the returns from volunteer work made for lively discussions and this furthered the goal of bringing to the group the opportunities for activities which were theirs to use, if they so wished.

The writer made reference earlier in this chapter to the importance of "using what one has." In line with this, one goal of these discussions was to bring to the group members information about entertaining or stimulating programs which were available either for little money, or free of charge. Another goal was to help them to realize that if one has a small budget, it is important to set aside part of it so that one can enjoy these activities. Those group members who were more outgoing, or had had more interests of this nature throughout their lives, mentioned concerts, movies, free or otherwise, house tours, the sights of historical Philadelphia, as well as the publications which would give information about these matters. The problems of going out at night, which were always mentioned in that connection, were discussed in terms of "using what one has," that is, of allocating part of available funds for taking a taxi home, at least part of the way.

Encouraging group members to involve themselves in social relationships was also closely connected with the question of "using what one has." In the discussions of the necessary reciprocity of social relationships, if the latter are to be ongoing, it became quite clear that it was not the lack of money which prevented group members from entertaining friends, or from going to a movie or to a show with them, but their lack of skill in planning such activities by using their available resources to best advantage. "The cup of tea" became a symbol for entertaining friends at minimum expense. One member of this group who had little money but many friends explained to the others that she asked her friends to have tea with her.

It is possible, of course, that those group members who felt that they did not have the means for entertaining, did not really want to do this because they were not sure of having positive relationships with other people. It is also possible that they were withdrawing from relationships with others, as a form of the disengagement which is one of the ways in which many older people cope with the experience of aging (Cumming et al., 1961, pp. 15-105). The disruption of social relationships of many older people has been found to be one of the factors leading to suicide, and it can certainly be assumed that it contributes to the depression of the elderly in general (Bock and Webber, 1972, p. 28).

An additional goal of these discussion series was related to the different attitudes which people can bring to an identical experience, in this case, the attitude which older people can bring to the experience of the later years. Age is one of the factors in one's life which--like having a handicapped child--must be accepted. The way, however, in which it is accepted and incorporated will make all the difference in the person's happiness, or at least in his tolerance for these problems during the later years. His approach to aging and his attempts to cope with its problems can rob him of the pleasures which are his to enjoy or can make the later years enjoyable in spite of their difficulties. This is not achieved by glossing over these problems, or by denying their existence, but by facing them and by finding the best solutions for them. One of the leader's functions was to encourage group members to apply these solutions wherever possible. Unfortunately, knowing what to do is not automatically followed by doing it but one can only offer one's professional service and must leave the use made of it to those to whom it is offered.

THE RELATIONSHIPS OF GROUP MEMBERS TO THE LEADER

Since loneliness was a problem which many members of the group had in common, they were ready to relate positively to the leader. Brief individual contacts, either before or after the meetings, seemed to be an acceptable solution and one which satisfied the needs of group members. These contacts were often used to report on something which had happened in the interval between meetings--a visit from a grandchild, a trip by bus to a nearby point of interest, etc. The leader expressed her pleasure at such news, and encouraged the person who had had these enjoyable experiences to tell the group about it. Such reports often sparked discussions of related topics, and they also served to encourage the more timid group members to participate in the discussions, or to venture on such excursions. One tends to forget the hesitance of many older people to try new experiences, and the satisfaction it gives them when they have done this successfully. Reports of illness or of impending operations were received by the leader with expressions of sympathy, with an inquiry of where the group member would be so that the leader and the group could send her a Get Well card. The leader never visited the sick group member but members of the group sometimes followed through in this fashion, or sent Get Well messages of their own.

These contacts were brief because the leader did not plan to get involved in problems of group members which needed more intensive help. This was not possible because of the nature of the professional service she was offering, and because of the limitations it had, one of which was also that of time. Group members were aware of the counseling service which Family Service of Philadelphia offered, and several of them made use of it. The leader was also called by a few group members when emergencies arose, such as a friend's psychotic episode, and she did what was necessary to be of help in these situations. The calls indicated that the group members knew that they could count on the writer's interest and on her help, outside of her group discussion leadership, and that was exactly what she wished to convey.

Instead of encouraging a closer relationship to the leader she made every attempt to encourage closer relationships among group members. Many of them followed her lead, and some also took the initiative, for instance, by asking the leader for lists of all group members with their addresses and telephone numbers so that they could keep in touch with each other, by calling or visiting, in the intervals between the discussion series. Group members who were active in other organizations asked if they could announce special events before the meetings started. This served a twofold purpose, in the leader's opinion, in that it reinforced intergroup relationships and also brought new activities to the attention of group members. One very active Senior Citizen Club in Center City had been founded by one of the members of the earlier discussion series, and many group members joined it later on.

SOME SPECIAL PROBLEMS OF THE LEADER FOR GROUPS OF OLDER PERSONS

While these problems depend in the main on the personality of a particular leader, one that will be encountered frequently is a rejection of older people, based on fear of getting older oneself, or on other dynamic reasons such as unresolved parent-child conflicts. Another problem is a "false jollity," that is, the attempt to deny or to minimize the threat which aging, physical deterioration, along with the loss of employment, the loss of members of one's family, and the loss of friends, bring to a person. These threats, if brought out, need to be acknowledged, but this should be done, and can be done, in such a fashion that the person receives emotional support and is helped, as far as that is possible, to look for positive components in the situation and to find new means of coping. Admittedly this is not always easy, and sometimes it is not possible, but it is a rare situation which has only negative elements and which cannot be improved by the attitude of the person involved in it. If self-pity, depression, a resentful attitude toward younger persons can be replaced by a pride in one's achievements, past and present, by an involvement in the world around one and by an acceptance and enjoyment of other people, the later years can be more meaningful and more satisfying.

A third problem is the leader's inability to accept the limits within which older people can be helped. This is somewhat similar to the problems of the parents of handicapped children, in that aging brings with it immutable factors, such as the ones mentioned in the preceding paragraph. It is essential, in this writer's opinion, that group members be helped to express some of their negative or painful feelings about these matters, that the leader acknowledge the validity of such feelings, but that the discussion then go beyond this and take up possible ways of dealing with the difficulty the person is experiencing. Any attempt, however small, to cope with a problem enhances the individual's capacity to deal with additional problems, and is therefore an Ego strengthening experience.

Recognition of the limitations within which older people can be helped, along with the recognition of the dangers of becoming over-involved with the members of these groups, led the professional people involved in planning these series to adopt a specific format for them. The use of movies to start off discussions of specific topics was one, and it was successful because it helped group members to focus on such questions as the ability to change in the later years, the advantages and disadvantages of life today as compared with life when the group members were young; positive aspects of the later years such as being in control of one's time, being entitled to refuse to get involved in activities which one does not enjoy, etc. Another device was the introduction of outside persons as speakers who were experts on such topics as hobbies or gardening, as mentioned before, but also a representative of the Social Security office and the vice-president of a well known department store who spoke on becoming clothes and suitable grooming for older persons. Bringing these speakers to the group had additional benefits: it brought helpful information in areas in which the leader could not offer it; their coming made group members feel important and such feelings tended to affect low self-images positively; finally, it conveyed to them that other professional persons than the leader were interested in them also.

Following is the record of the fifth meeting with a group of retired persons, which is part of the tenth discussion series offered to them.

SESSION V

November 3, 1969: Twenty group members attended this meeting; two of them, Mr. and Mrs. B.G., had not attended the earlier meetings of this discussion series although they had come to meetings of earlier discussion series. The other group members present were: Mrs. K., Miss T., Miss E., Mrs. M., Miss K., Mr. W., Miss O'N., Miss C. who sat around the table, in the "first row," while the other group members sat in a circle in Mr. and Mrs. B.G. were the only married couple present; Mrs. G. was not related to them. Miss M. was not related to Mrs. M. Mr. W. and Mrs. W. were not man and wife, nor were they related. Mrs. M. and Mrs. G. were the two black group members who attended this session.

Eight of the women present were unmarried; a ninth had recently been divorced and

back of them. They were Miss R. who said she wanted to sit in the back because she has a cold, Miss F. who sat next to her, with the explanation "we are friends," Mrs. W., Mrs. G., Mrs. Sch., Miss M., Mrs. McK., Mrs. K., and Mr. N. and Miss J., who explained that Miss O., a friend of hers and another group member, had asked her to take notes because she could not come today. I offered her a seat next to me so that she would be more comfortable but she thought her notetaking might "distract the others."

I welcomed Mr. and Mrs. B.G. back to the meetings and then summarized the questions which group members had checked off for discussion on their registration sheets. Their choice of topic for today was: How to Live a Full Life in the Later Years, although group members "took off" from this topic into other areas of concern to them. The discussion of "The Full Life" covered Volunteer and Other Interesting Activities; the Importance of Learning to Adjust to Different Patterns of Life in Retirement, and of Concentrating on These Activities Which are of Interest to One. This gave me an opportunity to stress the Greater Freedom One has to Make Choices in the Later Years as One of the Assets of These Years.

Other areas discussed were What Can Other People Contribute to the Full Life in the Later Years: What Kind of People Would One

had asked everybody to call her by her maiden name, with the prefix "Miss." One of the two men was widowed, the other had never married. Six of the seven women present today who had listed themselves as Mrs. on the registration sheet lived by themselves; the seventh lived with a sister. She was widowed, as were two of the other women. Another was divorced, as the writer knew because she had also been a member of her discussion series for Parents Without Partners, which was described in an earlier chapter.

All but four group members (Mrs. G., Mrs. M., Mrs. McK., and Miss T.) had attended these discussion series in earlier years.

The leader did not summarize last week's discussion because the members of this group were likely to return to it, and she knew from her previous experience that the discussion of leisure time activities and of related topics would probably take up two or more sessions. Since a movie was to be shown at the seventh meeting, it was helpful that the group members had selected this topic for today. Had they not done this, the leader would have asked them to plan with her how the remaining four sessions were to be spent, and what main topics they wished to discuss in these meetings.

If a leader plans to review the material discussed at the next session, it is often helpful to list the main points which

Select for Closer Contacts; The
Importance of Not Giving in Too
Much to One's Bad Moods, and of
Not Complaining Too Much if One
Wants Other People to Like One;
The Many Ways in Which One Can
Meet New People; and The Impor-
tance of Accepting Brief and Cas-
ual Contacts with Other People also
Because They Can Contribute to
Making One's Day More Pleasant.

In addition, the group took up
Adjustments to New Situations, and
What Would Help One to Make Them,
as well as The Opportunities Which
the Later Years Bring to Find Out
About One's Talents or Skills Which
One Had Not Developed Before,
and the Importance of Realizing
That One Has Something to Offer
and to Contribute to Others.

In line with the discussion of
activities and of Mrs. K.'s ques-
tion: "How Do Other People Meet
the Problem of Going Out Alone at
Night?" I could bring out the point
that Even On A Tight Budget, One
Can Make Choices and Decide on
What One Wishes to Spend Money.
An additional statement I made was
that Another Advantage of the Later
Years is the Freedom to Indulge
Oneself because One is Free of
Certain Earlier Obligations. Sav-
ing Money to Leave to One's Chil-
dren, or to a Cause in Which One is
Interested, is One's Privilege But
It Is Not an Obligation.

were brought out in a meeting.
This also helps the leader and
the group in the following meeting to take up related questions
or concerns which were overlooked, or which occur to them
at that time.

Mr. W. started the discussion of
of "The Full Life" off by mentioning
"a man who has had a full-time job
and is told at the age of 65--we don't
need you." Finding meaningful
work, which need not be paid employment, is in his opinion "essential
to keep you out of the clutches of
depression and illness." When I
asked him what he was doing now,
Mr. W. told us that he has for the

It was important to ask
this question so that Mr. W.
would give the group more
specific information about his
work. The discussion of
generalities, such as the
importance of meaningful work,
can very easily lead to plati-
tudes, and it would also lack
concrete suggestions, along
with the example of how one

past eight years acted as secretary of an organization of businessmen. He helps plan their meetings and other activities, sends out notices, takes care of other correspondence, collects dues. "This has meant so much to me."

Mrs. G. disagreed with Mr. W.: "A job is not necessary for the kind of people who create work for themselves." Miss F. said that whether it was a job or something else: "you must do something when you retire." Miss O'N. spoke with warmth of her experience when she was volunteering in a hospital which was closing, and helped to move the patients. Mrs. K. mentioned that "ill people are very appreciative of what you do for them." Mrs. B.G. spoke of her and her husband's work for a church for deaf people in the city and explained--in answers to questions from Mrs. G., Mrs. W., and Miss F.--that they went shopping with some of the people who attend the church, type the correspondence and said "we help in any way we can." They spend either two or three days a week there, depending on what needed to be done.

Mrs. W. then described her own volunteer activities; she gives one day a week to the Thrift Shop of her synagogue and another day to a children's hospital. She belonged to several clubs, "I am a bridge fiend" and took classes in Spanish.

person coped successfully with the problem of finding a satisfying activity after retirement. The leader should, however, have returned to Mr. W.'s introductory remark about meaningful activities which keep one out of the clutches of depression and illness, as it merited some further exploration by the group.

The discussion got under way after Mr. W.'s remarks. This was a group that needed very little encouragement to participate and the leader let the discussion develop. If no one had reacted to Mr. W.'s remarks, she would have asked the group members individually what they did now.

Mr. B.G. had a slight hearing and speech impediment which may have been one of the reasons why the couple volunteered in that particular setup. He participated occasionally in the discussion; Mrs. B.G. used to watch him anxiously when he did this. She had explained to the leader when the couple first came that her husband might not participate very much because of these handicaps; the leader had encouraged them to come since both were eager to do that. Many group members took time to chat with the B.G.'s who seemed to be lonely and were pathetically appreciative of any attention paid to them.

This is another comment which the leader could have picked up but, on the other hand, to do so would have interrupted a very active discussion, with much group interaction, which is often more

Mrs. Sch. said approvingly that "to be busy with something which interests one, like you are, is what counts. To be busy otherwise is not enough." Miss J. commented--in her usual reflective manner--that "the meaning of what you are doing, its value to you and to others, are more important than the time spent.... If one has worked five or six days a week, this pattern is hard to break and one tends to feel guilty if one does not have to work anymore." It took her some time to adjust to her "new style of life" and it also took her some time to learn to be able to turn down requests to do "things which I thought were not interesting and not important." People would say to me--"you have the time to do this!"

Mr. W. agreed that many requests come to one "because you are an easy mark. I have learned to say: 'I have done my share of the work of the world--let somebody who is younger do this!'" These comments gave me opportunity to develop the concept of the Freedom of Choice, as One Asset of the Later Years.

Mrs. M. leaned back, smiled and said: "I am not looking for more to do!" She described her present life very positively. She belonged to several organizations, was active in them, went on trips with them and "now I see things which I have never seen before!" Mr. W. asked if the members of this group had ever been to Fort Tryon Park and to the Cloisters in New York; he wrote out directions for Mrs. G. on how to get there at her request. (Group members

important than anything which the leader may have in mind as a topic to explore.

Miss J., another group discussion member of long standing, had given a great deal of thought to her new way of life. She was also intelligent and well educated as was evident from the way she expressed herself. The same description applied to Mr. W.

Concepts of this kind are more meaningful to group members if they originate in some of their own comments. This interweaving of the group members' contributions with the leader's professional knowledge facilitates the group members' learning and gives them recognition which also, in turn, encourages many to try new approaches to the problems they are facing.

Perhaps Mr. W.'s question was a little patronizing since quite a few group members had probably been there. On the other hand, he and Mrs. G. were obviously widely separated by education, income and social class, and his question proved to be helpful to her.

As previously mentioned, sharing such information reflected the group members' positive relationships to each

provided information of this kind for each other quite frequently.)

I used this opportunity to make reference to the leaflets, Philadelphia in the Fall, which group members had received earlier which describe many interesting things to do and to see in the city. I had brought along additional copies of the leaflet which several group members took along.

I went on to say that we had heard about many interesting activities but what about people--do they contribute to one's full life? Mrs. G. reacted to this question: "That depends. With some people it's best to just say: 'How are you? ' because you would not want to encourage a closer contact." She went on to talk about people "who are narrow and don't have any interests;" they are in her experience usually "the kind of people who stay at home and 'who have not learned to mingle with other people. '"

Mrs. K. agreed with Mrs. G., adding the example of "people who are depressing to be with because they complain so much about their troubles." Mrs. B.G. returned to her chief interest, which is obviously her work with the deaf, and explained that they had recently gone on a walking tour with this

other.

Material of this kind was made available to group members in order to encourage them to engage in new activities. Since older people sometimes lose or misplace these materials, the leader found it helpful to bring them to the later meetings. This also enabled persons who joined the group later to receive this information.

In addition to the above mentioned leaflets, copies of a free center city newspaper, reading lists, announcements of free movie showings in a variety of library branches or in other settings, pamphlets explaining Medicare and Social Security, etc. had been used in this fashion.

The ease with which Mrs. G. participated in the discussion was a response to the group's acceptance of her. The leader wondered, however, whether the statement about people who are "narrow" did not contain an oblique reference to racial factors. Since they were not the focus of the meetings, she did not explore this possibility.

group: "going places, you meet
people."

I said that all of us knew that
some people had few interests, or
complained too much, and certainly one would not want to select
people of this kind for closer contacts. Miss M. nodded and added:
"They would not have anything to
contribute and contacts with them
would be depressing. Maybe we
should be careful also and make
sure we don't complain too much!"
Mr. N. turned to her and said: "I
cannot imagine you being anything
but your cheerful self." Miss M.
smiled and said: "Sometimes I
don't feel cheerful but I try not to
show it." I said that certainly one
did not always feel cheerful, because many things happened in the
course of life which troubled one.
It had always seemed to me that it
did not help if one gave in too much
to one's bad moods, and certainly
it did not help one to complain all
the time. Miss J. added: "You
alienate people if you do that and
very often you, yourself, feel
worse also."

I then said, I would like to
return to something Mrs. B.G. had
said earlier, namely, that one met
people if one went places. Many
members of the groups with which
I worked--not only our group here
--found it hard to meet people.
What did our friends here think,

It was very helpful that
Miss M. took the topic under
discussion one step further
by relating it to the importance
of one's own behavior and
attitudes. If she had not done
this, the leader would, but
such statements are usually
more meaningful if they are
made by a member of the group.
If that person is well liked by
most group members, as was
the case with Miss M., the
statements carry even more
weight.

With this statement the
leader wanted to recognize the
problems which everyone has
to cope with, while encouraging more self-control and an
approach which would be likely
to lead to more positive responses
from other people. One of the
reasons for the social isolation
of older people is their tendency to dwell on their mis-
fortunes, real or imaginary.
The intent may be to ask for
sympathy, but the results are
usually avoidance of contacts
with such persons, partly
because one does not wish to
listen to their complaints, to
share their depression which
can be threatening to the
listener, and often also because
the latter feels guilty if he is
more fortunate than the other
person.

Many members of this
group were always ready to
react to a question from the
leader and, very often, they
helped to put this question in
a clearer focus as happened
here.

The examples given, as

and what had their experiences been? <u>Was it hard to meet new people</u>? Mrs. W. asked: "Did I mean new people to become friends with? I have met them here in our group!" She described how she got to know Mrs. K., Mrs. Sch., Miss F. when she started to come to the meetings a few years ago. Now they saw each other between the meetings or after the discussion series had ended, and "if we don't see each other, we call each other up." Mrs. McK. added: "Last week we did what you had suggested before--some of us went out and had coffee together." Miss F. said that she and "Anna"--she pointed to Miss C.--met in the group, and they had also become friends and now went out together. I said, I was so pleased to hear that and <u>I hoped that our group members would find friends in our meetings, and would also meet new people in other situations. How else could one meet people</u>?

Mrs. W. explained that she went on a trip to New York recently, started to talk to the woman who was sitting next to her and they exchanged addresses. They are planning to meet soon to go to a show together. Mrs. K. mentioned that she had known Mrs. G. before both came to the meetings because of their musical activities. She added, "being ready for people and for new experiences is one way of enlarging one's circle of friends or of meeting new people." She gave the example of the piano tuner who came to her house "on a routine job." They started to talk and he turned out to be very knowledgeable about music. Miss O'N. spoke about "sharing a pleasant experience with another person" even if it was only somebody with whom

well as the leader's encouragement of the friendships which had developed in the group would, hopefully, free some of the more timid, or more withdrawn group members to reach out in similar fashion.

The leader did not want the discussion to stop with the opportunity the meetings gave for meeting new people, and "took the discussion one step further."

Mrs. W., Mrs. K., Miss O'N., and Miss M. were obviously the kind of people who would find it easy to meet other people and to develop new social relationships. The leader hoped that their positive experiences in these areas would encourage the more timid group members to venture out a little more in their attempts to meet people. This is especially important for older people who have usually lost many of their former friends and who tend to have fewer social relationships than in earlier years. This happens because many of these relationships were connected with and derived from their employment and very often came to

you happened to share a table.
Miss M. mentioned volunteer work
as another way of meeting new
people. Mrs. K., turning to Mrs.
W., commented that she also liked
to talk with the people who sat next
to her on a bus or on a train, and
she had met many interesting people in that fashion. Miss E. said
approvingly to Mrs. K.: "You and
D.--she used Mrs. W.'s first
name--see interesting people
because you have open eyes," to
which Mrs. McK. added: "and an
open mind." Mr. W. commented:
"If our friend Mr. F. were here
today, he would say--these qualities
make an author." He explained
to the group members that Mr. F.
wrote poetry, which had been published, and plays which had been
performed. Mrs. K. and Mrs. W.
were very pleased by these comments.

I said: "There are many ways
in which we can meet new people
and have interesting experiences
also. It is good to have contacts
with others, and while some lead
to getting better acquainted, as we
have heard from Mrs. W., even to
exchange a few words with another
person in the elevator, or to talk
to someone with whom one sits at
the same table, can make the day
more pleasant."

Mr. N. said: "Retirement
brings many adjustments and,
sometimes, they are hard to make."
Mrs. G. agreed: "It is hard because what you do often becomes
second nature." Mrs. McK. said,
in her soft voice: "If one loses a
husband, that adjustment is hard
to make!" Mrs. W., turning to
her said, in a reassuring fashion:
"But many of us have made that

an end with retirement.

This exchange was another
indication of the good relationships which some group members had developed with each
other.

The leader thought it
important to stress that brief
and casual contacts with other
people should not be scorned,
because they can also add to
the pleasure of a day but,
mostly, because contacts with
others tend to draw out a person and are one way to counteract the withdrawal and concentration on oneself, symptoms
which many old people develop
and which reinforce their isolation and loneliness.

Mr. N.'s comment gave
the discussion a new turn,
which was welcome to the
leader, because many people--
old and young, incidentally--
find it difficult to adjust to
new situations.

The leader did not encourage
the discussion of inner security,
or of a person's inner strength
because it is very difficult to

adjustment." Mrs. K. commented "One's inner security helps one to adjust throughout one's life." (She had a tendency to make comments of this kind, as I knew from my extensive contacts with her. I thought they were made to impress the other group members and, perhaps, also the leader.) Miss J. replied "That is true, <u>if</u> one has inner security." Miss E. said: "But adjusting is nothing new, all of us have had to adjust from the beginning of our lives." Mrs. G. said, very thoughtfully: "It is the inner person, one's inner strength, which helps us to adjust."

I said to Mr. N.: "It is <u>certainly often very difficult to adjust to new situations and, perhaps, we can try to find out together what would help one to make such an adjustment.</u>" Miss M. said: "Not to wallow in self-pity." Mrs. M. added: "And try to find pleasure where you can find it." Mrs. Sch. spoke in considerable detail--and very helpfully, I thought--on "the effects on one's morale" if one feels sorry for oneself and "looks at the negative side of things only," and Mrs. W. added: "If you do this, you hurt yourself more." Mrs. K. said: "You also hurt others, because it hurts us if we like somebody and are unable to help them." Miss O'N. turned to Miss E. and said: "You were right when you said all of us had to adjust. Our generation had to be ready to make adjustments." Mrs. McK. agreed, with reference to "the fast progress" of the last decades.

I said that it was true that <u>all of us had to make many adjustments and I often wondered what was of the greatest help in doing that?</u> Miss J. said: "Absorbing interests." Mrs. G.: "God and faith in

acquire these attributes. She thought it would be more helpful to steer the discussion toward specific approaches which would help one to adjust to a new situation.

The leader could have reinforced this statement.

Many older people, particularly those who were strongly identified with the labor movement, or with political causes such as socialism, are not religious, and sometimes

him, " a point with which Miss O'N. agreed. Since I knew from my previous experience with groups of older people that many older people were not religious, I said, I would like to say something and I commented that it was indeed a great support and comfort if one was religious and had a strong belief in God. It did not matter which religious faith it was which gave one strength, but many people we knew did not have such faith and we should, perhaps, look for additional ways than one's religion to help us to cope with the changes which life brought.

Mrs. G. said: "If you try to do something for others, you forget yourself and your problems. " Miss E. "You must learn to understand yourself, " and she added how much more she knew about herself after coming to the meetings. Miss M., Mrs. W., Mr. N., Mr. W. made similar comments, and I said that I was glad if our meetings had been helpful.

Mrs. M. now said: "Nobody has mentioned a sense of humor" which helped and which she had. "I enjoy life and people and I can see good in everybody. " She went on to say that she lost most of her family in an accident several years ago, but "I made a new life for myself. " She found out that she could sing, she belonged to two choir groups, and she also belonged to two Senior Citizen Clubs. Several group members (Mrs. Sch., Miss E., Miss M.) asked Mrs. M. how she found out that she could sing, and what the choirs sang (hymns), and Mrs. Sch. added, approvingly: "Singing is an outward directed activity and it does much for people. " I said, we were all very grateful to Mrs. M. for telling

opposed to religion altogether.

us about her present life because <u>we heard so much about the problems of getting older, but getting older also had many assets, and one of them was that one had the time and the opportunity to find out what one could do, what talents or skills one had, which one had not developed before.</u>

Miss J. said: "If you are proud of yourself, you will make the adjustments more easily." Mr. W. added: "Others will appreciate you more, too." I said, I was very glad that Miss J. and Mr. W. had reminded us of these points, and <u>I stressed the importance of appreciating oneself, seeing oneself as a person who has something to offer and to contribute to others.</u>

It is always important to help people to see their assets as well as their liabilities in a particular situation, and this is particularly true if one works with older people. They, as well as the others around them, tend to see only the negative sides of getting older, and this contributes to the depression from which many old people suffer.

The writer made this point for the same reason for which she stressed the assets of the later years.

The problem which Mrs. K. raised was, of course, one with which many group members had to cope. It seemed well worthwhile to the leader to extend the session for a while so that it could be taken up.

I was getting ready to terminate the meeting, since our time was almost up and also because the last points made seemed good ones on which to do this, when Mrs. K. asked if she could bring a problem to the group. She explained that she lived with her mother, who was housebound, so that she went out by herself. <u>"How do other people meet the problem of going out at night?"</u> This question got a considerable response.

Miss F. said: "I don't; I only go out in the afternoon." Mrs. K. added: "Many organizations meet in the afternoon!" Mrs. McK. added: "You can usually find someone to go with in the afternoon." Miss T. made her only comment in today's meeting: "It does not do to be terrified all the time." Mrs. W. said: "I take the streetcar as far as I can, and then I walk the four blocks to my home!" Miss J. said: "I am inclined to take taxis at night." Mrs. G. turned to her and said: "But if you are on a budget, that is difficult." Miss F. added: "Some people, they think you are indulging yourself, if you take a taxi!"

I said, we could certainly talk more about the whole question of going out at night, and also about living alone, which many of our group members had checked on their registration sheets. I would like to add just one comment: "Another advantage of the later years was that one should feel free to enjoy the good things which came one's way and to indulge oneself also. Surely a little juggling of even a tight budget would make it possible to take a taxi, if one wished to do that, and sometimes going out did more for one than getting a more expensive cut of meat. What I was trying to say was that in the later years, one was free of certain earlier obligations. For instance, if one had children or grandchildren, and would like to save some money to leave to them, or if one would like to leave some money to friends, or to some cause in which one was interested, that was one's privilege, but it was not an obligation.

Mr. W. then reminded us that he was going to take a picture of the group today, which he did. This pleased the group members very much, who kidded each other about how they would look, that they had not worn their best clothes, etc.

Several group members came to talk with me after the meeting. Mr. N. told me how he had enjoyed "being back with the group," and added that the next meeting of the Senior Citizens Club would be at

the time when we met, so that he
could not come, because he was
responsible for that meeting. I
told him that we would miss him
and that I hoped he could come again
in two weeks. Miss R. apologized
for having coughed so much. Miss
O'N., Miss J., Mrs. G., and
Mrs. M. made positive comments
about the meetings.

Group participation was good, as
usual. Seventeen of the twenty
group members participated, in
varying degrees, of course. I was
very pleased that Miss T. spoke up
because although she and Miss C.
came regularly, they listened only.
Miss R. was handicapped by her
cold, and Mr. B.G. spoke up very
rarely, as previously mentioned,
probably because of his hearing and
speech difficulties.

PART THREE

A THEORY OF LEADERSHIP

XVI

The Discussion Content: How to Prepare It For and How to Handle It with Different Groups

The importance of preparing oneself for specific group discussion leadership assignments cannot be overestimated. One phase of doing this deals with the possible and probable content of the discussions and with the most helpful ways of handling this content.

First of all, the leader must be aware of the concerns and problems of the members of the group; appropriate ways of eliciting them were outlined earlier. Awareness, however, is not enough; these concerns or problems must also be evaluated, assigned an order of importance if they are to be part of the group's discussions, or eliminated, if that is not indicated. Evaluation means that the leader must determine whether the concerns or problems expressed on the registration sheets, or verbally--concerns which will be, necessarily, as different as the members of the group are--can be considered representative, that is, are shared by the majority or at least by a large number of the participants. If this is the case, they should be part of the discussions.

Next, it is helpful, in the writer's experience, if these concerns or problems are taken up in a certain order. For instance, stealing and lying belong together in a discussion of how to cope with the problems of children who engage in these activities, since the child who steals is likely to lie about it when confronted with the matter. Similarly, the discussion of how to answer young children's questions about pregnancy, birth, sex relations, and related matters can be extended to include the most helpful ways of explaining death to them, as these topics fall under the overall heading of how to answer difficult, embarrassing and--in the case of death--painful questions in ways which will be informative and nonthreatening. Aside from this logical connection between discussion topics, it is very often contributive to productive meetings if the leader can steer the discussions toward the less threatening topics in the earlier meetings, particularly if the group is starting, and can save the topics which are likely to be more difficult, for the group to tackle at later meetings when good intragroup relationships and good relationships to the leader have had opportunities to develop. Using the above-mentioned examples, one can assume that stealing and lying will be easier for the members of most parent groups to discuss than sex education and

death. Again, the leader's training and experience will suggest whether
such an approach is indicated. For instance, one can often discard
it when a group has been meeting for some time, as mentioned previously, but also if some event in the life of a group member, such
as a pregnancy, or the death of a family member, has brought these
problems to their attention.

GIVING FOCUS TO THE DISCUSSION

This subtitle covers a wide area, because it deals with relevant
techniques and problems. This is necessary because the latter very
often determine the former.

In the process of evaluating group concerns, the leader must be
prepared to cope with group members who raise questions or describe
problems which are unrelated to the overall focus of the meetings,
which may be the discussion of parent-child relationships, or of
adjustment to the later years. The unrelated problems and questions
are sometimes also quite inappropriate for the group discussion
setting, either because they express a group member's very personal
concern, or are related to a cause with which he or she is so identified that every interaction with other people is looked upon as an
opportunity to further this cause. It goes without saying that concerns and problems of this nature do not belong in the group discussions, and that it is the leader's responsibility to make this clear to
the group member who brought them up.

If a very personal problem was mentioned, it is usually best to
suggest to the person that help of a more specific nature is available
for it and to offer to assist him in contacting such a resource, if
that is what the person would like to do. This makes it easier for
the person to follow through on such a referral, because it is more
personal than just to give the name and address of an agency or a
psychiatrist. Going beyond this is proof of the leader's interest in
the group member and of his encouragement of seeking such help.
The cause mentioned can sometimes be ignored, but if the group member persists, the leader must explain that while it is worthwhile, it
is not the overall focus of the meetings, to which leader and group
members committed themselves when they planned and joined the
discussion series.

The overall focus of a discussion series deserves further consideration at this point. In the writer's opinion, it represents a
contract--however loosely binding and open to change it may be--
between the leader and the members of a group. This focus has been
decided upon in a variety of ways many of which were described in
earlier chapters. It is the major reason why participants attend the
meetings and as such, it should not be taken lightly. While group
members, as well as the leader, may move away from this focus, if
new concerns come up and questions are raised which are not related
to it, this should be done only after the leader has faced the group

with this development and if the participants or at least the majority of them decide to pursue the new areas opened up for discussion. This happens sometimes when group members know each other and the leader well and feel secure in this knowledge; it is a sign of group confidence when it does so and it is to be welcomed. What is important, however, is that the group members--and the leader!--must realize what is happening, and that the decision to pursue a different course should be made in a planned fashion, and not because the discussions started to wander aimlessly. Examples of situations when a group decided to turn to different areas of interest were given in earlier chapters.

One of the tools used to elicit the concerns and problems of group members are the registration sheets, which were discussed previously with reference to the factors to take into account in their preparation for a specific group. In this chapter their role in relation to techniques of group discussion leadership will be taken up. If the basis of leadership is a helpful relation which is to be established between the leader and the group members, the preparation, the filling out, and the planned use of these registration sheets play an important part in the development of these interrelationships. Three points should be kept in mind: first, the fact that these sheets are made up with specific reference to the group indicates the leader's desire to be helpful and his investment in his work; second, the filling out by the participants is an act of trust and something which they in turn give to the leader; third, the leader's response to and handling of the content of these registration sheets reflect his respect for them and acknowledge their part in deciding on the material to be taken up in the meetings.

The first two points made in the preceding paragraph need little elaboration, but they are worth mentioning because some leaders do not quite see why they should go to the trouble of preparing special registration sheets for each group when the use of a general form, for instance, for all parent groups or for all teen-age groups, would save time. In reality the time saved is not considerable, and one wonders whether it is not a reluctance to invest too much of oneself which is often the basis for a leader's preference for this briefer procedure. Be it what it may, if time spent furthers relationships as is the case here, it is time well spent.

How a leader will use registration sheets depends on the particular way in which each person works--his work style, to paraphrase the life style of which we hear so much--and the writer wishes only to share her own experience with the reader of this book. She has found it very helpful to come to the meeting following the one when the registration sheets were filled out with a summary of the questions or topics checked off or raised. Many group members commented approvingly: "you read what we wrote," expressing in this fashion their gratification that their efforts served a purpose, and that they received the leader's time and attention. This procedure represented not only recognition of their efforts, but was also proof of the leader's confidence in them and in their ability to use his knowledge in ways which will be helpful to them. It was particularly important for group members from low socioeconomic backgrounds who are all too often asked to fill out forms without being told what their purpose is. These requests engender a feeling of futility and lower the self-image of those to whom they are made. However, group members with middle class or upper middle class background reacted positively also to this use of their registration sheets, partly because they, like everybody else, wished to receive attention, and partly because they were assured in this fashion that their comments and questions would decide to a great extent the content and focus of the following meetings. "To a great extent" means that the leader should use his judgment in this area, both by organizing the material in some logical order, and also in the handling of inappropriate questions.

A few meetings before a discussion series is to end, the writer has often used a similar approach by bringing to the group a summary of what they had discussed so far and of the questions they had raised originally and which had not been covered. The participants could then decide whether they wished to proceed with the topics they were discussing or preferred to take up some of those they had listed when the meetings started. Here too the leader must use his judgment. For instance, if a group has moved on to some different but relevant topics, which will require the use of the remaining meetings, he may not wish to interrupt this development. In such a situation, however, the leader should pay particular attention to anything which indicates that the new and unplanned content does not meet the needs of most of the group members at any point. Should this develop, this should be discussed with the group so that they can be helped to select those questions which will be most helpful to the majority of the participants.

It sometimes happens that a group changes the overall focus, for instance when parents of schoolage children start to discuss problems with teen-agers, or with in-laws. Here too the leader should take up with the group members what is going on, should help them to clarify whether enough of the material they originally wished to discuss was covered or whether they wish to return to it. The latter usually makes it possible to move on to another overall topic--such as the one the group members brought up--for a following discussion series, which then has enough meeting time to explore the new focus fully, that is, if the leader and the group members decide that they wish to plan such a project. When to offer another group discussion experience and what factors to take into account in making such a commitment will be discussed later.

PRESENTATION OF MATERIAL AND GROUP PARTICIPATION

At this point the writer wishes to take up techniques of group discussion leadership which deal with such questions as the amount and form of material presented to a group on a specific topic, if such material is to be presented at all; ways of involving group members in the discussions; how much direction to give to a discussion as well as the reasons why this should--or should not--be done; how this can best be done, if indicated; how to use oneself with the group, that is, whether the leader's experiences--from his work with other groups or from his personal life--should be brought to the participants; if this is to be done, for what reasons, and what are the ways to make this most productive for them; how the leader can planfully use his appearance--clothes, manners, language, etc.--so that it will be most helpful for a specific group.

The relationship between the amount of material to be presented and the group composition was mentioned earlier. The examples used--the "silent majority" parents and the parents of physically handicapped children--were discussed mainly with regard to the orientation to learning in a more formal sense of the former and of the anxiety and grief of the latter, but other factors such as the educational level of a group must be taken into consideration when one prepares oneself for group discussion leadership, specifically if one has not met with the group before. As a rule of thumb, one can assume that groups with a lower educational level will prefer more presentation of material. Once group members have been meeting over a period of time, however, thus having developed good intragroup relationships, and are comfortable with each other, the need for presentation of material by the leader usually lessens. As they get to be more at ease with the leader also and are sure of being accepted and understood by him, this contributes further to their greater freedom to participate in the discussions. Some groups whose members have very little education, and to whom the exploration of their family relationships is a new experience, may move on to the stage where they initiate such discussions spontaneously when the meeting is starting. This is a step which should be encouraged, even though it may upset any plans which the leader might have had, because anything which is of concern to group members at a given moment, and of such concern that they wish to share it with the total group and with him, is vastly more important than anything which he had in mind as possible questions to be taken up. Any rigidity on his part in such a situation would be detrimental.

Should the leader feel that a good deal "was left hanging" at the preceding meeting, a brief reference to that fact coupled with the assurance that the loose ends will receive due attention later on will handle any fears of group members that this might not happen. It will also be helpful in handling the leader's own anxiety about this matter.

The growing ability of participants to involve themselves in the discussions, to raise questions and contribute different points of view to the topic under discussion, will do more than further their learning in the areas of family and social relationships. This skill will be transferable to other areas of their lives, such as their participation

in community activities, and will in this fashion enlarge their world
and contribute to an improved self-image.

In similar fashion, it becomes possible to present more intricate questions and situations or to guide the discussions toward them,
as group members progress. For instance, many mothers of acting
out children as described in this book were using the system of cash
rewards--a dime or a nickel--for good behavior, when the group
started to meet. After a number of discussion series, the leader
could discuss with them other and more appropriate ways of coping
with behavior problems, as well as some of the phenomena which
cause them. They would have rejected such a discussion earlier,
but were ready for it at a later point, as a result of their confidence
in each other, in themselves, and in the leader.

If one offers leadership to group members who are well educated, one can dispense entirely with the presentation of per-
tinent material. A statement such as: "You wanted to discuss today
some of the difficulties which in-laws can cause. Does anybody wish
to start?" may be enough to get the discussion under way. If this is
not so, the leader can ask: "Would you like me to bring to you some
of the things which members of other groups have brought out regarding in-laws?" This is one of the ways in which reference to other
groups with whom one works is helpful.

Groups who get the discussion going are usually very vocal,
very active, and the leader needs to make sure that it does not wander too far afield and that all those who wish to participate in it have
opportunities to do this. Groups of this kind are very challenging to
most leaders, of course. In working with them, the writer has found
it very helpful to summarize the content of the discussion either at
the end of the meeting, or at the beginning of the next one, so that
the ideas and viewpoints presented can be grouped in some sort of
logical order, which facilitates their retention. Such a summarization also offers an opportunity to bring to the group some of the
leader's knowledge of the topic which was discussed, and if he thinks
this will add to their learning, also some of the points of view of
other similar groups on the same subject. Summarizations of this
kind are helpful to almost all groups, but they have a special place
in very free wheeling discussions where the very desirable spontaneity
may sometimes result in a lack of cohesion.

In regard to the form in which the leader presents any material,
the first requirement is that the members of this specific group must
be able to understand and to accept it. The form can, and should,
include new ways of expressing the ideas back of it, because an extension of one's knowledge is an experience which is enriching and which,
as a result, increases one's self-confidence and feelings of competence and mastery as well as one's ability to contribute to others.
It should never, however, be beyond the comprehension of the participants; nothing is as frustrating and as discouraging for them as
to be unable to follow the leader's presentation. This undermines
their self-confidence, makes them feel inadequate, not up to the

leader's expectations and thus rejected by him. The result is a
negative atmosphere in the group which is not conducive to learning
and thwarts the goals which the group members and the leader have
set for their joint endeavor. As mentioned previously, the leader
should share some of his knowledge with the group, but this should
be done on a selective basis and in more appropriate ways.

In the writer's opinion, knowledge in the areas to be taken up
by the participants, expertise, and experience in leading group discussions are the most important parts of a leader's equipment. They
can be acquired in a variety of ways, such as keeping notes on meetings which eventually become a storehouse of one's various experiences, good or bad; self-examination; training; supervision and
consultation. All these matters are taken up in more detail later
on. What the author wishes to stress at this point is that the best
use of his knowledge which a leader can make should be comparable
to the iceberg: its tip only shows above water, but its strength and
impact come from the infinitely larger part which is submerged and
which propels it.

A brief word should be added here with reference to group
members who are well educated, knowledgeable in the questions
under discussion, and who give evidence of this in their contributions. If all the group members are at the same educational level,
the leader should adapt his presentation to that situation, but if this
is not the case, he must be a bridge for those who would otherwise
be left out. An example of such a situation was given in the chapter
describing the meeting with the separated, divorced, and widowed
persons.

Ways of mobilizing group members were presented earlier in
this book, but mobilizing a person to come to a meeting need not
always mean that he is ready to involve himself in the discussions.
It should be pointed out at the onset that some among those present
at a meeting may not wish to do this and this should be respected by
the leader. This is sometimes difficult, especially for inexperienced
leaders who may feel that verbal participation is a prerequisite for
a learning experience and who interpret their inability to engage
group members to the point where they are willing to do this as a
failure of their leadership. To be met with silence tends to make
many persons--not only inexperienced leaders!--anxious, but if this
happens, the anxiety must be contained and may not be permitted to
affect the professional service which is to be rendered. The ways in
which people learn differ widely, and listening is one of them.

Even more erroneous than to consider verbal participation a
prerequisite for learning is the assumption that the amount and intensity of verbal participation equate the gains of group members. The
replies on questionnaires or other evaluation forms confirm this
statement, since quite frequently the most detailed and astute comments are made by those participants whose verbal participation
was limited, and sometimes nonexistent.

To recognize this fact is different, however, from the attempts

which every leader should make to get the group members to participate in the discussions, and only after these attempts have not
received any response can a leader desist from making additional
overtures to certain participants.   There are several ways of doing
this, and the first one, which is also the simplest and often the most
effective, is to watch for any sign by which group members indicate
an interest in the material presented or discussed.   Such signs can
be a smile or a frown, a nod or a shaking of the head to indicate
disagreement; some people also start to whisper to their neighbors
if they are stimulated by what they are hearing.   Anyone of these
cues gives the leader an opportunity to pause, if he happens to be
talking, to turn to the person who gave out such a signal and to say:
"You were smiling (or frowning, etc.), did you want to say something?   All of us here will be glad to hear what made you smile, or
with what you disagreed, etc."   In similar fashion, the person who
whispers to a neighbor can be encouraged to share his comments
with the group if the leader says something like: "All of us here
would like to hear what you are saying."   In many instances, comments will be forthcoming but, while a leader may try such techniques
once or twice with a person, he should not bring further pressure on
the participant who prefers not to react to this approach.   This
usually leads only to the withdrawal of the one who feels pressured.
Should the leader get a response, however, it can be used to involve
the other group members in the discussion, by asking for their reactions to it, their points of view in this matter, and whether they had
any experience of a similar or different nature which they would like
to share with the rest of the group.

If no one indicates interest in the material presented, beyond
listening to it, the writer has found it helpful to stop and to ask if it
is what the group wanted, or if she should approach the topic from
another angle, or in another form.   If a suggestion for such a change
is made, it should be picked up.   Incidentally, such a suggestion sometimes enables a leader who is not familiar with the group members'
educational level to adjust his presentation accordingly.   In the more
frequent situations, however, when the leader is told to "go on," it
is best to follow through here also, but only for a while so that the
whole time will not be used up for a lecture.   A little later, the
leader can again attempt to draw the group members into the discussion and sometimes they are more ready to do this at that point.

Another way of involving group members who are not very
spontaneous in their contributions is by giving an example of the
question or topic discussed, which is close to their life situation and
has probably been at one point or another something which they
experienced.   This can be followed up by the question: "I wonder if
something like this has every happened to anyone here?"   This approach
usually gets a response, which the leader can then use to attempt to
involve the other group members in the ways described previously.

If none of the techniques mentioned so far get results, the
following question usually does: "You know, the example I gave is

something which happens quite frequently. I wonder what anyone who is here with us now would do, if this happened to you?" One of the reasons why this works is that this question brings the matter under discussion close to the group members and therefore encourages them to use their imagination and to identify with the situation presented and with the people who are part of it. (The writer is aware of other techniques for involving group members, such as asking them to write down their questions, or role playing, but she never used them in her own professional work, because the devices described above did not fail to work.)

Once a group member has responded in whatever fashion, his comment must be accepted, even if the leader is momentarily at a loss in what way it can be used--if this can be done at all--and even if he cannot figure out the connection between the response and the material which preceded it. If the comment would be rejected, this would probably discourage the other group members from involving themselves in the discussion, since they would fear that the same might happen to them, as they would identify with the rejected person.

The leader's acceptance of such a comment does not imply that he is lying to the group since every comment made, however odd it may seem at first glance, represents a participant's concern. However, acceptance does not preclude the leader's suggesting that the comment might well be taken up in another connection, at a later time, if that is indicated.

Acceptance can take simple forms, such as saying: "I am grateful to...for bringing this to our attention," or "This is a new point which I had not thought of before," but it should be followed by turning over to the group members the comment for their reactions, to find out if they had similar or different experiences, or in any of the other ways described previously as techniques for involving participants in a discussion. This is not necessary, of course, if they react spontaneously to the opportunity to do this.

The counterpart, so to speak, of helping group members move into a discussion is helping them to terminate it at a given point. This may be necessary for a number of reasons: other related questions were raised which should be covered; the meeting time is used up; the discussion takes a turn which threatens or upsets some of the participants, and termination is indicated for their protection. While the leader should not be so protective of the group members that he wants to prevent the arousal of all emotions, he must evaluate the depth of these feelings and most of all, whether the feelings which are aroused will be helpful to the person. To give an example, from the meetings with the parents of physically handicapped children, it was essential to give them opportunities to express their grief, their anxiety, their feelings of being helpless and overwhelmed by their own and their children's plight. However, the physical handicap was a constant factor in the family situation and could be expected to remain so, unless radical new medical discoveries were made, and for that reason unlimited expression of these feelings would not be helpful to these parents. It would weaken them if they were encouraged to focus on their distress, while they would be more able to deal with the difficult problems facing them if they directed their energies and abilities toward finding some better ways of coping with these problems within the range of the possible. In similar fashion, most older people experience negative feelings about aging, its diminishing physical capacity, its loss of status in a world where youth as well as work are highly valued, the impoverishment of life which follows the death of a spouse, or of friends. The problems of aging were presented in more detail in the two chapters which described meetings with older people. Here too one is faced with constant factors in the experience of growing old and here again, opportunities should be provided to express grief, anger, feelings of loneliness and of bereavement, but this should not be the only purpose of the discussions. If this were so, it would weaken and not strengthen the aged person, whose efforts to make a better adjustment to that experience and to find better solutions for their problems must be encouraged as a next step following the expression of the emotions which aging aroused.

It is often difficult for leaders to determine whether, and if so at what point a discussion should be given a different turn. Training, supervision, consultation, and experience can be helpful here.

If such redirection of a discussion is necessary, because the leader would like the group members to move beyond the expression of feelings as previously described, this must be done gently, with kindness and with acceptance of the emotions which are troubling the participants. The writer usually recognizes the feelings in a brief statement, but takes matters further: "We all know that aging is very difficult, but we also know that what one does with a situation which one is facing will make a great difference. It can help one to be more comfortable with it, or at least to accept that which one cannot change, and to see if there are any compensations for the losses one suffers. Perhaps we can look together at ways which will help make the later years better for all of us." This, or a similar approach leads the discussion away from the contemplation of the problems toward looking for solutions to them, and if that is not possible, for better ways of coping with the difficulties one is encountering. Doing this contributes to the greater well being of the persons who achieve this goal and as a further result, to an increase in their self-confidence because their coping capacity was strengthened.

The author would like to elaborate at this point on the use of "we" and "our" which she made in several examples given previously. This is one of the techniques of leadership which encourage group members to relate positively to the leader. It draws them closer to him and helps them to identify with him and to believe in his desire to be of assistance to them. If group members are addressed as "you" all the time, they tend to feel that the leader considers them different from himself and indeed an unconscious, and sometimes conscious, feeling of superiority on his part is often the reason for such usage. To say "we" is particularly meaningful when the leader recognizes that the participants are faced with difficult experiences. The use of "you," however, has a legitimate place also in the interaction between leader and group members, as several examples of such use in this chapter show.

Reference was made earlier to the protection which a group member sometimes needs because he is threatened, either by the direction which a discussion is taking, or because some of the other participants turn against him. In the former situation, the leader must decide on the spot whether interference is indicated, or whether it is more important for the group members who chose that course to continue with it. His diagnostic evaluation of the threatened person and his understanding of the others in the group and of their goals are the tools which he must use in making this decision. If it is advisable to go on with the discussion, the leader can usually reassure the person who is more vulnerable in a specific area than the other persons present by talking to him after the meeting, by pointing out that what was being discussed needed to be discussed, for the good of the group, although this was a difficult thing to do. In some instances, a group member leaves earlier than usual in such a situation. This is a self-protective device which should be respected.

If a group member is threatened, however, because the others-- or some others--turn against him, this requires different action on the part of the leader. "Ganging up" against one in their midst, or scapegoating should not be permitted to happen, or if it happens, to go on unchecked, in a group where learning--even if this term is used with much latitude, as in this book--is the group goal. It is interesting that incidents of this kind are very rare--if they occur at all--in groups whose leaders are positively motivated and wish to help the members without hurting anybody because most participants unconsciously, and sometimes consciously, adopt this attitude also in their interaction with each other.

COPING WITH DISRUPTION

A third category of group members, namely the unruly, disruptive or openly aggressive persons are often a concern to leaders. They are found mostly among teen-agers; the exception among adult group members are those who are disturbed, and who have to be excluded from attendance by the leader if this behavior continues. In rare instances, an example of which follows, the author has found it necessary to do the same with teen-agers.

If teen-agers are unruly or disruptive, this may be due to the restlessness which is a characteristic of many young people, or to the anxiety aroused by the topic under discussion, or to a desire to test the leader and to put him on the spot. If restlessness and anxiety are at the root of the group members' behavior, a leader who is kind but firm can usually calm them down without too much trouble. The writer has found it helpful to suggest--and to insist if necessary-- that the participant who disturbs the group sit next to her; in some instances, placing one's hand on the hand of the young person while saying that we all need a little quiet now, is effective. A next step, if the teen-ager does not quiet down, is to explain to the group that we must interrupt our discussion, until everybody is ready to calm down. This always leads to protests--legitimate ones by the way-- by the other group members who have not been disturbing the meeting so that group pressure is exerted on the deviant group member to make him desist from interfering with the ongoing discussion.

The desire to test the leader and to put him on the spot, which was mentioned as another reason for disrupting a meeting, often takes the form of very personal questions which teen-agers ask, and which they insist be answered at once. This matter is related to other areas of leadership--such as the use of the self, the leader's role as a model for behavior--and will be discussed in that connec- tion.

If aggression, especially uncontrollable aggression, causes the behavior which affects the meeting negatively, the above- mentioned measures of inviting the group member to sit next to the leader, etc. may be tried, but the chances of success are much smaller. Exclusion of the group member may be the only answer so that the others may not be the losers. An example follows, which is taken from the author's work with teen-age girls who attended a dis- ciplinary school because their behavior made it impossible to have them attend classes in the usual school situation. In this school con- certed efforts were made to offer help to the students by intensive individual counseling, by the use of psychological and psychiatric facilities, by keeping classes small with specially trained teachers in charge, and by using services outside of the school system among which was the group discussion leadership which the author offered to small groups of participants. The members of these groups with whom the author met for several years were unusually restless and often unable to sit in their places. They tended to start arguments with each other which led to shoving or pushing in some instances.

Because of the problems of aggressive behavior of the members of these groups, the leader decided to tolerate more disruptive behavior from them than from other teen-age girls of comparable age and background. She let the participants move around in the room a great deal and overlooked much of the by-play between them, unless it developed into actual physical fighting, which she explained was not permitted in the meetings. This always worked. In addition to accepting aggression, however, it was equally important to set limits to this behavior of the group members and it was never allowed to continue beyond a few minutes. The admonition to stop and to join "all of us who want to talk about..." always worked also.

Some girls expressed aggression to the leader very openly, as was to be expected. This was done by talking loudly, while she was saying something, by making derogatory remarks about her clothes, or by saying: "I am bored, I am leaving." She handled these situations by ceasing to speak until quiet was reestablished, by ignoring derogatory remarks, and by explaining to the bored member that she was free to leave the meeting, but would not be able to return because other girls were waiting for an opportunity to join the group. These methods were effective.

In one instance, the aggression took the form of a physical threat. One group member stood up, came close to the leader who was sitting at her usual place and said: "Leroy--her boyfriend--and I could wait for you after class and stick a knife in you." She did this after several admonitions to stop shouting at her neighbor to whom she had just showed an open penknife; the leader had told her to put this away at once. She was aware that she could not permit herself to show any fear, which she certainly felt; this was next best to not feeling threatened at all. Her answer was: "I am not afraid of you nor anybody else. You are not going to put a knife into me, and nobody else will do that either, but you are going to leave the room at once, because I do not permit such behavior in my girls." The disruptive group member tossed a few derogatory remarks at the author, and left the room, followed by her closest friend. The other group members jeered at them, and one said to the leader: "She is no good, we want to talk with you." This was obviously an attempt to reassure her and it was most welcome by the way.

This incident shows the importance of controlling aggression where it is indicated, and of keeping in mind the goal of one's work with a group which is not only to offer help to the participants with their problems, but also to offer it to the largest number of persons who can use it. It also demonstrates the need to be aware of one's own attitudes and possible reactions in certain situations ahead of time; for instance, if one is threatened by group members, and, furthermore, to clarify with the representatives of any organization with whom one works whether the procedure one intends to adopt will be backed up. In this situation, exclusion of a group member who could not function in the group discussion situation had been agreed upon; it was, of course, followed by a conference between the leader and the girl's counselor so that the latter could help the girl who needed to be excluded with her special problem. This incident is also an excellent example of the way in which group members and leaders interact, in that the girls who remained reassured the leader and rallied around her in a situation which was explosive and had elements of danger.

If the writer told "a white lie" by saying "I am not afraid of you..." she hopes she may be forgiven for departing from the principle of telling a group the truth only in this particular instance. This was the first--and only--time she had been threatened in this fashion and this seemed the best thing to do. It was also an example of relying on one's professional judgment of the factors at work in an unexpected situation and it was comforting to see that the approach to it was effective.

XVII
Use and Control of Interpersonal Dynamics in the Relationships of the Leader to Group Members and of the Group Members to Each Other

Group discussion leadership is based on an ability to relate to the group members and to help them in turn to develop good relationships to themselves and to each other. In order to achieve this, the leader must, first of all, understand the members of the group as individuals with their different personalities, their positive and negative feelings and attitudes, their biases--what one calls hang-ups today--and their problems in family and social relationships, since everyone has these problems to a major or minor degree. Second, it is essential to see the group members as part of their social, economic, educational, religious, and racial background and to give proper, but not undue recognition to what they bring with them as a result of belonging to the subgroup determined by this background. This belonging can be likened to an invisible but nonetheless existing burden of tradition which each of us carries with us into our lives and which affects to a considerable degree what we say or do in many situations especially if they are part of our family or social relationships. It goes without saying that the individual's adjustment to his environment, or his ease in relating to others might often be helped greatly, if change could be brought about in parts of the attitudes which are rooted in this background, for some of them are amenable to change. Others, however, are not and one of the responsibilities of the leader is to evaluate what, hopefully, can be changed through exposure to a group discussion experience and what cannot be changed, or at least cannot be changed at this point. Failure to do this will impair the development of positive relationships to him, because he will be perceived as a person who is neither understanding nor accepting of the members of his group, or even as someone who is looking down and rejecting them.

A leader's professional training, or if that is lacking, in-service training and supervisory help are invaluable in assessing group members in regard to the two areas mentioned above. In addition, the experience which he obtains in leading group after group results in a growing fund of knowledge which will enable him to formulate for himself the diagnosis of the individual and of his background as a member of a specific subgroup of the population more easily, more quickly, and also more accurately as time goes on. The passages

devoted to the description of Group Characteristics in the chapters
dealing with meetings with groups contained information of this kind
for these groups, while some of the interpersonal and intrapersonal
conflicts and problems of the participants were pointed out in the
running commentary which accompanied the presentation of the course
and content of these meetings.

RELATIONSHIP BETWEEN GROUP DISCUSSION LEADER AND GROUP MEMBERS

The ability to relate to group members merits some elaboration. Unless a leader can develop good relationships to the participants or at least to most of them, he cannot offer them a helpful
experience. Good relationships do not imply unqualified acceptance
of the participants, nor must they consist only of positive feelings
for them, although the latter, where they exist, will further the growth
of good relationships considerably. What is essential to the development of good relationships is the understanding of the group members
and of their concerns and problems, coupled with a desire to help
them. If these elements are not present, good relationships cannot
be expected to come to the fore.

The term "good relationships" which was used so far should
be clarified also to avoid any misconception in this important matter.
For the purpose of this chapter, and indeed of this book, relationships are good if their purpose was to offer help to the participants
in a group discussion experience and if some of this purpose was
achieved at least for a number of them. The term "positive" can be
used interchangeably with good in this connection. If the statement
is qualified by the addition of "at least a number of them" this is due
to the fact that no leader, however well trained, experienced, and
well motivated, can or should expect, or be expected, to be helpful
to every person in the group. This is impossible for several reasons:
the problems of group members are different, so are their expectations of and reactions to the group discussion experience, and so is
the interaction between the leader and each participant. The latter
is partly conscious, since there are group members whom even the
best leaders dislike, and leaders whom some participants reject
although they may be highly motivated, and partly unconscious, based
on intrapsychic phenomena which are set in action by the group discussion experience.

If the writer stated in the preceding paragraph that totally
positive feelings of the leader toward the group members are not a
prerequisite for a helpful relationship, this means that ambivalence
has its place here as in all other relationships between human beings.
What is required of a leader in his professional work, however, are
three items: first, knowledge about his ambivalent feelings; second,
exploration of their cause in this given situation, and third, control
over their expression. The latter is particularly important, because

negative feelings toward a group member have no place in the group discussions which are the subject of this book. Self-examination can often uncover the causes of these negative feelings, and so can supervisory or consultative help. In some instances, and especially when a leader finds himself experiencing such negative reactions repeatedly, psychiatric treatment is an excellent tool not only for the uncovering and facing of unconscious feelings and for help with professional difficulties resulting therefrom, but also for an increased understanding of the total self, which often affects a person's private life and happiness to a considerable degree. In the discussion of negative feelings which sometimes develop between a leader and a group member, one last caution should be added, which is that professional as well as nonprofessional persons must have realistic goals for themselves. The goal of liking and of being able to help everybody one works with is as unrealistic as that of liking and receiving help from every group discussion leader.

The above-mentioned intrapersonal problems between a leader and a few members of his groups are different from a leader's inability to offer helpful experiences to categories of people, such as teenagers or older people, to name two subgroups that some leaders find difficult to work with. This is mostly due to problems of overidentification or of rejection, which in turn are based on unsolved conflicts in the leader's own relationships to members of his own family, mostly his children, or his parents, and sometimes his siblings. These conflicts are usually not easily accessible and generally require personal help in the form of a treatment experience. Trying to "overcome" this by repeated exposure to working with such groups does not produce any results except that it increases a feeling of failure in the leader, who is often very skillful with other groups. In addition, such an approach to the leader's problem results in a negative experience for the group members who are entitled to the assignment of the best available leader. More about this follows in the discussion of supervision of group discussion leaders.

If we proceed to look at the relationships which the group members can be expected to develop to their leader, the first point to be made is that these relationships will vary greatly, and that allowance must be made by the leader for these differences. A statement of a general nature in regard to these relationships can be made with reference to the frequency of the contacts, since it is clear that relationships tend to grow and to deepen the more opportunity for interaction is offered. This is particularly true in group discussions with voluntary participation, which are the subject of this book, because group members who do not like the leader or the other group members usually leave the group after the first, or the first few sessions. Examples of growing and deepening relationships of group members to the leader can be found in situations where a leader offers leadership to a group which is essentially of the same composition for several discussion series, some of which were described. The members of such groups will develop more confidence and more trust in the leader, will be more ready to involve themselves and to commit themselves to the discussions more deeply.

While such deeper relationships are desirable since they help the group members to move toward their goals of learning more about themselves and the other persons in their lives--members of their families, friends, etc.--with whom they interact, they also present certain dangers. The chief one is that they can be a heady draught for the leader, especially if he is not yet very skilled in working with groups, where the impact of many relationships and many interactions come to him simultaneously. This experience is even more difficult to handle for the leader who is unsure of himself as a professional--and probably also about some other areas of his functioning--and who finds it reassuring. Even a very competent leader has his vulnerable spots and if this happens to be a neurotic need for love and reassurance, more intensive relationships of group members may seem to offer what he is seeking. Such a development does not take care of the leader's inner problems, however, since neurotic needs which are based on earlier conflicts, as exaggerated demands on others for love and support are, cannot be satisfied by experiences in adult life without some uncovering of their causes. In addition, such an interaction between leader and group members has a negative impact on the latter who sense the misuse made of their offering.

At the opposite end of the scale is the leader who, again because of his personality problems, finds it difficult to have people come too close to him. He usually withdraws his emotional investment in the group and aims for more distance between himself and the group members, leaving the latter baffled and feeling rejected as indeed they are. In both situations, self-examination and supervision may be useful although the personality problems of the leaders which are at the bottom of these phenomena usually require the acquisition of insight which comes as a result of a personal treatment experience.

The statement made earlier that the relationships which group members develop to a leader will vary widely deserves some elaboration. Some will relate spontaneously and warmly to him, will express their feelings of appreciation for his contributions verbally on various occasions and also through their replies on the questionnaires. Get Well cards if the leader is ill; the telephone calls of some mothers of acting out children during the interval between discussion series, which were mentioned in an earlier chapter of this book are expressions of such feelings. So are gifts, which are taken up in more detail later. Most of the examples given--but not all--apply to adult group members.

Teen-agers, in turn, find different ways of showing their positive feelings for a leader. Some wish to sit next to him; others offer to carry his coat or briefcase, or to set up a room for the meeting, or to help serve refreshments. If teen-agers who do not have many social skills make these efforts, this is even more meaningful.

Many leaders are baffled as to the appropriate response to

such manifestations, and again their work style and their personalities determine what is to them an appropriate response. In the writer's opinion, the decision of how to respond to such expressions of positive feelings must be guided solely by the leader's professional judgment of what will be most helpful for the individual group member in the situation. Again, the examples which follow are not the one and only answer to these questions; they reflect, as does the entire book, her experiences, but also her work style, personality, and hang-ups.

If an adult group member said: "Mrs. Pollak, you are wonderful!"--which, alas, is music to one's ears!--the author always replied: "I am so glad you like the meetings and find them helpful." This removed the group member's comment from the personal to the professional and related it to the service offered, which was the basic reason for the relationship, and this was done without hurting the group member's feelings. On the other hand, if a teen-ager who was very much in need of emotional support made this or a similar remark, the leader's reply was: "I am glad you like me, and I like you too." Once a teen-ager with an unhappy home situation said: "I wish you would adopt me." Her reply was: "I like you too, but you know parents who adopt children are much younger than I am." To say: "I wish I could adopt you" would have been a lie, since the author had no desire to do this, and one of her basic rules was that one only tells the truth to the members of one's groups, an obligation of which all members of helping professions are aware and which needs no explanation. (The girl's statement might also have been used for an exploration of the causes of dissatisfaction with the home situation of most of the group members, since the writer knew that this dissatisfaction existed, but she missed the opportunity to do this.) When a discussion series ended, some teen-age girls kissed her and she kissed them too, but she never initiated this form of leave taking.

When Get Well cards were sent to her, she acknowledged them with thanks at the next meeting; the aforementioned telephone calls were accepted and handled according to the problems which caused them. These, and other responses of the writer, were based on her evaluation of the needs of individual group members at a given point and on the best way in which she could meet these needs, within the range of a professional relationship and only if this was indicated.

Following is an example where the author decided that it was inappropriate for her to do something which the members of a specific group obviously wished her to do. The separated, divorced, and widowed persons used to go out together for coffee after the meetings and usually continued their discussions at that time. She thought it indicated not to join them, partly because the great need for supportive relationships of most participants might have made it difficult not to become involved too deeply with their personal problems and partly because these get togethers were different from the group discussions she led, which were a professional service. She also confesses to a certain preference for meetings which have a starting time and an ending time, although both are usually quite flexible, and last but not least she always liked to terminate her working days and especially her working nights at a reasonable hour, and more or less when planned. These are elements of her work style, but they were not discussed with the group. When the meetings were mentioned to the leader, several times, and also with a certain wistfulness, she replied that she was very happy to hear that the group members enjoyed them. Nothing further was said, and the participants continued to attend the group discussion meetings with the same involvement as before.

The dangers of becoming involved in too close relationships for the leader were mentioned, but such experiences can also do harm to the group members, if they are offered without a clear understanding of how far meeting the need for supportive relationships will be helpful to them. While considerable support is often necessary in order to enable a person to learn, grow, and change patterns of coping, such support, if overdone, can be crippling because it encourages him to continue to depend on the helping person. This is contrary to the goals of therapeutic help of any kind, which should contribute to the strength of the person using it so that he can eventually become independent of the services of the therapist.

One of the problems with which the author was coping in some of these situations was that of defining the boundaries between professional and personal relationships. This is a difficult task with which every person must come to terms by himself; how this is done, depends on one's personality, one's personality problems, one's values, one's work style, and one's experience. These boundaries are sometimes drawn less sharply in work with groups than in other treatment relationships and the writer has no quarrel with people in the helping professions who feel that these boundaries are not important or should not even exist. The theories of, and approaches to, the task of helping people are as different as the modalities of treatment offered and the persons who deliver these services. What one person found effective and comfortable need not be so in other situations, or for other professional people.

The group members mentioned so far responded very positively and warmly to the leader. However, every group has some participants who are more guarded and more reserved and the leader must respect the individual group member's differences as they affect his readiness or ability or wish to involve himself more closely with him. The purpose of meeting with a group is not only to help its members to develop relationships to the leader and among themselves; it is to offer them, based on these relationships, a learning experience in the areas of their concerns or problems regarding their family or social relationships. The relationship to the leader is no more than a tool in the pursuit of this goal which enables them to mobilize their strength to cope with their difficulties and to find better solutions for their problems. People learn in different ways, so that to some the relationship to the leader may be more important during the process

than to others and some may need closer relationships to achieve
their goals, while others may do better with more distant ones.
This is equally true for the different speed at which people learn,
for the different skills they acquire, or the different solutions which
are appropriate for them. The group members, and not the leader,
decide, sometimes consciously, and sometimes unconsciously, what
is right for them in these matters. It is sometimes a puzzle to a
leader why some group members are more guarded and more reserved,
but it should not be if he understands the members of his group.
Certainly any feeling of rejection which a leader might experience
if he compares the different ways in which the participants relate to
him are unrealistic and are usually also a reflection of his personal
problems.

THE USE OF THE SELF BY THE LEADER

Another area of group discussion leadership which often causes
problems for leaders, and which is also quite controversial, is the
use of the self with groups. This covers such questions as whether
one shares one's professional and personal experiences with a group
and, if so, why and how much; the language and terminology one uses
with a specific group; the impact of one's appearance on group members. Related to these matters are the leader's role as a model for
identification leading to new attitudes and changed behavior and the
ways in which he discharges his responsibilities for setting the tone
for the meetings. His goals in working with a group and his values
will determine the answers which a leader finds to these questions.

For instance, if the goal of one's work is to help group members to find more appropriate solutions to their difficulties with
family or social relationships, so that their coping capacity is
increased and any low self-image strengthened, the way in which the
leader uses himself will be one of his best tools for working toward
that goal. He can, and he should, enable the participants to identify
with him, always keeping in mind that the goal of such identification
is not the pleasant glow one may experience in being the object of
such gratifying emotions. The writer's philosophy in this matter
can be stated in one sentence: The leader should be ahead of his
group, but not out of reach. In other words, the model for indenti-
fication he presents must be carefully adapted to the particular group
with which he is working, must present traits he wishes to strengthen
in the participants, or behavior which is not part of their present
mode of action but which they can accept in his opinion. Never,
however, should the model for identification stress something which
the leader knows to be in the realm of the impossible for the members
of this group. An example of the latter would be to start a discussion of the impact of a happy first sexual and love experience with a
group of unmarried mothers, who have given up their children for
adoption, since this procedure almost always indicates an unhappy

relationship with the children's fathers.

If one keeps in mind the goals toward which one is working as well as the kind of model for identification which will be most helpful to a specific group, one can usually determine very easily whether, and if so, what kind of personal experiences should be shared with its members. This applies to questions about being married, or about having children, which should be answered truthfully, but even more important, in such fashion that these answers are related to and can be used by the group members in dealing with their special problems. To give an example, teen-age girls from deprived backgrounds who are engaged in a variety of sexual realtionships or who are unmarried mothers usually find food for thought if the leader says, in answer to the question: "Are you married?" "Yes, I have been married for thirty years, and happily too, to the same man." The questions which they tend to ask following such a comment often reveal a searching for ways to find more satisfactory, deeper and more lasting relationships than the ones in which they are currently engaged: "Do you still love him? What do you like about him?" Sometimes, the question follows: "Don't you get bored with him?" which is also a polite way of asking if the man would not like a little more spice and variety in his life! This is best answered with the true statement that everyone is boring, or annoying, or infuriating at one time or another, if one lives with that person, but that one can put up with this, if one loves and likes him, or her, most of the time. If group members are helped to delve into this matter further, and are able to do this, this leads to the exploration of love, of sexual and marriage relationships on a deeper level, and within the context of the total life experience of the two people who are part of these relationships.

If the writer met with a group of adults who were dealing with marriage and its problems, she would not stress the length or the happiness of her own marriage, but would share with them as she felt indicated, some of the unavoidable difficulties which living in close contact with a person must bring, ways which can contribute to their solution if possible, or at least to an improvement of the climate in the family.

The author has never answered questions which teen-agers have asked about her own sexual experiences before her marriage. Ignoring these questions was her way of handling them, and this never failed, because they were not repeated. She came to this decision partly because of her own values, which place certain topics outside of the professional area and which consider the right to privacy and to the respect by others of the lines which an individual draws in these matters, one of the privileges of every human being. She also felt that information of this kind, whatever its content, would not help the group members in any way, and last but not least, she realized that such a question was an attempt to put her on the spot. It was therefore an expression of aggression which should not be encouraged.

The leader's selection of language and terminology are related in similar fashion to the goals of working with a specific group.

Using the language of the teen-agers is often recommended, based on the theory that this makes the leader "one of us" as far as group members are concerned, and facilitates his acceptance and the establishment of relationships. This procedure may be helpful if one begins to work with a group of teen-agers who have no other way of expressing themselves, its purpose being to be understood by them. In the writer's opinion, this should not be continued beyond the point at which communication is established, even in such a situation. It is a fallacy to believe that teen-agers, for instance, will accept more readily the person who uses their language, because they know that this is something which is artificial, and some also feel that they are being "talked down to" by this usage. As mentioned previously, the language used with a group should always be adapted so that the participants will be able to understand it, but it can go beyond their immediate knowledge, with some explanations of both the language, and the reasons for the leader's selection of it.

To return to teen-agers--which lend themselves so well to an illustration of the matter under discussion--the correct, that is, medical, terms for sexual organs and sexual acts can very easily be introduced into a discussion of such matters, which are bound to come up when one meets with teen-age groups. The writer has done this consistently, with the explanation of the terms; the reason given for her bringing them to the group being that they are used by doctors and nurses and that it will be helpful to the participants if they are familiar with them. Teen-agers are not the only ones to express themselves in what were formerly known as four letter words; other groups such as unmarried mothers, or some parent groups do this also, mostly simply from ignorance. The writer usually acknowledged the use of such words by stating that she was familiar with them, but went on to present material or make her comments in proper terminology, always explaining that knowing these terms will come in handy, in the contacts of group members with doctors, hospitals, and clinics. No one ever questioned--much less ridiculed!--this procedure, which reflected her conviction that any tools which a person acquires to cope more effectively with reality experiences will increase his self-confidence, his coping capacity, and will give him the often much needed encouragement to tackle other problems also.

The appearance of a leader, if it is given some thought, as should be the case, is another example of the use of the self with groups. Appearance covers such items as the clothes, make-up, and jewelry which a female leader wears, the clothes a male leader wears, etc. These matters are subject to similar considerations as the use of terminology; always, the determining factor is the purpose of working with a group. Along with this, the values of the leader, his work style, will be codeterminants. The author has preferred to "tone down" her appearance when offering leadership to economically deprived groups and she never wore expensive clothes or valuable jewelry in such a situation. She planfully selected clothes, however, which were becoming and not out of style. She did this in her work with the mothers of acting out children described in this book, and a number of these participants identified with her eventually by abandoning house dresses in favor of better clothes, and by ceasing to wear curlers when coming to the meetings. One member of this group even went as far as to get a set of false teeth, which she needed badly! Since a poor appearance usually reflects a depressed state of mind and one's negative feelings about oneself, these improvements reflected the progress and emotional gains which these group members had made.

For her meetings with teen-agers, the writer did not feel it important to wear miniskirts or pant suits, because she does not like them. Only a few openly aggressive teen-age girls made negative remarks about her appearance as described in the preceding chapter. In her work with teen-agers, however, the author found it helpful to pay special attention to any jewelry she wore. A bracelet with a charm which said "I love you more today than yesterday" rarely failed to be noticed and to start off discussions of love and marriage, since many group members got curious about the inscription--which was in French--and wanted to know what it meant.

Reference was made earlier to the leader's role as a model for new behavior, and much of what was described as use of the self belongs in that category. Other aspects of group discussion leadership through which one wishes to present to the participants different ways of behaving from those which they habitually use can be added here. For instance, listening to what other people have to say without interrupting them is important to facilitate the interaction of group members, but this is not part and parcel of everybody's life style. This statement does not apply to teen-agers only, by the way. The leader's comment: "we take turns here and everybody will have a chance to speak up, but we don't interrupt the person who is speaking" not only brings order into a discussion which might otherwise develop into a shouting match, it also teaches restraint, where this is appropriate, and consideration for others. Suggesting that food be passed around, and that some of it be saved for the participants who will come later, if one works with deprived teen-agers, is another example of providing a model for behavior and of setting the tone for their interaction, since many of these young people have a tendency to grab whatever is available without thought for the needs of others.

The leader fulfills a teaching function here, and much of this can be done indirectly. Such an approach is particularly important if one would otherwise offend a group member whose standards of living are vastly different from one's own. The writer remembers vividly a participant in a group of economically and socially deprived women who, in addition to being poor, was not clean and had a body odor. In her eagerness to prepare coffee, she tested the temperature of the water by immersing her thumb in the pot. The author thought it appropriate to accept the coffee with thanks and to drink it. When seconds were suggested, she said casually that she believed the pot had a light which turned red to indicate that the water was hot. The group member replied that she had not known this, and from then on, she watched the light to determine when she could serve coffee.

Another aspect of this teaching function is related to other, less concrete matters, since one goal of the group discussions is to leave the members better informed, more aware of others and of themselves, of their actions, of the reasons for the latter and of their effects than when the leader started to meet with them. There are many ways of working toward these goals, and one is to help the participants to look for motives and causes for peoples' actions. For example, if a teen-age girl says: "Married people fight with each other," the question "Why do they do this?" leads to exploring, and hopefully to understanding some of the causes of marital friction, just as the question: "Why do children fight?" can be used to seek for the many reasons which can cause such behavior. Such understanding usually--although not always--increases the capacity of the persons involved in such situations to deal more effectively with these problems.

The questions raised by group members play an important role in connection with the teaching function of the leader, if they are used as "grist for the mill," as far as that is possible. The writer discussed previously how inappropriate or unrelated questions can be dealt with. At this point, it is essential to remember that the questions of the participants indicate their concerns, and that their exploration--which need not take place immediately, but should take place eventually in the course of the meetings--will broaden the knowledge and enhance the understanding of all group members.

Other ways of teaching are the reformulation of some of the questions raised by the participants, so that they will include related topics also, the summarization of what group members discussed in a preceding meeting, to which the leader adds such of his own knowledge as will be helpful to them. These procedures were discussed previously in other connections.

Providing models for behavior as well as setting the tone for the meetings should be done as soon as possible and preferably when the occasion to do this presents itself. This--like many other aspects of leadership--takes different forms, depending on the group with which one is working. It often "gets across" to the group members to an amazing degree, sometimes without being discussed, simply by the leader's methods of approach. An example was a retarded teen-ager whose friend was found stealing in a dime store, an act in which she had not participated. She explained this with the statement: "Mrs. Pollak does not want her girls to get into trouble by stealing," but stealing had not been discussed with the members of this group. Another example occurred in a meeting with the separated, divorced, and widowed persons, when a new member asked whether first names were used in the group. A participant answered: "We call each other by our first names, but Mrs. Pollak uses last names." This was said very matter of factly and was not questioned by the new or by the old group members. It reflected the leader's practice in working with adults, and she had never discussed it with any members of her groups.

GROUP REACTIONS TO THE LEADER'S ABSENCE

These reactions belong to the smaller problems of group discussion leadership which are worth mentioning, however, because they often puzzle less experienced leaders. One can safely assume that any absence of the leader from a meeting will be experienced as a rejection by the group members, even if illness or some other event outside of his control precipitated it. This holds especially true for teen-agers. They also often have fantasies about his unlimited power to meet their every wish. One example of such unrealistic expectations--which may also have been based on dependency needs or aggressive drives--were some girls with disciplinary problems, who wanted to go on a trip to New York with the author. She was unable to do this, partly because such a trip would have to be financed, a bus would have to be chartered, insurance taken out, parental permission obtained, not to mention her reluctance to assume responsibility for fifteen girls whose difficulties to start out with were such that they could sometimes not be contained in a small room. A few group members accepted her--carefully chosen-- explanations why she could not plan such a trip, but many were offended and the statement: "If you liked us, you would make it possible" reflected the belief in magic which is characteristic of many young--and sometimes older--people whose adjustment to reality is poor and who find it difficult to meet its demands.

It is only fair to add also that some members of adult groups who are better adjusted to reality are more guarded, less ready to involve themselves in the discussion and more distant if a leader has missed a meeting. Needless to say, such incidents should be avoided and notices of the leader's inability to meet with a group should reach them ahead of time. Even if this was done, however, many group members resent a leader's absence. One wonders if he does not become endowed with imaginary qualities by the participants, such as being always here, never ill, and always available to them, similar to the way in which small children see their parents.

THE GIVING AND RECEIVING OF GIFTS

The often complex question of gifts--both those given by the leader and those which group members may wish to give to him-- also needs to be taken up. The question is complex, because the giving, as well as the acceptance, of gifts is an emotionally charged activity which is likely to be caused by, as well as to unleash, a variety of feelings in the donors as well as in the recipients. The decision

on these matters will again be based on one's goals of working with
a particular group, and the common problems of its members as well
as the group's characteristics. To give some examples, in leading
discussions with emotionally deprived mothers who also came from
low socioeconomic backgrounds, the writer gave them a paperback
on sex education, partly as an expression of her concern for and
interest in them, but much more to reinforce the discussions they
had had on these topics, and to make sure that these participants,
most of whom had only scant knowledge in these matters, would be
better equipped and feel more capable in answering their children's
questions in turn. She also decided to accept the gift which these
mothers gave her at the end of each discussion series--an umbrella,
a pen and pencil set, etc.--because it is important for deprived persons to learn to give and to have their gifts accepted (Neisser, 1973,
pp. 294-301). Once, when she was given six dollars--with the explanation that the mothers were at a loss what to buy, and with the injunction,
which reflected the tight economic situation in which they were living,
"not to buy pots and pans"--she wore a new blouse at the first meeting
of the following series, and the participants were pleased to hear
that it had been bought with this money. They also approved of her
taste, and this started off a discussion of the impact of one's appearance on how one feels about oneself, of the children's positive reactions "if you look good" and similar matters which were related to
the goals of discussion leadership for these participants, who are
described in more detail in the chapter on the work with the mothers
of acting out children.

The retarded teen-age girls with whom the author worked for
several years were helped by their school counselor to select a gift
and to sign a card whenever a discussion series ended. The importance of learning to give and to see one's gift accepted was one of the
reasons here also why this was done. In addition, acquiring some
social skills, such as gift wrapping a box of talcum powder, selecting
a gift card, signing it, were new activities for most participants and
they were proud of their achievements in these areas. Since one of
the goals of meeting with this group was to help the retarded girls to
develop a better self-image, this newly found competence as well as
the leader's expressions of pleasure and appreciation furthered this
goal. She also used another device toward that purpose in that she
sent individual handwritten Thank You notes to every group member.
The counselor distributed them and the girls always received them
with surprise and with delight, partly because they did not receive
much personal mail, and partly because the notes were evidence of
the leader's interest in and positive feelings for them. These notes
were also an example of techniques in social relationships which
would, hopefully, provide a model for the behavior of the participants
in similar situations later on in their lives.

The material presented regarding use of the self, the role of
the leader as model for behavior and setting the tone for one's meetings represent the values of the author, her goals and her work style.

In the numerous institutes and training workshops she led for professional and paraprofessional staff members, much time was always devoted to the discussion of these questions, and the answers were as different as the people who contributed them. Life styles differ, so do work styles, and no one should force himself to do something which "goes against the grain." The author would like to add that she did not find her own answers easily; they were the result of much thinking, of trial and error, and of gathering experience in group discussion leadership. Furthermore, one must be able to cope with one's anxiety about being accepted or rejected by a group, or about being able to reach it and to be helpful to it, before one can find these answers. The writer is sharing throughout this book her own experiences and her own thinking regarding group discussion leadership, and the former cover those she found helpful to the participants, as well as those which were not helpful. In no way does the book attempt to provide final answers to the many questions which every leader must ask himself. If it assists the reader in this task, the work which went into it was well worthwhile.

HELPING MEMBERS OF HETEROGENEOUS GROUPS TO FIND COMMON GROUND

Group homogeneity--or the lack of it--must be mentioned in connection with leadership problems. Many leaders prefer to work with homogeneous groups. This is undoubtedly easier as it permits one to assume a certain commonality of socioeconomic and educational background, a more or less comparable life style, some and often many shared concerns and problems. Groups which are not homogeneous, either because the members come from different sectors of society--such as the group of retired persons described in this book--or groups with members who are of different ages, require a different approach if the leader wishes to enable all, or as many of the participants as possible to become involved in the discussions. This is usually best done by relating the material which they bring out to some factors which they share. In the case of older persons the common experience is aging which comes to everybody be they rich or poor. If several age categories are represented in the group, the leader can draw on the younger members in a group and ask them to bring out their concerns and problems in the area under discussion, and then on the older ones to share their experiences with these same problems, and any solutions which they may have found. A similar approach works with groups which are interracial, if their focus is on family and social relationships. Such an exchange usually achieves several results: it enlarges awareness of other people's problems and may help other members to anticipate, or to cope better with such problems, if they should come their way; it breaks down some of the cliches which we often apply to those who are different from us, and which reflect unrealistic fantasies, or hostility: "If I had money, I wouldn't have any problems;" "Young people don't understand old people;" "Our children have problems in school because they are black." What is more important, these encounters often--not always, of course--help to form a bridge for those who wish to cross it, so that they will enhance their knowledge of the world around them.

If the leader wishes to work toward such goals, he must make special efforts. First and foremost, he must expect and be willing to cope with the aggression which is likely to be present in greater amounts and closer to the surface in groups of this kind, since the projection of one's own difficulties on such factors as money, race, age is challenged by meeting persons who embody them, whose experiences are similar and who share them in the meetings. He must therefore guide the discussions so that they will go beyond the expression of negative feelings toward the young, or the old, or whatever the case may be, in order to enable group members, or as many as possible, to move toward an understanding of those who are not part of their own in-group. This step results in learning more about "how the other half lives" if the writer may use this somewhat shopworn term, and beyond that, in learning how persons who belong to a group different from one's own cope with life's difficulties. In addition, the leader must see to it that the members of one subgroup do not overwhelm the others and that representatives of both are given ample opportunities to share their experiences and to present their point of view. These tasks require firmness coupled with tact, an ability to shift gears quickly in one's thinking while keeping the goals of the discussion in mind, and strict discipline of oneself, so that one's identification with one subgroup--which may well exist-- does not affect the service which one offers to all participants. Leaders who find aggression difficult to tolerate and to handle, or those who are not in control of their own identifications and pre- ferences, which may be in regard to young people, or to parents, for instance, will find the leadership of nonhomogeneous groups dif- ficult. If these difficulties persist, a leader may do well to work with homogeneous groups only. In the writer's opinion, no one is required to be equally effective in all areas of one's professional work, but one has an obligation to make every effort to achieve this goal and, most important, one must desist from delivering services which are not helpful to those one serves.

It should not be forgotten, however, that nonhomogeneous groups present considerable challenge to the leader, because of the demands made on him and also because quite frequently new and totally unexpected material is brought out as a result of the interaction in such groups. Working with them often brings about a spurt of pro- fessional growth which then results in improved discussion leader- ship with homogeneous groups also.

SOME GROUP CHARACTERISTICS WHICH AFFECT DISCUSSION
LEADERSHIP

The material presented so far on group discussion leadership
techniques has stressed the importance of adapting them to the specific group with which one works, in a variety of areas, such as
amount and form of material presented, if any; language used, etc.
In addition, certain characteristics must be taken into account which
many participants who belong to subgroups tend to have. If one works
with teen-agers, for instance, the leader must accept that their
attendance will usually be more irregular than that of adults, and that
their intragroup relations will be fluid. One must expect that a date,
or dance, or some other attractive social activity will prevent teen-
agers from coming to a meeting. It becomes equally clear if one has
many contacts with them that today's best friend can be tomorrow's
enemy, and one will do well to take such statements of their emotions
with a grain of salt.

Accepting teen-agers' negative feelings toward each other is
quite different from permitting the open expression of aggression,
through hitting, scapegoating, and other actions which were discussed
previously. They have no place in groups where learning in the areas
of family and social relationships is the goal; this is different in some
therapy groups planned to effect deep seated changes in the membership. To be effective in coping with aggression, the leader must be
very sure of his stand in the matter, and in the situations presented
here, this means he must be sure that he will not permit the expression of aggression in certain forms. Any unconscious--and certainly
any conscious!--doubts he may have about the desirability or appro-
priateness of such an approach transmit themselves to the group
members, and lead to their disregard of his verbal statements pro-
hibiting this behavior. The analogy to the famous "Do as I say,
don't do as I do" which children interpret so correctly, when parents
send out contradictory signals, is very clear here. Since many adults
are quite conflicted in regard to their own aggressive drives, they
may find it very difficult to help others cope with these drives, and
this applies especially to the work with young people. If the leader
is free from such conflicts, he will find it possible to help group
members to look at aggressive actions from the angle of what they
achieve and what they do not achieve, and to enable many of them to
find alternate and more constructive ways of expressing negative
feelings. If one values aggression and its expression through destructive acts as a way of life, however, one's professional work should
not be focused on helping people with problems of family and social
relationships within the framework of the structure of the society in
which they are living.

When one offers leadership to groups of older people, the
characteristics of that subgroup of the population must be similarly
taken into account. They are physical changes, loss of vitality and
energy, fears, which may be realistic or unrealistic, loneliness,

loss of status in a world which is youth and work oriented. The two chapters on the work with groups of retired persons discussed these matters in more detail. The reality of these problems must be recognized, if only because most aged persons react negatively when their complaints--be they justified or not--are met with the non-responsive cheerful admonition "to count your blessings and to think of others whose lot is worse." In regard to their attendance, one must make allowance for the hesitancy of many older people to come out in bad weather, or for their giving preference to visiting children and grandchildren, if they are on good terms with them and such an invitation was extended.

THE ROLE OF RECORDS OR NOTES

An important part of group discussion leadership techniques is the keeping of records; some written notes in whatever form are most helpful to the leader regarding one's work with a group. This enables one to see where the group is going as well as what it has achieved so far, and to relate both to the group's goals. These records or notes are also essential for the leader's identification of the group members, which in turn goes a long way toward helping them to develop a relationship to him. Group members can be identified by a brief description of their appearance or personality, or both, as well as by some relevant comments or contributions which they made to a specific aspect of the discussion. A reference to such a comment at a later meeting indicates the leader's interest in the participants and the time and thought he gives to his work as well as to them. As a consequence, they feel appreciated, know that their contributions are welcome, and this knowledge usually frees them even more to participate in the meetings.

Records or notes of this kind are also a valuable tool for the training and supervision of leaders, as well as for any self-examination in which they may wish to engage. Sometimes leaders are reluctant to take such notes, or to keep such records, usually on the grounds that they are too busy, that doing the work, that is, leading groups, is more important than keeping notes. Needless to say, leaders who have these attitudes are even more reluctant to share any such material, sketchy as it may be, with another person for training, consultative or supervisory purposes. This is usually due to a lack of belief in one's professional competence, or to unrealistic expectations of oneself, or to fears of the evaluation from the training person or supervisor. Other more deep seated personal factors, most of which are related to problems in giving of oneself and compulsive withholding, are also at work in many such situations. Training and supervision can be helpful to leaders who do not have the last mentioned problems, particularly if the training person or supervisor stresses that the purpose of his activity is improved performance on the job and in the delivery of a certain service. For those group discussion leaders who have inner conflicts of anal origin, or residues of infantile magical thinking, or problems with authority, to name only a few causes, a treatment experience will in all likelihood be necessary to enable them to deal more effectively with these conflicts. This statement is of course equally true for helping persons who use other treatment modalities. Since conflicts of this nature are certain to affect the nonprofessional part of a person's life also, help in dealing with them goes far beyond achieving greater professional competence.

INTRAGROUP RELATIONS

Leadership techniques are of great importance also in the area of intragroup relationships because they contribute greatly to the development of positive and supportive relationships among the group members. Everyone who has worked with groups knows how different each group is in regard to its climate which is, in turn, closely related to and caused by the quality of the relationships which its members have developed to each other. Their relationships to the leader are another cause for the different climate of different groups. These two relationships are so interdependent that it is almost impossible to look at one without looking at the other. The writer's aim at this point is to discuss those techniques of group discussion leadership which will foster the growth of positive relationships among the participants of a group discussion experience.

Some examples will probably be useful here. If the leader listens with attention and courtesy to each group member while he is speaking, he conveys his respect for this person as well as for the contribution made, and this usually stimulates most of the others in the group to do the same. This approach has an additional result in that it allays any anxiety which they might experience at the thought that they might not be able to express their concern or might not receive their due share of the leader's attention. A decrease in anxiety leads to better functioning in the group, and this positive experience often gets transferred to other areas of a person's life, again with the result of better functioning and increased coping capacity. Another example is also related to the contribution made by a participant, and goes beyond listening to it. If the leader gives recognition to it, verbally, by quoting it, or recognizing its meaning, whenever that is realistic, the person's self-confidence is increased and his further involvement in the discussions is encouraged. This in turn affects the other group members in similar fashion, particularly if the leader is objective, impartial, and careful to give equal attention to all. An increase in self-confidence often eliminates, or lessens, a person's need to be belittling or hostile to others, and a readiness to give to others as well as to acknowledge their contributions and achievements may replace this need. As a result, the leader who is kind but firm in his dealings with the participants will

encourage kindness and discourage acting out behavior among them.
Here too, intragroup relationships will benefit those persons who
can accept such limits, and again, the relationships of the participants in other areas of their lives may reflect some of these changes,
with positive results for them and for those with whom they are in
contact. Since many members of the groups with which one works
tend to have a limited outlook on life, and narrow points of view, the
leader's ability to tolerate very different approaches to a problem or
even to bring them to the group is not only an exposure to these different approaches, but encourages tolerance, which has a place in
good intragroup relationships as well as in one's contact with the
world outside of the group discussion situation. An example is the
leader's capacity to accept the presence of a disturbed person, since
some of them often come to group meetings. If he can do that, most
group members will follow suit. The writer remembers a group of
mothers to which one woman came who was in psychiatric treatment.
Her contributions, which were fortunately infrequent, were rambling
and mostly unrelated to the topic under discussion, but she seemed
to find comfort in being with the other mothers. If one of her contributions happened to be topic related, the leader acknowledged it,
and she let the others pass. The participants followed suit; they
were aware of that woman's disturbance but it did not frighten them.
This experience drew them together and resulted in closer intragroup relationships. As they were also rather unfamiliar with the
meaning, causes, and treatment of emotional disturbances, beyond
applying the word "crazy" to people who suffered from them, one
can assume that this exposure had effects which might go further
than their group discussion experience. The writer should perhaps
add that the disturbed person would have been excluded from the
meetings, if attendance had obviously upset her, as well as if it had
upset the other participants, since a leader has an obligation to protect group members from damaging experiences wherever possible,
and may also not permit one group member to frustrate the others
and to inhibit the group's progress.

Perhaps one can say that the example which the leader sets in
his selective use of group discussion techniques is another powerful
tool in his efforts to encourage group members to develop positive
intragroup relationships which will enable them to learn from each
other, support each other, and reap the gains of such emotional
support. The author would like to go further and to contend that the
leader's example--the model to which reference was made earlier--
is one of the components of group discussion leadership which will
affect his professional work more deeply and more consistently than
any of its other elements will.

Example, however, is used in a special sense here. It means,
in addition to actions and words, convictions, attitudes, and feelings.
If the former are not the expression of the latter, that is, if the
leader's actions and words are "lip service" only, the group members
will sense this and will in all probability obey the unspoken command

rather than his spoken word, just as the previously mentioned children do when parents present them with a similar dilemma. This means that the leader must be truthful, as well as understanding and accepting of the members of his groups. This requires a high degree of self-awareness which, as the author knows from her own experience, is often difficult and painful to obtain. It is, however, essential for one's professional work, and here too, supervision, training, and consultation can be of great help. In some instances, a personal treatment experience will enable one to face one's hidden and often unconscious feelings, which is another way of gaining self-awareness along with the ability to control consciously the expression of feelings which might interfere with one's being helpful to the participants in a group discussion experience.

Intragroup relationships begin to develop, when the group starts to meet. In view of this, considerable consideration is often given by leaders to the problems of the latecomer, that is of the person who joins the group after it had one, two, or several meetings. They are often apprehensive that this person may interfere with the development of good intragroup relationships, may disturb the group, not be accepted by them or not accept them. In such situations, the leader's techniques, as well as his own attitudes and feelings about the fact that a person joins the group later, will affect and determine the group members' reaction to him. If the leader makes him welcome, offers to bring him up to date on what was going on before he came, does not make him feel guilty about missing earlier sessions, and draws him into the discussions, the other group members will follow the leader's example. If the leader is annoyed about a person's coming to later meetings, if he experiences this as a rejection of himself, as a lack of interest or if he is rigid and resents "having to shift gears," group members will sense this and usually their treatment of the newcomer reflects the leader's inappropriate reactions. The methods of helping a leader come to terms with them are the same as in the other previously mentioned examples of difficulties experienced in the delivery of one's services.

The material presented elaborated on the statement that leadership affects intragroup relationships, but the reverse is equally true. Most leaders respond positively to the positive climate in a group, which is largely the result of positive relationships of the group members to each other, and they give with ease and enthusiasm their best professional leadership to groups of this kind. This in turn affects intragroup relationships positively and furthers the growth of the positive group climate. A different situation arises when intragroup relationships are strained and when conflict exists between the participants. Many leaders find it difficult to work with groups under such circumstances, partly because they present more problems of leadership, and partly because some blame themselves and their shortcomings if the group climate is not positive. Such an attitude is not realistic, because groups differ as much from each other as the individuals who are part of them. Unavoidably, the members of some groups will relate more closely to each other than those in other groups and, as a result, the group climate in the former will be more positive than in the latter. The leader will do well to accept such differences without always assuming that he is to blame for them. Since the most expert leader is not entirely nor solely responsible for what happens in a group, he will need to keep his perspective in a situation of this kind. What he owes to such a group--as to any group with which he is working--is his best knowledge and experience in order to help its members to develop the most positive relationships to each other which they can achieve. Any fantasies about one's omnipotence will only be harmful to this endeavor.

Occasionally, intragroup relationships are affected by the presence of a member who, by a quirk of his personality, irritates most of the others in the group. The clash of personalities, which may occur in one-to-one contacts, occurs also in group situations when the participants find it very difficult, or even impossible, to tolerate one in their midst. This phenomenon is different from scapegoating, and while it is not one which is frequent, it should be mentioned, because the leaders to whom this happened--of whom the author was one--sought for errors they had made in their techniques with and approach to these groups. Conscientious examination showed, however, that this was not the case; an unknown factor sparked negative attitudes of the majority of group members to one particular person. As a consequence, this participant usually withdrew from the group. Since the leader could not recommend further attendance, joining other ongoing groups of similar interests was suggested wherever possible. It was interesting that the person who could not be tolerated by the members of one group was sometimes very acceptable to those of another group. One can only surmise that the different composition of the latter, and the different group discussion leadership produced this desirable result.

XVIII
Evaluation of Past and Planning of
Future Group Discussions

GOALS AS A BASIS FOR EVALUATION

The goals of group discussion leadership vary with the group
with which one is working. The overall goal is a better understanding
of family and social relationships, as stated previously, but what
this means differs vastly in every specific situation. It is in this
area that some group characteristics such as the level of education
and the life style play their most important role and group discussion
leadership which fails to take these factors into account cannot be
helpful. The "step forward" which one hopes group members will
take is related to where they started out just as the progress of a
client or patient in individual therapy must be evaluated in terms of
where he was when the treatment experience began. To give some
examples, if the teen-age girls described in this book gained a little
understanding of what marriage means, what to look for if one is
considering getting married to someone, if they learned a few facts
about sex relations, conception, and birth, and if along with this they
acquired a few skills in interacting with each other and with the young
men in their lives, this was considerable progress for them. If the
mothers who belonged to the "silent majority" learned that it is possible to discuss sexual relationships and related matters with their
children and how this could be done, this was progress for them.
The persons who were separated, divorced or widowed, on the other
hand, were quite able to handle the latter topics with their children,
but they were troubled about and unsure of themselves in their relations to members of the other sex and baffled by the conflicts between
their expectations of a second marriage partner and the reality of
what he, or she, had to and was willing to offer. Learning in these
areas was progress for them.

The goals which one can expect a group to achieve sometimes
present problems for leaders who wish to help their group members
to find fast solutions to their difficulties or who wish to achieve more
far reaching results. This desire may be due to lack of experience,
or to a wish to change the conditions under which a specific part of
the population is living, or to their enthusiasm for their roles as
helpers and enablers. Sometimes a wish to "save" others is at work

here, and this is generally based on the leader's personality and very
often on his own problems. It is essential to help leaders who are
coping with such difficulties to uncover and untangle their motives
so that their difficulties, needs, and conflicts do not interfere with
the delivery of their services to the participants. If this is not done--
through supervision, or through a personal treatment experience
where indicated--the latter will feel increasingly frustrated because
they will not receive recognition for what they have achieved, or will
feel, in spite of verbally expressed recognition, the leader's disappointment with them. Such attitudes do not foster positive relationships between leader and group members, nor are they conducive to
a favorable group or learning climate.

     In connection with the different goals of different groups, two
other factors should be mentioned which are important and which
also create difficulties for some leaders. One is that group members
use the group experience in different ways, with different speed and
to different degrees; the second is that they express, or show in non-
verbal fashion their gains from participation in the meetings in different ways also.

     The first mentioned factor should not come as a surprise to
persons from the helping professions, who realize from their one-
to-one contacts that changes in attitudes and feelings--not to mention
insight!--are acquired in various ways and with varying degrees of
ease which in turn determine how much time must be spent to obtain
such results. In similar fashion, each group member will take out
of a discussion of love, or of marriage problems, or of the adjustments to old age that which is important to him and has meaning for
him and will bypass and ignore those elements which do not apply to
his situation or which are too threatening. For this reason, it is
likely that if every participant wrote a report on the same discussion,
few if any of these reports would be alike. This is also reflected in
the replies on questionnaires which participants fill out at the end of
a discussion series, and which were discussed previously in another
connection. If, for instance, a leader takes the time to compare
the replies dealing with the stealing by children and to tie in this
material with his notes and his memory of that discussion, the different ways in which group members use the group discussion experience will become very apparent. This is due to many factors, such
as the different problems each person is facing in this area, to the
fact that a participant may not have this problem now, but is fearful
that it may develop later, to his understanding of the meaning of
children's behavior and of their needs, to his standards and values,
to his methods of parenting, to name only a few.

     The leader must accept such differences as soon as they become
apparent and use them to focus his service on those areas which need
to be explored more in his opinion whenever this is possible. Hopefully, a later rediscussion of the same topic as well as the reactions
relating to it will show growth and movement on the part of most
group members. He will always, however, find some who move more

quickly, others who took different parts of the material discussed
from the meetings, and some who learn slowly and laboriously that
which others assimilate easily. Any expectation that these differences will diminish as a result of the group discussion experience
are unrealistic and are therefore bound to lead to his and to the
group members' frustration. They are, furthermore, in conflict
with the respect which every helping person owes to the individuality
and uniqueness of the client, patient or group member to whom he is
offering his service.

GAINS

        Some gains from participation in a group discussion experience
are not expressed verbally, but become evident without being put
into words. Examples are some changes in attitudes, such as learning to take turns and learning to share, and reference was made to
them when the role of the leader as a model for behavior was discussed earlier. Many participants of groups which the author led
went beyond waiting for their turn, however, and saw to it that others
had opportunities to participate in the give and take of the meetings.
The writer remembers one instance when a new discussion series
with the mothers of acting out children started; some women were
present who had not attended previous meetings. One of the "old"
participants turned to them and said: "Why don't we let you say
what bothers you?" This met with a very good response and, incidentally, started a discussion on a topic which the leader had not
expected. Needless to say, this was one of those instances when it
is sound to forget one's own plans for a meeting. In a group of
retired persons who met in a library, it happened quite frequently
that one group member suggested to another that she bring to the
group what they had discussed on the way home, and the participants
in the discussion series for the separated, divorced, and widowed
persons did the same. Such encouragement went a long way with the
more timid persons in these meetings; beyond this, it gave them
self-confidence and made them feel that they had something to contribute. Since they could transfer these attitudes and their new
approach to others to a wider circle of relationships with people outside of the meetings--which some of them obviously could--and one
can assume that these relationships also profited from such change.
        Change also became evident in the appearance of some group
members in adult groups. (It was probably due to the great difference
in age between the author and the teen-age groups with which she
worked that no change of this kind appeared in the girls.) Some
mothers from economically deprived background began to dress more
carefully for the meetings; others went on diets. One school counselor with whom the writer cooperated for a number of years put it
very succinctly: "The curlers came down and the stockings came up."
Several women who participated in a discussion series for retired

persons who had presented a rather drab appearance at first began
to wear more stylish clothes and some make-up. This was perhaps
because of the way in which the author dressed but may also have been
due to their contacts with some other members of these groups who
were carefully dressed and made up. Compliments for these changes--
which other participants made--as well as a casual remark from the
author about them were received with appreciation and reinforced
these attempts to look better.

In those situations where the discussion series were planned
jointly with professional people from other organizations--counselors
or teachers in a school, for instance--their observations were valuable assets in evaluating progress made by the group members or
by members of their families. Some of the children who had been a
concern in school because of their acting out behavior did noticeably
better as the meetings with their mothers continued. As this behavior
disappeared or became less pronounced, they developed better relationships to the other children and to their teachers, and their school-
work improved. The attitudes of some of the mothers to the schools
changed also; they complained less of the school's failure to do its
job and were more ready to listen to what the teacher or counselor
had to suggest so that a child's learning might be encouraged and
facilitated. They also began to participate helpfully in the schools'
activities, in parent meetings, or as school aides, etc. When this
happened, it brought the school, the child, and the family closer
together, while offering outlets to the mothers for their time and
energy and involving them in an important part of their community.

Several librarians reported also on more interest in the library's
programs--not only the discussion series--an increased book cir-
culation and a greater readiness to volunteer on the part of some of
the retired persons as well as some of the teen-agers who had participated in projects in their branches.

A number of teen-age girls in schools to whom several discussion series on love, sex, and marriage were offered showed gains
from these experiences, such as less aggressive behavior, a greater
readiness to use the variety of services which the school made available to them and to turn to the faculty and the counselor when they
found themselves in difficulties which they could not handle. Furthermore, there were no pregnancies among the members of these groups
while they were in school. While it was of course not possible to
establish a cause and effect relationship in this matter, the results
were certainly to be welcomed from the point of view of the girls'
present and future happiness.

The writer should add at this point that no funds were available
for research so that the above-mentioned indices--replies of group
members on questionnaires, observations by leaders and by cooperating
professional persons--were used for the evaluation of gains of participants from their involvement in the discussion series.

In summary, if one is offering group discussion series, the
three most important factors to keep in mind are, first, to think

through what one plans to do, before one does it; second, to tie this in with the needs, problems, group, and personality characteristics of the recipients of this service, and third, to relate both to the goals of one's professional activity at a given time. This comment should not be taken as excluding any statement or action based on one's intuition and made following an impulse "on the spot." They certainly have their place in one's professional work. They should not, however, monopolize it and rule over it, nor should they take the place of reflection, examination of the group members and oneself, or of basing one's approach to and the methods selected for the leadership of a particular group on thoughtful planning.

PLANNING FUTURE SERIES

If one is leading groups, many decisions must be made which are not part of the techniques of group discussion leadership, but since they are closely related to them, the author will take them up in this connection. An example of such a decision is whether to plan another discussion series for a group, or to terminate the contact with the participants at this point. Factors to be considered in that connection are first of all, whether they are interested in and eager to continue, second, whether this would be helpful to them, that is, would lead to additional learning experience, and, finally, whether this is feasible in terms of available leadership. Questionnaires were discussed previously, and one of their uses was seen in the indication of the group members' interest in continuing to meet after the end of the discussion series which they evaluated, as well as in their selection of possible questions and topics for a next series of meetings. If all, or the majority, of the participants favor such a plan, the leader has a clear picture of the situation. If only a minority do this, it is usually best not to plan such a project, at least not at this time. Groups which meet for several discussion series often benefit from an interval to consolidate their gains, to turn to other concerns or for whatever purposes, until they may be again ready to involve themselves in another group discussion experience. The separated, divorced, and widowed persons, a meeting with whom was presented in this book, had more than twenty discussion series, usually two a year in successive years. Intervals of six months or a year before the group met again, gave the participants such opportunities; the meetings were resumed when the membership and the organization's planning committee felt that another experience of this kind would be helpful to those who would attend them.

A desire to continue to meet is generally, but not always, an indication that such a plan would be of benefit to the group members. In some situations, the leader may feel that certain goals have been reached and that their consolidation could best be achieved by applying that which was learned to the life situations of the participants.

In other instances, the leader may sense a reluctance to part with him, particularly if the relationships of most group members to him have been very positive, and this reluctance may be the real motivation for the wish to continue the group discussion experience, rather than the desire to extend or to deepen a learning experience. While it is certainly flattering to be perceived in such a favorable fashion by the members of one's group, the leader should not be tempted to base the decision to continue or to discontinue working with them on their need of him; if he were to do this, he would weaken them by encouraging their dependence on him as an end, and not as a sometimes necessary tool for learning. While it is true that dependence on the leader is part of the relationships of most participants to him, this should be only a bridge to make possible their progress to greater understanding of family relationships, better coping capacity, greater self-reliance, and greater competence. It is essential that the dependency needs of the group members should be met, but this must be done in a carefully planned and controlled way, and should be a passing phase of group discussion leadership only, and not one of its permanent facets.

We should remember at this point that just as some group members are reluctant to give up a beloved leader, some leaders find it difficult to give up their groups. This is an understandable and sometimes touching phenomenon, because the leaders who get into this bind seem to be mostly those who are very task involved. Nevertheless, leaders must be helped to separate themselves from their groups if that is indicated from the latter's point of view, just as group members must be helped to terminate their relationships to a leader who has fulfilled his task and whose continued professional service would not be helpful to them. In those instances where the leader finds this task difficult because of narcissistic gratification or over-identification with the group or for whatever nonprofessional reasons, it is doubly essential that he give up this tie. To do this, he must gain some understanding of his motivations for remaining, or wishing to remain, involved in a relationship with the recipients of his service.

Finally, administrative considerations are often decisive in the matter of continuing or discontinuing to work with a group. Evening meetings are a good example of such considerations, because assignments of this nature need to be limited so that they will not be too exhausting. Even the most enthusiastic and vigorous leaders cannot take the strain of working evening after evening, partly because of the physical toll this takes and partly because this imposes restrictions on their family and social relationships. Another example is that of receiving more requests for leadership than one can meet, so that one must decide whether it is indicated to move on to another group rather than to continue to work with the same group. This is often a difficult decision to make, and is affected by such factors as the needs of the different groups for the service, relations with the community in which one is working, the importance of offering different group discussion leadership training experiences to staff members, etc.

TRANSFERRING A GROUP TO ANOTHER LEADER

This question will be taken up here, since it is often connected to that of continuing to offer service. For instance, in situations where a leader finds it impossible to continue to work evenings, or leaves town, it is appropriate to make available to his group the leadership of another person, if that is possible and if the group wishes to avail itself of such an opportunity. Transfer is also indicated if a leader and a group do not work well together. If the leader recognizes this and if the group is willing to have another leader, this can usually be arranged. Wherever possible, such replacement should be made at the end of a discussion series. If the leader is reluctant to face this problem, supervisory help, and in some instances more intensive personal help will usually enable him to do this.

If a group is transferred to another leader, considerable attention must be devoted to the task of helping the participants to adjust to and accept him. Some of this can be done in the planning process for the discussion series which he will lead, for instance, by having him present so that they can meet him. While the leader who is about to leave should inform the group members of the impending change, should express his regret that this is necessary, and should talk in positive terms of the person who will succeed him, it is the latter's task primarily to facilitate the adjustment of the participants to him. In their meetings with the new person, some of them will need opportunities to express their positive--or negative--feelings about the former leader as well as about their present one, and these feelings must be accepted and recognized. Only after this has been done will the group members be able to "settle down" with their present leader and to work with him. If he should get competitive with or defensive of his predecessor, or feel rejected during that stage of his interaction with them, confusion or anger on their part would result, and would interfere with their ability to relate to him as well as with his ability to relate to them.

XIX
Staff Development: The Training of
Group Discussion Leaders

Training leaders for group discussion leadership can be done in various forms, depending on the facilities which can be used for that purpose--of which time available is one--and on the background and experience of the trainees and of the person who is working with them. The writer has offered training to staff members of the agency employing her and to staff members of other counseling agencies, all of whom were experienced family counselors and had Master's degrees in Social Work. She has done the same for graduate students of that discipline and has also been called upon to prepare para-professional staff who sometimes had not graduated from high school for group discussion leadership. In all situations the goals were the same and she used the same methods which will be described later. However, the expectations of what trainees could learn had to be related to where they were when the leadership training programs started, just as one has different expectations if one works with groups of parents with different group characteristics. Again, the author presents her own experiences only in this area of profes-sional activities and the reader will wish to keep in mind that opinions as well as methods used for training professional and paraprofessional staff members for group discussion leadership differ as widely as the goals of and methods used in working with the group themselves.

If one is training group discussion leaders with graduate degrees who are family counselors, one can take certain basic knowledge for granted. This includes the physical, emotional, and social phases through which the child goes in his development from infancy to latency, the problems and tasks of adolescence, the adjustments which young adulthood, the establishment of love, sex, and marriage relationships and, later, parenthood require, as well as the changes which the later years bring. One also assumes an awareness of the community to which a service is being offered, an ability to develop helping relationships and to work toward carefully planned and well defined goals. This is a brief sketch only; depending on the individual person's special interests, or on his particular professional experi-ence, or on the slant of teaching in the school of social work attended, one or the other aspect of these elements may be more or less pro-minent, or missing, or rounded out or replaced by other skills, such as that of working with groups. What matters is that the person in charge of training can after some preliminary exploration count on all or on parts of this information and can therefore concentrate essentially on adding the knowledge and techniques which will be useful to the trainees in offering group discussion leadership. In the writer's experience, this can be done in two ways: One is to have individual conferences with a trainee, while the other is to have several meetings with a group of staff members. The latter method is by far the better, partly because it offers a group discussion experience to those who participate in the training program, partly because it gives a demonstration of group discussion leadership, and last but not necessarily least, because it is also time saving.

If one has several meetings with a group who have experience in counseling and wish to take up group discussion leadership, it is useful to find out at the start whether they had some experience of this nature, either by leading some groups or by participating as members and, if so, what the purpose and approach used and what their reactions to this experience were. Such information, if available, will contribute to the best use of the teaching materials and, thus, to the learning of the trainees. Next, the leader will find it helpful to develop with the members of the training group a plan for the content to be taken up in the meetings, which will include their questions and concerns as well as what he wishes to bring to them. The approach described here resembles a planning conference with a group to which leadership is to be offered, and this is not the only instance of such similarity. The fact that training sessions for group discussion leadership are in many ways comparable to the work with groups is one of the elements of the training experience which the author wishes to stress in this chapter. She will also point out where the leader's methods differ from those used, say with a group of parents, and will give the reasons for this--the different purposes of the meeting, the different knowledge of the parents, counterindications for discussing certain facets of the work such as defense mechanisms which become apparent, transference phenomena, etc. One must also keep in mind in this connection that the time factor is important, because the number of meetings available for staff training of whatever nature is almost always smaller than the number of times groups of parents, for instance, can meet to discuss their problems.

The combination of questions and concerns of the trainees and of the material the leader wishes to present provides the overall focus for the training sessions, a focus which allows for many digressions, if group members wish to move away from it, and if this fits in with the purpose of the meetings.

In the writer's experience, trainees tend to raise questions about how to mobilize groups, how to prepare oneself for a meeting, how to involve the participants in the discussions, what to do with those who tend to monopolize it, and how far to go in the handling of problems which group members present, to name only a few. Much of this, and other material of interest to trainees is presented in the

preceding chapters of this book, as the latter is based to a considerable extent also on the numerous leadership training workshops and
institutes which she led. What specific facets she would select
depends necessarily on the knowledge which the trainees bring to the
situation--another similarity to the work with community groups.

The author has found an additional approach to staff training
very helpful, and that is to bring to the trainees an unidentified record
of a meeting with a group. Each person gets to read this record
between sessions, and it is discussed by the trainees as well as by
the leader. The selection of this record depends on the interests,
level of knowledge, and probable future work assignments of the
trainees. The questions which they raise in connection with the
record can cover anything, but a large part of the material which the
author attempts to cover is contained in the comments which appear
in the chapters of this book where meetings with parents or teen-age
groups or groups of older persons are presented and discussed.

It has been the writer's practice to use her own records, that
is those where she was the group's leader, for teaching purposes.
She did this for several reasons. First, one usually knows much
more than is recorded or written up in whatever fashion, about a
group with which one has had direct contacts. This information,
which covers that gained in earlier or later work with that group,
makes available much additional detail to the participants on such
matters as intragroup relationships, the development and growth--
or attrition--of the group, learning that took place. It is not possible to have similar information if one is connected only indirectly
with the group, that is by supervising the leader. Second, the use of
one's own record makes it easy to give reasons for one's actions at
given points, such as intervention, redirecting the meeting, or silence,
and last but perhaps most important, one can point out one's mistakes along with the reasons for them. It is essential that the training
person discuss these mistakes, partly to prevent the participants
from seeing them as desirable techniques or approaches, but also
because it is discouraging to see the so-called expert doing his or
her job perfectly. Such discouragement may well lead to the feeling:
"Oh, what's the use of trying, I can't do that!" Most of all, the
presentation of a record in which there are no mistakes of any kind
would be untrue, because no one's professional service is flawless,
or at least could not be improved upon, once hindsight is at work.

In addition, the "perfect record"--if it existed--would undo the
second purpose of any training program. As mentioned earlier, its
first purpose is to offer a learning experience to the participants so
that they will acquire new knowledge, new tools, new techniques to
assume the new professional responsibilities of group discussion
leadership. The second purpose is to help them feel more confident
of their ability to discharge these new obligations. The opportunity
to raise questions, to express their concerns and their doubts, often
their anxiety, to hear the points of view of the other participants and
to share experiences with them usually results in an increase in self-

confidence. In addition, if the training person is perceived as looking for better ways of doing her own job, as making and admitting mistakes, this encourages the more hesitant trainees to use the new professional approach as well. If the training person were to be seen as far removed in terms of knowledge and experience, fantasies might develop about him or her as someone who is perfect, who knows everything, who has magical powers--again like the all powerful parent of one's childhood--and whom one cannot hope to satisfy. Some trainees--and some group members also--may develop fantasies about the training person or group discussion leader, fantasies which may also take other forms, but the growth of unrealistic attitudes and emotions should never be fostered by anything which the training person or group discussion leader elects to do, or not to do.

The author prefers the use of a record which can be read to that of tapes to which one listens. It is true that the latter have many advantages: one hears the voices, which often reflect the emotions, they are often more lively also, but the written word anchors a discussion more effectively. Furthermore, it appeals to one's vision, and many of us--she among them--can more easily assimilate and retain what we see than what we hear. Whatever form the actual record of a meeting with a group takes, however, is less important than that such a record be used for staff teaching purposes.

In addition to making a teaching record available, the writer has also found it useful if the trainees receive, and keep if they wish to do this, samples of registration sheets, of questionnaires, of publicity materials. The purpose here was not to encourage copying them, but rather to make the task of developing one's own material easier, since having a draft, however inadequate it may be, generally facilitates developing related material. If time permits, she has also discussed the preparation of material on specific topics. All these activities had two purposes: She attempted to share her knowledge with the participants in these workshops or institutes and she hoped to allay the understandable anxiety which most of us feel when embarking on new ventures.

The training of staff members who do not bring to the task the professional background which social workers with Master's degrees have, is somewhat different in content but not in approach. This statement is again based on the author's experience, and one must keep in mind that different leaders will tackle the task of training very differently. Content, as used in this connection, covers the planning process, much of the material presented in earlier chapters of this book, including the present one, sharing with the trainees copies of the materials used in working with group. It also covers the use of an unidentified record of a meeting with an appropriate group, appropriate in the sense that the group is either of the kind with which the trainees are working at present, or one with which they are planning to work in the future. This selection helps, because it ties in the teaching material to the immediate concerns of the trainees.

The discussion of the record with the trainees who do not have Master's degrees in social work--or related training which gave them familiarity with intrapsychic phenomena, such as psychologists bring to a training experience--is different, because the unconscious factors at work, which were pointed out in the chapters presenting meetings with groups and which are discussed with other members of training institutes, are not taken up with the formerly mentioned trainees in full detail. They would be touched on very lightly, if at all, and if so by referring to attitudes and feelings, without reference to their possible origin in childhood experiences. Neither would the writer try to discuss what defenses the group members are using in given situations. Should a member of the training group bring up such material--which happens very rarely only--she would not go beyond what came out in such fashion. The reason for this guarded approach is that it is not possible, nor desirable, in her opinion, to encourage the participants to bring out material of this kind, which can lead to the uncovering of personal problems, since neither the time available nor the situation permit working through of such content. Opinions differ widely on the purpose of leadership training workshops, and there is room for all of them, but the author has defined her role in such undertakings as that of teaching, which is imparting knowledge. Of course, and comparable to the work with certain community groups which forms part of this book, insight may develop as a by-product of one's participation in a leadership training institute or workshop. Whenever this happens, it is a valuable gain for the member who acquires it, but this is not the primary goal of the training experience described here.

Professionally trained family counselors are usually better able than paraprofessionals to cope with any painful or disturbing revelations about themselves which may affect the delivery of the services which they are offering, partly because they have theoretical knowledge about personality development, intrapersonal conflict and its causation, and partly because experience in working with persons who need help with problems in family relationships or of personal adjustment rarely fails to mobilize some of the unconscious feelings, attitudes, and problems of the helpers. Furthermore, supervision--during the student years as well as when they become staff members--is responsible for bringing this to their attention, as well as for suggesting ways in which they can cope with this situation. In addition, as staff members in family counseling or other agencies offering help for problems of this nature become more experienced, they are usually called upon to supervise less experienced staff members, students from schools of social work or paraprofessionals, and this tends also to mobilize reactions and conflicts of which the supervisor was not aware before. For these and for other more personal reasons, many persons in the helping professions undergo treatment experiences, which may be of different intensity and of different nature, but which have as their goal to make one more aware and more accepting of one's own and of other peoples' problems. This in turn enables one to look for more helpful solutions to these problems, within the realm of the possible.

As previously mentioned, training depends on the time available for it, and if the training person is not a member of the agency or organization employing the trainees, also on funds available to pay for this service. There are considerable advantages to using a person from the outside, the greatest of which, in the writer's opinion, is that he or she is bound to bring a different point of view and different experiences to the training program. Of course, the person called in should be briefed on where the trainees are, in terms of their background and experience, what groups they will be working with, and what particular aspects of group discussion leadership should be emphasized. It goes without saying that the outside person called in should be qualified to do this in terms of background and experience.

If one decides to use a person from within the agency or organization to do such training, the greatest advantage is the familiarity with it, as well as with many of the factors mentioned in the preceding paragraph. On the other hand, existing relationships between staff members will affect the training experience, sometimes positively and at other times negatively. Furthermore, trainees seem to be more curious and to look forward with more anticipation to the coming of a person with whom they have had no previous contacts.

The training experience can be limited to one exposure although more can be accomplished in several training sessions than in an isolated experience. What is essential, however, is that training be followed by actual experience in offering discussion leadership to groups. The author would like to warn against training that is extended over too long a period of time because such an extension does not result in returns proportionate to the investment of all concerned. Rather, it tends to dampen any enthusiasm which the trainees brought to the training experience, and this may result in a reluctance to venture into the field of working with community groups which was, after all, the purpose of the training program. In the author's experience, six sessions of two to three hours each are quite sufficient to give a sound preparation to trainees for group discussion leadership, if that amount of time can be made available. If this is not possible, less time will have to be used to best advantage.

Once the participants have acquired some knowledge of how to work with groups, have had opportunities to ask the questions which are troubling them, and to which they will, hopefully, find some answers, so that the anxiety one feels if one starts on professional work with which one is not familiar is lessened, nothing can take the place of gaining experience in working with groups. If at a later time, they or the agency or organization which employs them, feel the need for an additional leadership training program, the latter will be much more fruitful because it can--and should--be built on the experiences of the staff members in their group discussion leadership activities, and deal with the problems they have met and solved, or been unable to solve in their work with groups.

The writer would like to add a word of caution in regard to students of social work and younger staff members who are to participate in a training experience for group discussion leadership. Many schools of social work have changed the courses offered in recent years and as a consequence, little if any teaching is done in the areas of personality development, intrapersonal conflicts and their causes and related topics. A person who is asked to offer such an experience will do well to ascertain the level of knowledge in these fields for his or her preparation and adjust the material used accordingly.

SUPERVISION

Next to training and experience, supervision is the most important tool toward the achievement of expertise in group discussion leadership. Much has been written about the purpose, content, and methods of supervision, and this author does not propose to add to the existing literature on these topics (Burns, 1965, pp. 789-795; Feldman, 1950, pp. 156-161; Getzel et al, 1971, pp. 155-163; Judd et al, 1962, pp. 96-102; Kadushin, 1968, pp. 23-32; Leader, 1957, pp. 462-468). It has always been clear to her that the purpose of her supervision was to enable the supervisee to function better in whatever task he, or she, was engaged, and that supervision should limit its concerns to the area of service delivery. In other words, attitudes, feelings, values, problems, interpersonal or intrapersonal conflicts of the person one is supervising become part of the supervisory process only if they interfere with the performance of the professional assignment. Should that be the case, these matters need to be pointed out to the supervisee, as briefly as possible, with reference to their effect on the delivery of the service offered, and with suggestions of ways in which they can best be dealt with. The latter range from the discussion of their existence to the supervisee's seeking professional help in the form of a treatment experience.

The other aspect of such a situation with which the supervisor must cope is to prevent as much as possible the potential damage to group members since the professional services discussed in this book are intended to be helpful to those who use them. If the author qualifies this statement by adding: "as much as possible," this is realistic because neither the supervisor nor the supervisee are always instantly aware of what is happening in a given situation. If it has become clear, however, that a leader does not work well with certain kinds of groups, this knowledge must be taken into account in the assignments for this person. Such a restriction of the use of staff members will not meet with universal approval, since in many cases the training of professional or paraprofessional staff members determines to a considerable degree which tasks are to be performed by whom. Granted that staff training is important, it should not be so important that the recipients of the service to be offered do not receive the most helpful service which can be made available to them.

The remarks made in the preceding paragraph take the writer and the reader of this book into the area of one's values and standards as a professional person, and it can well be argued that the training of staff members will eventually result in having larger numbers of helping persons available, so that it justifies the price to be paid for this training in the here and now. The author was caught in this dilemma, as is most everybody at one point or another who has administrative, supervisory, and training responsibilities, and she developed, by trial and error, a rule which worked out well for her and for the program which was her responsibility. First of all, since everybody may make one mistake, one group discussion series of a specific kind--such as a parent group or a group of older people--may not go well with a leader. This is discussed by leader and supervisor. If a second group of the same kind does not go well either, that deserves more careful examination by the leader, by the supervisor, and by both of them together. Should the leader wish to work a third time with a similar group, after having acquired some understanding of what happened previously and why things went wrong, that may be worth trying. After three attempts which are not successful, however, groups of this specific nature should not be assigned to this leader anymore. Instead he or she should be given opportunities to offer leadership to groups of different composition. It is often surprising and rewarding to see what excellent service a person can offer in situations in which he feels more comfortable and more competent, for whatever reasons.

A comparable statement can be made about groups, because a group which did not develop and grow under the leadership of one person may make considerable progress, if another leader takes over. The combination of many factors will determine whether this happens, most important of which will be the ability of the new leader to offer helpful relationships to the members of this particular group as well as their readiness to relate positively to him. It seems sometimes as if there were some special alchemy at work to bring such change about, but the writer is inclined to think that the essentials for such a very desirable development are contained in the development of positive relationships--both those between the leader and the group members, and those between the group members themselves, which almost invariably follow the former. It is the responsibility of the former leader and of the supervisor to face this and to make better plans for such a group.

Supervision also includes recognizing that some professional or paraprofessional staff members, however well motivated, are not suited by temperament, by personality, or for other reasons to offer group discussion leadership. They usually become aware of this themselves and withdraw from such endeavors. As a matter of fact, many very skilled and competent therapists are not attracted by and do not feel at ease in work with groups, and this reaction should be respected. In the situation where a person continues to wish to offer group discussion leadership although this is obviously not a good use of his potential, the supervisor has the difficult but necessary task of helping him to face this.

SELF-EXAMINATION

In addition to training, experience, and supervision, leaders, and especially experienced ones, possess a valuable tool for their professional growth and development: self-examination. If used regularly and honestly, it can lead to amazing discoveries. It is particularly helpful when a meeting did not go well. This should be followed, as soon as possible and before one forgets conveniently what went on, by a long look at what happened, and especially at the way in which one discharged the leadership function. Granted that factors beyond one's control may be at work--such as a race riot in the city, which is surely not conducive to a positive atmosphere, if a group of teen-agers get together to discuss problems of sexual rela-tionships--one will usually find that for these or some other reasons, one did not do one's best job at that time. The reasons are, of course, what counts, accounting more than anything else for the out-come of the meeting; they can be simple things such as the leader's fatigue, or his coming down with a cold, but they can also be the failure to hear what group members wanted to achieve in the meeting or the negative interaction between the leader and the group members, to which reference was made previously. Uncovering the reasons for one's failure to do one's best in a given situation generally leads to a better discharge of one's professional responsibilities in the future.

Leaders who keep records, or at least some notes on their work with groups, receive from this material considerable aid in the evaluation of their leadership. The written word is invaluable in this connection, because it is not amenable to those changes which one's memory might otherwise permit, and which are usually in one's favor. In other words, one tends to forget or to minimize one's mistakes, to shift cause and effect relationships and to gloss over the unpleasant memories unless the written word anchors the reality for a candid examination. Although this is not done consciously, it is nevertheless not conducive to professional growth, nor to the delivery of improved services to the group members. In similar fashion, the replies on the questionnaires which group members fill out regarding leadership, freedom to participate in the discussions, any help which they received from the meetings can contribute very much to one's evaluation of one's work with this group, if this mate-rial is used judiciously, as described earlier.

Very often the question is asked what qualities or personal characteristics persons should have who wish to lead group discus-sions. Drawing from her experience in training professional and paraprofessional staff members for many years, the writer would list first the ability to offer helpful relationships to the members of a group. The capacity to think quickly and to verbalize one's thoughts quickly also, the willingness to experiment with new ways of using one's knowledge and an interest in the unique ways in which group members relate and react to each other and to the leader are others. Experience in service delivery geared to problems of family and social relationships on a one-to-one basis is essential and so is the knowledge of when to be permissive and when to direct a discussion, a knowledge which is largely based on this experience and which grows, as one works with groups. Clarity about one's own values and standards and their roots is important, and so is the lack of fear when taking a stand as indicated by these values and standards. Compassion controlled by professional behavior, empathy, an ability to live with the imperfections of others, of the world around us, and of oneself is necessary. So is the ability to accept limited and reachable goals, for oneself as a leader and for the group, as opposed to the desire to be the savior of those with whom one works. Last but not least, keeping one's perspective and one's sense of humor, in regard to others as well as to oneself, are among the qualities which make group discussion leadership helpful to the group members and enjoyable and stimulating to oneself.

COLEADERS

The advantages or disadvantages, benefits or problems--for the leaders no less than for their groups--of using two leaders simultaneously have been discussed in the literature. Such matters as whether they should have the same professional background, be of the same sex or not, what their roles with the group should be have received considerable attention. The writer cannot contribute to these questions from her own professional work, since it was the agency's policy to assign only one leader to a group. This was due to the fact that requests for group discussion leadership were too numerous to permit tying up the services of two staff members with one group, when by having only one leader two groups could receive the service they desired. It was also based on the agency's focus on helping those members of the community who wished to use help; while training of staff members and students was important also, it was of secondary importance. The author can, however, report on a coleadership experience in which she participated herself with a psychiatrist and a psychiatric social worker, both of whom were men. Its purpose was somewhat different from that of the Family Life Education groups discussed in this book in that the team met with the faculty of a school to increase their understanding of the children whom they were teaching along with helping them gain some insight into their own personalities and personality problems. She found the experience exciting, stimulating, and also very self-revealing. In the latter area, it offered more insight into the self than anything

except a personal psychoanalysis. As a result, she would consider
a team leadership an excellent, although sometimes painful training
device which would deepen one's self-understanding, and be of great
assistance to the team members in working through some of their
personal problems which are activated through their interaction.

References

Bernard, J. (1956) Remarriage - A Study of Marriage, Dryden Press, New York.

Bernstein, R. (1971) Helping the Unmarried Mother, Association Press, New York.

Black, S. (1972) Group therapy for pregnant and nonpregnant adolescents. Child Welfare, LI (No. 8): 514-518.

Bock, E. W. and Webber, I. L., Suicide among the elderly: Isolating widowhood and mitigating alternatives. Marriage and Family, 34 (No. 1): 28-29.

Bowlby, J. (1960) Separation anxiety. Internat. Psychoana., No. 41: 89-113.

Burns, M. E. (1965) Supervision in social work, in Encyclopedia of Social Work, 15th Issue, H. L. Lurie, Ed., National Assoc. of Social Workers, New York.

Child Study Association of America (1965) What to Tell Your Children About Sex, Pocket Books, New York.

Cohen, P. C. (1962) The impact of the handicapped child on the family. Social Casework, 43 (No. 3): 137-142.

Cumming, E., Henry, W.E., Dean, L.R. and Newell, D.S. (1961) The evidence for disengagement in attitude and orientation, in Growing Old - A View in Depth of the Social and Psychological Processes in Aging, E. Cumming and W.E. Henry, Eds., Basic Books, New York.

Education for Social Work with "Unmotivated" Clients (1965) Proc. of an Institute sponsored by the Children's Bureau and the Florence Heller Graduate School for Advanced Studies in Social Welfare, Brandeis University.

Feifel, H. (1973) The meaning of dying in American society, in Dealing with Death, R.H. David and M. Neiswander, Eds., Ethel Percy Andrews Gerontological Center, Univ. of Southern Calif.

Feldman, Y. (1950) The teaching aspect of casework supervision. Social Casework, 31 (No. 4): 156-161.

Freud, S. (1965) The Complete Introductory Lectures on Psychoanalysis, J. Strachey, Ed., Norton, New York.

Getzel, G.S., Goldberg, J.R. and Salmon, R. (1971) Supervising in groups as a model for today. Social Casework, 52 (No. 3): 155-163.

Gladwin, T. (1967) Poverty U.S.A., Little, Brown & Co., Boston.

Glick, P.C. (1957) American Families, Wiley, New York.

Goode, W.J. (1956) After Divorce, The Free Press, New York.

Gursslin, R.O., Hunt, R.G. and Roach, J.L. (1959-60) Social class and the mental health movement. Social Problems, 7 (No. 3, Winter).

Harris, M.W. (1972) The child as hostage, in Children of Separation and Divorce, I.R. Stuart and L.E. Abt, Eds., Grossman Publ., New York.

Hilgard, E.R. (1956) Theories of Learning, Appleton-Century Crofts, New York.

Hunter, K. (1968) Pray for Barbara's baby. Philadelphia Mag., (Philadelphia), 59 (No. 8): 48-55, 98-105.

Jacobson, P.H. (1959) American Marriage and Divorce, Rinehart & Co., New York.

Judd, J., Kohn, R.E. and Schulman, G.L. (1962) Group supervision: A vehicle for professional development. Social Work, 7 (No. 1): 96-102.

Kadushin, A. (1968) Games people play in supervision. Social Work, 13 (No. 2): 23-32.

Kaufman, P.N. and Deutsch, A.L. (1967) Group therapy for pregnant unwed adolescents in the prenatal clinic of a general hospital. Internat. J. Group Psychotherapy, 17 (No. 3): 309-320.

Kennedy, J.F. (1970) Maternal reactions to the birth of a defective baby. Social Casework, 51 (No. 7): 410-416.

Klatskin, E.H. (1972) Developmental factors, in Children of Separation and Divorce, I.R. Stuart and L. E. Abt, Eds., Grossman Publ., New York.

Kolodny, R.L. and Reilly, W.V. (1972) Group work with today's unmarried mothers. Social Casework, 53 (No. 10): 613-622.

Leader, A.L. (1957) New directions in supervision. Social Casework, 38 (No. 11): 462-468.

Leslie, G.R. (1967) The Family in Social Context, Oxford University Press, New York.

Lewis, O. (1967) La Vida - A Puerto Rican Family in the Culture of Poverty - San Juan and New York, Random House, New York.

Lidz, T. (1968) The Person - His Development Throughout the Life Cycle, Basic Books, New York.

Loether, H.J. (1964) The meaning of work and adjustment to retirement, in Blue Collar World - Studies of the American Worker, A.B. Shostak and W. Gomberg, Eds., Prentice-Hall, New York.

Mandelbaum, A. and Wheeler, M.E. (1960) The meaning of a defective child to the parents. Social Casework, 41 (No. 7): 360-367.

Mayer, H. and Schamese, G. (1969) Long term treatment for the disadvantaged. Social Casework, 50 (No. 3).

Miller, S.M. and Riessman, F. (1964) The working class subculture:
    A new view, in Blue Collar World - Studies of the American
    Worker, A. B. Shostak and W. Gomberg, Eds., Prentice-Hall,
    New York.
Miller, W.B. (1958) Lower class as a generating milieu for gang
    delinquency. Social Issues, 14 (No. 3): 15-19.
Minuchin, S., Montalvo, B., Guerney G.B., Jr., Rosman, B.L.,
    and Schumer, F. (1967) Families of the Slum - An Exploration
    of Their Structure and Treatment, Basic Books, New York.
Motivation in Health Education (1949) N.Y. Academy of Medicine,
    Health Education Conference 1947, Columbia University Press,
    New York.
Neisser, M. (1973) The sense of self expressed through giving and
    receiving. Social Casework, 54 (No. 5): 294-301.
Neubauer, P.B. (1952) The Technique of Parent Group Education:
    Some Basic Concepts, Child Study Assoc. of America, New York.
Ohrbach, H.L. (1963) Social values and the institutionalization of
    retirement, in Processes of Aging, Social and Psychological
    Perspectives, vol. II, R. H. William, Ed., Atherton Press,
    New York.
Olshansky, S. (1962) Chronic sorrow: A response to having a
    mentally defective child. Social Casework, 43 (No. 4): 190-193.
Pochin, J. (1969) Without a Wedding Ring: Casework with Unmarried
    Mothers, Schocken Books, New York.
Polansky, N.A., Boone, D.R., DeSaix, C. and Sharlin, S.A. (1971)
    Pseudostoicism in mothers of the retarded. Social Casework,
    52 (No. 10): 643-650.
Pollak, G.K. (1956) Principles of positive parent-child relationships.
    Social Casework, 37 (No. 3): 131-139.
Pollak, G.K. (1963) New uses of a family life education program by
    the community. Social Casework, 14 (No. 6): 333-342.
Pollak, G.K. (1964) Family life education for parents of acting out
    children: A group discussion approach. Marriage and the
    Family, 26 (No. 4): 489-494.
Pollak, G.K. (1970) Sexual dynamics of parents without partners.
    Social Work, 15 (No. 2): 79-85.
Pollak, O. (1957) Design of a model of healthy family relationships
    as a basis for evaluative research. Social Service Rev., 31
    (No. 4): 369-378.
Reiner, B.S. and Kaufman, I. (1959) Character Disorders in Parents
    of Delinquents, Family Service Assoc. of America, New York.
Reiner, B.S. and Kaufman, I. (1956) Handling of early contacts with
    parents of delinquents. Social Casework, 37 (No. 9): 443-450.
Rexford, E.N. and van Amerongen, S.T. (1957) The influence of
    unsolved maternal oral conflicts upon impulsive acting out in
    young children. Amer. J. Orthopsychiatry, 27 (No. 1): 75-85,
    489-494.
Ripple, L. (1964) Motivation, Capacity and Opportunity: Studies in
    Casework Theory and Practice, University of Chicago Press.

Spiegel, J.P. (1964) Some cultural aspects of transference and
    countertransference, in Mental Health of the Poor, F. Riessman,
    J. Cohen, and A. Pearl, Eds., The Free Press, New York.
Stein, M.H. (1973) Acting out as a character trait. Psychoanalytic
    Study of the Child, 28: 347-364.
Steinzor, B. (1969) When Parents Divorce - A New Approach to New
    Relationships, Pantheon Books, New York.
Streib, G.F. and Schneider, C.J. (1961) Retirement in American
    Society, Cornell University Press, Ithaca, New York.
Weisman, A.D. (1962) On Dying and Denying - A Psychiatric Study
    of Terminality, Behavioral Publications, New York.
Williams, T.M. (1974) Child rearing practices of young mothers:
    What we know, how it matters, why it's so little. Amer. J.
    Orthopsychiatry, 44 (No. 1): 73.
Yarrow, M.R. (1963) Appraising environment, in Processes of
    Aging, vol. I., R.H. William, C. Tibbits, and W. Donahue,
    Eds., Atherton Press, New York.
Young, L. (1954) Out of Wedlock, McGraw-Hill, New York.

Index

Acting out behavior
  as caused by parental acting out,
  173, 195-196
  of children in school, 102, 169
  of disadvantaged inner-city boys,
  124
  of retarded teenage girls, 78, 82
  of unmarried mothers, 103
Adolescents
  general problems of, 12
  problems of disadvantaged inner-
  city boys, 118, 130, 132
  problems of retarded teenage
  girls, 78-80, 81-82, 89-91,
  92-93
  problems of teenage girls from
  deprived backgrounds, 47-49, 50
  problems of unmarried mothers,
  102-103, 104-105, 108-109, 111-
  112, 113-115
Aggression
  of acting out mothers, 169, 173
  coping with teenage girls' aggression, 323-325, 334, 336, 342
  of divorced, separated and
  widowed persons, 227-230, 239-
  240
  of retarded teenage girls, 82,
  84-85, 89, 92
  of teenage girls from deprived
  backgrounds, 47, 54, 56
  of unmarried mothers, 103, 104,
  105, 112
Aging
  as a common bond, 28, 298
  problems of, 254, 255-256, 257-
  258, 259-260, 268, 271, 279-280,
  285, 286-287, 288, 289, 290,
  291, 293-294, 298, 304-305,
  307-308

Ambivalence
  of leader, 328-329
Anomie, 17, 18
Anxiety
  of acting out mothers, 17
  of disadvantaged inner-city boys,
  126
  of divorced, separated and
  widowed persons, 228-231, 245,
  248-249
  of mothers of handicapped children, 199, 206-208, 220-221, 224
  of retarded teenage girls, 78, 89,
  92
  of older persons, 287, 291
Apathy
  as reason for non-attendance, 18
  in seeking out resources, 9
  of underprivileged persons, 17
Attendance at meetings
  of disadvantaged inner-city boys,
  120-121
  factors affecting it, 18, 170-177
  of low income groups, 7
  of low income mothers' group,
  176-177
  of low income older persons'
  group, 265, 270
  of lower middle class mothers'
  group, 138
  of mothers of handicapped children, 204, 208
  of older persons' group from
  various backgrounds, 290-291
  of retarded teenage girls, 84-85
  of separated, divorced and
  widowed persons, 226
  of teenage girls from deprived
  backgrounds, 57, 58
  of unmarried mothers, 105

teenage girls from deprived backgrounds, 52, 53, 54-55, 72
unmarried mothers, 103-104,
109, 116
ways of expressing positive
feelings for leader and appropriate responses of leader, 330-
332
Relationships of leader to group
members (general)
ambivalence, and how to cope
with it, 328-329
components of positive, 328
coping with aggression, 323-326,
342
definition, 328
defining boundaries between professional and personal relationships, 332
inability to have people come too
close, 330
inability to work with specific
groups, 329
reluctance to give up group, 354
Relationships of leader to group
members (special problems)
with disadvantaged inner-city
boys, 119, 123-125, 127-129
with divorced, separated,
widowed persons, 236-238
with low income mothers, 183,
195-196
with low income older persons,
256, 262-264
with lower middle class mothers,
142-143, 157, 165-166, 196
with mothers of handicapped
children, 206-209
with older persons from various
backgrounds, 295-296
with retarded teenage girls, 81-
84, 85, 88, 90, 93-94
with teenage girls from deprived
backgrounds, 54-55, 59
with unmarried mothers, 103-
104
anxiety, 319, 320, 340
Resources within the self
of older persons, 20
Retardation, 77

characteristics of disadvantaged
inner-city boys, 118, 120, 121
characteristics of retarded teen-
age girls, 78-80, 83
Retarded Teenage Girls' Group--
Problems of Dating and Impulse
Control of Retarded Teenage
Girls, 77-99
attendance, 84-85
attendance, selection for, 77-78;
see also exclusion
characteristics of group members, 78-79; anxiety, 89, 92;
dating problems, 89-91; familiarity with violence, 92, 95, 97;
inability of evaluating results of
own actions, 89-90, 92; lack of
skills in handling social relationships, 89, 92; parents, expectations from, 90-91; peers, nature
of relationships to, 89; sex, attitudes toward, 87-88, 94-95;
stereotypes (cliches), use of, 87-
88; self-image, low, 79; suspi-
ciousness, 86
concerns, 78, 87-88, 89-91, 94-
95
exclusion of group members, 85
goals, 80
intragroup relationships, 82
leadership techniques and mistakes, 81-83, 84-85, 85-88, 90,
91, 92-93, 94, 95, 96-98, 99
learning experiences and other
gains of group members, 89-90,
93, 94-95, 98
planning and setting, 77-78, 79-
80, 84-85
relationships to leader, 80-81,
83
school counselor, role of, 84
special problems of leadership,
81-84, 85, 88, 90, 93-94
Retired persons, 10, 13
discussion with retired persons
from low socio-economic background, 283-311
discussion with retired persons
from varied socio-economic
background, 283-311

DATE DUE

SEP 2 2 2008			